British working-class movements and Europe
1815–48

To Marian

British working-class movements and Europe

1815–48

Henry Weisser

Manchester University Press

Rowman and Littlefield

© 1975 Henry Weisser

Published by
Manchester University Press
Oxford Road, Manchester M13 9PL

UK ISBN 0 7190 0608 2

USA

Rowman and Littlefield
81 Adams Drive, Totowa, N.J. 07512

US ISBN 0 87471 721 3

BFT

Printed in Great Britain
by Butler & Tanner Ltd
Frome and London

Contents

		Preface	page vii
		Introduction	1
1		The ultra-radical press and European affairs, 1815–29	
	I	Cobbett's journalism	7
	II	Themes of sadness and hope	12
2		The early thirties	
	I	The July revolution	32
	II	Cobbett's last act	42
	III	The Belgian revolution	47
	IV	The Polish revolution of 1830	48
	V	Owenism and Europe	53
	VI	Continuities	57
3		The Chartists and Europe, 1836–44	
	I	The LWMA and Europe	66
	II	Bronterre O'Brien and Europe	78
	III	Chartism at its height and European affairs at the periphery	84
	IV	Newport, Beniowski, Urquhart and Russophobia	99
4		The Chartists and Europe, 1844–8	
	I	The Polish exiles	118
	II	The German exiles	125
	III	A triumvirate of leaders and their newspaper	129
	IV	The Fraternal Democrats: origin, organisation, and outlook	134
	V	The Fraternal Democrats and the Cracow uprising	140
	VI	Marx and Engels and the Fraternal Democrats	144
	VII	Feargus O'Connor's role	150
	VIII	The Fraternal Democrats' rivals	154
	IX	The Fraternal Democrats in perspective: some conclusions	163
	X.	An epilogue: Tiverton	172
		Appendix. The historiography of Chartist internationalism	193
		Bibliography	200
		Index	215

Preface

The following pages contain a detailed account of one aspect of the growth of the British working class from Waterloo to the outbreak of the revolutions of 1848. This study examines much of what British workers thought, said, wrote, and did about Europe and Europeans, and thereby affords some new insights into class consciousness, nationalism and internationalism in this vital formative period. Attention is focused on the Continent; both Ireland and the United States, each with special relations to England, are omitted from these considerations.

Acknowledgement for the assistance and encouragement of several persons and institutions must be made. I wish to thank Professor Harry Rosenberg, chairman of the history department at Colorado State University, for encouraging research and allowing me to work reasonably unimpeded. Professor Sidney Heitman, of the same institution and managing editor of the *Rocky Mountain Social Science Journal*, has given helpful advice for many years, and his concern is greatly appreciated. I must always be indebted to two scholars at Hartwick College, Oneonta, New York, Professors Daniel Allen and Alban W. Hoopes. Dr and Mrs Ralph Brown of Cooperstown, New York, have been helpful friends all through my career. Much kind, considerate assistance was freely given by Professor Peter Brock, formerly of the Russian Institute at Columbia University and now at the University of Toronto. I relied upon his expertise when dealing with the Polish exiles in London. I must acknowledge, too, the assistance of Professor Ludwik Krzyzanowski, editor of the *Polish Review*.

Several faculty research grants from Colorado State University were most useful for gathering microfilmed and xeroxed material. A Research Associate's Grant from the Social Science Foundation at the Graduate School of International Studies, University of Denver, allowed a second research trip to Britain, and a grant from the American Philosophical Society helped with a third venture.

My greatest debt is owed to Professor R. K. Webb of Columbia University, now the managing editor of the *American Historical*

Review. This study began as a dissertation which grew out of his doctoral seminar of 1958. From that time until the present, and despite enormous professional responsibilities, he has always managed to find time to provide advice, encouragement, and criticism. He was never too busy, even when on leave, to criticise carefully whatever I sent. What seems most remarkable, especially after working with some of my own graduate students, is how Professor Webb was able to insist on such high standards while being so kind and patient. In recent years disenchanted graduate students have regretted, among other things the lack of time or concern on the part of their professors. Such resentments have made me realise all the more how fortunate I was to have the guidance of Professor Webb. He is, of course, free from responsibility for the errors in these pages.

HENRY WEISSER

Introduction

Europe was one of many concerns earnestly taken up by the British working class in the first half of the nineteenth century. Social, political, and economic developments on the continent were often noted in the colourful working-class press to provide readers with lessons, examples, and diversions, and attempts were made to integrate these observations in the framework of evolving working-class thought. In addition, the British government's European policies came in for detailed criticism in the press, on the platform and, undoubtedly, at the cobbler's bench and local alehouse. In these years growing class consciousness embraced not only various kinds of English workers in the bonds of fellowship, but went on to include foreign workers as well. But concern with Europe evolved beyond opinion and thought; after 1830 there was action. Europeans received British working-class addresses, and, in some cases, hastily gathered funds. Finally, by the mid-1840s, special bodies were created in London to organise the mingling of European exiles with British workers and to proselytise international understanding.

These developments were merely one aspect of the profound transformation of a society based upon interests and orders into a society based upon classes.[1] Semantic indicators of this change, such as the use of the term 'the people' in the twenties, 'the working class' in the thirties, and, increasingly, 'the proletariat' in the forties, were applied internationally as well by leaders of the British working class, as was the pejorative use of 'middle class' and its variants. All of this was supposed to be part of that great march of the mind, a rational progression which was intended to destroy old fears and superstitions and undermine despotisms. Enlightened workers believed that eventually truth, justice, and freedom were destined to triumph as a result of it. Along the way, workers' heightened class consciousness would enable them to perceive that they were indeed superior to those who sought to hold them in economic and political subjection. Such class consciousness came to be projected to foreign countries as well, as an international identification of exploiters and exploited emerged.

A*

None of this could have happened without that tremendous initial surge of industrialism which allowed an ever-increasing number of ordinary men to break with ancient provincialism and to think beyond the neighbourhood to the nation, and beyond the nation to Europe and the world. Among the first tasks of working-class leaders in this new, unevenly industrialising England was the encouragement of an enlightened self-awareness and class awareness on the part of workers divided by occupation, living standards, immediate environments, and geographical distance. Reaching out to workers in other countries was in many ways merely a continuation of these initial tasks.

Undoubtedly the most important instrument in creating a new class consciousness, national and international, among British workers was the cheap, popular press. Without it, concern for Europe and Europeans would not have developed. Consequently, most of the source material for this study is drawn from the editorials, commentary, reports of meetings, and accounts of other activities lodged in this colourful medium.[2]

Between 1815 and 1848 the newspaper trade was open to democratic, plebeian newspapers willing to struggle against the law. The cheap, accessible hand press was not yet seriously challenged by expensive technological innovations such as steam-driven presses and the telegraph. Enormous amounts of capital, especially in the form of advertising revenue, had not yet been able to dictate giantism to journalism. In these years a newspaper produced by poor men could rival the circulation of any publication of the establishment. Cobbett's *Political Register* was a giant among postwar periodicals. Hetherington's *Poor Man's Guardian* sold 16,000 copies of one issue in 1833 and the famous Chartist *Northern Star* was a truly national newspaper. There was nothing ephemeral about these publications, although the adjective could be applied aptly to many other products of the working-class press.

Both durable and ephemeral publications from this press tended to be highly idealistic. Most of these newspapers were published to instruct rather than to gain profits. Influence was more important than affluence, and editors often assumed the roles of teacher or crusader instead of businessman. Most of them ran one-man shows, and were true sons of the working class. There is no parallel in journalism with the gentry or quasi-gentry leadership that flourished in working-class politics, except, of course, Feargus O'Connor's *Northern Star*. These editors plied their trade for rapidly swelling ranks of literate workers, haphazardly and fitfully educated by dame schools, charity schools, day schools, workhouse schools, Mechanics' Institutes, some Methodist class meetings, and by countless informal efforts, mostly of the self-help variety.[3] Idealistic motivation and a serious readership did not always guarantee quality, however. Readers often got the ill-disciplined, endless ruminations of turgid sages as well as some bad poetry. Yet much else was quite perceptive and well written, or at least well stolen. Quality was in general higher in 1830 than in 1820. In some respects quality was actually much less important than rapport. It was most essential that a portion of the early nineteenth-century press had a class-conscious position, speaking for and of the working class and thereby serving to broaden horizons and deepen understandings.

Since class was such an active cultural battleground in the early nineteenth century, this popular press had to emerge defiantly, embattled and heroic. The radical hand press—not the middle-class weeklies and dailies—drew the blows of governmental repression, and resistance managed to make the repressive laws of criminal libel inoperable in the twenties and reduce the stamp duties to insignificance in the thirties. Richard Carlile, a former tinsmith's apprentice, ground down the teeth of the law of criminal libel at the cost of a cumulative total of ten years' imprisonment. Henry Hetherington was the central figure in the second phase of the struggle for a free press, which is known as the war of the 'great unstamped press'. His style of resistance as proprietor of the remarkable *Poor Man's Guardian* also featured open, defiant bravado. Both editors, incidentally, included much information about Europe in their valiant publications.

Much more than the forging of class consciousness was at stake in these struggles. They reflected profound ideological differences as well. The government, Whig or Tory, really wanted the masses to stay on the loyal paths, seen as the paths of their own best interests, rather than stray on to the dangerous roads leading to treason and civil war. Ministers held the conviction that blasphemous, seditious working-class scribblers were making profits by driving the masses to dire ends. Yet it can be argued from hindsight that instead of increasing the danger of revolution, the popular press actually helped to prevent it by doing the very thing that the law prohibited— bringing institutions and rulers into contempt. Such criticism was what was actually needed to transform and thereby preserve the ancient institutions shaped in the green, paternalistic, preindustrial world. In the years of extreme social tension brought on by the impact of industrialism, the British working-class press, in conjunction with the platform, provided outlets. In countries where criticism could not splash into print or rise in speeches it grew more bitter and went underground to fuel truly revolutionary agitations. In Britain there were newspapers, clubs, meetings, and speakers for nearly every point of view, and although arguments clashed, analyses drastically opposed each other, and the 'knowledge' passed on was often worse than second-rate polemic, dialogue existed. The other side, or the other class, was at least heard. A war of words sharpened minds, not pikes. Political democracy in Britain was foreshadowed by a democracy of print. The British working class fought for both at one and the same time.

As a result of these and other struggles, considerable working-class consciousness had developed by the thirties. The ranks of the British working class were formed, and the class enemies were clearly in view. A working-class culture, expressed in manners, sports, attitudes, traditions, and value systems, existed in the thirties and forties. There was an articulation of common interests, and class was institutionalised. Many trade unions, clubs, friendly societies, and educational efforts were organised by and for the working class. A small but significant part of institutionalised working-class activity, largely confined to London, involved increasingly formal dealings with groups of European exiles and occasional contacts with European workers' organisations. Another aspect was the formulation of working-class pronouncements on foreign policy, which were often crude but always resounding.

These developments in class consciousness were largely responses to the new economic world erupting from industrialism. But many of the ideas and much of the inspiration for British working-class leaders were derived from the politics of the past. Most influential of all was the thought and style of Thomas Paine. His rationalism, deism, belief in natural laws and rights, pacifism, internationalism, and his enthusiasm for the French revolution were adapted by numerous working-class imitators in the early nineteenth century.[4] He armed them with clichés, slogans, an inflated rhetoric and a ponderous style. Paine's writing centred on the French revolution, and it is no wonder that after a quarter of a century of French revolutionary turmoil British workers should continue to be very strongly influenced by those Gallican events. Principles, issues, examples, vocabulary, songs, heroes, and villains, were all drawn wholesale from that era. British workers flew the tricolour, hung it on walls, placed it in buttonholes, and put it on hats. They called each other 'citizen', and closed their meetings with the 'Marseillaise'. Standard rhetoric for working-class agitations came from the French revolution: the future was to be a time when 'the dominion of kings, aristocrats, and priests would give way to the rule of law and reason'. People would be 'awakened' so that they would 'break their fetters'. Such preoccupation with the French revolution meant that British workers would have much more interest in France than in any other European nation in the early nineteenth century.

One organisation that existed during the French revolution came to provide an inspiring model for subsequent working-class groups. The London Corresponding Society was the first working-class organisation created for political activity, although it might be called a 'popular radical' organisation instead, because not all of its members were workers and the artisans enrolled might more readily identify with the lower middle class.[5] Nevertheless, certain features actually made the LCS the first prototype of the Fraternal Democrats, the working-class group which was the most class conscious and internationalist before 1848. First of all, funds were drawn from a weekly penny subscription, a method derived, no doubt, from the little journeymen's clubs of London. Secondly, the secretary, Thomas Hardy, was a workman—the lineal ancestor of dozens of working-class secretaries, including George Julian Harney, secretary of the Fraternal Democrats. In the third place, the benefits of reform were depicted in economic terms—bread, meat and butter—as well as in the commonly expressed inedible intangibles. Perhaps the most striking feature of the LCS was that it welcomed 'numbers unlimited'. They also fostered what has been grandiloquently called the 'British Jacobin tradition of internationalism'. The phrase should not imply that internationalism was a special cause of the LCS as it was for the Fraternal Democrats forty years later. Internationalism in the 1790s was merely part of the philosophy of the rights of man. Nevertheless, the organisation, along with several others, busied itself with sending advice and encouragement to governmental bodies in France, thus inaugurating a practice that was resumed with similar enthusiasm in the thirties and forties.

The London Corresponding Society, Thomas Paine, the French revolutionary style, the working-class press, and class consciousness all helped to shape the content and the style of what is taken up in detail in the following chapters. British working-class concern for Europe and Europeans was but one of many aspects of change in that dramatic, massive, unfinished transformation of Britain, Europe, and the world by the politics of the French revolution and the economics of the industrial revolution.

Notes to Introduction

1 The subject of class consciousness receives a classic treatment in E. P. Thompson, *The Making of the English Working Class* (London, 1963). Important aspects are also in: E. J. Hobsbawm, *The Age of Revolution, 1789–1848* (London, Cleveland and New York, 1962); Asa Briggs, 'The language of class in early nineteenth-century England', Asa Briggs and John Saville, ed., *Essays in Labour History* (London, 1960); R. S. Neale, 'Class and class consciousness in early nineteenth-century England: Three classes or five?', *Victorian Studies*, vol. XII, no. 1 (September, 1968); Dorothy Marshall, *English People in the Eighteenth Century* (New York, 1956); R. J. White, *Waterloo to Peterloo* (New York, 1957); R. Currie and R. M. Hartwell, 'The making of the English working class?', *Economic History Review*, vol. 18, no. 3 (December, 1965), pp. 633–43; R. F. Wearmouth, *Some Working Class Movements of the Nineteenth Century* (London, 1948); E. J. Hobsbawm, 'Methodism and the threat of revolution in Britain', in *Labouring Men: Studies in the History of Labour* (London, 1968); most recently, Harold Perkin, *The Origins of Modern English Society, 1780–1880* (London and Toronto, 1969).

2 Two recent studies treating the early working-class press are: Joel H. Wiener, *The War of the Unstamped: The Movement to Repeal the British Newspaper Tax, 1830–1836* (Ithaca, 1969) and Patricia Hollis, *The Pauper Press: A Study in Working-Class Radicalism of the 1830s* (Oxford, 1970). The struggles of Carlile and Hetherington are found in detail in earlier studies: A. Aspinall, *Politics and the Press, 1780–1850* (London, 1949); W. H. Wickwar, *The Struggle for the Freedom of the Press, 1819–1832* (London, 1928). Also E. E. Kellett, 'The Press', *Early Victorian England*, G. M. Young, ed. (London, 1934); J. H. Rose, 'The unstamped press, 1815–1836', *English Historical Review*, vol. 12 (1897). For Carlile's resistance, see Thomas Alfred Jackson, *Trials of British Freedom* (London, 1945), pp. 99–109; G. D. H. Cole, *Richard Carlile* (London, 1943). There is a sketch of Hetherington: Ambrose C. Barker, *Henry Hetherington, Pioneer in Freethought and Working Class Struggles of a Hundred Years Ago for the Freedom of the Press* (London, n.d.).

3 See R. K. Webb, *The British Working Class Reader, 1790–1848: Literacy and Social Tension* (London, 1955); 'Working class readers in Victorian England', *English Historical Review*, vol. 65, pp. 333–51; R. D. Altick, *The English Common Reader, A Social History of the Mass Reading Public, 1800–1900* (Chicago, 1959).

4 Julius Braunthal included a chapter entitled 'Thomas Paine, internationalist' in his *History of the International*, vol. 1, *1864–1914* (New York and Washington, 1967). Braunthal concluded that Paine's *Rights of Man* 'belongs to the history of the International, because it implanted the idea of international solidarity for the oppressed deep in the minds and hearts of English workers.' (p. 13). See also 'Paine's Address to the Republic of France, September 25, 1792' (London, n.d.).

5 For the London Corresponding Society, see Henry Collins, 'The London Corresponding Society', in John Saville, ed., *Democracy and the Labour Movement, Essays in Honor of Dona Torr* (London, 1954); Carl Cone, *The English Jacobins: Reformers in Late 18th Century England* (New York, 1968). For an earlier treatment, see P. A. Brown, *The French Revolution in English History* (London, 1918).

I The ultra-radical press and European affairs, 1815–29

I COBBETT'S JOURNALISM

Continental connections, against which our forefathers were so anxious to guard, are now really sought after with eagerness; . . . Come back to your former doctrines; disclaim all connection with a continent where we never can have power without the ruin of this island: . . . [leave] the French, the Italians, the Neapolitans, and the Swiss, and the Belgians, and the Russians and the Spaniards and the Prussians, and the Austrians, and the Hungarians, and the Dutch, and the Hannoverians, to settle their own affairs in their own good time and manner.[1]

No one will ever know just how many British workers read these pronouncements of William Cobbett in 1815. Some surely did by the light of ale-house candles and others heard them read aloud while they toiled. Workers had no other regular sources of information about Europe and Europeans at this time. They called no meetings for any European cause; they sent no petitions about criticising foreign policies; they sent no addresses to foreign workers or to foreign governments; and there were no working-class organisations established to fraternise with foreigners.

Workers did show up at meetings called to celebrate such events as the Spanish revolution of 1820, but these gatherings were held under the auspices of people from other classes, and were likely to have a high admission price and a Member of Parliament or some other dignitary in the chair. A Crown and Anchor meeting to celebrate the Sicilian, Portuguese, and Neapolitan revolutions in 1820 heard Major Cartwright, the old reform campaigner, but an ultra-radical editor present resented the fourteen-shilling admission, the abundance of noblemen present and the 'emasculated' nature of the declarations and toasts.[2] Workers might contribute their pennies to a foreign cause, but men from other classes stepped forth to manage these funds. A meeting called to help the Spanish resist French invaders in 1823 called upon Englishmen 'of every class and station' to contribute, but half of the managers were Members of Parliament.[3] While ultra-radical editors called for separate meetings, contributions, and even the sending of guns, deputations, and volunteers to southern Europe, these exhortations to action were empty.[4] There was no practical advice on how and where to volunteer or send weapons, and no reports of working-class meetings or special contributions.

Since neither working-class suppers, banquets, and meetings nor regular organisations stimulated interest in Europe or Europeans, British workers had to rely upon the ultra-radical press to maintain their interests in these topics.[5] The platform, often subject to harassment, was largely given over to English affairs. References to English history rather than to contemporary Europe were used by its popular speakers, including the most popular of them all, Henry Hunt, in order to drive home particular points. Moreover, there was no popular lecture series or lecturer who used European affairs as his theme.

How did the ultra-radical press maintain workers' interest in Europe? The quantity of information they printed about Europe was considerable, although, of course, it only took up a small percentage of the total output. Some material appeared inconspicuously, such as excerpts taken from the regular newspapers. Much information was scattered—a reference here, a comment there—sometimes competing for space with medicinal advertisements. Other material appeared quite prominently, as when editors devoted their lengthy letters, which were actually feature articles, to such topics as France or the Spanish revolution. Some of these letters consumed nearly all of the issue, but such treatment was spasmodic, and usually occurred when news from England was exceptionally dull. When English news was exciting, editors tended to offer excuses for neglecting important European developments. A statement made by William Cobbett in 1820, the year of fresh revolutions abroad and the trial of Queen Caroline at home, serves as a good example: 'Our attention has been so entirely absorbed by the affairs of her majesty that we have scarcely been able to look at the glorious events which have taken place in Spain, Naples, and especially Portugal.'[6]

John Wade of the *Gorgon* went further. He wrote that 'foreign politics is a subject on which we do not remember to have once occupied the attention of our readers: This has not risen from an indifference to the affairs of other states, but from a persuasion that our own country afforded matter much more attractive for political speculation.'[7] The Peterloo massacre provides a case in point. Although each of the ultra-radical publications filled many pages with commentary, none tried to connect Peterloo with European politics in any way. Instead there were elaborate discussions of

Anglo-Saxon history and the British birthright. On the other hand, a fair quantity of information dealing with Europe is attributable to the habit of looking to Europe for important news and excitement that had been built up in the decades of continental revolution and war. Also, the new, radical, press could find another way to imitate the established press by providing European coverage. Another reason is that readers who were discouraged by repression at home could often find consolation and encouragement by reading about hopeful developments abroad. As Wooler wrote in the *Black Dwarf* in 1822, 'Our rights and privileges have long been dwindling, together with our ardour and resolution: and if not yet countenanced, inspired and encouraged by the noble examples of French and Spanish patriotism, we should soon be completely at the mercy of domestic despotism.'[8]

Setting the style and tone for ultra-radical opinion at this time was William Cobbett, an important figure in early nineteenth-century British history, which is something that cannot be said of his competitors, who widely and frequently imitated him.[9] The vicissitudes of his career freed him from insularity; he fled to the United States twice and *petit bourgeois* France once; earlier he had been a British soldier stationed in New Brunswick and Nova Scotia. He emerged from French exile as a Francophile and the author of a best-selling French grammar. Although his fame as a journalist and popular intellectual distinguished him from his chief competitors for working-class pennies, there were other differences as well. Other editors tended to be Paineites—rationalistic, revolutionary, proponents of natural law. Cobbett's position was that of a constitutionalist and patriot who based his views on an historic if mythical conception of the British constitution.[10] His Tory radicalism reached vast numbers of Englishmen who were, like himself, unreconciled to the sudden changes of industrialism and attached emotionally to a world of small producers. Cobbett's *rapport* was magnificent. He called his readers simply 'men and women' instead of 'workers' and actually had a relationship that involved his audience with himself. He wrote with a brilliant conversational style, although modern critical readers might chafe at his blatant egotism, specious arguments, blind prejudices, contradictions, and his use of bludgeoning arguments.

Because of his popularity among readers and imitators, Cobbett's pronouncements on European affairs are highly significant. While he set the tone and direction of working-class attitudes towards the

French revolution, its wars, and the restored world of the Congress of Vienna, he did so with a purpose in mind. His main preoccupation was to explain the distress of post-war England in terms of a demonology that held parliamentary corrupters, called boroughmongers, responsible for the high taxation, staggering national debt, paper money system, and the prevalence of such parasites as fundholders, placemen, and speculators. Cobbett blamed the wars against the French revolution and Napoleon on these boroughmongers. He explained that if the French revolution had been allowed to run its course without interference, France would have been free, and such an inspiring example to Englishmen that the boroughmongers' position at home would have been in grave danger. So English boroughmongers hired, 'without any consent on the part of the people', any allies who would help to 'kill people who were endeavouring to be free'.[11] The wars which followed were stupid, because French principles could not be uprooted. These 'twenty-three years of violence and fraud' had extinguished three republics, re-established the Jesuits and the Inquisition, and, in general, had propped up despotism 'in every part of Europe where freedom had made her appearance'.[12] Cobbett insisted that something must be terribly wrong if British blood and treasure were lavished upon the restoration of the Bourbon family and the Pope, traditional enemies of England for centuries.[13] Cobbett thought that the boroughmongers had been busy behind the scenes at the Congress of Vienna as well, 'where they took all the despots into their pay to get the kind of settlement that would leave them secure in England'.[14] To Cobbett, English dishonour abroad and distress at home were two aspects of the same problem—the corruption of the boroughmongers. The remedy Cobbett prescribed for Britain's international relations was the same one that he prescribed for domestic, economic, and social ills—reform of the House of Commons. The following paragraph from the *Political Register* of 1822 shows how Cobbett linked foreign and home affairs:

Those who have called themselves statesmen in England . . . have but one object . . . *that of preventing the people from being* fairly represented in Parliament. . . . This has been the pivot on which their measures, abroad as well as at home, have constantly turned. All their wars on the Continent of Europe . . . their alliance on the Continent; their aggrandisement of the Autocrat and the Austrians. . . . The question with them has constantly been, not whether they were providing for the permanent power of the country, but whether they were doing that which would check the cause of Reform in England.[15]

In Cobbett's view, reform would restore England's position in Europe, and despots would have to fight French principles without British aid. However, if reform did not come speedily, and if Parliament did not get 'a set of men elected by the people' soon, Britain would have to fight in other costly wars, for French principles were at work in Europe, inspiring the peoples of various countries to fresh efforts.[16]

Other ultra-radical editors shared his views when writing about the aftermath of the French wars. Like Cobbett, John Wade's *Gorgon* recounted the blessings of the French revolution and called upon Englishmen to press towards reform to 'redeem their honour', which was lost while Britain was the 'chief instrument' in reducing Europe to 'slavery'.[17] Similar expressions appeared in Thomas Davison's *Medusa*, *The Cap of Liberty*, the *White Hat*, a periodical associated with Henry Hunt, and in the ancestor of Carlile's *Republican*, *Sherwin's Political Register*.[18]

None of these publications could give the *Political Register* strong competition. Thomas Wooler's *Black Dwarf* could, and Richard Carlile's embattled *Republican* drew a considerable following as well. Together these three publications shouldered most of the burden of informing the British working class after Waterloo. They were the only ultra-radical publications to break through to a national circulation; most of the rest circulated in London and a few did in Manchester.[19] When Cobbett fled to the United States in 1817, the *Black Dwarf* replaced the *Political Register* as the chief ultra-radical publication, and, after his return, remained a friendly rival.[20] Wooler was from Yorkshire, a disciple of Paine, a crusader against borough-mongering and, some implied, a drinker. His *Dwarf*'s small, closely printed pages contained many articles and items about British foreign policy and situations on the continent. In fact, one of the charges that brought Wooler to court for defamatory libel was an accusation based on his writing that 'now the war was over the people saw that they had won no glory and had conquered themselves and not France'.[21] Generally, the *Dwarf* was pessimistic about European conditions after Waterloo, as expressed in a poem that appeared in 1817, which found:

> The British Banner Furl'd o'er freedom's Tomb,
> A mournful presage of the days to come,
> When mad revenge shall bare his bloody hand,
> And scatter wild destruction thro' the land:—
> When Britain's strength shall with her freedom fall;
> 'And universal darkness bury all'.[22]

II THEMES OF SADNESS AND HOPE

Europe inspired two main themes in the ultra-radical press from 1815 to 1829. One theme, sounded in sad, disillusioned tones, was preoccupied with the aftermath of the French revolution, its wars, and its Corsican hero. The second theme, hopeful and enthusiastic, looked to a brighter future of improved European politics and a hastened passage of Reform in England. It was inspired by the burst of fresh revolutions in southern Europe in 1820, the date which came to serve as the dividing line between the dominant periods of each theme.

Before the outbreak of the Spanish revolution in 1820, preoccupation with France was the rule, for obvious reasons. Other major States were remote; many areas of Europe were pulverised into small States; France was the home of modern revolution, and it was believed that if anything of the sort were to succeed in Europe again, Frenchmen would lead. In *The Making of the English Working Class*, E. P. Thompson seeks to make the point that English radical preoccupation with France was broken by Napoleon's imperialism:

In 1802 Napoleon had become First Consul for life; in 1804 he accepted the crown as hereditary Emperor. No true follower of Paine could stomach this. The hardened Jacobin was cut as deeply by this as more moderate reformers had been dismayed by Robespierre. However much they had sought to maintain a critical detachment, the morale of English reformers was closely involved with the fortunes of France. The first Empire struck a blow at English republicanism from which it never fully recovered. The *Rights of Man* had been most passionate in its indictment of thrones, Gothic institutions, hereditary distinctions; as the war proceeded, Napoleon's accommodation with the Vatican, his king-making and his elevation of a new hereditary nobility, stripped France of its last revolutionary magnetism. *Ça Ira* faded in the memories even of the Nottingham crowd. If the Tree of Liberty was to grow, it must be grafted to English stock.[23]

This assumption does not hold true because France retained much magnetism for ultra-radical editors after 1815. They believed that revolutionary changes were immutable and went to great lengths to show that defeated, Bourbon France had much to recommend. Cobbett was pleased to note that since the breakup of large estates during the revolution there was an increase in the numbers and the collective strength of 'proprietors of small parcels of land, well dressed, well fed, bold in their manners, sensible in their remarks, understanding their rights and duties'.[24] Because France had 'no hereditary magistracy, no dominant church, no feudal tenures . . . one code civil and criminal, to which all men are subject', Frenchmen were better off after 1815 than they had been before 1789, regardless of the restoration of the Bourbons. To prove this point, he cited numerous statistics—comparative prices and the considerable number of Englishmen who lived in France. A corollary drawn from this proposition, and stated acidly, was that Englishmen were worse off after the war than the Frenchmen they had defeated.[25]

Richard Carlile emphatically agreed. He felt that during the French revolution the people of France were 'truly regenerated; their follies evaporated; their character changed. . .'.[26] The restoration of the Bourbons could not alter this condition: to use Carlile's metaphor, the tree of liberty had been too deeply rooted in France, even if its 'blossom were blasted'.[27]

Napoleon, like France, continued to be something of an inspiration to British ultra-radicals after 1815, and here another of E. P. Thompson's implications may be questioned, for Thompson wrote: ' "Boney", if he was admired, was admired as a "warrior", not as an embodiment of popular rights.'[28] To be sure, post-war ultra-radical editors were not blind to his shortcomings. Cobbett pointed out in 1815 that the Napoleon who fell was 'an Emperor and a King; the son-in-law of the House of Austria . . . the associate, preserver, restorer, creator of Nobles and Kings, crowned by the Holy Father, re-establishing, in some degree, Bishops and Priests. . . '.[29] An article in the *Black Dwarf* of 1817 declared that Napoleon's 'tyranny' was still alive in Europe, drawn up in lots and bid upon by his conquerors. Russia received 'greatness and ambition', Prussia had to be content with 'military mania', while the 'folly' of Napoleon's rule was divided between Ferdinand VII and the Pope. 'Absurdity' went to Austria.[30] Nevertheless, from 1815 to 1819, Napoleon was held in some esteem. Cobbett, in particular, remained fascinated by Napoleon after Waterloo, and filled many pages of the *Political Register* with remarks about him. Cobbett's point of view was that although Napoleon was a despot, he was an enlightened one, and good for France. Surely, enlightened despotism was not capable of bringing reform in Britain, where traditions of freedom and liberty were so strong, historically, but perhaps it had to serve to bring change in France, since that nation had been inured by centuries of despotism. Cobbett loved to contrast the way Louis XVIII was restored 'in the rear of those overwhelming foreign armies' to the manner in which Bonaparte regained power in the Hundred Days by 'virtue of the people's consent'.[31] He thought that the English people had been deliberately misinformed by their government about Napoleon, to the extent that the '*far* greater part of the people of England' really believed that Bonaparte was 'hated and detested by the people of France' and that conscripts were 'dragged in chains to his armies. . .'.[32] At best, Cobbett saw Napoleon's regime as 'a republican government with a chief called an emperor'.[33] He declared that Napoleon ought to receive 'the admiration and gratitude of every brave and every free man in every nation in the world'. He had 'established forever the superiority of talent over insolent birth . . .' and thereby 'laid the sure foundation for future freedom'.[34]

Carlile and Wooler repeated these sentiments and added some of their own.[35] An editorial in *Sherwin's Political Register* in 1817 revealed the simple reason for admiring Napoleon after his downfall: the legitimate rulers were much worse. 'How contemptible legitimates appear when contrasted with the noble-minded Napoleon! . . . a professed despotism administered by him is preferable to a pretended freedom under the care of an ass of the hereditary school.'[36]

Ultra-radical editors certainly thought that the Holy Alliance was much worse for Europeans than Napoleon's system had been. It contributed considerably to their pessimistic outlook, and they could never dismiss it as lightly as Castlereagh, who, in that famous phrase, called it a 'sublime piece of mysticism and nonsense'. They thought that the British government was either a member or a supporter of the Holy Alliance and that the boroughmongers worked for its ends.[37] As the *Medusa* announced, British ministers 'have leagued with the other tyrants of Europe to annihilate the liberty and to persecute all who have the boldness to resist them'.[38] Such fears made it impossible for the ultra-radical press to consider the Holy Alliance without resorting to a torrent of invective, heavy sarcasm, and ridicule. Carlile, a militant deist, was particularly offended because of its publicly declared religious basis and objects. He announced to his readers that the purpose of the Holy Alliance was to 'encourage the progress of fanaticism in the public mind' in order to 'convert Europe into one great state prison. . .'.[39] The *Black Dwarf* described the organisation as 'majesty wrapped up in flannels, hobbling on crutches, decked out in stays and whiskers, or beautifully strutting about in embroidered petticoats and caps, and feathers'.[40]

While no individual foreigners associated with the Holy Alliance were held up for special and persistent execration—not even Metternich nor Tsar Alexander—one English statesman, Lord Castlereagh, was singled out by these journalists as the arch-proponent of the organisation.[41] The widespread unpopularity of this solitary, unapproachable, misunderstood minister is well known, and the ultra-radical press was but one of many sources of abuse. What was remarkable, though, was the extreme degree of vilification, perhaps most strikingly revealed in the positive glee expressed at the news of his suicide in 1822. 'Let me express to you', wrote Cobbett, 'my satisfaction that Castlereagh has cut his throat.' Cobbett pondered the official explanation that 'his intellect was impaired' and wondered how he could have prepared to go to the continent as the king's representative the day before his suicide if this had been the case. Cobbett concluded that 'men would no longer wonder at the miserable state in which they are; no longer wonder that famine and overproduction of food should at once oppress the land. Here should be the solution to the whole wonder—A Mad Secretary of State and A Mad Leader of the House of Commons.'[42] Carlile urged people to show up at his funeral to cheer, and hoped that the body would be buried in the fashion of ancient suicides—at a crossroads with a stake through the heart. He was convinced that Castlereagh would 'have gladly introduced fifty thousand Russians into this country to establish absolute power . . .' if he could have got away with it.[43] The change from Castlereagh to Canning, a change now known to have involved method rather than principles, did not raise the confidence of the ultra-radical press, which expected him to continue Castlereagh's supposed co-operation with Russia, Prussia, and Austria. Surprisingly, Canning's humble origin was impugned by pointing out that a man who had risen so far under such a system must have exercised an unprincipled devotion to his own interests. Hence, Canning would take up 'coaxing, truckling and fawning' to get his way, and receive a 'tweak of the nose' if he had to.[44]

Preoccupation with the Holy Alliance and nostalgia for Napoleon suddenly disappeared as news of fresh revolutions began to flash across Europe. In 1820 and 1821 several minor upheavals occurred, beginning in Spain in January, and eventually including outbreaks in Portugal, Naples, Sicily, Piedmont, and Greece. The reaction of ultra-radical editors was immediate, vociferous, wildly enthusiastic, and out of all proportion to the events themselves.

This overwhelming preoccupation with revolution in the early twenties became the second main theme inspired by Europe in the ultra-radical press from 1815 to 1829. Popular urban outbreaks were more formidable in the early nineteenth century than later, when governments came to rely upon superior technology. From 1789 to 1848, Europe's modern age of revolution, barricades, muskets, and determination often provided sufficient force to topple kings. Moreover, revolutionaries appeared in abundance—Carbonari, Masons, members of a dozen secret societies, dissatisfied bourgeois, and countless unorganised thousands. In the words of E. J. Hobsbawm, 'never in European history and rarely anywhere else has revolutionism been so endemic, so general, so likely to spread by spontaneous contagion as well as by deliberate propaganda'.[45]

For the ultra-radical editors, any upheaval on the Continent seemed portentous because the nature of revolution was believed to be so swift, so sudden, so dramatic, so contagious, and so mysterious. A revolution in Spain or Italy or elsewhere would usually be considered with the possibility of an English revolution in mind, and would always be considered for its effect on the reform movement. For this reason, revolution was not an esoteric theme in the ultra-radical press. Ordinarily, editors did not urge their readers to strive in emulation of European revolutionaries. Instead, revolution was depicted as a consequence that had to be faced if government ignored 'public opinion' or the 'popular will'. Revolution was seen as the natural, unavoidable corrective of the ills of society, and where it occurred depended upon the unwillingness of governments to grant concessions.[46] To put it quite simply, if reform were not granted, revolution would occur. The situation was often put as bluntly as in the *Gorgon* in 1818: 'There are only two means of salvation—either radical reform or revolution.'[47] Frequently more elaborate declarations about the necessity of reform or revolution were made, as in the *Republican* in 1820: 'Society, like the human mind and body, has a continual tendency to corruption, unless it be placed on a self-reforming basis', and there was nothing like a revolution to 'remove a deep rooted corruption'.[48]

Revolution inspired much murky, turgid, and almost mystical writing in the publications popular with the working class. There was something like a language of revolution, for a set of stock phrases and metaphors were used over and over to describe it. Revolution was 'the sun of liberty' and 'electric fluid', 'the spirit of liberty', 'the wholesome thunders that would purify an infected atmosphere . . . of . . . pestilential vapours', 'the progress of reason', 'the march of the mind', 'the march of intellect', 'the light', and on and on. The principles of the first French revolution were declared to be alive in Europe and rapidly spreading, like unquenchable embers or seeds of a thrashed thistle. Resistance to these principles was condemned as 'kingcraft and priestcraft', 'despotism', 'the temple of hypocrisy', 'the stupidity and ignorance of antiquated systems', 'superstition', and 'darkness'.

Ultimately, revolution would triumph over all. It was common to speak of 'a better age . . . fast dawning . . . though the preceding night may have been dark and dangerous and stormy'.[49] Precisely how this age would dawn was a matter of speculation. There was a common radical belief that a grand world war of royalty against republicanism would take place throughout Europe, and a common anticipation that it would be initiated in France. In the words of Carlile, a revolution in France would 'decide the fate of the whole continent instantly . . .'.[50] It would also force a change in British politics. It was argued that a corrupt House of Commons would again be unable to tolerate a free France, but this time the hard-pressed boroughmongers could not wage war. In Cobbett's words, a new French revolution would give 'a furious shock on this side of the water'.[51]

The ultra-radical press was taken by surprise when the initial outburst occurred in Spain, but enthusiasm developed rapidly— a sentiment shared by middle-class editors.[52] Viewed in historical perspective, the Spanish revolution of 1820 was not a grand event. It began with a soldiers' mutiny, then, spreading, forced a liberal constitution on the Bourbon king, Ferdinand VII, and finally destroyed itself through the bickerings and inexperience of two groups of liberals, the *exaltados* and *moderados*. The reactionary forces in Spain and the Eastern powers allowed a French army to invade in 1823 in order to quell the liberals. Intervention was successful and bloody; brutal repression by reactionary Spaniards followed. After that, revolution in Spanish politics blurred into a cruel, boring, and seemingly perpetual civil war, involving various factions, each supporting some royal contender to the throne.

Unarmed with historical perspective or hindsight, the ultra-radical press became immensely excited over the Spanish revolution, at least until 1823. Oddly, the revolutions in Portugal, Naples, Sicily, Piedmont, and Greece received comparatively scanty treatment. Richard Carlile was the foremost enthusiast. He began to date his publications 'in the Year One of the Spanish Revolution'.[53] He explained: 'This year will certainly form a new era. It is the year for the emancipation of the human race. Nothing has ever occurred to resemble the present era.'[54] He came to see all history divided between the time before and the time after 1820, and assured his readers that the former period would 'be referred to only to excite our contempt. . . '.[55] The Spanish revolution was celebrated in song in the *Republican*:

> Who can now the Spaniards see,
> Boldly rearing Freedom's tree;
> A nation struggling to be free.
> And not assist their cause?
> Now they have the standard shown,
> To all the world it shall be known
> We fight for equal laws.[56]

A verse in the *Black Dwarf* concluded:

> Spain rises, awful and sublime,
> O'er slavery, error, woe and crime.[57]

Before 1820 ultra-radical journalists had been contemptuous of Spain. In 1819 Carlile had feared that Englishmen would 'become a band of hypocritical and contemptible slaves, crawling about, like the reptiles of Spain, at the feet of their oppressors. . .'.[58] In 1820 all of these opinions vanished. The Spanish people became heroic and confirmed the belief in the miraculous regenerative powers of the revolutionary impulse. After all, the country in Western Europe least likely to have a revolution was the first one to obtain its benefits.[59] The *Dwarf* exclaimed: 'And to see Spain do this! Spain, the most bigoted, the most ignorant of nations! Spain! Hitherto held in awe by a cowl, and governed by a band of sottish monks.'[60]

One apparent novelty about the Spanish revolution that attracted ultra-radical interest was the role of mutinous Spanish regiments.[61] Hitherto, regular armies had been regarded as props of despotism rather than potential revolutionary forces. Carlile responded to this situation by printing a number of appeals to British soldiers, and asked: 'Soldiers—shall you plunge your bayonets into the bosoms of fathers and brothers? . . . Turn your eyes toward Spain and there behold the happy effects resulting from the union of citizens and soldiers.'[62] He threatened that 'there is nothing wanting in England but a good understanding between the soldiers and people'.[63]

Another seeming novelty hailed in the ultra-radical press was the swiftness and relative bloodlessness of the upheaval. Wooler was happy to announce that the 'general characteristics of the Spanish revolution were providence, mildness, and moderation',[64] and Carlile boasted that 'not a drop of blood was spilt' in changing the government of a nation 'not celebrated for pacific dispositions'.[65]

Therefore, 'the dread and fear of revolution will pass away. . .'.[66] The ultra-radical press also expressed delight in the promulgation of a written constitution, the replacement of the hereditary principle with the principle of merit, the abolition of primogeniture and the confiscation of church property.[67]

Although British reformers' hopes were inflated by Europe in 1820, deflation began as soon as March, 1821, when Austrian armies lumbered into Piedmont and Naples, easily crushing the revolutionary regimes in those places. Some moves against Europe's new republics by the Holy Alliance had been confidently expected, so intervention in Italy came as no surprise.[68] What Wooler, Cobbett, Carlile, and others did not anticipate was the ease with which the Neapolitan revolution was terminated. The editors busied themselves, several hundred miles from the scene of the events, exhorting the Neapolitans to stout resistance. Carlile urged 'every inhabitant' to 'sell his life as dear as possible', for 'death is by far the least of two evils when slavery is the alternative'.[69] Cobbett hoped that 'not a man of the Austrian army would escape, not even a single man to tell the tale . . . Spare none!' he insisted.[70] Ignoring his advice, the Neapolitans spared nearly all of the Austrians in their frantic efforts to spare themselves, and thereby earned the derision of the ultra-radical editors.[71]

The Austrian advance made the principle of intervention a topic of concern for the whole British press. It seems that the ultra-radical segment merely followed its middle-class counterparts in criticising this principle.[72] Even so, Cobbett was unusually outspoken on the subject, for it touched a raw nerve. He felt that the Austrians were doing the same thing in Italy that the boroughmongers had done in France from 1793 to 1815. He despised the invaders: 'The Austrians, the implacable foes of the very names of freedom; the Austrians; the terrible, the horrible Austrians; the never-forgiving Austrians, have put their whiskered battalions in motion, and, by hundreds of thousands, like moving wall after wall, they are marching. . . .'[73] The *Black Dwarf* called them 'war hounds . . . disciplined slaves . . . barbarians of a distant clime' and inserted this mock advertisement in 1821:

> States Depopulated and Property, Commercial and
> Agricultural, Ruined, Upon the Lowest Terms and at
> The Shortest Notice. Liberality of Sentiment,
> Generosity of Character and Sympathy of Nature
> Expeditiously and Radically Exterminated in All Countries.[74]

Curiously, the statesman inseparable from Austrian politics, Prince Metternich, was ignored.

Although the British government clearly disapproved of Austrian action in Italy in 1821, the ultra-radical editors believed just the opposite at the time. They were sure that the boroughmongers were at work on the 'Austro-Russian' side,[75] and passed on rumours that English loans were financing the venture.[76] At the same time, British neutrality was criticised as being tantamount to support of Austria,[77] and, one step further, action was called for to save the Neapolitan revolution from the Austrians. This amounted, of course, to a call for intervention to prevent intervention.[78]

Despite the defeat of the Neapolitans in 1821, ultra-radical optimism persisted as long as Spain remained under a revolutionary regime, that is, until 1823.[79] Thereafter, disenchantment with Europe and pessimism about Europe's future returned as dominant notes in the ultra-radical press. When French troops massed at the Pyrenees in 1823 ultra-radical editors were sure that the world was about to see truly momentous events. Perhaps the long awaited war of peoples against the despots would result.[80] At any rate, there were good reasons for supposing that French intervention would end in disaster for the invaders. Had not Napoleon's legions failed to subdue Spain? How could French soldiers led by 'ultras' succeed against Spanish republicans? These troops were expected to come back from Spain quickly, and wearing the 'tricoloured cockade'. Should the French win—a most unlikely contingency—the Holy Alliance would then be so powerful that the British government would have to restrict liberty further or be the next nation to suffer invasion.[81] For these reasons the fate of the Spanish revolution was inflated to be the fate of western man; a Spain saved was 'a Europe saved'. So, when Englishmen helped Spain in some way, they were, according to Wooler, really helping themselves.[82]

The momentousness was not real—the French marched into Madrid with ease, and soon Ferdinand VII was busy torturing those liberals who had not made their escape. The initial response of the ultra-radical press was not to accept defeat. For a while they pinned their hopes on Spanish guerilla tactics to save the revolution. When the truth of the defeat was obvious and inescapable, they responded by ignoring Europe. Until 1830, when the July revolution suddenly created excitement that exceeded that displayed in 1820, there were very few prominent articles and editorials about Europe. Occasional reports about Iberian or even Greek developments appeared after 1823, but they were neither prominent, interesting, nor original.

The French invasion brought more than disenchantment to the ultra-radical press; it also broke up the united front that the most influential editors had maintained towards European developments. The formidable voice and pen of William Cobbett consistently denounced the Spanish cause, cheered the French invaders and thereby brought on heated disagreements. Cobbett's divergence has been the subject of some historical speculation. Arthur Aspinall had this to say in *Politics and the Press*:

It has been thought that even Cobbett may have accepted money from the same source [the French government] in 1823, in view of the fact that this ardent democrat was then defending the French invasion of Spain. But there may be another explanation.[83]

Aspinall referred to Harold W. V. Temperley's *The Foreign Policy of Canning*, which contains these remarks:

The *Political Register*, like the *Courier*, seems to have profited by French information, perhaps by French gold. On the fifth of March, 1823, Cobbett wrote a letter to Chateaubriand, and added longer articles in the *Political Register*, defending the French invasion of Spain.[84]

There is, as Aspinall suggests, another explanation. The statement by Temperley mentions that Cobbett wrote a letter to the French minister Chateaubriand, but he does not say what kind of letter. In the *Political Register* of March 8, 1823, there appeared, in bold print, a letter signed by Cobbett that was addressed to 'Monsieur de Chateaubriand on His Speech in the French Chamber of Deputies . . . Relative to the War Proposed to be Undertaken by France Against the Revolutionists in Spain'. This was an open letter, of a genre particularly suited to Cobbett's style. In many such letters he unburdened himself directly to the dignitaries of the day, including the Prince Regent, the Duke of Wellington, and Lord Liverpool. These letters in his publications were, of course, intended for Cobbett's readers and not for the people saluted in them. If this is what Temperley meant by declaring that Cobbett 'wrote a letter to Chateaubriand', the statement is misleading.

It was not 'French gold' which made Cobbett cheer the invaders in 1823. The *Political Register* offers a more logical explanation. To put it simply, Cobbett held a grudge against the Spanish since the French revolutionary wars because they had taken British money to fight for the 'Bourbons and boroughmongers' and against good King

Joseph Bonaparte. Therefore the Spaniards had contributed directly to Napoleon's exile and to the prevention of 'the Reform of Parliament in England'.[85] Cobbett continued to see the Spanish as boroughmongers' friends in 1823 as in 1812 and, Bourbons or not, Cobbett saw France as a reformed nation in the twenties.

Once again, Cobbett's rule of thumb in taking positions over foreign issues was the calculated effect that events on the continent would have on English boroughmongering.[86] Whatever side did the most harm to the cause of the rotten boroughs was the side William Cobbett wanted to be on. He was frank about this in June, 1823: 'I want to see . . . the Spanish . . . subdued by the French; but it is with me a matter of doubt whether such subjugation or a defeat of the French would do the most harm to English boroughmongers. When that is no longer matter of doubt with me, I shall know which to wish for.'[87] By November he had reached a decision. The Jews and jobbers of London, he wrote, would profit from the Spanish Republican government, because they were busy '*mortgaging . . . the labour of all Spaniards for ages to come*'. Cobbett admitted that the Spanish priesthood, which was on the French side, represented bad principles, but, he insisted, these priests were not as bad as 'those monsters who . . . have brought the people of once happy England to a state of wretchedness absolutely without any parallel. . .'. The inquisition 'burned now and then a man: the Jews and jobbers starve hundreds of thousands to death'.[88] These attitudes caused his xenophobic reaction to public meetings designed to raise funds for the Spanish cause. He was furious because he found boroughmongers attending them and even giving them direction. He declared that he would not take up a single column of the *Political Register* by reporting the speeches made at such gatherings which were, he declared, events 'calculated . . . to deceive and to cheat the people of his country' and 'humbug' them the same way that they 'had been humbugged for the last thirty years'. These people were deceiving the English when they professed to assist the Spanish cause. Their real purpose was to 'uphold that system under which the English have so long groaned. . .'. 'I would not', wrote Cobbett, 'give the parings of my nails' to save the Spanish from 'being hanged by the Bourbons.' Liberals busy raising funds for Spain were 'hypcorites', who 'affect to pity other nations on account of their misery when there is not a country in the whole world containing a thousandth part of the misery which our country contains'. Cobbett insisted that there was little sense in having public meetings on behalf of groups of foreigners as long as 'our unfortunate fellow-subjects in Ireland are far more miserable. . . . The mischief all lies in the English boroughs . . . to pretend to have anxiety to spare for other nations is to do mischief.'[89]

Thomas Wooler led the counter-attack, but he prefaced it by politely declaring that he had long been one of William Cobbett's admirers. He then went on to say that, although he could be called 'a follower of Cobbett's opinions', he was 'totally at variance' with them over the Spanish cause. On this topic Cobbett's ideas were 'startling to the common sense of the case' and 'contrary to the feelings which exist upon the subject'. Wooler agreed that the Spaniards had been used before 1815 'by the boroughmongers of England . . . to perpetuate the English system of Parliamentary corruption. . .'. The point was that the Spanish would have fought against the *Grande Armée* anyway, since the French had sought to force a foreign government upon them. Now, Wooler argued, it was different. In 1823 the English boroughmongers wanted the Spaniards defeated, and that should have been 'sufficient to induce every enemy of the boroughmongers to wish for the triumph of Spain'. Wooler granted that many who 'appear earnest in the cause of Spain' were not enemies of the boroughmongers, but they were still entitled to thanks for their assistance, for even if they themselves wished for no real change in England, they were helping to produce one if they contributed to the triumph of the Spanish revolution. Wooler was angry that too many men, some of means, were 'keeping their money in their pockets' because they had heard Cobbett's arguments. Since Englishmen were in fetters at home, why should they not help others throw off their chains? Besides, Wooler continued, money subscribed would help 'invigorate national industry' because it would be spent in England to manufacture arms and ammunition for the Spanish.[90]

Disagreement about the Spanish cause led to clashing ultra-radical criticisms over British foreign policy. The editors all agreed that the British government was inept and powerless in the situation, whatever it was doing, but beyond that arguments became terribly confused. Basically, Carlile was sure that Britain wished to help the bad French invade Spain, but could not; Wooler thought the British government wanted to keep the bad French out but could not; Cobbett thought that Britain wanted to keep the good French out, but could not.[91]

Despite this discord in 1823, ultra-radical editors were able to keep alive the internationalism of the Enlightenment, via Thomas Paine, during the period stretching from Waterloo to the July revolution. The vocabulary of internationalism certainly remained Paine's; for example, 'the people' was a regularly used collective noun. 'Workers' or 'industrious classes' or 'labouring men' or 'proletarians' would not come into frequent use until after 1832. Perhaps the greatest stimulus for internationalism after 1815 was the apparent league of kings united to repress the liberties of people in all countries. Ultra-radical editors were quick to urge that old national prejudices between peoples be overcome to face this threat. Carlile argued that 'since old governments of Europe had laid aside their national and religious jealousies' in order to enter into 'a formal conspiracy for the atrocious purpose of holding the people of every land in slavery . . .', the 'peoples' should 'divest themselves of selfish and intolerable prejudice' to obtain their 'individual rights'.[92] Such popular internationalism required the inculcation of Francophile sentiments: Cobbett explained that in the past, 'to hate France . . . was regarded as a sort of duty amongst us. We sucked in the feeling with our mother's milk.' But this had changed because now there was 'reasoning in the minds of the people.'[93] Thomas Wooler was able to declare in 1823 that the idea of France as the 'natural enemy' of England would be 'laughed at by a boy of twelve years. . .'.[94] In that year the *Black Dwarf* called for an alliance of the peoples of France, England, Spain, Portugal, and Italy because in each nation 'despotism' and 'freedom' were most actively at war. The 'patriots' of all five nations were charged to 'melt down and amalgamate all national jealousies into harmony in the common cause. . .'.[95] Cobbett's internationalism was kindled by the Austrian invasion of Italy in 1821, which led him to declare that

If a powerful nation be suffered to invade or oppress a weaker nation with impunity . . . the weak must all in time be subjected to the strong. As men in civil society laudably combine their efforts to seize the robber and the murderer, so must nations combine to protect each other alternately in case of need against the acts of tyranny, perpetrated by a force too great for any one singly to resist.[96]

In subsequent decades working-class internationalism would build upon these sentiments, and share the feeling that communications between the British 'people' and the peoples of the Continent were inadequate. As early as 1818 *Sherwin's Political Register* pointed out that the ordinary press could not be relied upon for information about Europe, thus anticipating a common argument in the Chartist *Northern Star*:

The sentiments of the People of France or of Germany are not to be gathered from the English newspapers, all of which . . . are too much under the influence of the government at home, or have too great an interest in the existence of the 'present Governments abroad, to publish what they know on the subject. The foreign papers are under a similar influence, they dare not publish the state of England, the feelings of the people towards the government, or anything else which it is the interests of foreigners to be acquainted with, and thus, as far as the influence of the press extended, a system of delusive silence is preserved on both sides of the water.[97]

Another anticipation of later working-class internationalism was the propagation of pacifistic or, at least, anti-militaristic viewpoints. The *Black Dwarf* thus itemised the causes of war in 1817:

1. War cleanses the country of all the 'swinish multitude' who are apt to grow saucy in a long peace. Thus all reforms are procrastinated as being dangerous and ill-timed.
2. War enables the minister to provide places and pensions for himself and his friends.
3. It attaches the monied people to his interest by the prospect of beneficial loans and contracts.
4. Above all, it accustoms the country to an immense standing army. . . .[98]

Professional soldiers were often vilified, in the style of the pamphlet 'The Character of a Soldier', printed by Richard Carlile and probably written by him. The pamphlet described soldiers as 'erect monsters' who were rewarded according to how much in 'wounds and blood, mutilations and deaths, shrieks and screams, widows and orphans and gore . . .' they could produce.[99] The way to guarantee peace in the world was to replace despotisms with representative governments, because, according to a widespread illusion of the times, such governments would assure peace. As the *Medusa* put it, '*the right of voting taxes* is the right of *preventing war*'.[100] Nevertheless, ultra-radical pacifism was limited because 'just' wars and the right of armed self-defence were recognised. Therefore the militarism of a national guard of citizens who defended republican institutions was justified, and the Neapolitans and Spaniards who defended their revolutions were fighting in 'just' circumstances. Ultra-radical editors were not at all reluctant to urge these 'defenders' to the battlefields. For example, Carlile called for resistance to French intervention in Spain in 1823 in these terms: 'No truce, no amnesty, no patched up peace can again take place—War! War! War! Let that be the cry, until popular liberty finds no opposition.'[101]

B

These explicit statements of ultra-radical pacifism and internationalism are easier to perceive than ultra-radical xenophobia and nationalism. Another similarity with working-class internationalism as it developed in the next decades was that nationalistic and xenophobic sentiments were rarely overt. There was a resentment against foreigners who received British funds in the form of pensions, subsidies, or profitable offices, but these foreigners invariably belonged to other classes. Some were Hanoverians.[102] Foreign institutions, not foreign peoples, were held up for ridicule and criticism.[103] Cobbett, Carlile, Wade, Sherwin and Davison commonly used such terms as 'the Bourbon system' and 'Bourbon censorship'. Spies, secret police, *agents provocateurs* and centralised bureaucratic operations were all regarded as foreign and bad. Moreover, it was a common practice to make bad government or bad governors at home analogous with notorious examples drawn from abroad. Carlile, for example, declared that Castlereagh was 'as absolute' in England as the 'Emperor of Russia or the Sultan of the Turks'.[104] The 'Dey of Algiers' was a popular subject for comparisons. Friendliness rather than xenophobia marked published attitudes towards poor foreigners. Some inkling of this can be gathered from some chance remarks made in the ultra-radical press about Alien Bills.[105] It was felt that laws made to control the stay of foreigners in England were designed to help the Holy Alliance pursue its victims, and that such laws destroyed the historic British role as a hospitable asylum. Xenophobia did not even surface in the form of fears of foreign workers' competition in these years. In fact, there was anxiety that English workers would flock to other shores to escape from 'the borough system . . . test acts and libel laws'.[106] Such unpatriotic remarks were common. This declaration from the *Gorgon* reveals the attitude prevailing towards nationalism:

Who amongst us ought to love Old England, the land of the Borough-mongers? . . . Has not the poor man been robbed of the just reward of his labour, and insulted by the bounty of his plunderer? Is not England a den of thieves, of beasts of prey,—of an insolent and tyrannical aristocracy—of a plundering and hypocritical priesthood? Ought we to love such a country? Would it not be a spurious and superstitious patriotism, which knaves might preach, but, which fools alone could believe?[107]

For ultra-radical editors England's glory was a thing of the past, and while England had declined, other nations had gained in stature. An editorial in the *White Hat* in 1819 noted 'the contrast with other countries, once the objects of contempt, . . . who rise as we are sinking, and go on gaining fresh privileges as we are loaded with addiːional fetters'.[108] The old boast that the English constitution was 'the envy of surrounding nations and the admiration of the world' was denied; instead it was common to write that the constitution received 'the contempt of surrounding nations and the scorn of the world'. The point was that England's historic role as the leading nation in freedom and liberty could only be regained through reform.

Many of these ideas from the ultra-radical press were built upon in the thirties and forties by working-class editors and organisers seeking to develop class-conscious internationalism. Of course, their ultra-radical sources were often poor critics of British foreign policy and were sometimes grossly misinformed about Europe. Nevertheless, the accuracy of articles and editorials about Europe in this press is not what is significant. After all, this was a doubtfully legal, usually embattled press, led by editors whose education was necessarily short, whose funds were limited and whose staff was almost non-existent. What is important is that they broadened and maintained interest in European affairs, and made the Continent relevant to British workers. These ultra-radical editors laid foundations.

Notes to Chapter 1

1 *Political Register*, March 18, 1815, p. 325.

2 *Black Dwarf*, October 4, 1820, no. 14. See also the *Republican*, October 6, 1820, p. 200.

3 *Black Dwarf*, June 4, 1823, p. 812; June 18, 1823, p. 895.

4 Appeals to help the Neapolitans resist invasion appeared in the *Black Dwarf*, March 14, 1821, p. 381. Also, for Spain, February 5, 1823, p. 207; May 14, 1823, p. 713; June 4, 1823, p. 718; June 25, 1823, p. 900; July 2, 1823, pp. 16–17. Richard Carlile wrote frantically to enlist aid for Spain in 1823, calling upon Englishmen to 'cross the Channel in thousands. . .'. (*Republican*, April 18, 1823, p. 482. See also June 6, 1823, p. 710.)

5 Ultra-radical is a better term to use in this era than working class because working-class consciousness had not yet emerged clearly. The plebeian left included substantial numbers from the lower middle classes.

6 *Political Register*, November 4, 1820, p. 1108.

7 *Gorgon*, December 12, 1818, p. 1.

8 *Black Dwarf*, March 27, 1822, p. 468. Carlile wrote in the *Republican* of September 1, 1820, p. 6: 'Amidst the sorrows of home we find consolation in looking abroad. . . .'

9 For Cobbett's interesting political views, see G. D. H. Cole, *The Life of William Cobbett* (London, 1947); E. P. Thompson, *The Making of the English Working Class*, pp. 746–62; John W. Osborne, *William Cobbett: His Thought and Times* (New Brunswick, N. J., 1966).

10 Cobbett posed as a yeoman, idealised farming, and used homey rural analogues for explanations. Shorn of repetition, Cobbett is quite pungent.

11 *Political Register*, September 26, 1818, p. 233. As Cobbett wrote in the

Political Register of September 5, 1818, p. 69, the boroughmongers 'clearly saw that if a really free government were established in France, it would be impossible for them to retain their ill-gotten power . . . with the example of France before them, close under their eyes, the people of England, who had never ceased to demand a reform, would not remain in an unresisting state any longer'.

12 *Political Register*, September 12, 1818, p. 118 and April 15, 1815, p. 499. Also, March 18, 1815, p. 321; July 26, 1817, p. 534; March 24, 1821, p. 824.

13 *Political Register*, October 10, 1818, p. 234. Also November 22, 1817, p. 1034.

14 He disliked the way the statesmen at Vienna shifted sovereignty over areas without regard to the wishes of the populations involved. *Political Register*, September 5, 1818, p. 69. Also July 29, 1820, p. 67; March 24, 1821, p. 831.

15 *Political Register*, April 13, 1822, p. 110.

16 *Political Register*, November 22, 1817, p. 1055.

17 *The Gorgon*, November, 1818, p. 236; and December 12 and 16, 1818.

18 *The White Hat*, October 16, 1819, p. 3.

19 Wickwar, *The Struggle for the Freedom of the Press*, p. 73 and Thompson, *The Making of the English Working Class*, p. 676.

20 Webb, *The British Working Class Reader*, p. 48. Carlile preferred the *Black Dwarf* to the *Register*, probably because his deistical republicanism found Cobbett's Toryism intolerable (Cole, *Richard Carlile*, p. 12). Even so, there was little divergence from the *Register* about the aftermath of the French wars. See, for examples, October 6, 1820, p. 200; October 1, 1819, p. 82; April 11, 1823, p. 450.

21 Wickwar, *The Struggle for the Freedom of the Press*, p. 57; *Black Dwarf*, June 25, 1817, p. 337; The *Dwarf* ridiculed the peace: April 2, 1817, p. 385; August 4, 1819, p. 167; June 18, 1817, p. 331.

22 *Black Dwarf*, April 2, 1817, p. 385.

23 Thompson, *The Making of the English Working Class*, p. 454; see also pp. 455 and 456.

24 *Political Register*, April 15, 1815, p. 419.

25 *Political Register*, January 18, 1817, p. 83; April 13, 1822, p. 105; August 10, 1822, p. 334 and April 26, 1823, p. 194.

26 *Republican*, December 3, 1819, p. 233.

27 *Republican*, February 11, 1820, p. 110. He thought that post-war France was far ahead of England in matters of civil and religious liberty, and agreed with Cobbett that the French peasantry was much better off than comparable groups in England (*Republican*, December 3, 1819, p. 227). See also *Gorgon*, December 26, 1818, p. 256 and December 12, 1818, p. 234; *White Hat*, October 16, 1819, p. 3; the *Medusa*, April 10, 1819, p. 73.

28 Thompson, *The Making of the English Working Class*, p. 456.

29 *Political Register*, August 12, 1815, p. 164. A letter from a worker that appeared in the *Register* of July 1, 1815, p. 815, declared that Napoleon would not have met defeat had he remained 'General Bonaparte, Commander of the Armies of the Republic' and if he had trusted 'the people' rather than kings, nobles, and priests.

30 *Black Dwarf*, June 25, 1817, p. 339.

31 *Political Register*, April 1, 1815, p. 393; July 16, 1815, p. 36; June 24, 1815, p. 784.

32 *Political Register*, April 1, 1815, p. 392; April 15, 1815, p. 525.

33 *Political Register*, April 1, 1815, p. 394. In the *Register* of July 29, 1815, p. 97 Cobbett wrote, 'if the fame of all the other famous men that ever lived could become embodied in one man, it would not equal his individual fame'. In July, 1815, p. 815, he wrote that Castlereagh would never 'efface the memory of the prisoner's deeds' or 'even lessen the effects of those deeds'.

34 *Political Register*, August 12, 1815, pp. 165 and 166. See also January 14, 1817, p. 105.

35 See the *Black Dwarf*, June 25, 1817, p. 337; January 29, 1817, p. 10; *Republican*, August 27, 1819, p. 2. It seems that after the optimism of 1820 flashed forth Napoleon was not so favourably remembered. He was then seen as a more effective restraint upon the 'march of the mind'. See the post-1820 negative comments of the *Black Dwarf*, December 6, 1820, p. 824; December 12, 1821, p. 837; *Republican*, July 25, 1823, p. 66.

36 *Sherwin's Political Register*, March 14, 1818, p. 260.

37 *Republican*, January 14, 1820, p. 17; May 23, 1823, p. 643. The *Black Dwarf*

featured an article entitled 'England a member of the Holy Alliance', April 2, 1823, p. 493. In the July 16, 1823 issue, p. 73, the *Dwarf* claimed that one manifesto of the Holy Alliance was of English origin. Then again, on July 2, 1823, the *Dwarf* declared that England's adherence was 'not formal'. Cobbett thought that the settlement made at Vienna placed Britain in the alliance. See the *Political Register*, September 12, 1818, p. 120 and March 24, 1821, p. 802. Cobbett wrote in the March 8, 1817 issue, p. 194, that the boroughmongers were working with the Holy Allies to bring Englishmen to 'a state of quiet submission' through such measures as the suspension of Habeas Corpus in order to bring England into the continental scheme of things.

38 *Medusa*, May 15, 1819, p. 103.

39 *Republican*, January 14, 1820, p. 13; February 11, 1820, p. 109; August 16, 1822, p. 366; July 5, 1822, p. 174.

40 *Black Dwarf*, September 2, 1818, p. 588. For other comments against the Holy Alliance, see April 2, 1817, p. 146; May 9, 1817, p. 236; July 16, 1823, p. 105; July 28, 1818, p. 520; *Gorgon*, December 12, 1818, p. 234; *Medusa*, March 6, 1819, p. 23. The middle-class press was markedly calmer. See, for example, the *Leeds Mercury* of February 27, 1816.

41 See the *Black Dwarf*, September 2, 1818, p. 560; April 2, 1823, p. 493; *Political Register*, July 20, 1820, p. 50; *Republican*, August 16, 1822, p. 365; April 9, 1823, p. 527.

42 *Political Register*, August 14, 1822, p. 414; August 24, 1822, p. 479.

43 *Republican*, April 16, 1823, p. 450; August 30, 1822, p. 417.

44 *Black Dwarf*, April 19, 1824, p. 480.

45 E. J. Hobsbawm, *The Age of Revolution* (London, Cleveland and New York, 1962), p. 120.

46 *Black Dwarf*, February 16, 1820, p. 199; December 6, 1820, p. 823. *Political Register*, March 21, 1821, p. 798, warned the French Bourbons of a coming revolution and urged them to 'make it themselves'. Compare with the *Leeds Mercury* of March 25, 1820, which presented similar views.

47 *Gorgon*, December 12, 1818, p. 233.

48 *Republican*, February 11, 1820, p. 11.

49 *Black Dwarf*, September 2, 1818, p. 588; March 27, 1822, p. 465; *Republican*, December 3, 1819, p. 227; February 11, 1820, p. 110; *Political Register*, November 22, 1817, p. 1054. *The Briton*, September 25, 1819.

50 *Republican*, March 10, 1820, p. 260. For anticipation of a French revolution, see March 8, 1822, p. 307; February 21, 1823, p. 250.

51 *Political Register*, March 24, 1821, pp. 798–804.

52 For examples, the *Leeds Mercury* of March 24, 1820 and the *Manchester Guardian* of May 12, 1821, p. 2.

53 Perhaps imprisonment contributed to the feverish nature of his enthusiasm for the Spanish cause.

54 *Republican*, October 13, 1820, p. 229.

55 *Republican*, September 1, 1820, p. 7. In the November 17, 1820 issue, p. 447, he wrote: 'One year, such as the one we are now passing, . . . is worth a life of twenty ordinary years.' Also, October 20, 1820.

56 *Republican*, March 7, 1823, p. 319.

57 *Black Dwarf*, August 2, 1820, p. 179. See also March 15, 1820, p. 350; December 6, 1820, p. 824; December 12, 1821, p. 840.

58 *Republican*, September 3, 1819, p. 30; Cobbett had assured his readers that 'the improvement of society in Spain and Portugal . . . [was] . . . a century, at least, behind our own country' (*Political Register*, April 15, 1815, p. 466; *Medusa*, July 11, 1819, pp. 185 and 186; *Black Dwarf*, May 1, 1820, p. 167; *Republican*, July 28, 1820, p. 468).

59 *Republican*, March 10, 1820, p. 260; February 24, 1820, p. 196; *Black Dwarf*, July 26, 1820, p. 534.

60 *Black Dwarf*, August 2, 1820, p. 179. See also December 12, 1821, p. 840.

61 H. G. Schenk claimed that the 1820 rebellion in Spain was just one in a long series of officers' plots that began in 1817 and continued on into the thirties (*The Aftermath of the Napoleonic Wars* (Oxford, 1957), p. 143); also, Hobsbawm, *The Age of Revolution*, p. 116.

62 Richard Carlile, *The Character of a Soldier:* by Philanthropos, second edition (London, 1822).

63 *Republican*, October 20, 1820, p. 381. Also February 18, 1820, p. 145; June 9, 1820, p. 229 and June 6, 1823, p. 710.

64 *Black Dwarf*, March 15, 1820, No. 10.

65 *Republican*, December 8, 1820, p. 533.

66 *Republican*, February 11, 1820, p. 111. Also June 9, 1820, p. 230; July 28, 1820, p. 472; September 13, 1820, p. 604.

67 *Republican*, April 28, 1820, p. 14; March 31, 1820, p. 369; *Black Dwarf*, March 21, 1821, p. 408.

68 *Black Dwarf*, July 26, 1820, No. 4; *Republican*, August 11, 1820, p. 546; October 13, 1820, p. 230; October 20, 1820, p. 183; December 29, 1820, p. 623.

69 *Republican*, December 29, 1820, p. 623. Also September 15, 1820, p. 77.

70 *Political Register*, March 24, 1821, pp. 796–7. Also *Black Dwarf*, March 14, 1821, p. 378.

71 Carlile's hopes, which had been built so high, came crashing down hardest. He abused the Italians more bitterly than the Austrians after the latter had won: 'Slavery and death to such men, or such wretches, the disgrace of their species. They are unworthy of the fertile soil on which they tread' (*Republican*, April 18, 1823, p. 1). Wooler was more kind. He explained their lack of effective resistance by the fact that they had been 'degraded by a bad system', and had risen prematurely. Carlile was chastised for excessiveness: 'I regret that some *friends* of freedom should fall to abusing the Neapolitans at so unmerciful a rate for having failed to achieve all the good that some sanguine spirits have anticipated'. After all, 'that Naples should have breathed the word revolution would have amazed the statesmen of the . . . last century' (*Black Dwarf*, April 18, 1821, p. 535).

72 See, for a good example, the *Manchester Guardian* of January 18, 1823.

73 *Political Register*, March 24, 1821, pp. 792–826. Cobbett advised his readers to follow his accounts of the Austrian invasion 'by laying the small of your right leg upon your left knee. If you be not too fat, you will need no map to give you a rough sketch of the seat of war.'

74 *Black Dwarf*, March 14, 1821, pp. 376–8.

75 *Political Register*, March 24, 1824, p. 784.

76 *Black Dwarf*, December 12, 1821, p. 841.

77 *Black Dwarf*, April 25, 1821, p. 602.

78 Cobbett wanted 'a British fleet in the Mediterranean . . . to prevent the deadly Austrian from marching . . .' but assured his readers that British participation to help Naples could never take place even if the government wanted it, because 'this nation is itself in a very ticklish state . . . the people's distresses are great . . . war at this time would shake the paper-money system to its foundation . . .' and might 'compel the government to yield what they have hitherto refused', that is, reform (*Political Register*, March 24, 1821, pp. 826–7). See also the *Black Dwarf*, April 25, 1821, p. 602.

79 *Republican*, April 23, 1823, p. 1; *Black Dwarf*, April 18, 1821, p. 535.

80 *Republican*, March 7, 1823, p. 289; March 21, 1823, p. 384; April 18, 1823, p. 481. It is interesting to note that the *Manchester Guardian*, January 18, 1823, p. 289, expected a general war with British participation to result from French intervention. Also, *Republican*, March 24, 1820, p. 328; February 18, 1820, p. 151; August 2, 1820, p. 179.

81 *Black Dwarf*, July 2, 1823, pp. 15–16

82 *Ibid.*

83 Arthur Aspinall, *Politics and the Press*, p. 105.

84 Harold W. V. Temperley, *The Foreign Policy of Canning* (London, 1925), p. 299.

85 *Political Register*, March 8, 1823, pp. 716–17; 741–4.

86 John W. Osborne, *William Cobbett: His Thought and His Times* (New York, 1966), p. 12, notes that Cobbett's observations about foreign affairs were 'too clearly written with conditions in England in mind to be taken at face value'.

87 *Political Register*, June 21, 1823, p. 744.

88 *Political Register*, November 1, 1823. Cobbett used the device of a 'Letter from the People of Spain to the Jews and Jobbers, on the Abuse which the Jew and

Jobber Press of London has poured forth on the Spanish nation for Expressing their Joy at the Recent Events in Spain'.

89 *Political Register*, June 21, 1823, pp. 712–35; November 1, 1823, pp. 282–3.

90 These arguments are found in the *Black Dwarf* of June 25, 1823, pp. 893–9; July 30, 1823, pp. 160–4. Wooler offered as evidence of his respect the recollection that he had 'walked twenty-five miles cross-country on a winter day to be present at one of Cobbett's "rustic harrangues" '. In future disputes, both Henry Hetherington and Bronterre O'Brien would disagree with the same type of deference.

91 These arguments are set forth at length in the *Republican*, February 21, 1823, p. 248; March 7, 1823, p. 290; May 23, 1823, p. 643; The *Black Dwarf*, June 11, 1823, p. 844; *Political Register*, March 8, 1823, pp. 521–85.

92 *Republican*, August 16, 1823, p. 266. E. P. Thompson in *The Making of the English Working Class*, p. 829, made the claim that working-class internationalism was one of the important 'themes' that arose before 1832: 'Two themes only may be mentioned of those which arose again and again in these years. The first is that of internationalism. This was, to be sure, part of the old Jacobin heritage; and one which the Radicals had never forgotten.' Thompson characteristically followed this quick, clear generalisation by rapid-fire presentation of details and pithy excerpts drawn from a variety of sources. In the very next paragraph the author is in pursuit of another 'theme'. A purpose of this chapter is to fill out this theme and supply it with contrasts and textures.

93 *Political Register*, November 22, 1817, p. 1046.

94 *Black Dwarf*, July 30, 1823, p. 164.

95 *Black Dwarf*, July 16, 1823, pp. 105–8.

96 *Political Register*, March 24, 1821, p. 826.

97 *Sherwin's Political Register*, May 16, 1818, pp. 7–12.

98 *Black Dwarf*, November 26, 1817, p. 733.

99 Richard Carlile, *The Character of a Soldier:* by Philanthropos, second edition (London, 1822).

100 *Medusa*, March 6, 1819, p. 23.

101 *Republican*, June 13, 1823, p. 719.

102 *Political Register*, August 30, 1817, p. 691; July 29, 1820, p. 102; May 1, 1819, p. 1011.

103 A possible exception would be the Jews. There was considerable anti-Semitism, judging from the way anti-Semitic remarks peppered ultra-radical publications, particularly Cobbett's *Political Register*.

104 *Republican*, March 22, 1822, p. 355.

105 *Sherwin's Political Register*, May 16, 1818, pp. 7–12; *Republican*, June 9, 1820, p. 234; *Political Register*, September 5, 1815, p. 70; November 4, 1820, p. 1116.

106 *Political Register*, July 29, 1815, p. 110; April 15, 1815, pp. 463, 467.

107 *Gorgon*, October 31, 1818.

108 *White Hat*, October 16, 1819, p. 1.

2 The early thirties

I THE JULY REVOLUTION

Late in the year 1830, the family and friends of a British major stationed in Germany searched the Black Forest for his eleven-year-old son, who had run away from home. When they found him, with the traditional runaway's bundle in hand, he bravely informed them that had he escaped he would have made his way east 'to help the Poles'.[1] His name was Ernest Jones, a boy destined to become one of the most active Chartist internationalists in the mid-forties. Most of the other future Chartist internationalists were also youths in 1830, as were those Europeans who would become their friends and associates. George Julian Harney was 13: Karl Schapper was 17; Friedrich Engels was 10; Karl Marx was 12. On the other hand, the ultra-radical editors who had struggled against the libel laws had become middle-aged by 1830—Wooler was 44 and Carlile 40—and their most influential years were already behind them. The one exception was 68-year-old William Cobbett, who reached a new height of influence in the early thirties just before his death in 1835. Prominent leaders around 1830, James Bronterre O'Brien, 25; William Lovett, 30; Henry Hetherington, 38; were more sophisticated, class conscious and less exclusively devoted to Paineite rationalism. Their newer outlooks furnished concern for Europe and Europeans with distinct, working-class points of view. It was also in the early thirties that the first working-class meetings, that is, meetings held under the exclusive auspices of working-class leaders, were given over to the celebration or commemoration of events on the continent. These years also mark the appearance of the first post-war addresses by British workers to their fellows in Europe. All of this would become increasingly common in the Chartist period, and was really just one of the momentous changes of the early thirties. This was the time which saw the maturation of class consciousness through the formation of great unions, through the disappointment of the Reform Bill, and through the war of the great unstamped press. There was a semantic reflection: increasingly, the term 'people' was replaced with 'working men' or the 'productive classes'. In addition, the 'profitocracy' or 'middlemen' joined the kings, aristocrats, and priests in the ranks of workers' enemies.

At first British workers' joy over the July revolution in France blended in with the enthusiasm of the liberals, who felt that 1688 had come to France at last. The influence of this revolution on the Reform Bill agitation has been much debated by historians, and what can be concluded from the remnants of Elie Halévy's thesis, Norman Gash's revisions, and Joseph Hamburger's insights is that many British workers were prepared to draw analogies between France and Britain in the early thirties and agitate in a demanding, threatening, impatient manner.[2] James Mill and Francis Place were able to use them to impress the government that there might but be two alternatives—concession or revolution.[3]

Some of the plentiful analogies with the French situation from the working-class press are worth noting: the Duke of Wellington was told in an open letter in the *Penny Paper for the People* that he 'should no longer be surprised' if 'the people' turned to 'face the cannon and the bayonet, and either end their miseries in death; or live in freedom and equality'.[4] A satirical 'King's Speech, Intended to be Spoken on the Opening of Parliament', published in the same journal, had the king warn that Englishmen were ready to 'follow the example of their foreign neighbours' if that 'moderate relief which they will now be content to receive' were not given them.[5] In 1831 Bronterre O'Brien told a tavern crowd celebrating the return of Henry Hunt in Preston that Englishmen, so long 'foremost in the race of liberty', could now learn from Frenchmen and Belgians 'what her course in the future ought to be'.[6] Cobbett, during a lecture at the Rotunda, asked: 'Where is there a man in England who does not feel that the example of the Parisians is not to be without its effect?'[7] William Carpenter, an important working-class editor, made considerable use of the Gallican example. An open letter of his to the Duke of Wellington declared:

The fearful proceedings . . . on the Continent of Europe must speedily extend their influence to this country, unless this can be suppressed. . . . The march of liberty, which has for more than a quarter of a century been restrained by the combined efforts of the lovers of oppression, in all parts of Europe, is now recommenced, and the knell of despotism, whether clothed in the garb of a continental sovereign, or in the dress of an English borough-monger, gladdens the hearts of all.[8]

In a second such letter, he added: 'Should the young men of England be afraid of a prison, when the young men of France were not afraid to meet death at the cannon's mouth?'[9] When some workers in Kent were sentenced to only three days' imprisonment, without hard labour, in October 1830, Carpenter blamed the effect of the revolutions abroad: 'O brave labourers and artisans of France and Belgium, see what your noble example has effected! See and rejoice. You are the cause of this, . . . it was your example that made the whole of the magistrates tremble with fear, while they were in the act of passing even this "lenient" sentence'.[10] John Doherty's *Voice of the People* contained this blunt editorial statement in 1831:

Men of sense and reflection would pause before they drive an entire nation to desperation, while the heroic example of the patriots of France, the intrepid, prompt and successful struggle of the brave Belgian and the still more glorious achievements of the gallant Poles are before us. Do they imagine that England, the cradle of liberty, the asylum of the oppressed and persecuted of every nation and clime, will be the last in asserting her freedom and securing her independence?[11]

Working-class and radical leaders generally hoped that revolution in England could be avoided. Cobbett wrote in his *Two Penny Trash* in 1830 that he did not want to see Englishmen 'rise on the government as . . . [the French] . . . have done'. He wanted the preservation of 'the institutions and the tranquility' of England, while restoration of the 'happiness' of the nation was accomplished. Should the government grant 'radical Reform of the House of Commons' while Englishmen were still capable of being content with just that, the French could be left 'to settle their own affairs in their own manner'.[12] Henry Hetherington wrote that the kind of revolution he wanted to see in England was an internal revolution, or as he called it, a 'self-revolution, self-reformation'. To be sure, he wanted to see all the existing institutions of the world overthrown, because all were 'based on error and supported by prejudice. . . '. The 'sword or the bayonet' would not accomplish it, however. The 'march of intellect' and the 'force of reason' had to gain the victory. Hetherington believed that 'no violent revolution will ever increase the happiness of mankind' unless the people 'are capable of knowing what they really want'. He admitted that revolutions 'may often times be necessary to remedy some passing act of oppression or effect some immediate benefit', but lasting results could not be guaranteed unless mass self-reformation had taken place.[13]

Working-class enthusiasm for the July revolution was by no means all swallowed up in the Reform Bill crisis. It went on to add fuel to class consciousness both before and after the passage of the Bill. Working-class anniversary celebrations of the July revolution were particularly significant in this. The very first of them took place on August 1, 1831, at the Copenhagen Tea Gardens in London, at a time chosen to coincide with the festive opening of London Bridge. 'Work-people' had been asked to attend in the greatest possible number, to show that they could not be drawn to London Bridge to see 'an exhibition of monarchical folly and extravagance'.[14] To make it possible for them to attend, special efforts were made to keep the price low. As one correspondent of the *Penny Paper for the People* wrote, a 'cheap dinner was necessary so that every working man who respects his rights, and loves his country, may have the power of attending. . . . Numbers would not assemble unless the price of admission were low.'[15] Numbers did assemble—1500 according to the *Poor Man's Guardian*[16]—and there was, besides the 'intellectual repast', dancing, drinking, and singing. Much was said about the July revolution at this meeting, but at least as much about the British reform movement. There is no evidence that foreigners were present. Regardless of these factors, the meeting was a turning point in the history of British working-class involvement with European affairs, and not simply because of the theme. The chairman had the simple title of 'Mr', and some people who would be among the most prominent Chartist leaders later on—Lovett, Hetherington, and James Watson—made the arrangements, sold the tickets, gave the speeches, and wrote the reports. From the first plans to the last toast, this was a working-class affair, the first of many, to celebrate an event in Europe.

Two reports of it are available for the historian—one in the *Poor Man's Guardian* and the other in the *Republican or Voice of the People*.[17] Julian Hibbert was unanimously called to the chair. He was a noted speaker, a man of scholarly pretensions, a republican, but not a working man.[18] Hibbert's lengthy speech commented on the bloodlessness of the July revolution, and regretted that a republic had not been declared, with Lafayette as president. Immediately after it, an 'Address to the Brave People of France' was considered and voted upon. This was the only official act of the gathering, besides passing a resolution in favour of a cheap, free press in Britain. The rather brief address, along with a letter from Hibbert, was sent to Lafayette, in the hope that he would see that it received wide publicity in France, particularly among French workers.[19] It read:

Friends and Brethren,

   We, the working classes of London and its vicinity, congratulate you on this, the first anniversary of your immortal triumph over fraud, cunning and military despotism.

   We dwell with admiration and gratitude upon the principles you established in these 'three great days'—that an [sic] united people are irresistible, and that for a nation to be 'Free, it is sufficient that she Wills it'.

It continued by expressing the basic disappointment of the British workers at the outcome of affairs in France. They regretted that 'the principle of the Sovereignty of the People, for which you fought and bled' had not been 'consolidated before you suffered yourselves to be dispossessed' of force. A republic should have been established. Instead, and here the new class consciousness is revealed,[20] French workers 'suffered . . . hopes to be deceived, and . . . efforts paralysed by the worst of men—viz. stock-jobbers, law-mongers, and others of like character'.

You, the working people, who effected the revolution and carried it to a successful issue, what have you got! More poverty and less sympathy—a press much more fettered, and which exists only in defiance of the laws that are stretched to crush it.

It concluded by hinting at the possibility of another revolution.

   Vigorous speeches followed the introduction of this address. One dwelt on a romantic account of a French heroine who led her countrymen to victory despite the fact that she was 'covered with wounds on the front of her person'. John Cleave, a noted working-class editor, asked single girls to have no 'sweet-heart' who 'would not exert himself in freedom's cause'. He adjured mothers to teach the principles of freedom to their children, to 'engraft them on the mind' so that 'no bayonet' could remove them. The men present were urged 'to quit gin shops for six months' to bring on a 'moral revolution'. After these speeches the address was put to the meeting and carried with great cheering, including 'nine times nine for the French people', whereupon the band struck up the 'Marseillaise'.[21]

   This class-conscious address was eventually conveyed to none other than that famous aristocrat, the Marquis de Lafayette. He wrote in reply to Julian Hibbert, cautiously.[22] After a few pleasantries he stated:

I considered it as a very agreeable duty to make the Address known to my fellow citizens. Nevertheless, after having shown it to various of my friends in the Chamber [of Deputies] and to various of my companions in the Revolution of July, we were of the opinion, that the announcement of the address (so as to have it inserted in the Newspapers) was susceptible of some modifications; not, certainly, because the address blames some parts of our conduct, for our friends have an indubitable right to tell us, and to tell the public, what they think of us, but because, in the present situation of France, some of the expressions of the Address would be regarded by the public as a provocation to very great political changes, which we do not desire and of which the party of the fallen dynasty might take advantage against the Revolution itself. . . .

Enclosed with Lafayette's letter was a paragraph cut out from one of the French newspapers, which presented, in translation, the first and last sentences of the Address, and a modified summation of what was in between. Thereby one of the first clearly working-class addresses to their fellows in Europe was castrated by an aristocrat's editing. Future addresses would be sent to more sympathetic recipients.

The second anniversary of the July revolution was marked by a similar celebration, held in the same place, on July 30, 1832.[23] An 'imposing spectacle' of 'thousands', made up of contingents of the National Union of the Working Classes came from different parts of London. The units, with their bands and banners, converged in an open field as they advanced upon Copenhagen Gardens. This time a leader from the working class, Henry Hetherington, was called to the chair. 'It might be thought', he declared, in the words of the *Poor Man's Guardian*, 'perhaps, somewhat presumptuous in a working man like himself occupying so conspicuous a situation on such an occasion; but he felt proud that he had been thought worthy to be placed in it by his fellow countrymen, and especially when he remembered that the Working Classes of France had raised the seige of Paris. (cheers.)' An 'elegant' tricoloured silk cap that some of the ladies present had made rested on his head while he made his rather direct comments: he found the July revolution 'an event pregnant with most important consequences to the nations of Europe, and replete with instruction to the people of all nations who desire to work out the political salvation of their country. . .'. Since the 'Working Classes of the people of France' were the 'principal actors in the great event', it was fitting that they assemble, 'and express their esteem and admiration. . .'. He went on to spell out some 'very important lessons' from the July revolution:

. . . The working men of France showed what could be accomplished by union and courage, and proved that we could at any time beat down despotism. (hear.) But they also taught us that . . . if men had not know-ledge, designing rascals would come in and possess themselves of the vic-tory. (hear.) . . . The effects of that event, however, had not altogether been lost; both France and England were beginning to demand cheap govern-ment, and it was quite clear if they were united it would be all over with the Despots on the Continent. (cheers.)

Hetherington went on to describe how the assault by the Polignac ministry on the press had triggered events in France, and went on to present one of the earliest evocations of working-class international-ism:

. . . Since the despots were united for such despicable purposes, was it not right for the people—the Working Classes—to unite to oppose them? (cheers.) If the people were united on the principles of freedom, they must succeed in overthrowing their oppressors; and he hoped the day was not far distant when he should see even the Emperor of Russia driven from his seat to the plains of Siberia. (cheers.)

Hetherington was followed by Julian Hibbert, whose remarks reveal how class enemies had come into clearer focus since the last meeting. He declared how the French workers had been 'betrayed by the *juste-milieu* men—the *Whigs* of that country—and unfortun-ately the power acquired by the brave republicans fell into the hands of men, bankers and such persons, who used that power to subdue the people who won it for them.[24] Should there be any revolution in Britain, he 'hoped the Working Classes would keep the power in their own hands. (hear.)'

The French turned away Charles the Tenth and put Philippe in his place, and thought all was right; but it was a terrible mistake—it was like turning out the lion to put in the tiger. . . . 'Rogues all' was the game—the plunder and degradation of the people. (hear.) It would be the case with us if we submitted to be governed by the *shopocracy*. (hear.) It was certain France was more degraded now than under Charles the Tenth. . . .

Clearly, bitterness of British workers over the Reform Bill coloured these interpretations of developments in France. One speaker was quite direct:

He was rather surprised to see no Members of Parliament present.—(hear.) Where was Mr Hume, Mr Hunt and all those men who were raised into power by the people? . . . He would go further, and would say to Lords Althorp, Russell, and Brougham, you ought to be here, for had it not been for the blow struck by the people of France at despotism, you would not have been the Ministers of England. (cheers.) Who put the match to the gunpowder first, but the powerful arm of the people of France?

Before dispersing, the meeting passed this internationalist resolution:

Resolved, that we deeply sympathise with the persecuted patriots of France, Poland, and Germany, in their virtuous struggles to obtain the blessings of free government; and we declare it to be our opinion, that there will be neither peace nor happiness until the people of all nations obtain the inestimable right of a truly representative government.

As one speaker explained, 'they were not merely directing their attention to the liberty of Ireland, or Scotland or England or France, but to the liberty and well-being of the whole human race. (applause.)'

Even stronger notes of class consciousness were sounded at the third anniversary celebration.[25] Even the banners were militant: one read 'Holy Alliance of the People', and another 'Unite and Conquer'. James Watson gave a particularly vigorous speech in which he declared that 'he felt proud on this day, a day on which we were reminded of the superior integrity and honesty of the working classes, of the unflinching valour of their brethren in France. . .'. He pointed out that 'it had been said, by way of reproach, that Englishmen would never exhibit such conduct, but he did not think that his countrymen were deficient in any qualification necessary for such a purpose, and he was sure that when the proper opportunity should arrive they would not fail to exhibit as much spirit and good conduct as their neighbours. (cheers.)'[26]

Resolutions passed at this meeting contained these sentiments:

Resolved, that while we recur with delight to the three days of July 1830, when the artisans of Paris achieved so splendid and brilliant triumph over the powers of despotism, the fruits of which victory was wrested from them by the crafty middlemen and loan and money-jobbers of Paris . . . [the next time] not only the French but every nation in Europe will imitate the example of America, and barter extravagance and venality for good and cheap government.

and:

Resolved that the example of France and this country is sufficient to convince every rational mind that there is no hope for the people but in their own exertions. That Whigs and Tories, Ultras and *Juste Milieu* men are only so many terms to effect the plunder of the people. . . .

It can be seen from the content of these anniversary meetings that a highly class-conscious analogy was drawn from the July revolution which was used in the time of deep disappointment for British

workers over the Reform Bill. Hatred of 'French Whigs', a French
'profitocracy' and, in general, the French middle class, was strongly
expressed, because it was widely believed that these were the
Frenchmen who had stolen the victory from the brave Parisian
workers.[27] This analogy was honed to its sharpest by the man who
would become famous as the 'Schoolmaster of Chartism', James
Bronterre O'Brien. According to E. P. Thompson, 'O'Brien was, as
much as Cobbett and Wooler in their post-war years, an authentic
voice of his times'.[28] Without doubt, one of the reasons why the
early thirties mark a turning point in the outlook of the British
working class was that O'Brien's pen was busy in the *Poor Man's
Guardian*, the *Penny Paper for the People*, and many other unstamped
publications, pouring scorn on the Whigs and the middle class from
whose ranks he had emerged.[29] His bitter, class-conscious interpretation of the French Revolution of 1830 became the standard
account in the great unstamped press, and versions of it diffused into
the varied realms of working-class expression. Key portions of a
characteristic editorial reveal his reaction: Bronterre began an
editorial in Hetherington's *Two Penny Dispatch and People's Police
Register* by asserting that Louis Philippe had a false title, for he was
not king of three-fourths of the French.[30] He went on to describe
the one-fourth of the French for whom Louis Philippe was truly
king:

He is king of the Chamber of Peers, whom he creates and pensions at the
public cost; of the deputies, . . . of the electoral colleges, which [comprise]
160,000 proprietors and profit-mongers. . . . He has made the tricoloured
flag wave over the Bourse of Paris. . . . He is king of the Bourse, of the
rentiers, of the stock-jobbers. His government gorges them with the spoils of
French industry, . . . wrung in taxes from his victimised subjects. He is
king of the millionaire capitalists—of the Jews and bankers—of bullion
merchants, of hotel-keepers, and the pampered shopocracy of Paris—of the
great master manufacturers of Lyons, Rouen, St Etienne, Amiens. . . . He
is king of the municipal and national guards, of his army officers and
Bourbon police. He is king of all the French and foreign loungers in Paris,
who spend their days . . . at the restaurants, or playing billiards at the cafes,
or gambling on the stock-exchange, and who spend their nights . . . swelter-
ing in the arms of other men's wives, for which species of gallantry have
made Paris the envy and admiration of the world. He is king of the *Academie
Royale de Musique*, where the fair *artistes* exhibit themselves half-naked and
the government supports the proprietors to aid their vocation of debauching
youth, and debilitating the manhood of France. He is king of all the
theatres and exhibitions . . . where vice is reduced to a system, where
licentiousness is ingrafted in the national character. . . . To comprise all in
one word, Louis Philippe is king of all that is rich, and rotten, and rascally,

and corrupt, and cruel, and tyrannical, and anti-national, and anti-Christian, and anti-human in France. He is king of self-privileged robbers and assassins, who would rather die than work, and who would immolate not only France, but the whole civilised world, to prevent the reign of equal laws and general happiness.

Bronterre went on to tell his readers that Louis Philippe stayed in power by armed force hired by the 'base shopocracy'. A would-be assassin of the French king was chided for his foolishness, because killing Louis Philippe was not the way to kill the system:

The true way to attack the system is to attack the classes who support it—that is to say, the shopocracy, or monied orders. These are, in truth, the real assassins. By these, for these, all crimes are committed, all despotisms upheld, all oppressions practised. A successful blow at the monied orders is a death-stroke to all the tyrannies on the earth.[31]

Bronterre's themes reappeared throughout the unstamped press, particularly in Hetherington's publications, where many unsigned editorials were probably written by him. For instance, an editorial in the *Poor Man's Guardian* called workmen who believed that kings were the 'authors' of their slavery 'fools', and informed them that:

The tyrants of all countries are those who rob the labourer of his hire, or . . . seize the produce of his labour without giving him an equivalent. . . . Kings and armies are but tools in their hands. Priests and lawyers are the same.[32]

Another editorial in the *Poor Man's Guardian* declared:

The honest artisan, being himself sincere, believed in the sincerity of the shopocrat. He buckles his armour and fights for the middleman's rights, in the hope that he is fighting for his own. Alas . . . he soon finds . . . that the shopocrat was his friend and ally only because he could not do without him, for the battle won, the middleman throws by his weapon (the work-man) and only thinks of appropriating the spoil. Thus it has ever been in revolutions: the parties who achieve them are seldom or never the gainers.[33]

Such heightened class consciousness led to a revaluation of the National Guard. In the past, radicals and ultra-radicals had clamoured for a national guard, but by the early thirties, the idea of such a force had fallen from favour, chiefly because it seemed that the French national guard was a middle-class institution, designed only to preserve 'good order' and 'protect property', which meant, it was claimed, keeping the working class down. Hetherington's newspapers noted how common workers were excluded from the national guard by the great investment of time for drilling and money for uniforms and equipment that was required for participation. Therefore, Hetherington's journals called upon French workers to form 'undress regiments' as a counter-force to the middle-class national guard, even if this meant drilling in 'smock frocks' with pitch-forks for arms.[34]

A common conclusion about the July revolution, with obvious parallels for England, was that French workers were actually worse off under the 'French Whigs' than they had been under the tyranny of the Bourbons. As an editorial in the *Penny Paper for the People* declared, the July revolution left 'governors more experienced and wary . . . chains . . . more closely riveted . . . prison walls doubled in thickness . . . and . . . guards multiplied'.[35] In fact, it was sometimes stated that the worst of tyrannies were found not in Russia or Asiatic states but in France and England. As Hetherington argued, the real test of slavery was not the existence of 'religious tyranny' or the lack of 'freedom of speech', but whether or not men were unceasingly forced into 'unrequited hard labour'.[36] He saw the political and social conditions of France and England as identical:

Twelve parties in France! Nonsense. In France, as in England and everywhere else, there are but two parties, viz.—*those that will work for their living and those that will not. These are the only really distinct* parties that have ever existed in the world.[37]

In sum, the July revolution, like the Reform Bill, did not do enough; France would have to have a new revolution, and the work begun in the 'three glorious days' when working men reigned in Paris would have to be continued.[38]

II   COBBETT'S LAST ACT

Bronterre O'Brien did not monopolise the role of interpreter of the July revolution for British workers. Richard Carlile was still around, but reacting in the same style as he did in the twenties.[39] Like Carlile, William Cobbett was his old self in the early thirties. Boroughmongers, fundholders, Jews and jobbers, and the debt were kept to the forefront of his analyses of the July revolution. He did not shift to vehement denunciations of the middle class and the Whigs. The brief period between the July revolution and the Reform Bill was actually the last time that the ageing journalist and political leader was in the limelight. It was probably one of the most important and influential times of his career, second only to 1815 to 1817, as G. M. Trevelyan has suggested.[40] The *Two Penny Trash* and *Cobbett's Political Register* were mobilised in his last great effort to bring about Reform, and perhaps most important were his appearances in the Rotunda, a building which was a great centre for all kinds of radical and working-class activities at the time.[41] Cobbett gave a total of eleven well-attended Rotunda lectures on 'The French and Belgian Revolutions and English Boroughmongering', and copies of them were printed and, according to G. D. H. Cole, 'widely sold'.[42]

Cobbett, more than any other popular journalist, tried to bring the excitement of the July revolution to bear upon English politics. Norman Gash has noticed this, but minimised Cobbett's effect on the Reform Bill struggle by pointing out that only the 'proletarian radicals' would accept the July revolution as a direct political inspiration. Moreover, Cobbett 'began generally to elaborate the analogy of the French revolution and English Reform' after the Parliamentary elections were over.[43] Even so, Cobbett undoubtedly raised the political temperature in the period of the Reform Bill crisis by his use of the example of the July revolution.

Cobbett explained that it was his aim to 'clearly show' that recent events in France and Belgium were 'closely connected, and almost identified with our public affairs and with the interests of every man of us'. There was 'no knowledge . . . so useful as that which relates to the recent events in France. . .'.[44] He noted that 'all possible efforts' were being made to show that there was no analogy between French and English situations,[45] and observed that the British aristocracy and clergy were 'mute as mice' while other Englishmen celebrated the July revolution.[46] Here Cobbett came closest to a class-conscious interpretation of the event. 'Who is it,' he asked, 'that has shown friendship for the French? Who applauded the overthrow of tyranny in France?' The 'people of England', who specifically included 'farmers, tradesmen, labourers and journeymen', and specifically excluded 'the mayors of towns . . . the nobility . . . [and] . . . the gentry'. Those excluded 'kept aloof, and shared no friendship at all for the people of France'.[47] The 'people', so de-fined, were also the victors in France:

The revolution in France [1830] was accomplished—not by the aristocracy —not by military gentlemen—not by gentlemen with whiskers or long spurs—not by gentlemen of any description, but by the working people alone; by the men who quitted their shops, who laid down their needles and their awls, and their saws and, rushing out into the streets of Paris, said, 'If there be no alternative but slavery, let us put an end to the tyrants'.[48]

Cobbett stressed the idea that the deaths of the Parisian workmen in the 'three glorious days' was transcendental, that is, Frenchmen who fought and died were supposed to have fought against 'the grievances of all working people. He urged British workers to meet in their 'several trades' and 'subscribe . . . pennies' for 'the relief of the widows and orphans of Paris'. Cobbett insisted that very few men 'in work' would not give 'a penny or twopence', noting that thirty workmen from Kent had left ten pounds with him for the survivors in Paris.[49] This appeal circulated widely, and brought in substantial funds. Nottingham, for instance, contributed £200.[50] British workers should contribute, he declared, because Parisians had 'shed their blood, not for their own rights alone, but *for ours* also. . .'. He admonished 'every sincere reformer' to remember that the 'men and women of Paris have now bled for him and his children'.[51]

Transcendental message aside, Cobbett used the same old stock phrases and arguments to characterise the July revolution, so there was really not much that was new in his analysis, in contrast to O'Brien's. Cobbett admitted it. He told readers of his *Political Register* in 1830 that the July revolution had no 'new character' and arose from 'no new cause'. The French people had merely restated their determination not to endure 'those burdens which a profligate, and greedy, and insolent court and aristocracy had laid upon them'. Frenchmen in 1830 had, according to Cobbett, 'come back to that rock from which they had been forced by a million foreigners in arms'.[52]

The content of his eleven lectures on the July revolution, as well as his simultaneous journalism, can be boiled down to this: the Polignac ministry of Charles X had attempted to foist English conditions upon Frenchmen. 'I am going to prove to you', he announced to his readers in the *Two Penny Trash*, 'that the Bourbon family have lost their crown by attempting to force upon France a government like that which exists in England now.' The July revolution had occurred because the 'people of France' resolved 'to die rather than submit to a government like that of England'.[53] He saw the attempt to restrict representation further as the most important specific step leading to the insurrection. Polignac had been out to make 'rotten boroughs'.[54] The ballot had kept Frenchmen in the Chamber of Deputies from being 'slaves', and without it there would have been a French legislature 'corrupt enough for the boroughmongers of England'—a legislature eager to tax ordinary Frenchmen into servitude.[55] Cobbett brushed aside other well-known causes of the July revolution in favour of his one overriding concern: 'My lads of the working classes . . . it was not "seditious writings", it was not *"love of change"*, it was not *"want of religion"*, it was nothing but a conviction that the Polignac ministry intended to bend their necks to a boroughmonger system; rather than submit to which, they resolved to shed their blood. . . .'[56]

Cobbett went further than this by putting forth the 'Wellington legend' about the July revolution. According to this tale, English boroughmongers, in actual co-operation with the Duke of Wellington, encouraged and backed the ill-fated steps of Charles X which led to the July revolution. Both Halévy and Norman Gash have taken note of the 'Wellington legend' in England, but neither one, presumably, has singled out William Cobbett as one of its disseminators. Halévy says that it was 'widely believed . . . that Wellington was Polignac's accomplice in the *coup d'état*', because Polignac had been Wellington's frequent guest and 'intimate friend' while the Frenchman was ambassador to England.[57] Gash fits the Wellington legend into the ultra-Tory vendetta against the Iron Duke—they had never forgiven him for passing Catholic Emancipation. Gash concluded:

The fact remained, however, that scarcely a person of consequence was found to believe the charge. The Liberal party as a body preferred to leave the Polignac legend as the monopoly of the *Standard* and the rest of the ultra-Tory press.[58]

Yet there was no monopoly because Cobbett injected this story into the ultra-radical understanding of the July revolution. Cobbett presented the tale in this fashion to a Rotunda throng in 1830: 'There is every reason in the world for believing that these steps [of Charles X] were hatched by the boroughmongers of England.' Moreover, they 'set Polignac to work to carry it into effect'. Polignac himself was declared to be 'seven-eighths an Englishman, and of the worst sort', owing to his upbringing in England 'amongst the boroughmongers. . .'.[59] Polignac's promotions in the French government were attributed to 'the influence of the English government; and particularly to the Duke of Waterloo. . .'.[60] Furthermore, monied Englishmen were behind this fellow, and behind all others who were ready to move against the remains of representation in France. Why? To Cobbett it was the story of the 1790s all over again. As in that decade, when a French republic without 'nobility and tithes' had appeared, France was feared, because of the changes that nation might inspire in England. 'Though the French had got the Bourbons forced back again, they had not got the tithes back again, and they had . . . in addition . . . a chamber of deputies. Our government, therefore, was not at heart's ease. They said, if we suffer this to go on, we cannot hold our ground here in England, without a reform in Parliament; and therefore it was they that hatched this plot.'[61] They could not abide that 'bit of representation' that the French had had in the Chamber of Deputies, for that body had continued to resist the king by turning out his ministers, thus providing an example to urge on reformers in England. As long as this continued, Cobbett informed his Rotunda hearers, the boroughmongers 'could not keep off Reform in England. . .'. Had Polignac's plot come off successfully, boroughmongers would have turned to their opponents in England and said, 'Pooh! you are bellowing for Reform; why, the French had what you want, and you see they could not go on with it; they have been obliged to give it up!'[61] Had Polignac succeeded, Cobbett and others would have lost one of their 'great arguments' for Reform. After all, Cobbett had repeatedly used the example of France in the English struggle, showing how Frenchmen avoided distress, Corn Laws, and tithes, 'because, and only because, there are no rotten boroughs and no boroughmongers in France; only because the people choose their representatives themselves and choose them by ballot'.[62]

Cobbett made these points with characteristic repetitiveness, bursts of egotism and considerable showmanship. Perhaps his worst egotistical pronouncement in dealing with the July revolution appeared in his *Two Penny Trash* in August 1830.[63] What he did was to attribute the instigation of the July revolution to himself!

France owes her deliverance to the good sense and to the valour of her people; but that sense and that valour would not have been exercised had not the press pointed out the danger; and the press of France could not have pointed out the danger, notwithstanding the great ability of the writers, if those writers had not been in possession of the facts; and those facts were furnished by me, and *never by any-body else.*

One incident at a Rotunda lecture may serve to indicate Cobbett's showmanship:[64] Just after the tricoloured flag was hoisted 'amidst vociferous cheering', Cobbett produced two small cannon balls, and claimed that they had been sent to him from Paris by a French gentleman who attested to the fact that the 'deadly missiles' had been fired by Charles X's troops, and had actually killed several women and children. There were cries of 'Shame! Shame!' from the audience at this point. He then produced a cabbage and a turnip, and held them up in order to show what 'humane' people used to 'pelt their adversaries'. Cobbett kept on pelting the boroughmongers, fund-holders, and the debt until his death in 1835.

III THE BELGIAN REVOLUTION

Much less attention was given to the Belgian revolution of 1830, which altered the provision of the Congress of Vienna merging the former Austrian Netherlands with the Dutch Netherlands in order to form one of the new buffer states around France. Working-class leaders were aware of the shortcomings of this arrangement. Cobbett told an audience at the Rotunda that 'Belgium was no more con-nected with Holland than England is with France . . . the people were separated by the most deeply rooted antipathies. They spoke a different language, and they hated one another to such a degree that it is impossible to do justice to it by any description.'[65] Hetherington wrote in the *Penny Paper for the People* that they may 'bring the case home' by imagining a union of the British Isles under an Irish Catholic sovereign, in which England and Ireland were given equal representation. 'By linking a few recreant Englishmen, his Irish majesty would have no difficulty in securing a majority in his Imperial Parliament, and Britain, if she submitted, would become a province of Ireland. The ministers would be Irish, the bench would be filled with Irishmen, and the majority of the army and navy would be Irish. This is exactly what has taken place in the Netherlands.' The rebellion of 1830, he concluded, was merely a reaction against 'a brute arrangement of European diplomatists, in which neither the wishes nor the interests of the Belgians were thought of'.[66] William Carpenter explained the situation in the following fashion: 'The Belgium [*sic*] people were severed from the nation of which they were closely attached, and united to a people towards whom they bore the most unconquerable aversion.'[67] Cobbett declared that the struggle in the Lowlands was a 'contest . . . of the true, genuine character—a battle of the tax payers against the tax eaters; and the tax payers have prevailed'.[68] Hetherington concurred, pointing out in the *Penny Paper for the People* that the Belgians had been lightly taxed before the union, and heavily taxed thereafter.[69]

Working-class editors wanted to see a republic in Belgium, and, as in the case of France, they were disappointed by the new regime.[70] The solution worked out at the London Conference was viewed with disdain. Hetherington complained that the victory of the Belgians 'was a decided triumph for freedom. What a pity, that having become free, they could not remain so. But the decree of "The Five Powers" is that of fate: and Belgium being surrounded by kingdoms, must have a king.'[71]

The most impressive lesson learned from this other Western revolution in 1830 was that foreign troops could be readily defeated by insurgents. The prevailing assumption had been that they would be more effective than native soldiers in such cases. Hetherington enjoyed describing how regular Dutch troops could not put down the 'undisciplined canaille, or vulgar, as the aristocrats call them— meaning the working classes. . .'.[72] The point of his argument was that 'no armed force' commanded by governments 'will long withstand the necessities, or the outraged rights and "liberties" of the people'.[73]

IV   THE POLISH REVOLUTION OF 1830

Another revolution that occurred in 1830 created a *cause célèbre* that stimulated working-class concern with Europe and Europeans all through the thirties and forties and beyond. The Polish cause became a magnificent source of entertainment and interest for British workers, and eventually served as a catalyst to bring together proletarian internationalists, exiles of various nations, and foreign intellectuals. Even though the Poles were just one of many peoples struggling for national independence in the nineteenth century, they came to symbolise the struggle of light and justice against darkness and tyranny. Unlike the national cause of the Italians or Germans, the Polish cause aroused widespread, intense, and continuous enthusiasm among British workers from 1830 to 1848 and beyond. The main reason for the pervasive phenomenon of Polonophilism was the constant stimulation derived from a large number of emotional, loquacious, sentimental, and colourful Polish exiles who came to England after the fighting was over.

The uprising of 1830 was another major episode in the long, tortured effort to achieve Polish independence. After the collapse of the insurrection, many Polish exiles tramped westwards carrying a passionate conviction that they must go on struggling for the independence of their homeland and enlist any and all foreigners to assist their cause. Whether they were in legions or in exiles' depots or mixed in with the cosmopolitan swarms of the major cities of Europe, the Poles of the Great Emigration kept the Polish cause alive. They posed as the élite of the homeland and gave the impression that they led the Polish nation from abroad, although some of those who stayed behind disagreed.[74]

A glamorised view of the Polish cause came to be held enthusiastically by liberals, radicals and ultra-radicals in Western countries, particularly in France and Britain.[75] Poles were seen as the children of light who fought the champion of darkness, as the defenders of civilised Europe who had entered the lists against the barbarism of Asia. In reality, the Polish revolt of 1830 fitted none of these descriptions. The uprising was not a national war because the overwhelming majority of the peasants were unmoved by it, to say nothing of the Jews. The revolution was actually a war of the *szlachta*, or Polish noblemen, an order which had remained much more powerful and independent than its counterparts in Western Europe.[76] The *szlachta* organised and led the rebellion as another attempt of the old, traditional Poland to prevent Russian hegemony over the Polish part of the great eastern plain. Nevertheless, Western observers would have appreciated the creation of a Polish buffer state between Russia and the West. Liberals also regarded the uprising as one more attempt to gain better government by striving for the nation state, constitutionalism and limited government.

An explanation for the attachment of the British working class to the Polish cause seems less obvious. Poland was so different from their world. There were few Polish counterparts to English artisans and factory hands. Most of the exiles certainly were not, for they had mostly been landowning provincial noblemen before 1830, in many cases proud, pretentious, and arrogant individuals. British workers might have felt more akin to the handful of Polish emigrés who had been agricultural labourers or peasants in Poland, people whose dream was the perpetual dream of their class—to return to take up the plough. British workers could understand this; O'Connor's popular Land Plan was not far from the peasants' dream, and many British workers themselves were not far removed from the countryside in time and habits.

While the Poles were in the field against the Russians, the Polish cause gained less attention from the British working class than later on, for two reasons. First of all, the July revolution and its aftermath absorbed considerable working-class interest, and, secondly, eastern Europe had rarely been considered previously in the ultra-radical press. Polonophilism did not become central to working-class interest in foreign affairs until after the Russians arrived in Warsaw and the Poles of the Great Emigration arrived in London.

Even so, at least two of the frequently held working-class political meetings were given over to the Polish cause while the fighting was still going on. Their tenor reveals how the Polish cause appealed to members of the British working class in a non-specific, simple, and direct manner at that time. At one of these meetings, held in June 1831, a committee of the National Union of the Working Classes prepared a strong protest condemning British complicity in arming the Russians who were engaged against the Poles. It seems that a rumour had spread that the Russian Tsar, through the efforts of a Rothschild, ordered 200,000 muskets from a Birmingham manufacturer. The manufacturer could not fill it in time, so he tried, it was believed, to get the arms stock from the Tower of London sent instead by using his contacts in the British government. The understanding was that his factory would replace the Tower arms as soon as possible. The protest was presented to 'an assembled throng' and passed with cheers.[77]

In February 1831, there was a special public meeting to express admiration for 'the noble conduct of the Polish nation. . .'. and to raise money for the Poles. It was thinly attended and only £13 was collected, but it produced some rhetoric and an address that was sent to the revolutionary government in Poland. The Poles were told by it that British workers looked to them for 'deeds of heroism, worthy of . . . their ancient fame'. The Poles were exhorted to prove themselves 'entitled to inherit the wisdom of a Copernicus and the courage of a Kosciusko' in accomplishing their 'holy exertions'. Poles were declared to be in the 'vanguard of the heroes of liberty'. 'Every eye' was watching them, and 'every heart' was beating for them. It was observed that the Poles were fighting for liberty everywhere, because the cause of liberty, or the contest between 'the oppressors and the oppressed', was 'one and indivisible . . . Any victory of freedom fills the breast of every despot with dread and despair . . . and every patriot bosom with hope and joy.'[78]

Occasional remarks about Poland were also injected into speeches at the Rotunda and appeared at random in the editorials of the great unstamped press during the months of fighting. Some banners at Reform meetings were inscribed with slogans in favour of the Poles and toasts to them were offered at working-class gatherings.[79] In all of these observations, there was little perception of the political or social realities in Poland. There was not much to indicate an awareness that Polish nobles were leading a struggle for old Poland. In 1830 and 1831 no attempt was made to integrate the Polish cause into growing class consciousness, something done later on. While battles were fought on the banks of the Vistula, the contest was built up before the British working class as a vague, glittering thing that it was not. It was not, for example, a war of a united, invincible people who were bent upon the establishment of a republic. Neither was it a clear-cut war of right against might, nor of the oppressed against the oppressors.[80] These designations were nothing but the old, standard, and, by that time, threadbare clichés of the ultra-radical press. They had been used time and time again to describe the rash of revolutions that had swept Europe since 1789.

Henry Hetherington did show some exceptional and rare scepticism when writing about the Polish uprising in his newspapers, but perhaps this was merely a reflection of his disappointment over the outcome of the July revolution in France. When he published a 'Manifesto of the Polish Nation' in the *Penny Paper for the People* in January 1831, he added his hopes 'that the poor people—the mass of the population—are to be benefited by . . . a revolution a little more than the French have been by theirs'. As it looked to him then, in the event of a Polish victory, 'probably only a few will better their condition, while the country at large will merely change their masters'.[81]

Hetherington's views were singular. While the Polish revolt was going on, there was some rather heated and unsceptical working-class enthusiasm for British intervention on behalf of the Poles. Perhaps the most vigorous pleas for action appeared in John Doherty's popular *Voice of the People*, a Manchester publication. Arms were called for:

The conversion of Jews, Indians, Hottentots have cost immense sums of money, and much labour and exertion, without ever producing even a tithe of the benefit to mankind which a few thousand stand of arms and field pieces, presented at this time to Poland, would effect.[82]

And war:

The people [of England] will not stand and see the Poles quietly butchered. Let us see all Europe in a war before the catastrophe of a national slaughter.[83]

War was justified, the editor of the *Voice of the People* explained, because Polish success would 'infuse new energy into the advocates of liberty in every quarter of the globe, and pour fresh balm on the wounded spirits of oppressed millions'. A Polish defeat, on the other hand, would release tyranny and legitimacy to spread 'blood and carnage' everywhere.[84] Therefore, 'the liberty of Europe, may, the world, depends upon the issue of this desperate struggle. . .'.[85]

Speeches in the Rotunda and editorials in the unstamped press also called for intervention. Since the Polish struggle was viewed as a 'war of principle', it was argued that British intervention to help the Poles was imperative.[86] The unreformed state of the House of Commons was given as the explanation for Britain's cowardly foreign policy, as James Watson stressed in a speech given in the Rotunda in October 1831, when he insisted 'that if Englishmen were in possession of their just rights, the Autocrat of Russia dare not now occupy Warsaw'.[87] Without reform, Henry Hetherington wrote, the Poles would have to fight on unaided 'except by the good wishes and enthusiastic cheers of the surrounding millions. . .'.[88] The Whigs drew sharp criticism in the unstamped press for their unwillingness to help the Poles. Readers of the *Penny Paper for the People* were told that the Poles could have 'no hope of assistance from the Property Men', because they supposedly respected the Tsar's property rights over Poland.[89] John Cleave went so far as to declare in a Rotunda speech that the Whigs would betray good government wherever it appeared, in Poland or elsewhere.[90]

After the fighting was over, Polonophilism came into its own, celebrating a nostalgic lost cause—a cause that had displayed the heights of heroism and martyrdom and suffered from the depths of barbarism. A resolution passed at a Rotunda meeting in 1831 conveys this feeling:

RESOLVED That this meeting view with the bitterest indignation the events which have lately been permitted . . . to take place at Warsaw, in which a brave and heroic people, contending for their civil rights and national independence, have been atrociously slaughtered by hordes of barbarians brought from Tartary and Siberia, as the most convenient tools of an odious and overwhelming despotism. . . . This meeting blushes for the name of Englishmen that the power . . . of this country should have been withheld in arresting so frightful a career of despotism, injustice and blood. . . .'[91]

There was nothing particularly class conscious about these sentiments, and, indeed, the British working-class spokesmen were only going along with what was rather common among radicals and liberals of various shades in England. John Howes Gleason has shown in *The Genesis of Russophobia in Great Britain* how immensely popular the Polish cause was, and how 'constant reference to the unbearable wrongs and cruelties inflicted upon the Poles' was made by many and various sources of English public opinion during these years. Eventually, some editors called for intervention against the

'Muscovite barbarians', and radical members of Parliament pleaded for Poland in intemperate language on the floor of the House.[92] Working-class reaction to this revolution was, for the time being, unlike the special, unique, and often highly class-conscious reaction to the July revolution. Later on the Polish cause, so popular and enduring in working-class thought and activity, would receive its own particular class-conscious interpretations, but only after the arrival of Polish exiles.

V OWENISM AND EUROPE

Owenism led to a new and dramatic phase of the working-class movement in the thirties. Owenite socialists who attempted to organise the Grand National Consolidated Trade Union certainly strengthened and deepened class consciousness by attempting to project an alternative system to capitalism. The question is, did they strengthen and deepen that phase of working-class consciousness that looked to Europe?

The fact is that Owenites were out-and-out internationalists as part of their Utopian stance. Their plans were for all men for all times. They freely addressed Europeans or the world in their pronouncements, and talked often of international congresses or world government. Yet there was something terribly distant and abstract about all of this. Owenite internationalism had a hollow ring, as if it were broadcast into dead air. Moreover, their pronouncements were vague and diffuse as revealed in this excerpt from 'An Address to the Governments of Europe and America from the Congress of Delegates of the Cooperative Societies of Great Britain', dated April 1832:

We wish another system, derived from facts and experience . . . a system which shall remove the causes of evils which have so long afflicted humanity. We offer one capable of being applied most advantageously to immediate practice in every country; not only in Europe and America, but in every part of the world.[93]

In general, Owenite publications had a detached nature about them, as if they were concerned only with their own little co-operative worlds. E. P. Thompson, in *The Making of the English Working Class*, has noticed how the Owenite *Crisis* 'sailed through the waters of 1831 and 1832 carrying cargoes of reports on co-operative congresses and on trading stores, without noticing that the country was in fact in a state of revolutionary crisis'.[94] Ironically, the periodicals issued by the most frankly internationalist Englishmen, these Owenites, displayed the least interest in foreign affairs of any read regularly by the British working class. Neither the *Crisis* nor other Owenite journals took much notice of the July revolution.

Owenite lack of interest in foreign affairs ran the risk of veering into xenophobia, out of fear that concern for Europe would dissipate energies needed for the creation of new forms of society at home in England. An item in *The Pioneer* declared:

What care we for the squabbles of courts and diplomatists, for protocols and manifestos; whether Pedro or Miguel are kings of Portugal; or for the twaddle about Donna Maria. . . . We have our interests at home, in those near and dear to us. . . . If we care about the unfortunate condition of poor Poland, or detest the barbarity of the tyrant Nicholas, it is that we determine with our sovereign power . . . not only to render ourselves impregnable to such villainy, but to teach the Poles themselves how to work out their emancipation. We are serious when we say that the Builders' Trade Union have commenced, and will effect, the work of emancipating the world.[95]

Despite such xenophopic inclinations, an Owenite periodical, *The Pioneer*, was involved in what probably was the first direct exchange with a specific group of foreign workers.[96] An 'Address of the Workmen of Nantes to the English Trades' Unions' appeared in *The Pioneer* in June 1834.[97] It began with a variation of what would become a cliché of international fraternisation: 'The Working Classes in all Countries are Brothers'. It went on to declare appreciation for what the British workers had done:

We have heard . . . of the struggle you have begun in defence of your rights, and applaud you for it. You have behaved like men; and our hearts were with you through the whole.

A brief account of the French workers' struggles followed, and then a strong declaration of internationalism:

There was a time when every province of France had custom-houses and land of its own. At present, all France is one; and England is in a way of being more so still. But why are England, France, Spain, Portugal, Italy and the rest, to keep themselves separate either? All men in all countries who desire freedom, or, in other words, bodily and mental good; all who want to get rid of its yoke of absurd and antiquated laws; all who want to shake off their present misery—are they not brothers?

For the sake of humanity and civilisation, an Anglo-French democratic union was called for:

Brothers and friends!—A Union between you and us will bring about and compel another between England and France; and England and France united are strong enough to play the part of civilizers to all mankind; in other words, to protect and bring forth the liberty everywhere, by its exercise of a peaceful power over the rest of the world.

The first steps towards these goals, as might be expected, involved establishing lines of communication:

Brothers and friends!—Do not let our Union be stopped by the sea or rivers, that mark the boundaries of states. Let us put into communication with one another, London, Paris, Manchester, Lyons, Liverpool, Nantes, Bordeaux, Aporto, Lisbon, Madrid, Cadiz, Barcelona, Turin, and all the great centres of industry in the world.

The press was chosen as the instrument of communication on account of its cheapness, afterwards 'we can, when necessary, go to the expense of individual correspondence and special messengers. . .'.

It is no wonder that the exchange ended abruptly after the *Pioneer's* reply, for the Owenites responded in a nebulous manner, and filled a considerable part of their address with purely English concerns.[98] The opening paragraph affords a good example of its fulsomeness:

Brothers—Your voice came over the waters, and we listened to its melody with extreme joy. Our sorrows, our sufferings, and our sympathies are akin to each other. The sentiments which find peace in your hearts, have also taken up their abode in ours. The voice of the stranger from afar awakens in our minds the kindliest emotions, and it widens the range of thought, and enlarges our conception of extended brotherhood. . . .

French workers were congratulated for their struggles with reference to 'bloody sceptres', 'yokes', and the 'eternal spirit of progression'. The Owenists' response to internationalist overtures took this form:

O! God, that we could spread a spirit through the nations to act together— to beard the foe at every point at once—to meet him here and there and every where! . . . We want a little of your ardour, Brothers.

The world situation was described in this fashion:

The Cauldron boils; where is the witch to chaunt the incantation? There is a weight upon men's mind at present; a sudden change will shortly throw it off, and thick and hurried incidents will quickly follow. We are no prophet, Brothers; but the sky we think looks somewhat stormy.

The address concluded with these sentiments:

Dear fellow-workmen, do not let your pens like [*sic*; lie?] idle; write ever and anon to stir our sympathies. . . . Our cause can never sleep, and they are fools who hope to catch it snoring, but frequent intercourse makes men more social, and foreign news is always welcome. . . . Our best esteem to all your Brotherhood. And if the Females are in Union, our fervent love to them.

The Owenites also participated in an episode which was, as far as the history of the British working class is concerned, relatively unimportant and certainly little known. This episode was the visit of St Simonian missionaries in the early thirties, a story told fully in R. Pankhurst, *The St Simonians: Mill and Carlyle*. Various items about these French visitors were carried in the working-class press, including their addresses and some English replies, often heated, in the form of letters and editorials.[99]

Working-class contact with the St Simonians took place in the early thirties when two groups of symbolically costumed missionaries arrived in order to proselytise their economic religion. One of the many interests and activities of these missionaries was to enlist the support of the British working class. To do this, they planned to found a journal in London. Nothing came of it, but they were able to get some of their propaganda in the working-class press through the contributions of a sympathetic clergyman, and some of the missionaries' addresses were published directly.[100]

Extensive criticism of St Simonian propaganda was not undertaken by the Owenites, save for one who wrote in to complain of the missionaries' 'Jesuitical side-wind attack' on labour exchanges.[101] Instead, it was Henry Hetherington who considered the St Simonians' mission in great detail in the *Poor Man's Guardian*.[102] His lengthy editorial was entitled:

The Saint Simonians—Remarks on Their Politico-Religious Tenets—Their Good Points and Their Bad Ones—Wherein We Agree with Them and Wherein We Differ

He summed up the energetic efforts of the missionaries by explaining that 'like all other professors of a new faith, they are great zealots, and like all other missionaries, profess, of course, to preach truth, and truth only'. What Hetherington disliked about St Simonianism was the creation of a new 'political priesthood', the use of unnecessary 'hard words in explaining their system' and 'the desire to reconcile everything to a general theory. . .'.

We would do all that the St Simonians propose to do, but we would do it by plain and straightforward means. We want no new religion—no new priesthood—no newfangled theories—no ;abstractions—no mysticism. . . . We are for Equal Rights and Equal Laws—which every man can understand—we are for Universal Suffrage, which will enable the people to put society into any form they like, and to make and unmake whatever institutions they please.[103]

VI CONTINUITIES

Owenite communications, working-class commemorative celebrations, reactions to the revolutions of 1830 and, above all, the development of a class-conscious interpretation of European affairs were all fresh turning points in the thirties, but there were continuities from the past as well. For example, the old, vague internationalism calling for a league of peoples to face a league of kings continued to appear in the great unstamped press,[104] as well as expressions of Paineite republicanism[105] and Paineite pacifism.[106] Disenchantment with Iberian affairs also continued.[107] Some publications and speakers gave European affairs a prominent place; others virtually ignored the continent, as in the past.[108]

Criticism of the government's foreign policy certainly was not new; it had been popular in the press read by British workers and in speeches delivered to them since before Waterloo, and continued in the thirties, with greater asperity and, often, with a decidedly working-class point of view.

An ingenious device used by Henry Hetherington to criticise foreign policy was a 'King's Speech', supposedly found at Brighton, 'near the pavilion'. By this means, readers of the *Penny Paper for the People* were informed of the kind of foreign policy that Henry Hetherington desired in 1830 by reading words put into the mouth of the King of England![109] The speech included a pacifistic declaration: '. . . We have expressed . . . [to all foreign powers] . . . our firm determination not to plunge this country into war.' The King of the Netherlands was adjured to 'make amends for all past errors, by improving the condition of his Dutch subjects. . .'. Great Britain did not wish to become involved in his strife with his rebellious Belgian subjects, because 'our people would never consent to opposing this struggle of an oppressed people for freedom . . .'; besides, the British treasury was too deeply in debt for war. Non-intervention was also pledged in case of any troubles that might break out in Spain and Portugal, where 'tyrants' would probably lose their thrones in the future. Yet non-intervention was a policy intended only for the government; individuals would be permitted to volunteer on the side of revolutionaries, and there would be no restrictions at all on 'the raising of any loan or subscription generally

C

among the people, for the purpose of furthering the independence of any country which is labouring under a tyrannical yoke'.

Non-intervention was widely regarded in the working-class press as a sane policy because the spirit of freedom was felt to be operating well by itself in its tasks of changing Europe for the better; time was on their side.[110] A foreign war might bring a greater debt and greater repression at home, as it did during the first French Revolution. In fact, working-class spokesmen regularly entertained fears that the Whigs were out to embroil the nation in an unwanted war to strengthen their hold over the country. One meeting of the National Union of the Working Classes passed this resolution:

Resolved, that the members of this Union view with indignation the wily and hypocritical conduct of the Whigs, in their manœuvres to entrap the nation into a war, for the purpose of supporting monarchy and aristocracy, in opposition to the more important interests of the millions. . . .[111]

An interesting editorial in the *People's Conservative and Trades' Union Gazette* foresaw a war between 'those two sections of European society, the Holy Alliance or absolute government advocates, and the Whigs, or mock liberty partisans . . .' and concluded that 'the monied men all over Europe' had a stake in it, but the 'cause of the People' could not gain by the issue. The Whigs were blamed for this state of affairs:

From all this anyone can easily see into what a position the folly, the trickery, the irresolution and the swaggering of the Whigs have brought the country. . . . We do not know whether these Whigs are mere bunglers, or cheats, or cowards; but we believe they are a heterogeneous compound of all three. . . .[112]

The immediate cause of this particular crisis was the Eastern Question, that tangled set of problems that has taken up so much space in the diplomatic history of this period.[113] The *People's Conservative*, unlike the scores of diplomats involved, saw the Eastern Question in relatively clear and simple terms. It was simply that when the Sultan of Turkey had turned to England for help against rebellious Ibrahim Pasha the Whigs would not support him, and so he turned to the Tsar, who thereby gained domination over Turkey and the Straits. The Whigs had been 'too much engrossed at home in party intrigues, and corrupting majorities of our excellent representatives' to deal with the situation. Grudging appreciation of Tory strengths in handling foreign affairs was expressed, foreshadowing instances when Chartists would support them rather than Whigs:

The Tories, if in office, would have never acted so stupid a part in the first place, or so pusillanimous a part in the second. We are fully aware of the curses they have heaped on the country, but . . . they would have presented such a bold front as would make those Muscovite barbarians shrink back into their frozen morasses. By their superior skill in diplomacy, or their firmness, the storm that now threatens us would have blown over.

The editorial concluded: 'We detest a Whig war for Whig purposes, for which we must pay with our blood and money.'

Another editorial in the *People's Conservative* on foreign affairs concluded with a remark indicating what would become, in the decades ahead, an increasingly important reason for working-class concern with Europe:

We have given these sketches of the present posture of foreign affairs that the people may at one view see their real position, and be prepared for the interminable discussions upon them in the approaching session.[114]

This running criticism of foreign policies continued in the future, as did the new developments in dealing with European affairs that the turning points of the thirties mrked. All of these new and old elements were sucked along together into that varied and gusty political whirlwind of Chartism.

Notes to Chapter 2

1 *Ernest Jones' Diary*, Manchester Central Reference Library.
2 Halévy thought that the July Revolution was a major factor in bringing about the passage of the Reform Bill. See *A Short History of the English People*, Vol. II, *The Triumph of Reform* (London, 1947); New York, 1950 ed., pp. 3–7. Norman Gash has critically re-examined this contention in 'The July revolution in England', *Essays Presented to Sir Lewis Namier*, Richard Pares and A. J. P. Taylor, eds. (London, 1956), and found that elections to the so-called 'Whig' Parliament of 1830 were largely uninfluenced by the July revolution. Definite news of what had gone on in France arrived too late and moderate Englishmen, that is, the bulk of the electorate, were not prepared to draw an analogy between conditions in France and conditions in England in 1830. If the July revolution did anything, Gash contends, it brought a 'vague and diffused' excitement that probably diverted attention away from elections. Even so, Gash admits that ultra-radicals were prepared to draw analogies between French and English politics (pp. 262–3).
3 Joseph Hamburger, *James Mill and the Art of Revolution* (New Haven and London, 1963).
4 October 2, 1830, p. 3.
5 October 23, 1830, p. 3.
6 *Penny Paper for the People*, January 21, 1831, p. 2.
7 William Cobbett, *Eleven Lectures on the French and Belgian Revolutions and English Boroughmongering*, lecture 6, p. 9.
8 *Carpenter's Political Letters*, 'Letter to the Duke of Wellington', October 9, 1830.

9 *Carpenter's Political Letters*, 'Letter to the Duke of Wellington', November 11, 1830, p. 14, pp. 2–3.

10 *Carpenter's Political Letters*, October 29, 1830, p. 1.

11 *Voice of the People*, April 23, 1831.

12 *Two Penny Trash*, August 1, 1830, pp. 45–7.

13 *Penny Paper for the People*, February 26, 1831, p. 1. William Lovett told a crowd in 1831 that the July revolution showed 'the irremediable mischiefs which moral courage, and a blind rage . . . unaccompanied with prudence, would produce' (The *Republican or Voice of the People*, August 6, 1831, p. 5).

14 *Poor Man's Guardian*, July 23, 1831, p. 24. See also the *Republican or Voice of the People*, July 30, 1831, p. 8. Several historians have noted these meetings, but no secondary sources deal with them in detail. Fiodor Rothstein, *From Chartism to Labourism* (London and New York, 1929), pp. 126–7, quoted a portion of the address of the August 1, 1831 meeting, and a small portion of one of the speeches. His source was the *Poor Man's Guardian*. An almost identical account by the same author appeared in a supplement to *Die neue Zeit*, Nr. 17, October 31, 1913. This version was briefly quoted by Julius Braunthal, *History of the International*, vol. 1, *1864–1914* (New York and Washington, 1967), p. 63. Braunthal declared that the meeting of August 1 'marked the re-emergence of international solidarity among the English working class'. He previously mentioned that international solidarity was a feature of the corresponding societies in the era of the first French revolution.

15 *Penny Paper for the People*, May 21, 1831, p. 7. As Hetherington wrote in an editorial in the *Penny Paper for the People*, May 21, 1831, p. 7, those who would attend would be 'better satisfied with an intellectual repast than a City Gorge'.

16 *Poor Man's Guardian*, August 6, 1831, pp. 38–40; *Republican or Voice of the People*, August 6, 1831, p. 4.

17 *Poor Man's Guardian*, August 6, 1831, pp. 38–9; *Republican or Voice of the People*, August 6, 1831, pp. 4–5.

18 Mark Hovell, *The Chartist Movement* (Manchester, 1918; 3rd ed. 1966), p. 58. E. P. Thompson has called Hibbert 'brilliant and ill fated', in *The Making of the English Working Class*, p. 812, and notes that in the Reform crisis he was one of those who was preparing for an armed struggle, p. 814. Lovett admired him; see his *Life and Struggles of William Lovett* (Liverpool, London, and Prescot, 1967 ed., pp. 66, 72).

19 It is found in the *Poor Man's Guardian*, August 6, 1831, p. 38. An abbreviated version was printed in the *Republican or Voice of the People*, August 6, 1831, p. 5.

20 Moreover, a seconding speech regretted how French workers were induced to give their arms to those 'designing knaves, called shop-keepers or National Guards'.

21 The meeting did not end on this high note. There were more speeches, by William Lovett and James Watson in particular, and a resolution. But the primary concern of this was to support the struggle for a free, unstamped press. As this meeting ended, a dinner began in the 'large room' of the Copenhagen House, also to celebrate the anniversary of the French revolution of 1830, but it was 'independent of the meeting in the gardens'. Although Cleave and Watson attended, it was the affair of 'gentlemen' whose toasts did not display the class consciousness of the meeting outside. It is covered briefly in the *Poor Man's Guardian*, August 6, 1831, p. 39.

22 The reply appeared in full in the *Poor Man's Guardian*, September 24, 1831, p. 92.

23 An extensive report of the festivities is in the *Poor Man's Guardian* of August 4, 1832, pp. 482–3.

24 One speaker added: 'It was not the middle, nor the higher classes, but the working men of France who effected the glorious revolution they had now met to celebrate'.

25 The 1833 meeting was at the White Conduit House. A full report is in the *Poor Man's Guardian* of August 3, 1833, p. 247.

26 He hastily added the explanation that he advocated exhausting the opportunities available to bring change by moral force before turning to violence.

27 The British middle-class press was not so exclusive in hailing the heroes of July. The *Leeds Mercury* of August 7, 1830, for example, cheered liberal editors,

some French judges, some members of the chamber of deputies, students, and the national guard as heroes of the revolution, in addition to the 'unarmed multitude of Paris'.

28 Thompson, *The Making of the English Working Class*, p. 823. Thompson noted that historians will not go along with O'Brien's 'overcrude' linking of the post-reform Whig administration with middle-class interests. The same thing can be said of his analysis of the middle-class interests of the July monarchy. See also Alfred Plummer, *Bronterre: A Political Biography of Bronterre O'Brien, 1804-1864* (London, 1971).

29 Although many articles in the unstamped press were signed 'Bronterre', countless unsigned pieces seem to have been written by him as well. O'Brien's attacks on the middle class were especially trenchant because he knew their weaknesses from his own background.

30 Hetherington's *Twopenny Dispatch and People's Police Register*, July 30, 1836, pp. 2–3. Contempt and vilification of Louis Philippe were common in the great unstamped press. For examples, see the *Poor Man's Guardian*, April 19, 1834, p. 82, the *Republican or Voice of the People*, August 13, 1831, p. 3. *The Working Man's Friend and Political Magazine*, April 6, 1833, p. 128, declared that Louis Philippe was noted for his 'open, undisguised, and flagrant manner by which he manifests his extreme selfishness, and upholds and encourages . . . the most hateful tyranny. . . . Avaricious and grasping, he deludes the people with the word of promise on his tongue and the most heartless despotism in his actions. . . . He is the bane of freedom and the curse of France.' He was called, among other things, a 'royal animal', a 'citizen usurper', a 'dishonest shirk', a 'canting hypocrite', and 'an excellent Whig'.

31 Hetherington's *Twopenny Dispatch and People's Police Register*, July 30, 1836, pp. 2–3.

32 *Poor Man's Guardian*, April 19, 1834, p. 82.

33 *Poor Man's Guardian*, December 15, 1832, p. 641. An editorial of April 19, 1834 explained that 'the workers might have seized all the wealth of Paris to their own use. They might have imposed on France whatever form of government they pleased. They might have ample vengeance on the usurers for all the crimes of the past forty years. But no! They would not sully their victory with rapine, however just. They renounced for themselves all selfish objects . . . forgetful of the countless wrongs inflicted upon them by the middle classes since the death of Robbespierre. . . .'

34 *Penny Paper for the People*, October 14, 1830, pp. 1–3. Guardsmen were depicted as men of property from nobility to the lowest bourgeois, men who would 'not scruple' to pull triggers or use bayonets '*to preserve good order and protect property*' and, 'as for their feelings and consciences, they would justify their proceedings, even to themselves, by proclaiming workers murderers and robbers'.

35 *Penny Paper for the People*, October 14, 1830, pp. 1–3. A list of voting qualifications was studied in an editorial of January 8, 1831, p. 7, and the conclusion was that 'the people are as far from being represented or influential as in the reign of the great tyrant Louis XI! . . . And this is the result of the blood of eleven thousand victims!' Also, *Republican or Voice of the People*, July 9, 1831, p. 1.

36 *Poor Man's Guardian*, January 12, 1833, p. 14.

37 *People's Conservative and Trades' Union Gazette*, December 14, 1833, p. 383.

38 *Penny Paper for the People*, October 7, 1830, p. 4; October 14, 1830, p. 2; October 22, 1830, p. 3; November 3, 1830, p. 3; February 26, 1831, p. 1; April 15, 1831, p. 2. *Republican or Voice of the People*, August 13, 1831, p. 2. *Gauntlet*, February 24, 1833, p. 39.

39 In the name of a republic, he called for Louis Philippe's head, and sharply criticised Lafayette for his recent role (*The Prompter*, March 26, 1831, p. 326).

40 G. M. Trevelyan, *British History in the Nineteenth Century* (New York, 1922), p. 226.

41 The Rotunda, in Blackfriars Road, was described by Carlile as 'the capitol of public virtue . . . a real House of Commons in the absence of a better' (*The Prompter*, November 13, 1830, pp. 1 and 8). During the Reform Bill crisis it was used weekly for meetings of the National Union of the Working Classes, which were regularly reported in the *Poor Man's Guardian*. Regular speakers at the Rotunda in these years included William Lovett, James Watson, Henry Hunt, John Cleave, Henry

Hetherington, John Gast, and William Benbow. See Thompson, *The Making of the English Working Class*, pp. 811–13.

42 Cole, *The Life of William Cobbett*, p. 45. Carlile reported that after Cobbett began his lectures, 'the theatre became crowded to excess . . .' (*The Prompter*, November 13, 1830, p. 9).

43 Gash, 'The July Revolution in England', *Essays Presented to Sir Lewis Namier*, p. 263.

44 *Two Penny Trash*, September 5, 1830, p. 50.

45 *Two Penny Trash*, August 1, 1830, p. 50.

46 William Cobbett, *Eleven Lectures on the French and Belgian Revolutions and English Boroughmongering*, lecture 1, p. 4.

47 Cobbett, *Eleven Lectures*, lecture 9, p. 3. See also lecture 5, p. 9.

48 Cobbett, *Eleven Lectures*, lecture 1, p. 1. As Cobbett wrote in the *Two Penny Trash*, September 1, 1830, 'The condition of mankind depends especially on the conduct of the working people.' As the 'great deed' of overthrowing the Bourbon king had been accomplished by the working class, 'the working people here must finally . . . produce those salutary effects which every good man wishes to see produced'. Quoted in G. D. H. and Margaret Cole, *The Opinions of William Cobbett* (London, 1944), p. 120.

49 *Two Penny Trash*, volume 1, 1830, p. 70. Funds were to be left with Cobbett or with the editor of the *Morning Chronicle*. Donors, who would be given receipts, were allowed to send their names along with the money. He even solicited funds from Quakers by telling of how Parisian 'wounded, . . . widows and orphans called upon their generosity' (*Eleven Lectures*, lecture 1, p. 2).

50 Cobbett, *Eleven Lectures*, lecture 10, p. 1.

51 *Political Register*, August 7, 1830, p. 186. Cobbett's *Two Penny Trash* proclaimed: 'The slaves have been slain for you as well as for their wives and children . . .' (vol. 1, p. 64).

52 *Political Register*, August 7, 1830, p. 162.

53 *Two Penny Trash*, September 1830, p. 51.

54 Cobbett, *Eleven Lectures*, lecture 1, p. 2.

55 *Two Penny Trash*, August 1, 1830, p. 56.

56 *Ibid.*, p. 64. He was extremely annoyed that the July Monarchy continued to honour the French national debt. 'National faith', he remarked at the Rotunda, simply meant 'to keep on paying taxes'. He was sure the French would get rid of it, somehow, and that this would affect England profoundly. He called on his audience to 'recollect that the French debt is only a limb of the old lady herself. (Laughter.) Take off a limb, and it is quickly felt at the heart' (Cobbett, *Eleven Lectures*, lecture 6, p. 7).

57 Halévy, *The Triumph of Reform, 1830–1841*, p. 2.

58 Norman Gash, 'The July revolution in England', *Essays Presented to Sir Lewis Namier*, p. 269.

59 Cobbett, *Eleven Lectures*, lecture 2, pp. 3–4. His English wife, a previous ambassadorial engagement, and a period of exile spent in England were also supposed to be influential in Polignac's predisposition.

60 *Two Penny Trash*, August 1, 1830, p. 55.

61 Cobbett, *Eleven Lectures*, lecture 2, p. 3.

62 *Two Penny Trash*, August 1, 1830, p. 54.

63 *Ibid.*

64 The account is in *Carpenter's Political Letters*, 'A Letter to the Aristocracy of England', November 6, 1830, p. 20.

65 Cobbett, *Eleven Lectures*, lecture 9, p. 10. He declared his resentment for the way 'Lord Castlereagh . . . sat down at a table with the other ministers of the holy allies, with paper and pencil, and marked out Europe, in just such a way as they intended it should remain forever'.

66 He had to admit that the Belgians had not been oppressed in some specifics. The king, although he tended to be a 'wilful old gentleman', was 'good and popular', and the 'bulk of the people had a sufficiency of food'. In addition, 'their press was free to circulate publications and newspapers'. *Penny Paper for the People*, October 18, 1830, p. 2.

67 *Carpenter's Political Letters*, 'A Monitory Letter', October 15, 1830, p. 14.

68 Cobbett, *Eleven Lectures*, lecture 9, p. 1.

69 *Penny Paper for the People*, October 18, 1830, p. 2.

70 One of *Carpenter's Political Letters* had called for a republic in 1830: 'Why may we not have a Belgian Republic, as well as a Swiss Republic?'

71 *Republican or Voice of the People*, July 23, 1831, p. 8. See also the *Poor Man's Guardian*, August 20, 1831, p. 54.

72 *Penny Paper for the People*, October 22, 1830, p. 1.

73 *Penny Paper for the People*, October 2, 1830, p. 3.

74 Robert F. Leslie, *Polish Politics and the Revolution of November 1830* (London, 1956); Günter Weber, *Die polnische Emigration im neunzehnten Jahrhundert* (Essen, 1937), pp. 16–36; John Howes Gleason, *The Genesis of Russophobia in Great Britain* (Cambridge, Mass., 1950), chapter v, 'The Polish revolution', pp. 107–34; *Cambridge History of Poland* (Cambridge, 1951), vol. II, pp. 311–23; Alfred Stern, *Geschichte Europas seit den Verträgen von 1815 bis zum Frankfurter Frieden von 1871*, vol. v, Zweite Abteilung, vol. I (Stuttgart and Berlin, 1921), pp. 129–92. For a vast bibliography in several languages on the insurrection's repercussions in England as well as in various European nations, see Ludwik Krzyzanowski, 'Joseph Conrad's Prince Roman: fact and fiction', in Ludwik Krzyzanowski, ed., *Joseph Conrad: Centennial Essays* (New York, 1960), pp. 27–69.

75 For the popular impact on various groups in France, see Liza Cukierman, *Die polenfreundliche Bewegung in Frankreich im Jahre 1830–31, im Lichte der Volkersolidaritätsbewegung* (Warsaw, 1926). For the impact on various groups in England, but not the working class, see Gleason, *The Genesis of Russophobia in Great Britain*, pp. 107–34.

76 In material goods they may have owned, on the average, as much as a substantial British farmer, but the education of many was likely to be poorer. Leslie, *Polish Politics and the Revolution of November 1830*, p. 260.

77 *Penny Paper for the People*, June 18, 1831, p. 4.

78 *Penny Paper for the People*, February 4, 1831, p. 7. No acknowledgement of the receipt of this address has been found.

79 British workers would lift their glasses 'To Poland, successful may be the liberties of her people . . .' (*Poor Man's Guardian*, August 6, 1831, p. 40).

80 See the speech of Gale Jones at a Rotunda meeting, reported in the *Republican or Voice of the People*, June 4, 1831, p. 3. Also the *Poor Man's Guardian*, September 24, 1831, p. 94 and August 6, 1831, p. 44.

81 *Penny Paper for the People*, January 29, 1831, p. 6. He added that an English revolution might succeed as easily, but without a 'moral revolution' success would be questionable.

82 *Voice of the People*, August 6, 1831 p. 2. This was the organ of the National Association for the Protection of Labour. See the editorials of January 29, 1831, p. 36; July 30, 1831, p. 2; also a letter which appeared on August 20, 1831, p. 2.

83 *Voice of the People*, July 30, 1831, p. 2. He added: 'Have we not basely stood still, unconcerned spectators of the butchery of her best patriots, while she is fighting our battle?'.

84 *Voice of the People*, August 6, 1831, p. 2.

85 *Voice of the People*, January 29, 1831, p. 36. Editorials in this periodical urged subscriptions for the Polish cause.

86 *Poor Man's Guardian* December 1, 1832 p. 627. Also *Penny Paper for the People*, June 11, 1831, p. 5.

87 *Poor Man's Guardian*, October 29, 1831, p. 139.

88 *Penny Paper for the People*, June 11, 1831, p. 5. The British and French were urged to 'draw their swords for once in a good cause'. A republican France or a reformed England would go to war, according to the *Republican or Voice of the People*, July 2, 1831, p. 3.

89 *Penny Paper for the People*, June 11, 1831, p. 5. See the *Poor Man's Guardian* of October 29, 1831, p. 139 for the observation that the Whig ministers had sent ambassadors 'to coquet, to wink and look on until the Poles were sacrificed. . .'. Also, see the *Poor Man's Guardian* of December 1, 1832, p. 626.

90 *Poor Man's Guardian*, October 15, 1831, p. 127.

91 Henry Cleave proposed it: *Poor Man's Guardian*, September 24, 1831.

92 Gleason, *The Genesis of Russophobia in Great Britain*, pp. 115, 120–3. Gleason

found that from December 1830 to September 1831, 'hardly an issue of the metropolitan papers failed to include some more or less well-authenticated report or editorial commentary. From the very beginning the Poles were accorded unanimous sympathy . . .' (p. 113).

93 *Cosmopolite*, May 12, 1832, p. 19.

94 Thompson, *The Making of the English Working Class*, p. 783.

95 Quoted in the *Destructive and the Poor Man's Conservative*, October 19, 1833, p. 298. The date from *The Pioneer* was not given.

96 The French newspaper, *Echo de la Fabrique*, established at Lyons, has been noted for its internationalism in the early thirties. On May 27, 1832, it published an address 'To our brethren in England'. See A. Müller-Lehning, *The International Association* (Leiden, 1938), p. 2.

97 *The Pioneer*, June 7, 1834, pp. 395–6.

98 *The Pioneer*, June 14, 1834, pp. 401–2. The response was prominent on the front page.

99 St Simonian addresses appeared in *The Pioneer* of February 8, 1834, p. 188, January 11, 1834, p. 147 and January 18, 1834, p. 105. A reply appeared on March 1, 1834, p. 225. Pankhurst mentions that the address published on January 18 was also printed on that date in the *People's Conservative and Trades' Union Gazette*. See Pankhurst's chapter, 'The working class press debate', in *The St Simonians: Mill and Carlyle* (London, 1957), in which he notes that the response was generally tepid.

100 Pankhurst, *The St Simonians: Mill and Carlyle*, p. 132. The clergyman was Elishama Smith. The St Simonians strained to demonstrate that they were familiar with British conditions, but a patronising tone managed to insinuate itself. See *The Pioneer* of February 8, 1834, p. 188 and the address to the 'Working Men and Women of Derby' in *The Pioneer* of January 11, 1834, p. 147.

101 *The Pioneer*, March 1, 1834, p. 226.

102 *Poor Man's Guardian*, November 30, 1833, pp. 380–3. Pankhurst took notice of this editorial and quoted it briefly in *The St Simonians: Mill and Carlyle*, p. 137.

103 Hetherington did approve of association to replace the cannibalism of the existing system, but the apparent weaknesses of the new teachings led him to conclude that 'St Simonianism will make no progress in England'.

104 *Poor Man's Guardian*, December 17, 1831, p. 212; Hetherington issued this warning in the *Poor Man's Guardian* of June 8, 1833, p. 185: 'If the despots . . . maintain a permanent conspiracy to keep down the people . . . why, in God's name, should not the people (and the army, which is but part of the people) combine to put down their respective tyrants?'

105 See, for good examples, the *Republican or Voice of the People*, June 11, 1831, p. 7; *The Cosmopolite*, April 7, 1832, p. 2.

106 *Poor Man's Guardian*, July 16, 1831, p. 13; December 1, 1832, p. 626; *Gauntlet*, February 24, 1833, p. 39; *The Cosmopolite*, April 7, 1832, p. 2; *Penny Paper for the People*, November 3, 1830, p. 3; *The Radical*, October 15, 1831; *Republican or Voice of the People*, September 3, 1831, p. 3.

107 The *Destructive and Poor Man's Conservative* of October 19, 1833, p. 298, declared, 'Now we are amused with stories of a squabble in Spain. . . . The friends of freedom and social happiness both here and in Spain can of course take no interest in the success of either party. The carnage likely to ensue on both sides will only tend to diminish the enemies of the human race.' The issue of October 12, 1833, found 'Spanish Whigs' trying to establish 'a sham representation like that of Great Britain' which might 'serve as . . . an instrument of plunder for the middle classes'.

108 Fiodor Rothstein, a Marxist historian, has asserted that the *Poor Man's Guardian*, as well as its predecessor, the *Penny Paper for the People*, had 'from a quarter to a half of its eight small pages taken up with foreign affairs, reports and comments' (*From Chartism to Labourism*, p. 126). This is an exaggeration, except for some brief periods, such as in the aftermath of the July revolution. *Carpenter's Political Letters* should be examined in comparison with *The Poor Man's Advocate and Workman's Guide*, published in Manchester. The latter publication had only two brief items on foreign affairs in its fifty numbers from 1832 to 1833. A remarkable

exception was *Berthold's Political Handerkerchief*, which was printed on calico by a Saxon journalist in order to evade the newspaper stamp. It carried an unusual amount of information about Europe. See Joel H. Wiener, *The War of the Unstamped*, pp. 159–60.

109 The 'King's Speech' appeared in the *Penny Paper for the People*, October 23, 1830, pp. 1–3.

110 The 'King's Speech' did not even call for intervention if the Eastern powers were to move against France and Belgium.

111 *Poor Man's Guardian*, December 1, 1832, p. 626. See *ibid.*, May 19, 1832, p. 395; October 6, 1832, p. 555 for further criticisms. Sometimes the fear that Britain would be left behind other nations was expressed. See Doherty's Manchester publication, *Voice of the People*, January 1, 1831, in which 'the once free and happy, and deservedly proud England' was depicted as standing by, 'under the blighting domination of her boroughmongers' while the French, Belgians and Poles hurtled towards freedom and liberty.

112 *People's Conservative and Trades' Union Gazette*, January 11, 1834, pp. 394–6.

113 This newspaper's detailed comments on the Eastern Question are almost unique, since working-class publications generally did not take up this topic, except in passing, and except for Poland.

114 *People's Conservative and Trades' Union Gazette*, January 18, 1834, p. 400.

3 The Chartists and Europe, 1836–44

I THE LWMA AND EUROPE

Chartism was a movement of movements. Although its eclectic nature allows liberty in choosing a time at which to begin a study of the Chartists and Europe, June 1836, is convenient, because it was then that the London Working Men's Association was founded. Whether or not they came from the provinces, like their chief organiser, William Lovett, a Cornishman, they lived as Londoners. Their great, sprawling, cosmopolitan metropolis had much to do with shaping their organisation, its outlook, its influence, and also the nature of its contacts with Europeans and reactions to European conditions. The metropolis still had a vast congeries of workshops, providing hundreds of specialised trades, as in the eighteenth century, without new dominant industries as in the North. London's workers experienced a variety of wages, working conditions, and occupations that must have seemed infinite. Diversity spelled division. Diversity would push and pull away from any attempt at a monolithic mass movement and provide opportunities for variegated pluralism.[1] While London Chartists most characteristically sat in committees and issued manifestos, provincials manfully assembled at militant torchlit meetings, or manufactured pikes, and sometimes drilled at night.[2] London's Chartism did not feature these activities; it was different. London meetings tended to be smaller, and were held in dingier surroundings.[3] Like other London Chartists, members of the LWMA were apt to meet for quiet instruction rather than rousing speeches.

The LWMA had roots that went deep, tapping the rich experiences of the old, established crafts. For them Chartism was a logical continuation of the radical movement that went all the way back to John Wilkes and the ideas of the rights of man embodied in the French revolution and translated by Thomas Paine. They were the heirs of Cartwright, Cobbett and Hunt as well. The organisation sought to continue where Thomas Hardy and the London Corresponding Society had left off in the 1790s. They wished to work again at creating a body of intelligent, educated, rational, and democratic workmen, men who would seek to persuade all reasonable men of the justice of their demands.[4] Workers who enrolled were motivated by the conviction that progress, while assured, would be due in large measure to their own efforts in self-improvement, an attitude which fostered élitism among these self-declared 'sober and moral' workers.[5]

The LWMA seems to have taken on the characteristics of its founder and most outstanding leader, William Lovett, who was far from being a demagogue or even dramatic. His talents were those of a teacher or a secretary, and his strength was his quiet patience. Like the craftsman he was, he painstakingly and steadily worked at drafting manifestos, corresponding and checking up on others to see that assigned tasks were done.[6] A Methodist upbringing trained him to order and discipline and an apprenticeship at cabinet-making taught him craftsmanship. Lovett was deeply influenced by Paine, Owen, and the rationalist traditions of London artisans. He wanted the Working Men's Association to carry on calm deliberations and free discussion in a sober, unemotional atmosphere. His writings tell much about him; they were pedantic, rather pompous and dull, but sincere.

Regardless of his Owenist background, his reactions to Europe and Europeans lacked that nebulousness so characteristic of the Owenites. His enthusiasm for the July revolution had been so direct and vigorous that he was forced to withdraw from the Metropolitan Political Union because some members of the council thought that his responses had the 'savour of sedition . .'.[7] Thereafter, as the heart of the organisation, he was the person most responsible for the remarkable flurry of working-class contacts with European workers in the thirties.

He made impressive claims for these contacts: 'To the Working Men's Association belongs the honour, I believe, of first introducing the mode of *international address* between the working men of different countries that has since been practised by other bodies so beneficially on several important occasions.' This claim, found in his autobiography, is untrue,[8] but it cannot be denied that these contacts were significant; they provided the first cross-Channel working-class exchange to be widely noticed.

What brought on these contacts was the prosecution of a Flemish working-class leader, Jacob Katz, for holding a public meeting.[9]

British workers were first informed of Katz's punishment through an emotional account in the *London Dispatch*:[10]

Katz dared to assemble men of his own class of wealth producers, and peaceably to address them. This was high treason in the eyes of the wealth consumers. They first of all glutted their vengeance by keeping Katz a long time in a dungeon, whilst they debated what offence he had committed—we mean what offence by law, for the offence against the tyranny of classes was clear enough. A working man had dared to imagine that the millions had rights—that was offence enough in the eyes of priest and aristocrats.

The newspaper went on to describe how the authorities supposedly inspired by Louis Philippe's police spies in Brussels, sought to avoid trial by jury, and had Katz come up before several magistrates instead:

We need not say he was found guilty. Just imagine three wolves trying a ram who had protected the flock; he would be charged with violating the dignity of the wolfish functionaries, and be condemned to be eaten.

The sufferings of Jacob Katz inspired the LWMA's 'Address to the Working Classes of Belgium', a document that has been noted by several historians.[11] What is striking about the address is that it contains an early expression of the international character of the class struggle. It clearly declares the international solidarity of the rising working-class movements. This is by far the most important portion of the address:

Fellow Producers of Wealth—We are of the opinion that those who produce the real wealth of any country (by which term we mean the food, clothing, habitations and all the essentials of human happiness) have in reality but *one great interest.* . . . We believe, therefore, that our interest—nay, the interests of working men in all countries of the world—are identified, and consequently that principles of fraternal friendship should lead us to cultivate peace, industry, and the mutual interchange of kind feelings and benevolent actions. . . .

Ignorance was blamed for class oppression in all nations and for 'foolish' dissensions between nations:

Ignorance has caused us to believe that we were 'born to toil', and others to enjoy—that we were naturally inferior, and should silently bow to the government of those who call themselves superior. . . . The existence of their power depending on the ignorance, the instilled prejudice, the cupidity of the multitude, they have formed their institutions for hoodwinking and keeping them in subjection—their laws have been enacted to perpetuate their power, and administered to generate fear and submission towards self-constituted greatness, hereditary ignorance, or wealth, however unjustly acquired.

Yet the progressive march of the mind was taking place, and ignorance was in retreat:

> Happily, however, for mankind, the floodgates of knowledge, which the tyrants of the world have raised to stem the torrents, are being broken down. We have tested its refreshing stream; . . . we perceive the injustice practised on us, and feel the slavery from which we have not yet the power to free ourselves. Our emancipation, however, will depend on the extent of this knowledge among the working-classes of all countries, on its salutary effects in causing us to perceive our real position in society—in causing us to feel that we, being the producers of wealth, have the first claim to its enjoyment.

All should have the right to education, the right of running for office, and a voice in enacting legislation. Education was the real instrument of revolution:

> The object of those who now address you . . . is to unite the intelligent and influential portion of the working classes in town and country, and to disseminate a knowledge of correct principles among them, which . . . we conceive will gradually produce a *peaceable revolution* in the fruits *for our own* advantage, and not wholly for others.

The framers of the address took it upon themselves to explain recent Belgian history to these Belgian workers. They were informed that they had 'gained nothing' from their revolution because of ignorance of 'correct principles' and a lack of 'union'. They were urged to emulate the LWMA to remedy the situation. In addition, they were advised to work for a federation with Dutch and Rhineland workers. The address concluded on a note of vigorous encouragement:

> At all events, you should, in our opinion, cultivate fraternal feelings, and strive to disseminate correct principles among your own brethren. Be cordially united against the common enemy, and use the partial rights you have to the attainment of all that belongs to you.

The address produced a spirited reply from Belgian workers, which was broadcast in the *London Dispatch* after this enthusiastic introduction:[12]

> It is with feelings of great delight we publish this international document, which has for its object, not the marriage of one girl or boy, glorified with the name of royal, but the substantial benefit of millions of men. The time is fast arriving, when men will find that national animosities are fermented for the sole purpose of enabling aristocrats in every country to keep their own subjects in unremitting submission.

The reply continued warmly: the Belgians proclaimed that 'with gratitude and love we press the hand that you have held out to encourage and sustain us . . .' and went on to accept the premiss of the LWMA that ignorance was at the root of their mutual problems:

You have truly spoken—We, like you, are slaves. The cause of our degradation is the same as yours. The source of the polluted river of slavery is ignorance. Ignorance has caused our disunion.

A strong declaration of pacifistic internationalism followed:

Working men of the world, let us too have our 'Holy Alliance'. Let us resolve, never again to be persuaded, under the mad pretext of national dignity, to murder our brothers in our own or any other land in order to please a sanguinary oppressor, or to gratify the egotistical pride of a mere man, whose self-love has imagined itself affronted.

Thus will we answer those provokers of national animosities, when they shall endeavour to excite us against our brothers, and prate to us about 'love of country', and the 'common good of the nation'. We shall say, we know no nation but the whole world, no countryman but man throughout the universe; the only common good we recognise, is that of all the people of the earth, the whole human race.

This particular argument concluded with a striking analogy:

Nature has not created man to be separated by political botanists into genealogical classes, nor to be divided into separate species, according to the capricious limits of an imaginary frontier. The existence of these artificial distinctions, and the evils they engender, add only another argument for the necessity of beating them down instead of repairing them.

There was no doubt but that these Belgian workers felt the English were ahead of them in the pursuit of liberty. 'Children of Britain' were declared to be 'forerunners in the noble arena where the strife is for the emancipation of the working man'. The Belgians said they were seeking to copy British workers' 'noble *meetings*' and 'plans for instructing the people'. They vowed to struggle and suffer 'in the confidence that you, our brethren, who have already surmounted . . . most arduous difficulties, will continue to aid us with your benevolent sympathy'. There were several other specific goals cited in this address, including equal participation in the power of law-making, equal participation in publicly supported education, and the abolition of 'detestable' excise laws and taxes upon occupiers rather than owners of houses. In addition, there was also a demand for what could be considered to be graduated taxation:

Working men of every country, have we not the right of demanding the abolition of every tax which directly or indirectly affects articles of necessity, and to make every impost fall upon the rich revenue, the overpaid salary, and the opulent inheritance?

Great dissatisfaction was expressed at the operation of the law and the hypocritical 'equality' it proclaimed. Without economic justice there could be no legal justice:

'The tribunals are open', says the enemy. Yes, open to those who can buy. There is no justice for those who can not. [*sic.*]

When upon some absurd and unfounded suspicion we are thrown by an oppressive magistrate into prison, of what avail to the working man is the rich man's law, by which . . . [he] . . . can obtain his liberty on bail?

If abject hunger in the child compels the father of a perishing infant to take a morsel of bread to sustain his offspring's life, is not . . . the judge ready to immolate the victim of our detestable institutions—whilst the *money mopolist* daily commits crime after crime with the law in his hand, and dreading nothing from the aristocratically formed tribunals

Such inequality before the law 'exists in various shapes and forms' to the harm 'of the working classes . . . in every nation'. The root cause was exposed in this fashion:

Can we wonder that laws made by the wealth consumer, in whose enactment the wealth producer has no voice, should be framed for the benefit of the few who form them, against the many, who have no one to watch over their interest in the law manufactory?

The suggestion of a local federation as a step towards unity was accepted enthusiastically, as might be expected of Flemings in the new state of Belgium:[13]

We shall unit with our fellow working men in all our towns and all our own country; we shall add our united force to that of the labouring multitude of Holland, and the provinces of the Rhine in order to co-operate together for the retaking of our rights, and to obtain a just share of the fruits of our labour.

The major goal of workers' agitations was also agreed upon—representation, not revolution:

It is . . . necessary that the working men and the poorer portion of tradespeople of every land should employ all their energies to obtain a real representation of their interests by men of their own class. . . .

As with the LWMA address, appended signatures included the occupations of the signers. Most were craftsmen and most had obviously Flemish names.[14]

These addresses made a stir on the Continent. Copies were sent to many Belgian towns in order to gather workers' signatures at public meetings. All were then to be sent on, with the original, to the LWMA.[15] Later the *London Dispatch* reported that the exchange of addresses had caused a 'great sensation' in France. The 'myrmidons' of Louis Philippe were 'so stung' by the 'pungent truths' contained in the addresses that they prosecuted *Le Journal du Peuple*. The jury acquitted the publishers, thereby providing further publicity.

Further after-effects occurred in Britain. The Working Men's Association in Newcastle sent an address to the LWMA, cheering the 'philanthropic addresses' sent to Belgium. Editorial comments by the LWMA in the *London Dispatch* enthusiastically introduced it by proclaiming:

> If all the working men in this great country would but imitate this manly example, they would soon effect the emancipation of the producing classes, not only in Britain, but throughout the universe.[16]

Involvement with Katz and the Belgian workers went beyond addresses, meetings, speeches and editorials. British workers sought to pay Katz's fine with money raised through a twopenny subscription. Collection began at a dinner held on December 5, 1836, in honour of Henry Hetherington and John Cleave, where 'upwards of three hundred most respectably attired workmen' and 'others, friends of a free and unshackled press' dined together. The 'others' included several M.P.s.[17] When a subscription for Katz was presented to the meeting, they were the persons heading the list. The project was in the hands of Lovett, although Hetherington, Cleave, Watson, and Vincent and several others received funds. The *London Dispatch* urged workers to contribute to 'prove to Katz how his conduct is appreciated by honest men of the people's party in this country'. The committee in charge declared that the subscription gave British workers 'an opportunity . . . of marking their detestation of tyranny, whether foreign or domestic, and shewing [*sic*] our Belgian brothers that British working men are alive to their duty as members of the great family of mankind'.[18]

It took time to collect the money because class consciousness came into play. Although an offer had been made by sympathetic Members of Parliament and friends to pay the whole fine immediately, Thompson, Roebuck, Harvey, Francis Place and Augustus Beaumont had their proposal turned down by Lovett and his friends on the grounds that it would be better 'to have the amount raised principally amongst the working men. . .'. Therefore the subscription was strictly limited to twopence per person.[19]

Because of the Katz affair the basic position of the LWMA towards Europe was formulated and exposed. This outlook, stressing faith in progress through education and working-class unity, was repeated in several other addresses by the LWMA and its successor, the National Association for Promoting the Political and Social Improvement of the People. Lovett planned the latter organisation while he sat out a sentence in Warwick Gaol in 1839–40. It had even stronger emphasis on education, in part because Chartist political agitation was increasingly dominated by Feargus O'Connor's National Charter Association, whose emotionalism and demagoguery Lovett could not abide. At any rate, the National Association was the LWMA in a new wrapping, through which Lovett wrote and issued another string of addresses. Several of them were specifically brought to bear on European conditions and international affairs: 'An Address to the Working Class of Europe and Especially to the Polish People', 1838; 'An Address to the Working Class of America on the Subject of the War Spirit', 1846; 'An Address to the Working Class of France on the Subject of War', 1844. Each contained more or less the basic message wafted to the Flemish workers, so there is no need to repeat it, but some of the new elements or clearer formulations from the subsequent documents are worth noting.

The view of Europe revealed by these pronouncements is generally grim, with only a few bright spots to relieve the mosaic of tyranny and oppression. Promising developments in France, Belgium, Poland, Greece, Portugal, and Spain had been overcome by the old forces of reaction. Germany was despotically ruled and the 'intelligence and courage' of its harassed 'professors and students' did not yet permeate to the multitudes. In Italy there was a lamentable contrast between the 'greatness of the past' and the 'littleness of the present'.[20]

The bright spots were the few democracies in Europe. Lovett lauded Norway and Switzerland. After all, democracy was the panacea for numerous domestic and international problems, so it was natural that Lovett found 'facts and illustrations' to prove the superiority of democracy from these countries. A pamphlet he wrote with John Collins while in gaol included these remarks about Switzerland:

In the democratic cantons of Switzerland, agriculture and manufactures, being combined, produce prosperity in every cottage. Knowledge and Freedom, twin sisters, have caused them to outspeed their neighbours in most of the ingenuities and refinements of art. Their laws, based on equality, are few, just and respected; custom, excise and prohibitory laws are banished from among them; justice, cheaply and impartially administered, is every man's protecting guardian; morality, intelligence and comfort gladden every home. . . .

Praise for Norway included a contrast with Sweden:

> During the few years the democratic principle has prevailed in Norway, the rapid improvement and increased prosperity of her people have shown forth the more conspicuously by the dark contrast afforted by her neighbour Sweden, a country blessed by nature with far greater means of happiness, but wanting the stimulating soil of freedom to convert them to the mental and physical uses of her people.[21]

Free from 'exclusive and corrupt government', the democracies of Norway, America, and parts of Switzerland would be pacifistic because the 'venomous influences' leading to war were abated 'in proportion as the spirit of democracy forced its influence on the legislatures of governments'.[22]

In some instances Lovett used examples drawn from Europe to warn British workers of domestic dangers; at other times he used European examples to urge imitation. An LWMA address issued to the working class in 1837 on the subject of education contained warnings against Prussian centralisation.[23] Government support for British education was welcomed, but not to the extent that the central authority would choose and supervise teachers, superintendents, teaching methods, and books. 'We perceive the results of concentration of power and uniformity of system lamentably exemplified in Prussia and other parts of the continent, where lynx-eyed satellites of power carefully watch over the first indications of intelligence, to turn it to their advantage . . . to crush in embryo the buddings of freedom.' Lovett's petition to Parliament for opening the British Museum and other exhibitions on Sundays pointed out that in European countries 'every facility is afforded on Sundays for the rational recreation of the industrious population'. Instead of 'leading to vice and immorality', the 'mass of the working population . . . are confessedly more sober and moral than the same class of persons in our own religious country'.[24]

While Europe might have its dark and bright spots, Lovett's outlook on his own nation had its contrasts as well. He urged foreign workers to struggle for the right to use British methods and enjoy freedoms Britons possessed:

> And we know of no better means of effecting [enlightenment] than by availing ourselves of those great rights and privileges of humanity our

countrymen have achieved through persecution and death, . . . the right of investigating . . . through the means of public meetings and open discussions and the press (stamped and trammelled as it is). . . . All of the corruptions and anomalies of church, state and individuals [should] pass in review before the great tribunal of public opinion. . . .

Criticism accompanied this praise:

True it is that the friends of freedom throughout the continent have just cause to remember with feelings of execration the base conduct of the government of England in secretly undermining or openly opposing every attempt they have made to check the inroads of despotism, or to advance the cause of democracy.

This was because the British government was directed by 'the rampant spirit of aristocracy, which, by a corrupt legislative assembly, a hypocritical money-loving priesthood and a standing army of soldiers, placemen, pensioners, expectants, keep the working millions in ignorance and subjection. . .'. These Englishmen were the *persecutors of liberty throughout the world*'.[25]

They also fomented wars. One of the main purposes of these communications with Europe was to prevent war. When tensions between Britain and France raised the spectre of armed conflict in 1844, the National Association was quick to send an 'Address to the Working Classes of France on the Subject of War'.[26] It opened with this statement:

We are, for the most part, *working men* who now address you—men, who, intent on the political and social improvement of our brethren, conceive we have some claim to the attention of those of our own class upon any subject of mutual and vital importance. . . .

It went on to offer a programme of protest to be taken up by the workers of Britain and France for the confrontation of their respective governments in the hope of maintaining peace. First of all, they should protest against all war; they should urge their legislatures to set examples of 'forbearance, morality and religion' for other nations, particularly in setting declared limits to their territorial acquisitions and in seeking international arbitration. There was even an interesting approximation of the classic 'guns or butter' arguments:

. . . we urge on them [the governments] to devote the enormous sums now expended in war and warlike preparations to the *education* and *improvement of the people* of their respective countries.

Not only the old, aristocratic minions were singled out in this address as the 'vultures' who 'hope to thrive on the carnage of war'. The increasingly nationalistic press of each country came in for its share of criticism:

> The press . . . of both countries . . . has unhappily been administering to our combative feelings; and by sallies of wit, boastings, and threatenings, seeking to fan our old (and we trust never to be revived) animosities into a flame of destructive war.

Also held up as causative factors were 'gothic prejudices, . . . those who plan battles on paper, and prefer fighting by proxy', those who mouth the phrases 'glory', and 'honour', and the warlike proclivities of the churches. Moreover:

> We should remember that the warlike tales and toys of the nursery are the seeds of strife and battle; and that *our admiration* of warlike splendour and gory *'glory'* is fitting instruction for moulding our sons into soldier slaves, or tyrant chieftans.

In an address to the Working Classes of America over the Oregon boundary dispute, the National Association asked: 'Will the labouring population of the world submit . . . to . . . going forth at the bidding of their rulers to murder and destroy?' They wished that 'what is called *"honourable warfare"* and *"glorious victories"* ' would be 'properly designated to be *National Crimes!*'[27]

Unlike the ultra-radical press in the twenties, the National Association was not ambivalent about 'just' and 'unjust' wars. They admitted that Great Britain was pacifistic 'when despotism is crushing the liberties of a country', but warlike when 'liberty has chances in her favour. . .'.[28] Although particular wars were singled out for the label of 'unjust' war—British campaigns in China and Afghanistan and the French War in Algeria fell into his category—they condemned all wars:

> But our object is not the mere condemnation of particular wars, but of all war; believing *war in principle* to be *vengeance in practice*, a vice equally opposed to our *morality* and condemned by our *religion*; its tendency being to deteriorate the noble faculties of man, and strengthen those which level him with the brute. It stands the most formidable impediment to the civilization of our race, rendering nearly nugatory the best devised efforts for elevating humanity; for, by polluting the youthful mind with tales of blood, by stamping public approbation on deeds of vengeance, and idolising *as heroes* those who have excelled in crime, we sap the very foundations of virtue, and offer the highest premium to vice.[29]

Perhaps the most interesting aspect of these pacifistic messages was a proposal for an international organisation to settle disputes by arbitration rather than war. This proposal appeared in the 'Address to the Working Classes of France on the Subject of War' in 1844:

That we request them [the respective legislators of France and Britain] to use their influence with the nations of the world, to establish a *Conference of Nations;* to be composed of three or more representatives, chosen *by the people* of their respective countries, to meet annually, for the purpose of settling all national disputes that may arise, by arbitration, without having recourse to war.[30]

International accord already existed in one matter, according to the LWMA. Although they warred upon each other from time to time, rulers were united in keeping the workers ignorant and submissive. To oppose them, the LWMA appealed for an international workers' alliance. The 'Address to the Working Classes of Europe, and especially to the Polish people' of 1838 contained this declaration:

Fellow producers of wealth! seeing that our oppressors are . . . united, *why should not we, too, have our bond of brotherhood and holy alliance?* Seeing that they are powerful through your ignorance, why should not we unite to *teach our brethren a knowledge of their rights and duties?* Perceiving that their power is derived from our ranks, why should not we unite in holy zeal to show the injustice of war, the cruelty of despotism, and the misery it entails upon our species? . . . Let us, therefore, brethren, cultivate feelings of Fraternity among nations and brotherly union in our respective countries.[31]

The desire for greater international co-operation even carried over into the educational schemes of the organisations inspired by William Lovett. In an address to British workers in 1837 on education, 'living languages' were 'preferred to the dead' in order to 'promote a more intimate acquaintance with the inhabitants and literature of other countries, and thus help to break down those national prejudices which the tyrants of the world are too prone to take . . . advantage of in fomenting the evils of war and all its consequences'.[32]

The internationalism of these organisations was so developed that a class-conscious identity of interests for all workers throughout the world was defined. This definition was published in the address to French workers in 1844:

We address you, the *working classes,* because we believe that *the interests of our class are identified throughout the world.* Our interests are evidently in the peaceful cultivation of our lands, the feeding of our flocks, in the ingenuity and extent of every manufacture and production capable of administering to human happiness; the reciprocal interchange of our commodities, the full enjoyment of the fruits of our labour; and the cultivation of freedom, intellect, morality, religion and brotherly affection among all the nations of the earth; in all these we believe there is *an identity of interests*. . . .[33]

How significant were these addresses, manifestos and pronouncements of Lovett and his friends in their small organisations made up of superior artisans living in cosmopolitan London? Was their influence on the British working class lost in the vastness, the complexity and the diversity of the metropolis? Have historians exaggerated their role in providing programmes and guiding movements in the country because their leaders were the most coherent, educated, articulate and intellectual of the Chartists?[34] These questions are still subject to interpretation, of course, but even so, and even assuming the minimum estimate of their influence, there is a significance about these LWMA and National Association activities that cannot be denied. As R. H. Tawney wrote, long ago, these addresses and manifestos cover a remarkable range of subjects and give a 'broad and generous interpretation to the political aspirations of labour. . .'. His statement is certainly true of their preoccupation with Europe and workers' internationalism.[35]

II   BRONTERRE O'BRIEN AND EUROPE

Chartism's greatest intellectual was not the Chartist most preoccupied with Europe. George Julian Harney, Ernest Jones, William Lovett and Thomas Cooper each have a better claim to the latter accolade. To be sure, Bronterre O'Brien was a man with a world view, or, as E. P. Thompson described him, 'a theorist of stature to define the working-class predicament'.[36] His thought was enriched by the traditions of ultra-radicalism, Owenism, his Irish hatred of English Whigs, and by his highly class-conscious interpretations of French Revolutionary history. He knew several languages, including French and Italian, and · travelled in France in the thirties, for the purpose of collecting material for his major literary effort, a long rehabilitatory biography of his special hero, Maximilien Robespierre.[37] He only finished one volume, but he did publish a richly annotated translation of Buonarotti's *History of Babeuf's Conspiracy for Equality* in the thirties.

In spite of this rich background, Bronterre was not an active Chartist internationalist. He made no effort to organise working-class activities around continental themes or around groups of exiles in London—this was left for others to do—nor did he take up an exceptional amount of space in his newspapers with foreign affairs. There are several reasons for his lack of significant activity in this area: O'Brien was an intellectual first and foremost, and his popular journalistic efforts were largely uncombined with effective political leadership. In actuality Bronterre was more a lecturer and teacher than a political leader. Furthermore, he had the knack of falling out with the prominent working-class politicians of the moment. O'Brien had begun his Chartist career as a contributor to Hetherington's newspapers and as one of those honorary middle-class members of the LWMA. A violent dispute over Daniel O'Connell's attacks on trade union practices caused O'Brien to break with his old friends and link his journalistic career with Feargus O'Connor and his followers. From 1838 to 1840 Bronterre was highly successful, both as an outstanding writer for the *Northern Star* and as an important and serious platform speaker.[38] At this time the 'moral force' advocates, especially his former friends in the LWMA, felt the sting of his bitter, clever words. Shortly after the sad dissolution of the Chartist Convention Bronterre was clapped into gaol, and, like so many other Chartists in such circumstances, he gave up militancy[39] and his dreams of becoming the Robespierre of an English revolution. This swing took place during 1840 and 1841, and contributed to his break with O'Connor and his followers, a falling out marked by vituperation unusual even for Chartists. Francis Place, who thought O'Brien a 'three parts insane and savage man', observed that O'Connor and O'Brien 'abused each other to an extent . . . [and] . . . in as bad language as perhaps never before had been done by any two men since newspapers were first published'.[40] The upshot of these furores was that O'Brien was left high and dry. This meant that in the years of the most intense working-class activity with foreign affairs, 1844 to 1848, when working-class internationalists organised with continental exiles, O'Brien was exiled from the main Chartist organisations, a condition emphasised by his retreat to the Isle of Man, which lasted from 1844 to 1847. So O'Brien, unlike Harney and Jones, among others, did not have the advantages of close association with Marx, Engels, Weitling, Schapper, Mazzini, Worcell, and other continental exiles.

Perhaps the most important connection between Bronterre and Europe was actually in the realm of European history rather than contemporary European affairs. As Alfred Plummer has declared, 'O'Brien must . . . be regarded as the chief channel through which the influence of the French revolution reached the working people of his day.'[41]

His reflections on the France of Louis Philippe during the Chartist era were no different from his earlier observations: he continued to lament the loss of the principles of the Constitution of 1793, principles stolen from the French people by 'the armed sections of Paris; that is, by the pot-bellied middle classes'.[42] As a result, thirty million Frenchmen were 'robbed of their civil rights, and made hopeless prey of mammon and arbitrary power' by an 'armed shopocracy of commercial men'.[43] Louis Philippe's government rested upon their bayonets, and the king himself was 'a mere instrument in the hands of the monied classes. . .'.[44] It was therefore useless to attempt assassination, as Fieschi had, because Louis Philippe would merely be replaced by someone else who would rule in the same manner. This mistake of assassins was that they overlooked the fact that 'the fate of millions' no longer 'hung on the breath of one man'. Modern 'slavery' was due to 'whole classes of people whose interests are naturally in opposition to our own'.[45]

Several visits to France in the mid-thirties provided Bronterre with observations that he drew upon throughout his career as the Schoolmaster of Chartism. He found the stark contrast of workers' poverty and the way French 'profit hunters' spent their time 'guttling and guzzling' unbearable. It was to his 'wonder and amazement' that 'the poor of Paris could submit to such a horrible and inhuman state of things'.

Instead of being astonished at their repeated insurrections against the government this last forty years, my only wonder was, that they did not devise some means of reducing Paris to ashes, and thereby destroying their oppressors, though at the expense of perishing themselves in the flames. Death, in any shape, provided it was accompanied with vengeance, appeared to me preferable to such an existence.[46]

Such reflections on France afforded an opportunity to clarify his notorious 'physical force' position. In answering a letter in his *National Reformer* in 1837 which decried the use of physical force, Bronterre agreed that France had gained 'truly nothing' from its use in 1830, and declared that he was for physical force only as 'a last desperate resort against tyranny', and only after 'the popular mind has been fully enlightened beforehand'.[47] As E. P. Thompson has pointed out,[48] historians will not accept his identification of Whig administrations after 1832 with the interests of the middle classes. The same can be said for his exclusive identification of Louis Philippe's regime with the monied interests of France. Bronterre's class-conscious views went further than England and

France, for he found middle-class men at work nearly everywhere, defrauding the workers of their rights to life, freedom, and happiness. Bronterre had no difficulty in finding the same enemies of the people in the tiresome civil wars that were fought for the Spanish throne between two main parties, those supporting Don Carlos and those fighting for Queen Christina. The queen's 'Moderato' supporters were called 'a purely middle-class, mercantile, blood-sucking, money-mongering, fund-holding, tax-eating faction'.[49] He expected that their victory would mean 'a system of loan jobbing and national debts' for Spain.[50] British gold and British support were behind this faction in order to promote the importation of British manufactures under the aegis of Free Trade,[51] as well as the general assimilation of Spain to France and England. Meanwhile, Englishmen were being deluded into thinking that this was merely a struggle of despotism against constitutionalism.[52]

Dorothy Thompson has observed that O'Brien's 'writing stands in relation to Marx rather as Robert Chambers' *Vestiges of the Natural History of Creation* stands to the *Origin of the Species*', and that in both cases, 'it is a mistake to underestimate the contemporary influence of the earlier work'.[53] As far as Europe is concerned, Bronterre's contribution is largely confined to his emphasis on an international political and economic exploitation of the working classes by the middle classes. Such an outlook did lead him to call for working-class internationalism in a manner that does indeed seem proto-Marxian:

Is it not time that the productive classes of all nations should form a holy alliance amongst themselves to fight no more for landlords and money-lords? Is it not time to tell these landed and commercial demons henceforward to fight for themselves. . . ? Is it not time that nations should come to a common understanding that all war is sinful and an abomination in the sight of God, unless it be a war against landlords and merchants to save the human race from future crimes and carnage?[54]

O'Brien's other views on Europe in the Chartist years are not marked by such originality; they bear instead a marked similarity to old, ultra-radical observations. He feared that despotism's 'unnatural system' was everywhere,[55] and that capitalists had joined the ranks of kings, priests and soldiers.[56] All this would change if the subjects 'knew the truth'.[57] Dynastic marriages were meaningless bores, and should the liberal press warn that they endangered British influence on the Continent, 'we must heartily congratulate the Continent'.[58]

Bronterre was not at all nationalistic. In fact, he was convinced that England was worse off than continental states because middle-class rapaciousness was so much more developed. Bronterre had this to say to the 'conceited prigs' and 'vile coxcombs' who praised the perfection of England's constitutional monarchy and representative government:

The Government of England is the most atrocious form of government that ever did exist, or ever will exist, or ever could exist, for the unrepresented and poorer classes. There is no other form of government in which the proportion of tyrants to slaves is so great, or in which so large a proportion of the population is interested in the plunder and degradation of the productive classes. . . . There is more murder and robbery perpetrated by the higher and middle orders of this country, under forms of law, in one year, than takes place under all the absolute monarchies in Europe in ten years.

A working man in Austria, or in Turkey, has not to submit to a tithe of a tithe of the insult, wrong and degradation that a poor labourer or mechanic has to put up with every day from middle-class villains . . . who have usurped all the institutions of the country, to his exclusion, in order to keep him for ever the slave they have made of him. There is no power at the disposal of the Austrian Emperor, or of the Turkish Sultan, by which those rulers could, by any possibility, compel their subject to work as the English slaves work, to enrich-middle class villains, and the devils incarnate known under the names of landlords and capitalists.[59]

Despite the fact that British arms had won 'the richest and most extensive portions of the earth's surface', these wars for empire were waged 'for the landlord and the money lord'. The people of England should have fought against them instead of for them, because all they had to show for their efforts was:

A nation of slaves, without land, without homes, without education, without morals, without wealth, or worth of any kind, and almost without consciousness that they are slaves. . . .[60]

It was in dealing with this topic of war that his old, ultra-radical sentiments were most clearly revealed, particularly in one memorable dialogue between Bronterre and one *Quid Nunc*, a 'moral force' Whig who was a 'thorough-going liberal—a moral force man—a march of intellect man' and a 'greatest-happiness-principle man'.[61] Bronterre's avowed purpose in writing it was to have workers exclaim 'never' to the question of whether they would fight for 'the aristocracy and the shopocracy . . . in case a war be got up' by them. He wanted his views proclaimed 'in every Trades' Society, Radical Union, and Working-Men's Association in the United Kingdom', He had *Quid Nunc* declare:

Wars are often just and necessary; or why be at the expense of maintaining fleets and armies? Besides, a war is wanted just now, to give a stir, and a fillip, a new impetus to the country. We never had such prosperity as during the American and French wars.

Besides, *Quid Nunc* went on, wars were inevitable and they could not be had without killing and wounding. Wars had been fought before they were born and would be fought after they died. Bronterre replied to these declarations with grim, graphic descriptions of dozens of horrors caused by war, horrors that had been depicted time and time again in the ultra-radical press. He then went on to urge that those immediately profiting from a war be the ones to fight it. For example, if India were threatened by Russia:

Let the proprietors of the East India Stock, let the owners of East India merchantmen, let those English and Irish merchants and brokers and writers and underwriters and governors and judges, and naval and military officers, and liver-coloured nabobs . . . go and fight for our 'Indian Possessions', but let them not mock our degradation by asking us, working people, to fight along with them. . . .

Moreover, in contemplating French aggression over Mexican trade or 'Algerine' conquests in the Levant, Bronterre declared:

Let those who profit by foreign trade go and fight for it. Let the merchants, and shipowners, and big manufacturers and capitalists . . . go and fight for it. Or let our aristocracy . . . fight for it.

He would rather see commerce in these areas 'utterly extinguished' before he would 'see one solitary Working Man . . . lose a leg or an arm in a war to defend it'.

O'Brien cynically discussed what he saw as the causes of war. One of his most succinct statements appeared in the *British Statesman* in 1842, which informed workers that:

Having deprived you of the means of obtaining a living by your industry in the midst of your relatives and friends, they have kindly opened a door for your exertions by offering you the enviable boon of enlistment. There is too much young blood in the country, want and Poor Laws do not kill you off fast enough—emigration has lost attraction, because it is expensive, and unprofitable to the government; we must, therefore, have a war to thin us off. . . .[62]

Even though so many of these ideas were old, and regardless of the fact that so much of what was new was also crude and simplistic, Bronterre's striking journalism kept these views alive amongst Chartists. Although he was not as highly attuned to European affairs as some other Chartists, the Schoolmaster's influence in this area cannot be denied. He expressed his ideas about Europe as a somewhat isolated figure in the movement, in virtual exile in the most important years for Chartist internationalists, grinding away at one foredoomed newspaper venture after another. Such was the nature of his contributions.

III CHARTISM AT ITS HEIGHT AND EUROPEAN AFFAIRS AT THE PERIPHERY

The Chartist movement reached its peak in 1839, the year of the Convention and first great petition. Riots, an uprising, and repression followed the crest, and in the course of events bitter factions formed.[63] A second and lesser peak was reached in 1842, marked by a wave of strikes and riots and further repression. Thereafter Chartism endured a long downward slide, broken only by a temporary rally in 1848. It was in the period of decline and deep division that Chartism featured the luxurious growth of some highly developed special activities, such as Temperance Chartism and Feargus O'Connor's celebrated Land Plan. Not the least interesting autumn flower in the decaying garden of Chartism involved London workers under the stimulation of democratic continental exiles and visiting continental theoreticians, and produced organisations that made working-class internationalism their special concern. What about such interests when the movement was in full flower? To put it simply, European affairs were at the periphery from 1838 to 1842. English grievances, English conditions and, in general, the richness of the English past were drawn upon by the Chartists when they were carried along on a wave of hope and optimism. To be sure, Europe was not ignored. Their newspapers carried some editorials and news about the continent, and their speakers used some European examples to press their points home, but, with the exception of a burst of Russophobia engineered by David Urquhart, M.P., Europe and European exiles were in no way of central importance.

The Convention of 1839 provides an excellent example of the peripheral nature of European affairs. Despite the fact that its very name and some of its members' trappings were borrowed from the French Revolution, almost all of its speeches and concerns had nothing whatsoever to do with Europe. A close reading of Convention debates reveals that Europe was virtually ignored.[64] Plans, finances, procedures, the activities of missionaries, the preparation of the petition as well as a whole range of complaints, ranging from the

New Poor Law to the state of representation in the House of Commons, were all treated with hardly any reference to Europe. Historical arguments pertaining to the ancient liberties of Englishmen provided standard fare for comparisons.

At times delegates actually sounded patriotic: a manifesto drawn up by the Convention in the event that the petition should fail promised eventual success if 'there be yet within you a latent spark of that quality which was wont to distinguish Englishmen throughout the globe', a 'manly courage' with which 'our forefathers sacredly guarded our island . . . and arrested with their iron grasp foreign foe or domestic spoiler'.[65] Moreover, the delegates at one time proposed an address to the 'People of Great Britain' that contained regret that a speech from the throne was too preoccupied with Europe and insufficiently concerned with domestic matters:

While the mind of the sovereign has been anxiously directed to arrange the terms on which the separation of Belgium from Holland—begun by physical force—may be completed and established by negotiation; and while a like concern has been manifested in the affairs of other countries, only a few lines are given to the internal affairs of our own country.[66]

Members of the Convention made only sporadic use of sundry European examples. Debate on the Rural Police Bill, a measure designed by Parliament to improve the forces of law and order in the counties,[67] brought some comparisons with France into play on the floor. Mark Hovell has remarked that the speakers 'had the example of France before their eyes' on this issue,[68] but an examination of the speeches shows that there was a much greater use of Irish comparisons.[69] Dr John Taylor did recall what he saw in the way of police brutality in France in the twenties, and predicted that the Rural Police Bill would mean that 'the three glorious days of July' would be enacted in England. He and other delegates were afraid that the police would be agents of repression, either openly or in functioning as spies and informers. It was clearly an 'un-English . . . continental plan of centralisation. . .'.[70] A few foreign examples were cited in a manifesto of the Convention to British workers. It declared that the Chartist petition was not contending for a 'visionary or impracticable scheme' because the principles of the Charter were those of their ancestors, and its points were 'now in practical operation in different parts of the world', and 'wherever they are in practice the people are prosperous and happy'. This was the 'strongest argument' in favour of their 'general adoption'. Such allusions usually referred to Norway, Switzerland and the United States.[71]

On only one occasion did the Chartist Convention have direct dealings with Europeans. The assembly received, without comment, one address from a body calling itself the 'union of French Democrats in London', which claimed to speak for a majority of Frenchmen.[72] The French democrats wanted 'to convey . . . some words of encouragement . . . and sympathy' to the 'industrious classes' of Britain, through the members of the Convention, the 'natural mediators' for such communication. Their message, they readily admitted, was 'of little importance . . . in a numerical point of view, but important because we are expressing the sentiments of our brethren in France'. The message was clearly internationalist in the mode of Thomas Paine:

Men of the movement—the true friends of humanity see in other nations only parts of a great family, and in the members of each nation only the children of the same cause—only brothers. Democrats of Great Britain! our two countries were many years rivals. . . . Ah, be convinced that in our hearts there exists no longer this spirit of national hostility. . . . We desire with all our hearts, the intimate union of the two nations—the most civilised in the world—the result of which would be liberty. We wish for the universal brotherhood of the people. . . . All our thoughts, our efforts, tend to form one holy alliance of the people, opposed to the league of kings. . . . It is with joy we shall make the sacrifice of our liberty and our lives to defend our oppressed brothers.

The declaration went on to cheer the 'noble and beautiful' struggle for the Chartist programme and expected the anticipated Chartist victory to provide an international model:

We hope with confidence that having obtained this for yourselves, you will propagate the same doctrines amongst other people, and that you will place yourselves at the head of the mission, which, as a nation, you have to fulfil . . . in working without relaxation to create in the heart of Europe a state in which the inhabitants of its whole continent may enjoy the pure air of liberty, and experience the benefits of . . . political and social equality.

It concluded in rousing Napoleonic prose.

There was no response to this address, no stir comparable to the kind the Fraternal Democrats would muster to such communications in the late forties. Enthusiasm for international communications was not manifest when the movement was in its halcyon years, and only minor Chartist figures had anything to do with Europe at that time. Surely the most interesting and romantic of them all was Dr John Taylor, a physician from Scotland.[73] He was a militant

Convention delegate who was enveloped in a cloud of romantic stories about his former exploits. His appearance was fitting for them: Taylor was swarthy, tall, long haired, and frequently in sailor's garb,[74] and one observer commented on how he looked like 'a cross between Byron's Corsair and a gypsy king'. When he spoke it was 'lava-like eloquence that set on fire all combustible matter in its path'.[75] He was rich, and had experience as a naval surgeon. Taylor needs the attention of a biographer; it is almost impossible to sort out fact from fiction in tales about him. No small portion of his adventures have to do with Europe. He was supposed to have fought in the Greek war for independence with his own private vessel.[76] Afterwards he was supposed to have conspired with leading revolutionaries in France, activities that had him clapped into a French prison before expulsion from that country.[77] Except for occasional references to European revolutions in his Convention speeches, this rich background does not seem to have had much effect on his Chartist career, and his death at the height of the movement kept him from engaging in any activities with Chartist internationalists later on.[78]

Augustus Hardin Beaumont and his brother, Arthur James Beaumont, were somewhat less romantic, but more important for connections between the Chartists and Europe.[79] They were American by birth and Jamaican by rearing, and well-to-do. Both went off to Paris soon after the July revolution and joined the National Guard. Soon after they departed for the revolution in Belgium, where they fought in the streets and received wounds. Thereafter Arthur Beaumont became involved with French radical groups, to the extent that he became treasurer and member of the central committee of the *Société des droits de l'homme*. He was gaoled, and Augustus sought his release. Since the British Foreign Office was, at first, courteous but ineffective, Beaumont made his case publicly, through the use of several of his ventures in English journalism, including publications close to the LWMA. The story of the struggles to gain release of his brother and the eventual celebrations was presented in great detail in the *London Dispatch*.[80]

The brothers were most interested in gaining popularity amongst British workers, to the extent that they participated at meetings, translated addresses for the LWMA, and engaged in democratic journalism. Arthur Beaumont took over the *London Dispatch* in 1837 and Augustus Beaumont founded the *Northern Liberator* in Newcastle upon Tyne in the same year. The latter newspaper came to carry a higher proportion of information on foreign affairs than other publications popular with Chartists. Beaumont made a considerable stir as a platform speaker in the north-east, where the passionate intensity of his manner was probably better received than in London.[81] He died in 1838, and at least one Chartist was glad a year later that he was not around to provoke a Newport-style rising in Newcastle.[82]

Another figure who emerged to play a brief role in stimulating working-class interest in Europe was James Bernard, a Cambridge-shire farmer, a currency reformer and a rather bizarre egomaniac who helped organise the 'Central National Association' in 1837.[83] This organisation tried and failed to create a national movement for reform, although for a time it enlisted the support of O'Brien, Harney, Bell, and O'Connor behind Bernard's unstable leadership. Other Chartists warred on the organisation through the *London Dispatch* which sought to raise working-class suspicions about his activities.[84] At any rate, Bernard visited Paris in 1837 to discover the 'real' state of affairs in France. His return was celebrated by an extraordinary meeting of the Central National Association at which Bernard described how French reformers were looking towards England for change.[85] He toyed with the idea of welcoming Frenchmen into the organisation, and proposed that an address be sent to French leaders to initiate fraternal exchanges on the leading issues of the day. After lengthy debate, the association moved and carried these resolutions: that the association was happy to learn that the president had opened communication with leading reformers in Paris; that the association approved of an address to the French people and entertained hopes that it might lead to an 'intimate union between the two countries'; that the association was happy to enrol Frenchmen; and that the president was to act as 'the medium of intercommunication' between the association and the French people.

A revealing controversy surrounded this address. Several members made the point that it should not be sent because the matters treated would be 'beyond the comprehension of working men' because they knew 'little of the affairs of the Continent. . .'. A third of those present voted against these resolutions and John Bell, the *Mercury*'s editor, published a dissenting statement which was signed by several others. It gave these reasons:

Firstly, because the matters treated . . . affect the working men of England only remotely and indirectly. Secondly, because I am not satisfied of the soundness of Mr Bernard's views on the subject of continental policy.

Thirdly, because Mr Bernard's views, even if absolutely correct, can derive no additional force from the sanction of an association which has not carefully studied them:—whilst, on the other hand, the rash and hasty sanction of such views must tend to bring the Central National Association into contempt, if not to endanger its existence.

Bernard's proposals were indeed grandiose: he wanted to establish a whole new democratic 'balance of power' in Europe, and took upon himself the task of redrawing the map from the Black Sea to the English Channel. In his address he offered the services of British workers to intervene in the domestic affairs of France, but with conditions:

The intelligent portion of the English working classes entertains a deep sympathy for the working classes of the continent, and would, I think, be inclined to extend protection to them, if their own domestic affairs could be first satisfactorily arranged, and the business could be so contrived as to offer a reasonable prospect of its being accomplished without too great a sacrifice of either *life* or *money* and was likely to be permanent.

Bernard's influence on the development of working-class attitudes towards Europe and Europeans was probably minimal, for he was only a passing eccentric in the Chartist movement. The same can be said, to a lesser degree, of the influence of the Beaumonts and Dr Taylor. Much more important was the continuing role of the working-class press. Concern with Europe was peripheral there just as it was in the movement in general, but the extensiveness of the press guaranteed at least some space in editorial and news columns to Europe and criticism of British foreign policy.

Xenophobic responses were generally two-pronged: they were aimed at royal foreigners and at foreign systems believed to serve as models for centralisation in Britain. The latter variety was new, and associated with such recent changes in Britain as the introduction of the New Poor Law and more modern, efficient police forces. The older variety had as its prime target Prince Albert. He was described as the Coburg who 'played at "speculation" and turned up the Queen of Diamonds. . .'. He was a 'lucky young dog' who was 'the only trump card in the Coberg [*sic*] pack'.[86] The National Association's *Gazette* resented the way 'a lot of blubbery citizens' once cheered the Prince when he ceremonially performed the functions of a bricklayer's labourer 'with delicate hands and a silver trowel'.[87] Why, a writer for the *Charter* wondered, must 'Virgin Victoria' seek a foreign husband 'when her throne is surrounded by young,

D

generous, and handsome Englishmen'? And why must he be German?

In what virtue is Germany distinguished, that no king can, as reviewers say of a library on the publication of a new book, 'be complete without it'? Is it wisdom? See George the First. Is it magnanimity? Inquire of George the Second. Is it practical liberality? Why, for further particulars, see the husband of the late Princess Charlotte.

It was, however, of little consequence, because the age in which a German prince could do mischief was over. Therefore 'the Queen's husband is really of no more importance than the Queen's parrot'.[88] The *London Dispatch* was more bitter: Coburgs were 'alien by birth, alien in principles, alien by education, alien by German prejudices and German predilections to all that is free and just in Britain. . .'.[89] *McDouall's Chartist and Republican Journal* relayed a conversation of British workmen supposedly overheard while royal coaches were rumbling past them. 'It would be better for England', said one man in a fustian jacket, 'if the damned German crew had been sunk in the channel.' 'Ay', responded another, 'the curse of Cromwell on every mother's son of them.'[90] In addition to Albert, there was apprehension lest Victoria, described in one speech as 'a little girl who would be more usefully employed at her needle',[91] be too much under the influence of her uncle, the Belgian king.[92]

Royalty around the throne was not the only target of Chartist contempt. They disliked the hubbubs over royal marriages and how the speeches from Victoria's throne were so taken up with the affairs of other monarchs.[93] Royal visits, so overplayed in the established press, were a colossal bore.[94] The very worst visitor in the Chartist years was Tsar Nicholas of Russia. While the liberal press was upset when he subscribed funds for the completion of the Nelson monument as well as the statue of the Duke of Wellington, Chartists did not mind these donations. After all, as the *Northern Star* argued, Wellington and Nelson were representatives 'of the selfsame principle' because they had won 'the bloodiest struggle Europe has ever yet witnessed to prop up despotism and prevent the march of liberty'.[95]

Visiting and domestic royalty were generally the only foreigners who served as targets for Chartist xenophobia. There was one complaint against French and Italian shoplifters,[96] and disgust with Italian opera at Covent Garden, on the grounds that 'not one quarter of . . . [its] . . . rich patrons patronised this theatre when opened for native talent'.[97] A nasty murder of an English nobleman by a Swiss servant in 1840 elicited a snarl against 'noblemen and others who are so fond of having everything *foreign*, from a monkey to a mistress. . .'. Such employers were reminded of how 'revenge, cruelty and a total want of principle' were 'characteristics of foreign nations. . .'. It was a pity that they pampered 'their Swiss, Italian, and French servants—actors and refugees, etc.' while 'the poor English, who have many and superior claims upon their consideration' suffered under the New Poor Law and other forms of exploitation.[98]

Xenophobia was much more pronounced when it came to dealing with foreign systems rather than foreign individuals. The key word was centralisation. Richard Oastler and the Rev. Joseph Rayner Stephens were noted for their particularly vigorous resistance to it. As Oastler told a crowd in Leeds, 'It was centralisation that destroyed the liberties of the German Empire; and it will be centralisation that will destroy the liberties of Englishmen' by removing the authority of 'local patriots'.[99] Stephens urged Chartists to 'Give no hear [*sic*] to newfangled politics—centralisation politics—politico-economical politics—stick to the good old laws . . . of England. . .'.[100] Feargus O'Connor joined in this assault by pointing out 'the great dissatisfaction existing now in all the countries of Europe against the principle of centralisation'.[101] More telling were Peter McDouall's remarks in defence of himself at the Chester Assizes:

I can see approaching a train of evils which is calculated to level down the fundamental principles of the constitution, and the few remaining privileges of the people, in the new and arbitrary ideas of centralisation, copies from the despotic governments of France, Prussia and Russia.[102]

Police centralisation was regarded as the worst kind. The new 'blue bottles' were a 'Bourbon' police, according to the Chartists. A tin-plate worker got up at a meeting in Bristol to warn that this 'Bourbon police' was 'armed with bludgeons to beat their brains out'.[103] A meeting at Totnes condemned the use of the new police to quell the riots at Birmingham by calling them 'a brutal and un-English *gendarmerie*'.[104] There were other aspects of centralisation, or what was often the real issue, greater efficiency on the part of agents of law and order. There were complaints against disarming Chartists and preventing Chartist meetings on the grounds that these denials of the liberties of Englishmen would make them indistinguishable "from the inhabitants of Russia and Prussia".[105] Moreover, trials of Chartist prisoners for sedition were so perfunctory that there seemed to be no difference between them and those held in Turkey.[106]

Sporadic outbursts of xenophobia aimed at foreign royalty and foreign centralisation were unmatched during the height of the movement by manifestations of working-class internationalism. There was little of it between the early addresses of the LWMA and the flurry of internationalism towards the end of the movement. Internationalism was at the periphery during the Chartist peaks. There was no preoccupation with sending weighty addresses across the Channel, and whatever internationalist sentiments did appear in the Chartist press were generally vague echoes from the past.[107] At meetings it was common to make toasts and addresses expressing general internationalist feelings, hailing 'fellow men of whatever sect, class, country, or colour'.[108] Lovett and his friends periodically put in a good word for working-class internationalism, but in these years they had many other preoccupations.[109] There were a few glimmerings of it now and then. Chartists thought it important to make Europe acquainted with their wrongs and their struggles because they felt their movement had significance for 'the enlightened, the liberal, the humane of all countries'.[110] As a 'Chartist Soldier' wrote in 1839: 'On the death blow to tyranny in this country depends not only our own liberty and salvation, but the liberties and happiness of every nation on the globe. . . .'[111] George Julian Harney said much the same thing in a speech in Norwich in 1838: 'The eyes of all Europe were on England . . . for if England was made free, every country in Europe would establish the rights of man.'[112] All sorts of salubrious changes might take place in Europe as a result of achieving the Six Points. As an anonymous letter in the *Northern Star* declared, Russia might lose control of Poland, the Confederation of the Rhine 'would be but a fairy tale' or a 'dew-web', and the Holy Alliance itself would become 'no more than the dolorous meeting of political old maids assembled to talk and weep over their faded loveliness, withered charms, and departed power'.[113] An editorial comment in *The Charter* sums up this feeling: 'The movement in England is not an isolated one—it is the cause of the rights of man, which must ultimately triumph in every part of the earth.'[114]

At the height of the movement, internationalism was often indistinguishable from the ultra-radical expressions of the twenties, tending to be of the 'march of the mind' variety.[115] Even Feargus O'Connor had such views:

All nations were rushing forward into one great system of brotherhood. Mind was pushing forward to combine with mind. Steam and cheap postage had done much in producing that result. They could now shake hands with America and kiss France. The whole political world was on the eve of a convulsion. The rumbling of the mental earthquake could be distinctly heard, and he trusted that out of chaos and confusion, peace and prosperity would arise.[116]

Chartists felt England was the place for important changes; their own actions would be crucial for democracy in Europe. After Chartism was thwarted and swung into headlong decline, more attention was paid to Europe because hopes for decisive action were increasingly focused abroad. In the late thirties and early forties European states seemed to offer much less cause for optimism. France, that traditional well-spring of democratic and revolutionary hope on the continent, was seen as facing the same key issue as England: the extension of the right to vote. In France a shrewd monarch and 'French Whigs' manipulated 'rotten' constituencies, despite the ballot.[117] Chartists thought they perceived a cunning attempt of these French Whigs to head off democracy by a partial extension of the franchise, which was really another reflection of workers' disappointment over the bill of 1832. When the Birmingham Political Union sent an address to the National Guards of France congratulating them on their determination to gain the right to vote, workers from Bristol protested on the grounds that the National Guards would then oppress French workers both politically and militarily.[118]

The movement for French democracy was often called 'French Chartism', and not only in the Chartist press. The *Morning Chronicle* made the accusation that if 'French Chartism' succeeded it would only lead to a stronger hand for legitimists, because peasants and town 'rabble' would vote for rightists under universal suffrage. A writer in the *Charter* responded that it was common in England for Whigs to 'hold forth that Universal Suffrage would strengthen the hand of the aristocracy . . .' and admitted that new voters might make some initial mistakes. The Six Points offered means to correct these tendencies, and 'proper views' would soon 'become general'. They had to take their chances with 'the first ebullition of an excited people' hitherto 'deceived and humbugged by their enslavers. . .'.[119]

Louis Philippe remained a traditional target for the opprobrium of British workers during the Chartist years. They recognised the greater power of the crown in France, and attributed this circumstance to the unscrupulous craft and resolution of the monarch himself. He was thought worse than Charles X because he was able to mask the arbitrary nature of his tyranny.[120] A poor poem by a poor workman describes the situation:

I am king of the French
No one can deny,
And though my subjects oft cry, Liberty
I bend them to my will;

My dad was old *Egality*,
And the idol of the mob,
While I was in reality,
The man for any job;

I bribed the rich and crushed the poor,
Gold eloquently pleads,
Still I have got great wealth in store,
I am king of the barricades.
In spite of that republic cry,
That everywhere pervades,
My son shall reign when I shall die
The king of the barricades.[121]

Outside of France there was little to hold the interest of Chartists in Europe. Norway[122] and Switzerland were small bright spots, but Russia, Austria,[123] and Prussia[124] were despicable, along with the Pope.[125]

Lack of confidence in the governments of Europe contributed to Chartist impatience with traditional British foreign policy. Whigs received most of the running stream of Chartist criticisms of the way foreign affairs were handled, but this was because they were in office most of the time that the movement was at its height. Chartists believed that the Whigs were out to foster '*juste milieu*' governments throughout Europe, governments designed to exploit the workers on behalf of the men of property. Chartists were quick to point out that when Whigs spoke of helping countries obtain 'free institutions' they meant 'free according to Whig notions of freedom'; they did not mean 'democratic institutions'.[126] Chartists were actually so alienated from traditional means and methods of British foreign policy that they criticised the government regardless of what steps were taken. Action was careless warmongering; inaction was supine folly. Whigs could not claim credit for the peace of Europe. As one Chartist editor wrote: 'we . . . feel more inclined to laughter than anger, when we hear it impudently asserted that the tranquillity which Europe . . . continues . . . to enjoy is due to the address of a ministry so proverbial for their imbecility as ours'.[127] Old reasons were offered to explain the prevalence of peace: England did not have enough money to fight;[128] aristocrats feared that a war might unleash the oppressed peoples of Europe.[129] A newer idea was that banking and manufacturing houses would not be able to stand the shock of armed conflict.[130]

Preoccupation with the maintenance of peace was of considerable importance to Chartists, and was actually the clearest and most direct carry-over from ultra-radical agitations.[131] Chartists feared the same causes of war that were dreaded in the twenties: it might be used to divert the people from their campaigns for democratic rights;[132] aristocrats' 'cupidity, selfishness, and ambition' might lead to 'unjust and uncalled-for wars' at any time.[133] Such dangers would continue until democracy were established in the nations of Europe. Wars 'would seldom or scarcely ever occur' if aristocratic rule were 'put down'.[134]

The old pacifism of the twenties was alive in part because the old terrors of European statecraft were still perceived. Working-class Russophobia included the assumption that the British government co-operated with the Tsar to repress liberty in Europe.[135] Chartists believed that the Holy Alliance continued to operate on the continent, although some updated it somewhat, as in an editorial of the *Midland Counties Illuminator*:

. . . the foul conspiracy of the Holy Alliance still exists. That conspiracy (to which this hapless country was most unnaturally made a party by 'carotid-artery-cutting Castlereagh') first sets its iron heel upon Nap, and then threw the whole weight of its massive carcase [*sic*] upon the working-classes of all Europe. We have lived to see this traitorous policy repeated in our own day, by a Foreign Secretary: the 'Syrian War'—in which we have been leagued with Russia, Prussia, Austria, and Turkey against France and Egypt—is only a Whig imitation of this old Tory trick: the effort to *keep the people down*. How much longer will the trick last?[136]

Pacifist resolutions were often passed at Chartist meetings. For example, a meeting at Manchester in 1840 resolved:

. . . that no government has a right to declare war against any nation without the consent of the people who have to pay the necessary expenses attendant upon such unnatural and nefarious proceedings. . . .[137]

The 'Sturgite' Conference at Birmingham in 1842, that ill-fated attempt to reunite the middle and working classes for the substance of the Charter, without its name, passed this resolution:

To recommend all classes of society to withhold their support from government in no way representing the great body of the people, by refusing to enlist and to be used for the purposes of war, cruelty and injustice.[138]

Chartist songs called for peace. This was sung to the tune of 'God Save the Queen':

> Hush'd be the orphans' fears
> Dried be the widows' tears
> Peace is our cry;
> Despots, the people's foes
> Breaking the world's repose,
> Feel not war's bloody woes
> Where thousands die.[139]

At the height of the movement foreign affairs were in the hands of one of the most remarkable diplomats that the country ever produced, Lord Palmerston. Chartists fought him until the movement predeceased him. What was unique about these forays was that they singled out one statesman for attack. Except for Castlereagh, previous working-class criticisms of British foreign policy relied upon castigation of impersonal systems. This contest produced the most detailed and clear statement of Chartist grievances about foreign affairs. It appeared in the *Northern Star* in 1841, prompted by a war scare with France, and in the form of a set of scathing letters.[140]

Criticism of his policies centred on the charge that he was aggressive towards the weak and cowardly towards the strong:

There were several occasions, my Lord, in which it was said that you were disgracing and endangering your country by tamely submitting to foreign insults and acts of aggression. . . . You were nicknamed 'Protocol Palmerston' on account of your frequent use of written negociations [*sic*]. Your only weapons were 'quips and sentences, and paper bullets of the brain'. . . . How it comes that you rush into an opposite extreme—that you now forget, when, indeed, arbitration might settle the dispute; we can have no clue to your conduct but in your cowardice. It was cowardice that made you decline a war against potent Russia, and declare war against peaceful China; and what was it but cowardice that made you take odds of four to one against Egypt?

It was all part of an abnormal desire to meddle:

You must be meddling, nor will you take a plain course, but choose an intricate one, to display your talents for diplomacy, to out-devil the devil. . . . You must adjust the balance of power in Europe, as if it would not come to equilibrium of itself! and you must do this after a fashion peculiar to yourself; that is, by going to war to preserve peace!

And yet he avoided meddling in places where it might do some good: 'If my Lord loves interference, why did he not interfere in behalf of Greece or Poland?' As a result:

Brave men have been sent on services only fit for the vilest cowards; the British flag has been tarnished with guilt and sent round the globe to show its shame; the indignation and contempt of all humane and honest men excited; and all this because our foreign minister happens to be a busybody, a mischief-maker, a second marplot. . . . Had you been anything but a Whig, every cannon-ball fired at the houses and homes of the poor Chinese and Syrians would have knocked at your heart. The Tories love you because you are like them, and your middle-class partisans care not what cruelties you commit to spite the Chartists who alone pity your victims.

The one sure cure for 'Palmerian' policies—as for all else amiss in England—was the Charter. It was hoped:

. . . that what you have done will be a lesson to the country, providing the necessity of the Charter. Had the Charter been in force, you would neither have had the power, nor been permitted, to disgrace and endanger England, by your crusade against freedom and humanity, to lessen our inflence by lessening the respect of other nations.

Palmerston went on to win his victories—overseas, at the polls and over countless breakfast tables—undisturbed by his Chartist critics. The Anti-Corn Law League was similarly undeterred from achieving its great end by the uproar it created amongst the Chartists. During the League's coincidental agitation, 1838 to 1846, the movements clashed repeatedly and negotiated occasionally, casting up a welter of arguments and counter-arguments about the Corn Laws and free trade. The story of the League and its relations with Chartism has already been well told,[141] and the conclusion of one scholar, that 'the Chartist attitude to the League was . . . neither consistent nor clearly thought out'[142] certainly seems apt. Some Chartists supported the League, usually to continue the old radical demand to get rid of protection for the landed interest. Others opposed, sometimes in the violent form of smashing up League meetings.[143] Opposition was based on the assumption that the League was an organisation of middle-class men whose primary concern was profit, and who would seek cheaper bread in order to lower wages. Some Chartists felt that the League was an obstacle in the way of achieving the Charter because it sought to use them, and might thereby divert their energies from agitating for the Charter.[144] At best, the League was a red herring; at worst, a diabolical scheme.

The League forced Chartists to handle thorny economic questions and to consider European workmen as their competitors. It might be expected that such cogitations were likely to conjure up xenophobic attitudes towards continental workers, but such was not the case. European workers were nearly always considered dispassionately, almost as abstractions. Cold calculation of the economic world was the rule, with European workers counting as one of several factors. Hatred of them, even contempt, was rarely expressed. It was commonly assumed that foreign workers had a competitive advantage because they were paid less. Therefore, repeal of the Corn Laws would facilitate the competition of British manufactures because it would lead to the lowering of British wages to match those paid on the continent.[145] With or without free trade, British workers were at a disadvantage in facing foreign competition because taxation, the national debt and the costs of the aristocratic establishment burdened and shackled the whole British economy.[146] How could a 'state so oppressed' trade 'upon terms of equality with the free nations of the world?' asked Feargus O'Connor in an open letter.[147]

According to some Chartists, foreigners were already competing in manufactures successfully, or they were learning to do so rapidly, since they were opening the same kinds of factories as Britain had, equipped with the latest machinery and staffed with many skilled British workmen.[148] Such apprehensions actually led some Chartists to call for more, not less, protection—protection for industry. Lower prices for goods and unemployment were predicted in the *Northern Star* in 1842, when Peel reduced tariffs:

Foreign boots and shoes are to be admitted to this country at a greatly reduced duty. Foreign furniture, and foreign vegetable produce, are also to be admitted at a reduced duty. The operation of this portion of the tariff scheme will be, upon the shoemakers and cabinet-makers and upon the market gardeners, just what the reduction of duty upon foreign silks has been to the Spitalfields and Macclesfield silk weavers'.[149]

Since Europeans were erecting their own manufacturing establishments rapidly, and protecting them with tariff walls, would it not be wiser to produce and consume English goods in the English market behind English protection?[150] After all, competing for sales in foreign markets was a shibboleth to some Chartists, something that manufacturers used as a warning when Chartists asked for 'a measure of *Regulation*' to prevent such things as overworking children or when workers sought to resist reductions in wages.[151]

Speculations of this sort led to comparisons of foreign and British standards of living. Most depicted European labour as worse off— sometimes pointing out that these conditions prevailed where no Corn Laws existed at all,[152] and some argued that the wage statistics used did not take real costs and living conditions into account.[153] Some concluded that it made no difference anyway:

And after all, what matter it to the English Operative whether continental artisans are or are not better off than himself? For him it is enough to know that he is worse off than he ought to be, that a money-monger's repeal of the Corn Laws would not make him better off, and that if Frenchmen, Swiss, or Prussians choose to submit to semi-starvation, that is no reason why he should.[154]

Some Chartists raised the argument that foreign wage rates were immaterial because British workers were more productive. Their 'know-how', natural resources,[155] and 'spirit' enabled them to be 'equal to three or four of the men of any other country in producing goods'.[156] Therefore a somewhat tepid endorsement of the struggle to repeal the Corn Laws was announced in the *Gazette* of Lovett's National Association, 'on the ground that . . . all protective duties' were unwise and against the order of nature.[157] In both the past and the present protection had not protected:

Did the Spitalfields weavers profit by the prohibition of French silks? Do the peasantry at this moment fare sumptuously on the fruits of the food mono-poly? . . . Foreign nations close their doors against us . . . [but] . . . the Polish peasant is clothed like a half-savage amidst rotting corn. . . .[158]

Sometimes such endorsements led to the establishment of good relations between the League and certain Chartist groups.[159] On the other hand, relations between the League and O'Connor and his followers were notoriously bad.[160] Bronterre O'Brien called Leaguers 'Sham Radicals', middle-class types who were out to put Chartism down.[161] In the welter of thought and discussion other arguments were raised from time to time. Repeal was said to mean eventual dependence upon foreign foodstuffs, so that in the event of a war England could be starved into submission.[162] Another, more strained, was the declaration that repeal would cause the price of grain to go up abroad and this would lessen the purchasing power of foreigners buying English goods.[163]

All the arguments of the Chartists could not diminish the effective pressure of the League upon the people with political power—electors and Members of the House of Commons, so that its goal was achieved at the very time the defeated Chartist movement was falling into dissolution.

IV NEWPORT, BENIOWSKI, URQUHART AND RUSSOPHOBIA

The failure of the great Chartist petition in 1839 tempted some Chartists to try rebellion.[164] In contemplating drastic action,

Chartists did draw upon European experiences. Allusions to the efficacy of physical force on the continent were common,[165] as well as fears that British workers would eventually face force similar to that which crushed the Poles.[166] While examples of European violence were surely in mind in 1839 and the forties, London was never Paris and the Chartists were never French 'ouvriers'. Continental handbooks on street warfare did circulate,[167] but, as Reg Groves has pointed out, they did not relate to conditions in industrialised Britain.[168] Francis Maceroni's *Defensive Instruction to the People* was the most popular form of instruction about street warfare, purporting to show how an armed populace could defeat trained troops. An ex-trooper of the Scots Greys, Alexander Somerville, became alarmed over the optimism generated by such instructions amongst his militant friends. In contradiction he published a series of penny pamphlets, *Warnings to the People on Street Warfare*, which argued that trained troops and their artillery would be unresistible in England.[169] British troops, unlike continental troops in several revolutionary situations, were not likely to go over to the other side. When they fought mobs in the Chartist era they demonstrated their reliability and zeal. Of course they were never hemmed in by barricades and worn down by masses of insurrectionists operating in a maze of city streets. Instead General Charles Napier moved formidable numbers of troops from place to place in Britain to act against threats of disorder. They were not used to break up peaceful meetings or to force strikers to resume work, activities that might have played upon radical sentiments among the rank and file.[170]

Even so, Chartists can claim the only revolutionary outburst in England in all of the nineteenth century, the Newport rising—a sad affair in a poor part of the Welsh borderland that was noted for its violence.[171] Of particular interest is the legend that a colourful Polish exile was involved, which became a vehicle for the insane Russophobia of a strange Member of Parliament, David Urquhart. Perhaps it is fitting that the name, at least, of a Pole should be associated with the only armed uprising of the Chartists, since Polish exiles were so active in insurrections on the continent in the nineteenth century.[172] All told, the Newport rising caused from ten to twenty deaths and destroyed £100 in property. It was, according to the patient research of historians, a purely local outburst that was actually a cumulative reaction to several grievances, including the destruction of a local union, low wages, payment in truck, poor working conditions and the New Poor Law. Its leader, John Frost, reluctantly went along with the insurgents, and led only to the extent that he did not oppose. No unity of purpose was displayed in the affair. The rioters deluded themselves into thinking that British soldiers would join with them, or at least refuse to shoot at them. As it turned out, the rising was a 'pathetic, futile enterprise'.[173]

The Newport rising was something else in the imaginations of contemporaries, as a flock of rumours rapidly spread and grew. Some believed that this was an attempt to create an English republic with John Frost as its first president. Others saw it as part of a general revolution carefully arranged throughout England by the Chartists. The wildest tales—and these were stories that gained wide circulation—depicted the Newport rising as part of an international conspiracy that aimed at the conquest of England and Europe by Tsarist Russia.[174] It was reported that a Russian agent, one of many operating in Britain, was supposed to take command, or, as others had it, work through Frost, in the mountains of Wales. The object was to co-operate with a Russian fleet that was to effect the invasion of England.[175]

The suspected Russian agent was Major Bartolomiej Beniowski, a Polish exile. A painstaking search by historians has not turned up a single scrap of evidence that Beniowski participated in the Newport rising or that he was in Monmouthshire immediately before or after the riot.[176] At most, he may have helped to drill Welsh firebrands sometime in 1839, or he may have acted in the capacity of unofficial military adviser to them at some time before the uprising.[177] He did write some extremely dense and belligerent articles about military science that appeared in the Chartist newspaper, the *London Democrat*, which was edited by Harney.[178] This is as far as Beniowski's connection with Chartist violence could have possibly gone, according to all the evidence that has turned up.

It is clear that Beniowski had a stormy career in exile, but there is no evidence that he was a Russian spy.[179] Little was heard of him in the activities of Chartist internationalists in the forties, although he did speak at a Democratic Supper held in August 1845. Harney, the chairman, introduced him as 'a man who had been infamously calumniated', who had 'suffered terrible persecution even from some of the Chartists themselves', but who had demonstrated his 'unshaken fidelity to the good cause' by appearing at the supper. Beniowski's remarks consisted in part of a defence of himself. He declared that he had been 'cruelly slandered' and lamented that his accusers 'had never offered to prove their accusations'. The rest of his speech was taken up by a strong attack on various other Polish democrats, those who were 'humbugging' Englishmen.[180]

Beniowski was interesting. He was a Jew from a prosperous family who had studied medicine before the outbreak of the Polish revolution. He fought on the Russian side at first, because he came from Russian Poland. Beniowski rose to the rank of major, but went over to the Polish side in the midst of the struggle.[181] In exile, he studied military science in Paris for a while, and went to Palestine on behalf of a committee chaired by Lafayette that sought a homeland for the Jews. He arrived in London in 1836 and settled in Bow Street, where he occupied himself with eccentric occupations. He attempted to invent a system of logotypes, or printing type that combined common letter groupings on single pieces of type. He hoped the system would be adopted to simplify printing and lessen its cost.[182] He also tried to invent a new English orthography, and sought to teach languages in an original method known as 'phreno-typics'. All the while he termed himself a 'cosmopolitical Chartist'.[183]

Why did Beniowski become the villain of the Great Emigration? Why was this democratic, eccentric Pole who had, for a while, friendly relations with members of the Chartist left, so strongly suspected of being a Russian agent? The idea of a Russian conspiracy involving the Newport rioters and Beniowski probably came from the fertile, unstable mind of David Urquhart.[184] Urquhart had been for a time a diplomat at Constantinople. He gained some notoriety later when he became the correspondent and friend of Karl Marx. He was probably half-mad or all mad.[185] He had terrible obsessions, and was, according to Webster, in *The Foreign Policy of Lord Palmerston*, entirely unfitted for his diplomatic post, and therefore a serious problem for the foreign secretary.[186] Nevertheless, Urquhart was a fluent, charismatic, cosmopolitan Scottish aristocrat, a man who made a deep impression on some people.[187] Some critical comments by the editor of the middle-class *Spectator* about his performance in the House of Commons reveal something about the nature of his methods:[188]

Mr Urquhart has not gained by being in the House; he does not succeed as a public speaker: the impressive solemnity, the air of subdued precision, the pregnant mystery, the elaborated innuendo, which tell so much at a half-private gathering of selected listeners, go for nothing on the wide stage of the public meeting or Parliament.

Urquhart confronted the British working class in the pose of a Tory radical who was desirous of leading them in a crusade to save Britain and Europe from Russian designs.[189] Urquhart was appalled by the revolutionary rumblings of the most militant Chartists, and hoped that his activities would serve to circumvent rebellion.[190] He was not against the Six Points. When Robert Lowery once asked him whether the Chartists had a right to the Charter, Urquhart replied: 'You may as well ask me if they have a right to the air they breathe.'[191] Yet he wanted to change the tactics of the movement so that platform oratory and enthusiastic mass meetings would be replaced by steady, quiet activities stressing mutual improvement. Later in life he made the grandiose claim that he had frustrated plans for a Chartist rising by diverting workers from domestic discontents by focusing their attention on Russia.[192] After all, as Urquhart saw the situation, Russians were at work seeking to create a Chartist rising in order to paralyse Britain in preparation for a conquest of Europe by Tsardom. The thing to do was to arouse the British working class over the intrigues of that traitor Palmerston, the designs of Russia, and that other obsession of his, a romantic love of Turkey.[193]

In order to arouse workers, Urquhart busied himself with a number of propagandistic undertakings—fund raising, the establishment of working-class foreign affairs committees, and sending working-class speakers about the country with his message. He coveted space in publications, and captured the Chartist *Northern Liberator* of Newcastle upon Tyne for his purposes. The story of this publication's conversion has been told in J. H. Gleason's *The Genesis of Russophobia in Great Britain*. From April 1840 until December, when it folded up, this organ was filled with Urquhartite editorials, accounts of speeches by Urquhart and his followers, charts showing Russian aggression and letters from the leader himself. Russian plans for world domination were outlined, Palmerston's treason exposed, and even forebodings of a Russian invasion were declared.[194]

These activities apparently reached their height in the winter of 1840-1.[195] His groups seem to have been inactive during the period of the most intense Chartist internationalism, 1845 to 1848, although they revived prior to the Crimean war.[196]

George Jacob Holyoake was asked to join one of these foreign affairs committees in 1838. He recalled later that it met in a Birmingham bookseller's home and had the impeachment of Lord Palmerston as its object. As Holyoake put it, they wanted to 'cut off Palmerston's head' legally, and since 'things were bad in those days, I had no doubt somebody's head ought to be cut off and I hoped they had hit upon the right one'.[197]

Other workers' committees, variously called 'Committees for Investigating Foreign Affairs', or 'Committees for the Investigation of Diplomatic Documents'' appeared in northern cities, particularly Newcastle.[198] The effect of all this activity on the government was almost nil. The effect on Chartism was divisive, but not at all significantly divisive. Although Urquhart made the claim later in life that his activities had destroyed the Chartist movement, historians have asserted that his influence upon the working-class movement from 1838 to 1841 was actually slight.[199] Of course, some wild fantasies took hold. Some Chartists became convinced that Russian agents were at work in their movement or that Urquhart had secret documents proving that Lord Palmerston had betrayed England to Russia.[200] Nevertheless, those so influenced were not important working-class leaders.[201] Harney, Jones, Lovett, Cooper, and others who figured prominently in working-class internationalism were unmoved by Urquhart. In fact, the *Northern Star*, the most important of the Chartist newspapers, owned and operated by Feargus O'Connor, came out against Urquhart's 'Foreign Policy Movement' in no uncertain terms. The main thing that disturbed Harney, O'Connor, and other Chartist leaders, was that Urquhart's agitation would distract the rank and file from the fight for the Charter. As the *Northern Star* stated, the Charter was to come first, 'and then down with all foreign tyranny when you have the tools to work with. . . . We caution the people against going to work without the tools.'[202] Exhortations of this sort must have had effect, for workers began to cause commotions at Urquhart-inspired foreign policy meetings. One of the common tactics they employed was to attach amendments to resolutions, saying such things as: 'The people would not consent to join in any movement which had not for its object the obtaining of the Charter.'[203] While some Chartist leaders came to feel that the so-called 'Russo-Chartist agitation' was a Tory scheme to 'undermine the Whig government on the foreign policy question', and others concluded that it was a middle-class venture to direct attention away from democratic reform, none disapproved out of concern for Lord Palmerston.[204] The *Star* thought there was nothing wrong in 'cutting off the old beau's head', for he was certainly a traitor. What was wrong was spending energy in that kind of agitation when the Charter was obviously so much more important.[205] An address of the 'Democrats of Sheffield to the Polish Exiles in England' stated this clearly:

They [the British people] were appealed to by certain parties, who told them a certain minister was a traitor . . . and had sold his country to Russia! What said the people? 'Palmerston may be a traitor, but what then? Are not all his coronetted compeers traitors too?—have not the aristocracy, one and all, sold to slavery? We detest the Russian despot, but we have no power to prevent an alliance of our irresponsible rulers with him; we will not have our attention diverted from the obtainment of our Charter.[206]

Another argument advanced against the 'Foreign Policy Movement' was that foreign tyranny could be no worse than domestic oppression—and therefore British workers ought to worry first about the tyrants at home:

Let these questions be argued by those whose properties would be injured by the invasion of a foreign foe; for the poor we do aver, that neither Russian, Turk, German, Prussian, Jew, or Devil, could make their condition more deplorable than it is.[207]

Feargus O'Connor found the paid missionaries of the movement very annoying. He called them 'nasty fellows' who were paid £3 to £5 per week to 'get up a national feeling' on the Russian conspiracy, while they 'lulled the Charter into a comfortable slumber by giving it the go-by'. He warned fellow Chartists about these missionaries in this fashion:

We have always advocated the employment of paid missionaries, while, at the same time, we think the country ought to know who these missionaries are, whence they come, how they are paid and by whom they are appointed. We do confess that we feel an awkwardness about working men, not appointed by the people, going on expensive tours all over the country, having an abundance of money, their families well supplied at home and Russia—Russia their constant theme of declamation, while, in reality, they know nothing about Russia. We advise all local committees, previous to their proceedings, hereafter, to be satisfied of their having been appointed by some authorised Chartist Association, or otherwise to have nothing to do with them.[208]

The ridiculousness of much of what Urquhart was trying to pass on did not escape Chartist leaders. The *Northern Star* called Urquhart, among other things, 'a half-cracked, philanthropic, theoretical politician', and his assistant, Charles Attwood, the brother of Thomas Attwood, was dubbed a 'hare-brained theoretician'.[209] On the whole, it seems that Urquhart was discredited by many Chartists as a 'fraud' and his schemes were regarded as distracting delusions.[210] One of the unfortunate ramifications of this criticism was that any and all Chartist interest in foreign affairs became suspect, as the *Northern Star* lamented:

> The cause of freedom and progression in Eastern Europe was materially injured instead of aided by the 'Foreign Policy Movement'. The duplicity and exaggerations of the actors in that movement implanted in the breast of the English democrats suspicions and prejudices which are but now wearing away. . . . With some sound views, the originators of this movement . . . organised their own failure by indulging in the grossest exaggerations as to the power and designs of Russia.Their exaggerations caused men to doubt, and ultimately to reject the entire of their statements; and thus Russia was most effectually served by the very means intended to injure her. . . .[211]

Urquhart was not needed to create working-class Russophobia—it existed before he busied himself in the 'Foreign Policy Movement', and it continued long after his efforts were condemned. Without exception, all kinds of working-class leaders and their various newspapers were Russophobic as a matter of course. It was just as normal for them to dislike Russia and the Tsar as it was for them to appreciate the democratic elements in the first French Revolution. This Russophobia was generally for all Russians, from Tsar to peasant. There was no sympathy for the poor, ordinary peasant soldier because he was seen as a superstitious, blind beast—made so by the absence of a free press, public meetings, and free speech and by the priesthood's perversion of truth.[212] Of course, the Tsar was especially loathed. Hetherington's *Destructive and Poor Man's Conservative* even called for his assassination:

> What man that reads this [various stories of Russian atrocities] will not wish himself at the side of Nicholas with a dagger! . . . Think of vengeance! There are occasions when men shall arm themselves, and leave tears to women . . . One blow at the villain would be worth all the tears in the world.[213]

Working-class Russophobia reached one of its peaks when Tsar Nicholas paid a state visit to England in 1844. A huge meeting was held at the National Hall, High Holborn, 'to give the men of London an opportunity to express their feeling as regards the "Autocrat of All the Russias" '.[214] Henry Hetherington was in the chair and William Lovett was the principal speaker at this crowded meeting. An unruly, enthusiastic audience held up the proceedings several times and participated by shouting 'No, no, no' when they were asked whether the 'depopulator of countries . . . the enemy of mankind' would be welcome in England. They shouted 'O the monster, O the brute' when the sufferings of the Poles were recounted; there were screams of 'Horrid, horrid', mass groanings and 'sensations of horror'. Explanations were given for the cheers that greeted Nicholas: the police had been ordered to cheer. At this point a cry went up for 'a groan for the bluebottles', which was 'heartily' responded to. In addition, the 'base hireling' press was sharply criticised for urging public courtesy towards the Tsar out of respect for the Queen's wishes. It was argued that Victoria should not expect the British people to offer hospitality to a 'mass murderer'. Several resolutions were passed, one stating that Nicholas' presence was 'an insult to the great body of the people' on account of what he did to the Poles. Another warned of the 'infringement of the rights of humanity or public liberty' which might be in the offing from the visit. The meeting ended late with 'several rounds of groans' for Nicholas and 'astounding cheers' for the Poles.

British workers did not need this visit or the wild ideas and frenetic activities of David Urquhart to whip up such Russophobia— it was already there. So were many colourful Polish exiles of the Great Emigration, who would heighten these feelings in future years. They, and not the men of the 'Foreign Affairs Committees', would act as a catalyst to help create the Chartist internationalism of the forties.

Notes for Chapter 3

1 It was not uncommon for provincial Chartists to view distant London with great disdain. Some were as blunt as Feargus O'Connor, who declared: 'London is rotten'. *Northern Star*, July 4, 1840, quoted in Mark Hovell, *The Chartist Movement* (Manchester, 1966 ed.), p. 231. London's Chartists were seen as apathetic about reform and riddled with atheistic tendencies.

2 Brian Harrison and Patricia Hollis, 'Chartism, liberalism and the life of Robert Lowery', *English Historical Review*, vol. 83 (1967), p. 512.

3 D. J. Rowe, 'Chartism and the Spitalfields silkweavers', *Economic History Review*, second series, xx, no. 3 (1967), p. 493.

4 G. D. H. Cole, *Chartist Portraits* (New York, 1965 ed.), p. 33.

5 The declared objects and aims of the LWMA proclaimed a deliberate élitism. They wished to 'draw into one bond of unity' only the '*intelligent* and *influential*' portion of the working classes. This meant 'honest, sober, moral, and thinking' British workmen, whom they regarded as 'few compared with the viscious many . . .'. The LWMA, unlike 'an indiscriminate union of thousands', would be spared the contamination of the 'veteran drunkard' and the 'profligate railer at abuses'. It would also avoid the 'habits and associations' which mar 'domestic happiness' and destroy 'political usefulness' by shunning 'by every possible means' meetings in public houses. Another feature was that active membership was restricted to actual members of the working class. All of this is in William Lovett, *Life and Struggles of William Lovett* (Liverpool, London, and Preston, 1967 ed.), pp. 74–80. Also, the *London Mercury*, September 17, 1837. Several debates and questions about the organisation have been raised; see, in particular, E. J. Hobsbawm, 'The Labour aristocracy in nineteenth century Britain', in *Labouring Men: Studies in the History*

of Labour, 3rd ed. (London, 1968), pp. 272–315; Iorwerth Prothero, 'Chartism in London', *Past and Present*, no. 44 (August 1969), p. 84; D. J. Rowe, 'The failure of London Chartism', *The Historical Journal*, XI, no. 3 (1968), p. 486; Asa Briggs, 'Chartism reconsidered', in M. Roberts, ed., *Historical Studies, Papers Read Before the Third Conference of Irish Historians* (London, 1959), p. 45; D. J. Rowe, 'The London Working Men's Association and the People's Charter', *Past and Present*, no. 36 (April 1967), pp. 73–86; 'Debates: The London Working Men's Association and the People's Charter', *Past and Present*, no. 38 (December 1967), pp. 169–76. Controversies aside, members, compared to most other workers throughout Britain, whether urban or rural, were better paid, more secure in their employment, better educated and not as dependent upon the trade cycle. Their vast, diverse London environment and their deliberate segregation from potential mass movements meant that the LWMA would be but one small group of many groups in the metropolis. Still, they stood for much of London Chartism.

6 G. D. H. Cole, *Chartist Portraits*, p. 34. W. J. Linton remembered him as the 'gentlest of agitators, a mild, peace-loving man, whom nothing but a deep sense of sympathy with and duty towards the wronged could have dragged into public life'. W. J. Linton, *Memories* (London, 1895).

7 Lovett, *Life and Struggles*, p. 46. Lovett once lost his stock of household furniture because he refused to serve in the militia or hire a substitute to serve for him because he was not represented in Parliament. See Lovett, *Life and Struggles*, p. 53; Cole, *Chartist Portraits*, p. 37.

8 Lovett, *Life and Struggles*, p. 80. To deny Lovett's claim, see the Owenite contacts described in the previous chapter, and the introductory chapter of A. Müller-Lehning, *The International Association, 1855–1859*. He notes a manifesto addressed to British workers from French workers which was published in a Lyons newspaper, *Echo de la Fabrique*, in 1832.

9 Katz had founded a Flemish working-class society, 'Maatschappij der Verbroedering', in 1831 and spread socialist propaganda through his plays and in a Flemish working-class newspaper that he edited, the first of its kind: Müller-Lehning, *The International Association*, p. 6.

10 *London Dispatch*, October 30, 1836, p. 45.

11 The entire address is in the *London Dispatch* of November 13, 1836, p. 65. A significant portion of it is reproduced in William Lovett, *Life and Struggles*, p. 80. The Place Collection, Add. MSS 27,819 and Newspaper Clippings, vol. 51, gives the most complete account of these developments, including many of the responses from foreign newspapers.

12 The address is presented in full in the *London Dispatch*, January 22, 1837, p. 145. It was reprinted two years later in the *Working Men's Association Gazette*, no. 2, June 1, 1839. An appendix in Müller-Lehning, *The International Association* contains the original version in French.

13 An anti-French note was included in the address: 'We . . . are the victims of the united aristocracy of France and our own country, as you are the victims of your tyrants.'

14 There were four cabinet-makers and four weavers; three printers and three labourers; two tailors, two masons and two shoemakers; and one each of the following occupations: clerk, painter, hat maker, locksmith, cooper, soldier, waggoner, and porter.

15 One Belgian group, the workers of Ghent, sent a separate letter, which concluded with these sentiments: 'Dearly do we love to see these beautiful signs of the times. How delightful it is to witness the manifestation of brotherly love between nation and nation! How much more noble is the document we have translated than any marriage treaty between a girl Guelph and a boy Coburg, under the pretext of cementing love between the millions of two great peoples.' *London Dispatch*, February 26, 1837, p. 185.

16 *London Dispatch*, July 9, 1837, p. 340.

17 The meeting is reported in the *London Dispatch*, December 11, 1836, pp. 97–8. The M.P.s included Colonel Thompson, Thomas Wakeley, and W. Harvey. Augustus Beaumont was in the chair.

18 *London Dispatch*, December 18, 1836, p. 108; January 1, 1837, p. 123.

19 *London Dispatch*, January 22, 1837, p. 149. Apparently the rightist press in

Belgium taunted the followers of Katz over the fact that funds from Britain were not yet forthcoming. The *London Dispatch* described the arrangements of the subscription in order to explain the delay.

20 Lovett, *Life and Struggles*, p. 129. The LWMA's view of Europe is most explicitly presented in the 'Address to the Working Classes of Europe and Especially to the Polish People', issued in 1838 as a pamphlet, as were all of these addresses. For convenience, reference is made to *Life and Struggles*, where substantial portions of them appear; For this address, see pp. 125–31.

21 William Lovett and John Collins, *Chartism: A New Organisation of the People, Embracing a Plan for the Education and Improvement of the People, Politically and Socially*, 2nd ed. (London, 1841), pp. 14–15.

22 Lovett, *Life and Struggles*, p. 146.

23 Lovett, *Life and Struggles*, p. 116.

24 Lovett, *Life and Struggles*, p. 47.

25 Lovett, *Life and Struggles*, pp. 125–6. From the 'Address to the Working Classes of Europe and Especially to the Polish People'.

26 It is reproduced in Lovett, *Life and Struggles*, pp. 249–55. Lovett declared that he received letters from friends on the continent who said it had a wide circulation.

27 Lovett, *Life and Struggles*, pp. 260–5. The 'din and dazzle of warlike preparation' might 'speedily intoxicate the unreflecting thousands of our brethren having their worst passions loosened and excited', which would transform them 'into savage demons thirsting for blood'.

28 Lovett, *Life and Struggles*, p. 128.

29 Lovett, *Life and Struggles*, p. 252.

30 Lovett, *Life and Struggles*, pp. 253–4. This plea was repeated in the address to American workers in 1846, with slightly different wording. A 'Congress of Nations' was proposed, 'freely chosen by the people of their respective countries' to apply arbitration. The National Association hoped that 'through such instrumentality, universal peace and human brotherhood may be established, freedom expanded, commerce promoted, and the arts, industry and civilisation of *each* be made to contribute to the welfare of *all*'. Lovett, *Life and Struggles*, pp. 264–5.

31 Lovett, *Life and Struggles*, p. 125.

32 Lovett, *Life and Struggles*, pp. 119–20.

33 Lovett, *Life and Struggles*, p. 251.

34 Iorwerth Prothero, in 'Debates: The London Working Men's Association and the People's Charter', *Past and Present*, no. 38 (December 1967), p. 172. In 'Chartism in London', *Past and Present*, no. 44 (August 1969), p. 77, Prothero remarked that the 'chief contribution' of the LWMA lay 'in the country, where it sent missionaries to help found other working men's associations'.

35 R. H. Tawney, introduction to Lovett, *Life and Struggles*, p. xvi. On p. xxvi he wrote that they anticipated the idea of 'Workers of All Lands Unite'. One early historian of the Chartist movement held these preoccupations in very high esteem: Hermann Schlütter wrote that the LWMA was the organisation 'which first cultivated, in an entirely conscious manner, a feeling of international solidarity of the modern working class'. Herman Schlütter, *Die Chartisten-Bewegung: ein Beitrag zur sozialpolitischen Geschichte Englands* (New York, 1916), p. 213.

36 E. P. Thompson, *The Making of the English Working Class* (New York, 1966 ed.), p. 821.

37 R. G. Gammage, *History of the Chartist Movement: 1837–1854* (New York, 1969 ed.), pp. 71 and 73; Alfred Plummer, *Bronterre: A Political Biography of Bronterre O'Brien, 1804–1864* (London, 1971), pp. 66–8.

38 G. D. H. Cole, *Chartist Portraits*, pp. 241 and 248.

39 Asa Briggs, 'National bearings', in Asa Briggs, ed., *Chartist Studies* (London, Melbourne, Toronto, New York, 1967), p. 301.

40 Place Collection, Add. MSS 27,821 fo. 22. Quoted in Julius West, *A History of the Chartist Movement* (London, Boston, and New York, 1920), p. 72.

41 Alfred Plummer, 'The place of Bronterre O'Brien in the working class movement', *Economic History Review*, II, no. 1 (January 1929), p. 80. See also chapter four, 'Revolution in retrospect', in Alfred Plummer, *Bronterre*. Bronterre's enthusiastic preoccupation with Robespierre, Babeuf, and Buonarroti continued all through the Chartist era. See in particular the *Northern Star* of August 25, 1838, p. 4. Bronterre

wrote in *McDouall's Chartist and Republican Journal* that 'like the Saviour of the world he [Robespierre] immolated himself for an ungrateful people' (September 4, 1841, p. 181). See also the *London Democrat* of May 18, 1839, p. 42 and April 20, 1839, p. 11.

42 *McDouall's Chartist and Republican Journal*, May 22, 1841, p. 62.

43 *Ibid.*, September 18, 1841, p. 199.

44 *Ibid.*, May 8, 1841, p. 47.

45 *Ibid.*, May 29, 1841, p. 70.

46 *Ibid.*, May 15, 1841, p. 54. See also *Bronterre's National Reformer*, February 18, 1837, p. 56; February 25, 1837, p. 59; March 11, 1837, pp. 76 and 77.

47 *Bronterre's National Reformer*, February 18, 1837, p. 56.

48 E. P. Thompson, *The Making of the English Working Class*, pp. 822 and 823.

49 *The National Reformer and Manx Weekly Review of Home and Foreign Affairs*, April 24, 1847, p. 2.

50 *Bronterre's National Reformer*, January 15, 1837, p. 12. See also the *Operative*, November 18, 1838.

51 *The National Reformer and Manx Weekly Review of Home and Foreign Affairs*, April 24, 1847, p. 2.

52 *Bronterre's National Reformer*, January 15, 1837, p. 12; *The Operative*, November 18, 1836; *Bronterre's National Reformer*, January 15, 1837, p. 12; *The National Reformer and Manx Weekly Review of Home and Foreign Affairs*, April 24, 1847, p. 2.

53 Dorothy Thompson, 'Notes on Aspects of Chartist Leadership', *Society for the Study of Labour History Bulletin*, no. 15 (Autumn 1967), p. 29.

54 *The National Reformer and Manx Weekly Review of Home and Foreign Affairs*, May 22, 1847, p. 1. As he saw it, the landlords and capitalists were 'the veritable rulers of all countries', who used generals as their 'tools' and who hid 'behind the thrones of kings, the altars of priests [and] the parchments of lawyers'.

55 Hetherington's *Twopenny Dispatch*, August 27, 1836; *The National Reformer and Manx Weekly Review of Home and Foreign Affairs*, December 19, 1846.

56 *Ibid.*, December 19, 1846.

57 *McDouall's Chartist and Republican Journal*, May 22, 1841, p. 62.

58 *The National Reformer and Manx Weekly Review of Home and Foreign Affairs*, December 19, 1846.

59 *Ibid.*, January 9, 1847, p. 10.

60 *Ibid.*, May 22, 1847, p. 1.

61 *McDouall's Chartist and Republican Journal*, August 21, 1841, pp. 163–4; August 28, 1841, pp. 173–4. It appeared in the *Operative* three years earlier. Alfred Plummer quotes part of it in *Bronterre*, p. 229.

62 *The British Statesman*, April 24, 1842, p. 9.

63 It is too simple to say that there was a breach between 'moral force' and 'physical force' Chartists after 1839; each shaded into the other at some point, and most individual Chartists could be either, depending on the circumstances. There were many kinds of Chartism after 1839, so that the movement may be described as a seething hodgepodge, conforming to the diversity imposed by regional differences, responsive to the charisma of local leaders, and impelled by particular economic irregularities.

64 A motion was introduced and withdrawn disapproving of members wearing French emblems. It was probably prompted by the inflammatory activities of young George Julian Harney, who wore a phrygian cap while making his violent speeches. See Thomas Frost, 'History of the Chartist Movement', found in the *Bradford Observer Budget*, Newspaper Cuttings Chiefly Relating to Chartism and Local History of Hypperholme, unpaginated and undated, Manchester Central Reference Library. The debates of the Convention were closely followed in the *Charter*. It should be added that Julius West raised the question of the working-class nature of the assemblage. He found that twenty-four delegates worked for wages and twenty-nine did not.

65 Lovett, *Life and Struggles*, pp. 173 and 174.

66 *The Charter*, February 17, 1839, p. 54.

67 For a consideration of this bill see F. C. Mather, *Public Order in the Age of the Chartists* (New York, 1967 ed.), pp. 127–40. He points out that prejudice against the centralisation recommended by a Royal Commission was such that John Russell

had to bring in a measure which was less objectionable. Chartist dislike of this aspect of centralisation was shared.

68 Mark Hovell, *The Chartist Movement*, p. 128.

69 *The Charter*, March 24, 1839, p. 139.

70 From an editorial in *The Charter*, February 3, 1839, p. 24.

71 William Lovett, *Life and Struggles*, p. 176. Dr Bowring's 'Facts in Favour of Democracy' appeared in the *Charter* of August 18, 1839, p. 469, and depicted Swiss workers in peace and comfort under a democratic system.

72 In all probability this organisation was the body known as the French Democratic Society, founded in 1839 and merged with the German Workers' Educational Society in 1847. Camille Berrier-Fontaine and Jean Michelot, two relatively obscure French republicans, were prominent leaders of this group who became the representatives of the French exiles in the Fraternal Democrats. The address was published in *The Charter*, July 28, 1839, p. 428.

73 Gratitude must be expressed to Dr Alexander Wilson of the University of Manchester, who allowed me to study his material on Taylor for another project. He has written a sketch of Taylor in his *Scottish Chartist Portraits* (Wakefield, 1965). Taylor himself wrote little, outside of newspaper pieces.

74 Leslie C. Wright, *Scottish Chartism* (Edinburgh and London, 1953), p. 61.

75 W. E. Adams, *Memoirs of a Social Atom* (New York, 1968), p. 211.

76 Thomas Frost, 'History of the Chartist Movement', in the *Bradford Observer Budget*, chapter two, Newspaper Clippings, Manchester Central Reference Library; W. E. Adams, *Memoirs of a Social Atom*, p. 211.

77 Gammage, *History of the Chartist Movement*, p. 28; Wright, *Scottish Chartism*, p. 29.

78 One of the unsubstantiated stories about him is that he was at Newport at the time of the rising. Another is that he had a ship ready to intercept the vessel taking Frost and other convicts to Australia.

79 An article by William H. Maehl, Jr., 'Augustus Hardin Beaumont: Anglo-American Radical, 1798–1838', in the *International Review of Social History*, vol. XIV, part 2 (1969), pp. 237–50, provides interesting information on the subject. Some of it is used below.

80 *London Dispatch*, May 21, 1837, pp. 280, 283, 284; June 11, 1837, p. 305; June 25, 1837; July 23, 1837, p. 353; September 10, 1837, p. 412.

81 A conclusion of Francis Place, quoted in William H. Maehl, Jr., *op. cit.*, p. 250; also Gammage, *History of the Chartist Movement*, p. 15; Hovell, *The Chartist Movement*, p. 92.

82 Robert Lowery's remark in the *Weekly Record*, September 20, 1856, p. 210, quoted in Brian Harrison and Patricia Hollis, 'Chartism, liberalism and the life of Robert Lowery', *English Historical Review*, vol. 82 (1967), pp. 532–3.

83 His background is mentioned in R. N. Soffer, 'Attitudes and allegiances in the unskilled north', *International Review of Social History*, vol. X, 3 (1965), p. 448. For the Central National Association, see A. R. Schoyen, *The Chartist Challenge* (London, Melbourne, Toronto, 1958), pp. 17–21; Iorwerth Prothero, 'Chartism in London', *Past and Present*, 44 (August 1969), pp. 93–4.

84 *London Dispatch*, April 2, 1837, pp. 232–3; June 4, 1837; June 11, 1837, p. 305. Chartists were warned not to be 'gulled' into participating in his schemes, and the suggestion was made that the *London Mercury*, which Bernard took over, ought to be renamed the 'London Bacchus', for 'assuredly the spirit of the god of wine far more pervades . . . [it] . . . than the god of eloquence' (*London Dispatch*, June 4, 1837).

85 The whole matter of his report, the meeting, the resolutions, and the address is presented in the *London Mercury* of August 13, 1837.

86 *Northern Star*, February 8, 1840, p. 6.

87 *The National Association Gazette*, January 29, 1842, p. 38.

88 *The Charter*, February 3, 1839, p. 21.

89 *London Dispatch*, January 15, 1837, p. 137.

90 *McDouall's Chartist and Republican Journal*, April 3, 1841, p. 7.

91 From a speech at a Newcastle meeting of 1838, quoted in Gammage, *History of the Chartist Movement*, p. 25.

92 *London Dispatch*, June 23, 1837, p. 326. See also December 18, 1836, p. 108; June 18, 1837, p. 316.

93 *Northern Star*, February 5, 1842, p. 8.

94 *Northern Star*, June 15, 1844, p. 4.

95 *Ibid.*

96 *London Mercury*, October 9, 1836, p. 28.

97 *The National Reformer and Manx Weekly Review of Home and Foreign Affairs*, April 24, 1847, p. 2.

98 *Northern Star*, June 27, 1840, p. 3. One variety of Chartist xenophobia was Irish—and directed against the English! Just as 'Belgium was infected with Dutch placemen and Greece was swarmed over with German lice', Ireland was 'sucked by English leeches' (*Northern Star*, October 7, 1843, p. 5). Feargus O'Connor was at home with this topic. For an example, see the *Northern Star* of August 5, 1843, p. 8.

99 *Northern Star*, March 2, 1844, p. 8.

100 *Northern Star*, October 20, 1838, p. 7. Stephens, incidentally, had lived in Sweden from 1826 to 1830. He was a missionary and domestic chaplain there, and learned Swedish, Danish, and Finnish before returning to England. G. J. Holyoake, *Life of Joseph Rayner Stephens, Preacher and Political Orator* (London, n.d.), p. 29; Cole, *Chartist Portraits*, p. 65.

101 *Northern Star*, June 22, 1844.

102 *The Charter*, August 25, 1839, p. 495.

103 John Cannon, *The Chartists in Bristol* (Bristol, 1964), p. 2.

104 *The Charter*, August 25, 1839, p. 493. Goodwin Barmby called them a 'Frenchified Police . . . a Gendarmerie of spiers and slaves' in an address to British workers which was reported in the *Southern Star* of January 19, 1840, p. 3. In addition, the remarks of the Newcastle-upon-Tyne Radical Association speakers on the 'damnable French police spy system' are worth noting in the *London Dispatch* of November 27, 1837, p. 83.

105 *The Charter*, July 28, 1839, p. 424.

106 *The Charter*, September 15, 1839, p. 582.

107 'Ironpen's Vision', in *The National Reformer and Manx Weekly Review of Home and Foreign Affairs*, April 10, 1847, p. 5, is perhaps the vaguest example.

108 Examples are in the *Northern Star* of February 17, 1838, p. 7; February 24, 1838, p. 6.

109 The declaration of purpose for the new *National Association Gazette* included this provision: 'It will seek to create fraternal feelings between nations, so that those prejudices and animosities which enable the rulers of the earth to foment wars and national devastations may be abolished' (January 1, 1842, p. 1). Lovett re-expressed his internationalism in the *English Chartist Circular*, vol. 1, p. 11.

110 Letter from the Metropolitan Delegate Meeting, *Northern Star*, October 8, 1842, p. 3; also *McDouall's Chartist and Republican Journal*, April 10, 1841.

111 *The Charter*, March 24, 1839, p. 132.

112 *The Operative*, November 11, 1838, p. 21.

113 *Northern Star*, February 27, 1841.

114 *The Charter*, October 20, 1839, p. 622; also, the *Northern Star*, December 10, 1840.

115 For examples, see *The Charter*, October 20, 1839, p. 622; *McDouall's Chartist and Republican Journal*, July 3, 1841, p. 106. The old calls for an alliance of European peoples to resist the crowned heads of Europe were heard whenever a spate of royal visits raised apprehensions that the Holy Alliance was in the process of resuscitation. See the *Northern Star* of September 23 and 30, 1843, p. 4.

116 *Northern Star*, August 5, 1843, p. 8. O'Connor was not blind to the way workers' outlooks were broadened by foreign contacts. In Nottingham he noted how business connections with Europe of small lace manufacturers led to 'expanded minds' and improvement in their 'powers of reason'. He was struck at how many of the 'working people speak several foreign languages with great fluency' (*Bronterre's National Reformer*, January 28, 1837, p. 29).

117 *Northern Liberator*, December 2, 1837, p. 3.

118 The address of the Birmingham Political Union to the National Guards of France is in the *Northern Star*, September 22, 1838, p. 3. The response of the Bristol Working Men's Association appeared in the *Northern Star* on October 6, 1838, p. 3. The *Northern Liberator* of December 2, 1837, p. 3, warned Chartists not to be deluded by such talk of 'an extension of the suffrage'. The franchise in France

would be enlarged just enough to render it 'possible to make every elector's primary interest to support bad government'.

119 *The Charter*, October 13, 1839, p. 600; the *English Chartist Circular*, vol. 2, p. 26; vol. 2, pp. 14, 17–26; *National Association Gazette*, January 29, 1842, p. 38; the *London Dispatch*, December 25, 1836, p. 116.

120 The *English Chartist Circular*, vol. 2, p. 14; *Northern Star*, February 8, 1840, p. 6; September 2, 1843, p. 5. One of the many bizarre suppositions in the *Northern Liberator* was that English policy and major English establishment newspapers were controlled by French gold and royal influence. See the issue of December 16, 1837 in particular.

121 The *National Association Gazette*, April 2, 1842, p. 114.

122 The *National Association Gazette* of January 15, 1842, p. 22 carried a brief item extolling the Norwegians, who, as owners of small plots of land, and enfranchised, saw their taxes and public debt diminish.

123 Austrian despotism was discussed in detail in the *English Chartist Circular*, vol. 1, pp. 203–4. An editorial in the *Charter* in 1839 commented on problems of nationalism and hoped for the day 'when each nation will belong to itself . . .' (July 7, 1839, p. 376).

124 Some hope for Prussia was expressed in an article in the *National Association Gazette*, January 29, 1842, p. 39. The militarism of Prussia was severely dealt with in the *English Chartist Circular*, vol. 2, p. 9.

125 Anti-Papal feeling was common. Perhaps one of the most rational expressions of it was in the *National Association Gazette*, April 2, 1842, pp. 110–11.

126 *National Association Gazette*, April 2, 1842, p. 109. As Preston William Slosson noted many years ago, Chartists saw the moderate constitutional reformers on the Continent as the enemies of the working class because they were actually practitioners of Whiggery; *The Decline of the Chartist Movement* (New York, 1916), p. 204. Spain was a classic example because it seemed that England and France sought to foist *juste milieu* government on the Spanish people; *Northern Liberator*, December 16, 1837; *National Association Gazette*, March 26, 1842, p. 101. Whigs, Tories, French *doctrinaires* and French *juste milieu* all dreaded a democratic upsurge of the Spanish people, for such an event might overthrow 'the despotism of the lawjobbers and money mongers' hiding under 'the trammels of constitutional monarchy' (*London Dispatch*, April 23, 1837, p. 252). According to an editorial of August 13, 1837, p. 380, English Whigs admired French *juste milieu* institutions to the extent that they plotted to model England on them as much as possible.

127 *The Charter*, February 3, 1839, p. 17.

128 *The Charter*, June 9, 1839, p. 315. (The page is erroneously foliated p. 215.)

129 *Northern Star*, October 17, 1840, p. 4.

130 *The Charter*, February 3, 1839, p. 17.

131 Some examples of truly old-fashioned exhortations for peace in the Chartist press are: the *National Association Gazette*, February 26, 1842, p. 72; March 19, 1842, p. 92; April 23, 1842, p. 132; *English Chartist Circular*, vol. 1, pp. 14, 33, 74, 166; vol. 2, p. 32; *McDouall's Chartist and Republican Journal*, September 18, 1841, p. 196. An editorial in the *Northern Star* stated that rulers made wars 'to revenge a joke, to please the priests, to gain a bauble, or to maintain spiritual or worldly pride, or the imaginary balance of power, or the "Right Divine" of kings to govern wrong'. (December 10, 1840.)

132 *Northern Star*, November 10, 1838, p. 4; March 30, 1839, p. 3; December 10, 1840.

133 *National Association Gazette*, January 29, 1842, p. 33.

134 *Northern Star*, November 10, 1838, p. 4. Of course, condemnation of foreign wars as the aristocrat's way of promoting despotism at home was a common liberal denunciation at this time. Richard Cobden was noted for such accusations.

135 *The Charter*, June 2, 1839, p. 307; June 9, 1839, p. 315 (erroneously foliated p. 215); The *London Mercury* declared that the Tsar had the 'good wishes' of the 'reigning family' and the 'anti-national party in England' behind his 'gigantic projects, which in their completion, are to regild the faded crowns of Europe, and cause the nations to love and worship them . . . long years more' (October 30, 1836, p. 1). See also the Russophobic *Northern Liberator* of Newcastle upon Tyne, especially November 10, 1838, p. 3.

136 *Midland Counties Illuminator*, February 23, 1841, p. 8.

137 *Northern Star*, November 3, 1840, p. 3.

138 The *National Association Gazette*, April 16, 1842, p. 126. This resolution was to be altered if it were declared illegal. Cole, *Chartist Portraits*, p. 171.

139 *McDouall's Chartist and Republican Journal*, June 19, 1841, p. 96.

140 *Northern Star*, December 10, 1840; January 30, 1841. The letters were signed Junius Rusticus.

141 Norman McCord, *The Anti-Corn Law League, 1838–1846* (London, 1958); Lucy Brown, 'The Chartists and the Anti-Corn Law League', Asa Briggs, ed. *Chartist Studies*, pp. 342–72.

142 Lucy Brown, *op. cit.*, p. 351.

143 Norman McCord, *The Anti-Corn Law League*, pp. 38, 45, 48, 51–3, 55, 96, 97.

144 As George Julian Harney declared at an Anti-Corn Law meeting in 1842, 'What had they to hope for unless they stuck to the Charter, and established the sovereignty of the people on the ruins of the aristocracy? (Cheers.) . . . If the people lent their powers to the Repealers, they would find if they got repeal of the Corn Law they might whistle for the Charter. . . . The people . . . could afford to wait— not because they did not want cheap bread and meat, but because they wanted right above all. Let them stand by the Charter entire' (*Northern Star*, February 26, 1842, p. 6).

145 *The Charter*, September 22, 1839, p. 552; *McDouall's Chartist and Republican Journal*, May 29, 1841, p. 65; the *English Chartist Circular*, vol. I, p. 74; the *Northern Star*, July 2, 1842.

146 *The Charter*, March 6, 1836, p. 60; *The Operative*, February 17, 1839, p. 8: the *English Chartist Circular*, vol. II, p. 65.

147 *Northern Star*, June 25, 1842, p. 1.

148 *McDouall's Chartist and Republican Journal* declared that capitalists were erecting 'mills and manufactures in Belgium and parts of France' in order to gain advantages from hiring 'the low taxed operatives of the continent' (June 5, 1841, p. 73). See also the *Northern Star*, May 25, 1839, p. 7; the *English Chartist Circular*, vol. I, p. 33.

149 *Northern Star*, April 30, 1842, p. 4. There was a public meeting of journeymen and master boot and shoe makers to consider Peel's amended tariffs and demand protection from cheaper made French, Dutch and German goods: *Northern Star*, April 2, 1842, p. 7. The point is also made in Lucy Brown, *op. cit.*, p. 352.

150 *Northern Star*, September 2, 1843, p. 4; September 9, 1843.

151 *Northern Star*, September 2, 1843, p. 4.

152 *The Operative*, February 17, 1839, p. 8.

153 I. F. Mollett, a former secretary to the North London Charter Association wrote a letter that appeared in the *English Chartist Circular*, vol. I, p. 65, stating that the workers of Europe were much more favourably situated than reported.

154 *The Operative*, February 17, 1839, p. 8.

155 *Northern Star*, May 5, 1838, p. 3.

156 *National Association Gazette*, January 15, 1842, p. 23. These views were humbug to some other Chartists, including, at times, Feargus O'Connor, who argued that England's prosperity in the past was simply due to Britain being 'first among nations to possess . . . powers of artificial production' at the time that the country became the 'queen of smugglers'. This 'command of the markets of the world' was bound to end, repeal or no repeal (*Northern Star*, June 25, 1842, p. 1).

157 *National Association Gazette*, March 19, 1842, p. 85.

158 *National Association Gazette*, February 26, 1842, p. 72.

159 Lucy Brown, 'The Chartists and the Anti-Corn Law League', Asa Briggs, ed., *Chartist Studies*, p. 360.

160 O'Brien charged O'Connor with ambivalence on the subject when the latter attacked the Leaguers in 1847. See *The National Reformer and Manx Weekly Review of Home and Foreign Affairs*, April 17, 1847, p. 3.

161 O'Brien wrote that cheap bread was a specious lure, because capitalists would reduce wages so that 'all the world' would be benefited 'at the expense of England'. To the free traders' arguments that their panacea would result in less unemployment through a greater volume of exports, O'Brien asked: What would prevent foreign nations from setting up tariffs against British goods? See Alfred

Plummer, 'The place of Bronterre O'Brien in the working class movement', *Economic History Review*, II, no. 1 (January 1929), pp. 72–3. See also Lucy Brown, *op. cit.*, p. 349. *Northern Star*, February 16, 1839, p. 5 and the *English Chartist Circular*, vol. I, p. 24.

162 *Southern Star*, March 1, 1840, p. 3.

163 Lucy Brown, *op. cit.*, p. 352.

164 According to G. Kitson Clark, 'Hunger and politics in 1842', *Journal of Modern History*, vol. 25 (December 1953), p. 368, a 'full-blooded rhetorical tradition' prevailed: 'It coloured the language of many popular speeches and many rousing sermons. In such a style, scathing denunciations, manly defiance and solemn warnings about dread alternatives came easily and naturally, probably without a very close appreciation of the realities which underlie words threatening revolution and violence.'

165 For a typical example, see *The Charter*, November 17, 1839, p. 677.

166 For a common example, see the *English Chartist Circular*, vol. I, p. 39.

167 Mather, *Public Order in the Age of the Chartists*, p. 19; Hovell, *The Chartist Movement*, p. 128.

168 Reg Groves, *But We Shall Rise Again: A Narrative History of Chartism* (London, 1939), p. 108.

169 According to Julius West, *A History of the Chartist Movement*, p. 131, Macerone's book was first published in 1832 and a revised edition appeared in 1834. For a brief discussion of the diffusion of Macerone's and Somerville's ideas, see Alfred Plummer, *Bronterre*, pp. 108–9.

170 Mather, *Public Order in the Age of the Chartists*, pp. 180–1.

171 G. D. H. Cole, *Chartist Portraits* (London, 1941), maintains in his chapter on John Frost that earlier Welsh revolts, including the 1831 episode, were worse.

172 The following quotation from Eric Hobsbawm, *The Age of Revolution* (London, Cleveland, and New York, 1962), p. 130, is interesting: 'No rising or war of liberation anywhere in Europe between 1831 and 1871 was to be complete without its contingent of Polish military experts or fighters; not even (it has been held) the only armed rising in Britain during the Chartist period, in 1839.'

173 Quoted from David Williams, *John Frost: A Study in Chartism* (Cardiff, 1939), p. 289, also, pp. 247–50; G. D. H. Cole, *Chartist Portraits*, 'John Frost'; Peter Brock, 'Polish Democrats and English Radicals, 1832–1862', *Journal of Modern History*, vol. 25, 1953, pp. 146–8.

174 A Chartist cobbler named Cardo went from the scene at Newport to address large meetings in Manchester and Bolton and pass on fantasy. See Williams, *John Frost*, pp. 247–50; Brock, *op. cit.*

175 *Ibid.*

176 According to David Williams, *John Frost*, pp. 248–50, the only independent evidence of any connection between Beniowski and the Newport Rising was an anonymous letter sent from Bristol to the mayor of Newport after the rising. It stated that Beniowski had been sent to south Wales to prepare a march on Monmouth and had brought 138 pounds of ball cartridge with him. This is a rather dubious piece of evidence. Brock contends that Beniowski's movements in the months before Newport were 'obscure', but 'it seems certain that he was not present during the actual rising' (*op. cit.*, p. 147).

177 *Ibid.*, p. 146.

178 *London Democrat*, April 13, 1839, p. 2. See also April 27, 1839, p. 21. The *London Democrat*'s articles were quite technical and poorly written. Since there were so many other 'scientific' treatises in the *Democrat* and other working-class papers at this time, their inclusion does not seem extraordinary, especially since no attempt was made to apply the articles to any specific British situations.

179 He joined the Chartist left's East London Democratic Association, and he was elected to the stillborn Chartist Convention in 1840 (Schoyen, *The Chartist Challenge*, p. 37; Iorwerth Prothero, 'Chartism in London', *Past and Present*, 44 (August 1969), p. 79). When Beniowski was seen taking notes at a secret session of the Convention, Robert Lowery's objections forced him to burn his notes. Such an event indicates the suspicion he aroused. Brian Harrison and Patricia Hollis, 'Chartism, Liberalism and the life of Robert Lowery', *English Historical Review*, vol. 82 (1967), p. 509. He fell from the graces of the Literary Association after the

Newport rising and was thereafter refused a government allowance of £40 a year, both for taking part in the Chartist movement and for writing articles in the *London Democrat*. Henry Vincent wrote a letter in the *Operative* of December 16, 1838, p. 99, complaining of how Beniowski was hushed at a Crown and Anchor meeting held by Lord Dudley Stuart's group. See the *London Democrat* of June 8, 1839, for some details.

180 *Northern Star*, August 16, 1845, p. 8. Soon after the supper, an anonymous letter from another exile appeared in the columns of the *Northern Star*. It tattled on Beniowski by declaring that he had recently written in favour of the rightist Literary Association of the Friends of Poland, and had of late become a member of that group. The editor checked the democratic credentials of the writer, found them commendable, and asked Beniowski to respond to the charges. He stubbornly insisted that he would not answer an anonymous letter, which produced, in turn, an angry rejoinder from the *Star's* editor. In it, Harney accused him of attempting 'to get out of a decided fix' in a 'not very creditable manner'. After that episode, Beniowski's doings were never reported again in the *Northern Star*. The controversy is all on p. 6 of the issue of September 6, 1845.

181 Brock, 'Polish Democrats and English Radicals, 1832–1862', *Journal of Modern History*, vol. 25 (1953), p. 146. He wrote in the *London Democrat* of April 13, 1839, p. 2, that Jews were 'highly intelligent, industrious, peaceful human beings'.

182 Thomas Frost, *The Secret Societies of the European Revolution, 1776–1876*, p. 92.

183 Peter Brock, 'The Polish revolutionary commune in London', *Slavonic and East European Review*, vol. xxxv, no. 84 (December 1956), pp. 120 and 126. He relates how a Russian exile compared Beniowski to Oborski and found the former more intelligent by far. Another source, Thomas Frost, *The Secret Societies of the European Revolution*, p. 92, described him as 'audacious . . . fluent . . . aristocratic looking'.

184 Williams, *John Frost*, p. 248.

185 This opinion seems unanimous, except for Gertrude Robinson, *David Urquhart: Some Chapters in the Life of a Victorian Knight-Errant of Justice and Liberty* (Oxford, 1920). It does not seem balanced.

186 The *Spectator* declared that the general public looked upon him simply as someone who belonged 'to the testy class of discharged servants' (February 26, 1838). Webster, *The Foreign Policy of Palmerston*, p. 525, says that he got the post through the patronage of the king and a lapse of judgement on Palmerston's part. See J. H. Gleason, *The Genesis of Russophobia in Britain*, pp. 164–205.

187 His educational background was French, Swiss, and Italian. See J. H. Harley, 'David Urquhart', *Contemporary Review*, vol. 118 (September 1920), pp. 400–4.

188 *Spectator*, February 26, 1838. The article also declared: 'If Lord Palmerston still has whereon to rest his hat, it is not by any favour of Mr Urquhart. . . . The existence of one gentleman continually talking and writing at another gentleman's head is a striking historical fact—an oddity of contemporary history; but . . . Lord Palmerston wears his head . . . with as jaunty an air as if nobody at all were protesting his right to do it.'

189 J. H. Harley, *op. cit.*

190 Gleason, *The Genesis of Russophobia in Britain*, p. 260.

191 Brian Harrison and Patricia Hollis, 'Chartism, liberalism and the Life of Robert Lowery', *English Historical Review*, vol. 82 (1967), p. 517.

192 *Ibid.*, p. 516. Thomas Frost, no relative of John Frost, but a minor Chartist figure, interviewed Urquhart about the Newport conspiracy in later years. He could not give credence to Urquhart's interpretations in his 'History of the Chartist Movement', chapter four, in the *Bradford Observer Budget*, Newspaper Cuttings, Manchester Central Reference Library. The series began on June 5, 1886. He was less critical in his *Forty Years' Recollections* (London, 1880), pp. 103–17.

193 Harley, *op. cit.* Urquhart idealised the virtues of old, nomadic Turkey. He admitted that the central government of Turkey might be cruel and corrupt, but the local districts, or municipia, he felt, preserved the real vitality of the country.

194 Gleason, *The Genesis of Russophobia in Great Britain*, pp. 262–4. It should be pointed out that Urquhart was busy securing coverage in many non-working-class publications simultaneously. Also, Russophobia had not been absent from the

Northern Liberator before this period, but the intensity soared once it became converted.

195 Harley, *op. cit.*, p. 404.

196 From 1842 to 1848 he was hardly ever mentioned in the *Northern Star* in connection with working-class activities in foreign affairs. An exception is the account of his past activities in the June 4, 1846 issue. For Urquhart's activities between 1848 and the Crimean War, see John Salt, 'Local manifestations of the Urquhartite movement', *International Review of Social History*, XIII, 3 (1969), pp. 350-65.

197 G. J. Holyoake, *Sixty Years of an Agitator's Life*, vol. 2 (London, 1892), p. 77. The expression 'cutting off Palmerston's head' was a commonplace to describe Urquhart's schemes.

198 Harley, *op. cit.*, p. 404; Gammage, *History of the Chartist Movement*, p. 189. In addition, Urquhart sought the Tory seat from Marylebone, and Chartists of that area were also prominent in Urquhart's activities.

199 Kingsley Martin, *The Triumph of Lord Palmerston* (London, 1924), p. 54.

200 Williams, *John Frost* (Cardiff, 1939), p. 248. According to Williams, Urquhart published what he called incriminating documents in the *Free Press* in 1855 and the *Diplomatic Review* in 1872.

201 An article in the *Northern Star* in July 4, 1846, p. 7, recalled that 'two or three fourth-rate Chartist agitators' had been involved with Urquhart and Charles Attwood of Newcastle, the brother of Thomas Attwood. When Charles Attwood went to France he took two working-class committee men with him. One, a cobbler named Cardo, was the spreader of Beniowski-spy tales. The other, according to the *Star*, was 'a blind fiddler of Birmingham who said he never heard music he liked half so well as the jingle of Charlie's tin'. A possible exception was Robert Lowery, later noted for his connection with mid-century Liberalism. He lectured for Urquhart's group and accompanied Charles Attwood to France. See Brian Harrison and Patricia Hollis, 'Chartism, liberalism and the Life of Robert Lowery', *English Historical Review*, vol. 82 (1967), pp. 516-17.

202 *Northern Star*, August 15, 1840, p. 4. In looking back on the Urquhart agitation of 1839 and 1840, an editorial in the *Northern Star* of July 4, 1846, p. 7, had this to say: 'The people', when confronted with Urquhart's proposals, 'wisely said, if you are in earnest, help us to get political power, and we'll soon settle accounts with Russian despotism.'

203 *Northern Star*, August 15, 1840, p. 4.

204 *Northern Star*, August 8, 1840, p. 1; August 15, 1840, p. 4; July 4, 1846, p. 7.

205 *Northern Star*, August 22, 1840, p. 1.

206 *Northern Star*, December 13, 1841, p. 7.

207 *Northern Star*, August 15, 1840, p. 4.

208 *Northern Star*, October 23, 1840, p. 5.

209 *Ibid.* At one meeting in Newcastle, Urquhart was denounced as 'a sort of diplomatic magician, a kind of political Dr Faustus' (*Northern Star*, June 13, 1840, p. 8). See also, a defence of Urquhart by Charles Attwood in the June 27, 1840, issue. Further denunciation is found in the *Northern Star* of November 7, 1840, p. 3.

210 *Northern Star*, July 4, 1846, p. 7.

211 *Ibid.* These statements were made in introducing a series of articles about Russia. Subsequent remarks by the editor made it plain that he felt compelled to disassociate himself and the articles from Urquhart's teachings before presenting them.

212 See, for example, the *Destructive and Poor Man's Conservative*, November 30, 1833, p. 846.

213 *Ibid.* This seems to be the clearest call for the assassination of a specific victim in working-class newspapers. On the other hand, O'Brien was against it because he saw the Tsar as the replaceable result of the system in Russia, the 'tool-idol' of the church, nobility, and military, just as Louis Philippe was the tool of his 'blood-hound usurers. . .'. *McDouall's Chartist and Republican Journal*, May 8, 1841, p. 47.

214 The most complete account is in the *Northern Star* of June 15, 1844, p. 6, although portions of the proceedings appear in other sources: Lovett, *Life and Struggles* (1920 ed.), vol. II, pp. 303-6; Julius West, *A History of the Chartist Movement*, p. 229.

4 The Chartists and Europe, 1844–8

The Polish exiles were highly catalytic for Chartist internationalism because they were so romantic, colourful, and loquacious. In the forties, the Poles represented the forces of light and their Tsarist enemies the forces of darkness. Yet the Russians had to arrive in Warsaw and the Poles in London before the Polish cause took on the characteristics that kept it perennially alive in working-class circles. It was as a nostalgic lost cause—a cause that had displayed the heights of heroism and martyrdom and suffered from the depths of barbarism—that Polonophilism came into its own. Ever since the autumn of 1831, working-class public meetings in honour of the Polish cause, with appropriate toasts and resolutions and translated speeches of Polish guests had taken place regularly. Furthermore, working-class newspapers opened their columns to the frequent addresses of one or another group of Polish exiles, and commented upon the Poles' pronouncements editorially.

Polish exiles' politics were notoriously complex—kaleidoscopic would be a better word—and British workers were often deeply confused by Polish factional strife. For example, a reporter from the *Northern Star* had hoped to take some interesting notes on a 'Meeting in Favour of the Poles' in Theobald's Lane, June 6, 1839, but a terrible row erupted. Daniel O'Connell, M.P., was expected to be chairman but failed to arrive. After an hour, or so, the reporter related, someone proposed that Major Beniowski take the chair, but this 'was the signal for an explosion of frantic fury on the part of a portion of the crowd. . .'. Almost immediately, 'blows were dealt most energetically and indiscriminately, and a hundred voices, hoarse with rage, all shouting at once, rendered the scene as exciting as it was unaccountable'. The platform was stormed and taken over a dozen times. Some of its assailants were thrown headlong into the crowd, or, if they gained the platform, they were soon pulled down by the legs, but usually not before they had kicked someone. The reporter observed, here and there, 'innumerable single combats mingled with trios, quartets and every other description of pugilistic encounter . . . and many a bloody visage, battered hat and blackened eye betokened the sincerity of the combatants'. Eventually, 'all parties having bumped and bellowed themselves into exhaustion', they began to ask what it was all about. The reporter was unable to find out, but noted that it seemed to stem from the fact that some Poles did not like Major Beniowski.[1]

Such confusion was inevitable. It took time for the Polish exiles of the Great Emigration to sort themselves out and it took time for Chartists to recognise the most compatible groups. As Polonophilism matured, it became increasingly class conscious, leading Chartists and some Polish groups to find their mutual support heightened by intense dislike of other groups of Polish exiles. It took very few Poles to create a faction in exile and there were thousands of them in Western Europe after 1830.[2] The exiles' left and right wings were far apart, and within these wings factions formed with extra-ordinary speed and bitterness. Prince Adam Czartoryski, former head of the insurrectionary government, was at the centre of the right wing and the diplomatic activity on behalf of the Polish cause in Western Europe.[3] His followers in England came under the wing of the 'Literary Association of the Friends of Poland', a group founded in 1832 with the help of Whig aristocrats, among whom Lord Dudley Stuart was the leading light.[4] The Czartoryski Poles had little or nothing to do with the British working class, except to serve as targets for joint attacks by British workers and left-wing Poles. After a while the very name Czartoryski became pejorative. The more complex left wing formed in exile, after the differences which had appeared during the insurrection matured.[5] What marked this wing, apart from its more radical politics and social views, was opposition to reliance upon orthodox diplomatic activity in order to create an independent Poland. Left-wing Poles appealed directly to the peoples of Europe as their natural allies, and hoped for a general revolution or a dramatic change in Western govern-ments to bring on a war with Russia. These Poles, comprising more than half of the emigration, were the ones who engaged in all sorts of revolutionary activity in western Europe, hoping thereby to instigate the general explosion that would liberate Poland as well as other European peoples. They worked with the Freemasons, the Car-bonari, Mazzinian conspirators, and in the first groups to preach proletarian internationalism.[6] The Poles of this wing in Britain were the ones who came to know radicals and Chartists better than Whigs.

The Polish Democratic Society had been founded in 1832 and organised in sections, with one in London. This section was not among the most important; they were in Paris.[7] At any rate, one Chartist leader, George Julian Harney, became an honorary member of the Polish Democrats, and several Poles from this London section joined Chartist groups.[8] Among them, the exile most intimately associated with the Chartist internationalists was neither a conspicuous leader nor a brilliant intellectual, according to what little evidence there is about him. Colonel Ludwik Oborski was apparently quite colourless, except for his sabre scars and re-collections of the Napoleonic wars.[9] By the forties he had become converted to socialism and Slavophilism. He was secretary for the Polish sections of the Fraternal Democrats, and his signature usually appeared on the resolutions and addresses of that body. He spoke but rarely, and whenever he did make a speech reporters did not bother to take down much, if anything, of what he said.[10] Never-theless, Oborski was ubiquitous in Polish-Chartist activities in London.

Class consciousness made for mutually stimulating relationships between certain groups of Poles and certain groups of British workers. Each group discovered that their counterparts rejected both the English and the Polish ruling classes. Each group discovered that the other had a social-democratic programme for the regeneration of society. Both groups felt they represented the downtrodden. The self-styled English slave class and the Polish serf class were declared to have much in common, even though the former group lived in an industrial world and the latter in an agrarian environment. As the Democrats of Sheffield declared to the Poles in 1841, they were not slaves to a blood-stained autocrat, but 'to a host of plundering aristocrats, stock-jobbers, capitalists, state priests, pensioners and court parasites, who keep the toiling classes in political bondage, that they may deprive them of the produce of their industry and plunder them of the fruits of their toil'.[11] On the basis of such attitudes, working-class internationalism and Polish democracy evolved together.[12]

Essential class-conscious sympathies were aroused by the late thirties. At one radical meeting Henry Vincent boldly announced himself as a member of the working classes and declared that the Polish people ought to be sovereign in Poland. The aristocrats who led the insurrection in 1830 were 'as much opposed to the natural rights of man as the Russian aristocracy', and if a future revolution should succeed, arms had to be given to fifteen million Polish peasants first. Some of the Poles present responded with cheers and others shouted protests.[13] The East London Democratic Association, a group of left-wing Chartists associated with George Julian Harney addressed the Polish Democratic Society in 1837 in response to a manifesto by that organisation:

Your noble manifesto so well proclaims our own principles to the world, that were we to attempt to answer each section of that famous address, we should . . . echo yours . . . in many instances be compelled to use the same words in expressing our ideas.

. . . We agree with you that without equality, there is no liberty; for while a class or classes live on the labour of others, such men must of necessity be tyrants, and all who labour must be slaves. . . . We abjure the cant of treacherous politicians who talk to us of 'equality before the law' believing that laws cannot be just and equal while rich and poor exist. No, the equality we contend for, is the equality of rights, duties and condition.[14]

One of the first steps taken towards Anglo-Polish class consciousness was the rejection of the Literary Association of the Friends of Poland and their Polish beneficiaries by some Poles and English workers.[15] That step brought them to realise that they mutually condemned aristocratic principles in general, and, upon further examination, the Polish and English aristocrats in particular. As the *Northern Star* declared, 'the English democrats are not very likely to co-operate with the men who are patronised by the aristocratic oppressors of the English people; with men who, though they were anti-Russian, were anti-democratic; who, though they hated tyranny, hated still worse social freedom'.[16]

By the forties the idea was commonly held that only British workers truly cared for the Polish cause, and democratic Poles could not depend upon the British government nor upon the upper or middle classes.[17] Some Poles became convinced of this, advertised themselves as the only true representatives of the Great Emigration or as the only true representatives of the majority of the people left in Poland.[18] Some Chartists came to hail them as such,[19] but they could not go too far in rejecting aristocrats because majors, colonels, and gentry were in all the organisations mutually joined. Harney had to point this out in the *Northern Star* in 1846:

Once for all, let us say that we do not declaim against any section of the Poles belonging to the aristocracy because of birth and station; . . . we testify most heartily to the virtues of an immense portion of the Polish 'nobility'. Some of the most daring heroes and statesmanlike leaders have belonged to this body of the Polish people. Not a few of the Democratic

E

Society, and the most trusted of the democratic leaders belong by birth to the 'nobility'! veritable *nobles* in heart and mind. . . .[20]

A similar expression was included in a resolution carried at a working-class public meeting in favour of the Poles in 1846:

We are no admirers of aristocracies but many of the nobility have gloriously striven to redeem the errors of their class. Some of the chief of Poland's sons, great not only as heroes and martyrs, but also as champions of equal justice, struggling and suffering for the freedom of all classes, have belonged to the Polish nobility. . . . The agents of the usurping despotisms have industriously propagated the idea that the Polish nobles are still opposed to the emancipation of the serfs, but this is not true.[21]

The fundamental prerequisite demanded of a member of the Polish gentry for acceptance by the British working-class was that he believed in programmes of economic justice, which meant, for Poland, agrarian reform, and for England the end of the tyranny of capitalists over workers. The point stressed was that mere political rights were illusory if unaccompanied by economic justice. A portion of a resolution passed at an important working-class meeting held on behalf of the Polish cause in 1846 indicates this feeling:

The land in every nation is clearly the propety of the entire people, and whatever unjust appropriations have existed under worn-out systems of society, mankind will expect that a nation recommencing existence will set an example of equal justice in the appropriation of the soil.[22]

The new, socially and economically reformed Poland of their dreams was proclaimed to be the only Poland worth fighting for, either by British workers or Polish democrats. What sense was there in restoring the tyranny of Polish aristocrats in place of the tyranny of Russian, Austrian, and Prussian aristocrats? As Harney wrote, 'Tyranny is tyranny all the world over, and if the mass of the Polish people are to be trampled on, it matters little whether their tyrants are Poles or Russians.'[23]

Such views led to a critical revaluation of the very event which forced the Poles into exile, the celebrated and fabled revolution of 1830. Disenchanted Chartists like Harney and Jones, and Poles like Lelewel and Oborski came to see the insurrection of 1830 as a 'half revolution' whose failure was due to the deliberate attempt of the noble leaders to overlook the claims for political, economic and social justice. Harney once told a cheering crowd that the 1830 insurrection had 'failed because it was not committed to the Polish masses'.[24] At another time he declared that the Poles fell because of 'the slavery of the many and the corruption of the few'. In that 'glorious but unfortunate insurrection' the aristocracy were 'quite willing that the people should pour out their blood in combating the Russian invader' but they had 'no notion of establishing a state . . . in which the entire Polish people should be . . . sovereign. . .'. Had the object of the insurrection been liberty and equality, 'no power on earth could have prevented the triumph of the Poles'.[25]

Despite increasing class consciousness, many of the old forms, arguments and slogans to celebrate the Polish cause were not dropped in the forties. For instance, it was regularly repeated by many Poles and Chartists that Poland had saved the West in 1830 by checking the inroads of Asiatic despotism.[26] Ernest Jones added a bad metaphor when he shouted at a public meeting: 'Heroes of Poland! . . . Glory to you! Thanks! Thanks! for having lavished your precious blood on the ramparts of western civilisation, cementing its old stones. . . .'[27] The Polish cause remained transcendental— it continued to stand for the struggle of all men everywhere for liberty. The exiles themselves retained their status as a specially chosen people whose very scattering was supposed to hasten universal emancipation from tyranny.[28] *Lud Polski* proclaimed its members 'a dispersed people among all the people of the world, without home, without bread . . . we become like a tribe of Jews'.[29]

The exiles were aided by the romantic nature of the era, which relished adventures lying outside the experience of ordinary men, providing that they taxed the emotions and imagination.[30] The Poles had the image of chivalrous heroes who had struggled against the hordes of terrible, semi-oriental barbarism until overwhelmed. Since the contrast between the good Poles and the bad Russians was so great (certainly much greater than along the Vistula) and since the Polish uprising had created so much gore, there was much in it that orators and journalists could use for effect. The Polish cause provided innumerable opportunities for indulgence in the sentimental, the melodramatic and the sensational; thereby guaranteeing durable popularity at working-class meetings and in working-class newspapers. The very word 'gore', for example, had a way of getting into speeches or editorials about the Poles. Two examples worth citing are in the address of the Democrats of Sheffield to the Polish exiles, sent in 1841. It spoke of Polish heroes who 'sleep in their gory graves' and noted how the Polish struggle had brought on 'torrents of gore'.[31]

Although the Chartist George Julian Harney and his friends were the masters at expressing Polish-inspired sensationalism, even

William Lovett indulged in it. In a speech given before a large audience protesting against the Tsar's visit in 1844, Lovett told of how 'six hundred Polish females were hurried into the camp of Noznesenski [*sic*] and handed over to the Russian soldiers, who gratified their brutal passions on these innocent, virtuous, and helpless creatures'. A reporter from the *Northern Star* who was present noted that these words 'had an electric effect upon the audience who were roused to the highest pitch of phrensy by it'.[32] Remarks like these were so typical whenever the Polish cause was brought up at working-class meetings that the audiences can be suspected of looking forward to their 'electric effects'.

Harney's tales of Polish martyrdom were, in their way, classics. He recounted several favourite incidents time after time to liven up his harangues. One of his best, or worst, concerned the fate of forty nuns who were released among Russian captors:

When the Russian soldiers were drunk . . . all these helpless nuns were turned out amongst them . . . to treat as they saw fit. Then commenced a scene worthy of pandemonium—the shrieks and prayers of the victims mingling with the oaths, blasphemies, and ribaldry of the crowd, to whose brutal lust they were abandoned.[33]

Harney loved to dwell upon the details of atrocities, and his audiences probably relished them too. At one meeting he asked his hearers to recall 'the patriots who were quartered alive, their legs and arms broken with flails, their heads skinned, their eyes torn out and their living flesh chopped into mincemeat for hogs. (sensation.)'[34] Then there was the tale of the lady who, 'pregnant with twins, was killed with a dung-fork, and the twins torn out of the corpse; the assassins committing this hellish abomination that they might get the Austrian price for more than one head! (expressions of horror.)'[35] One patriot named Kierwinski gained notoriety through Harney when he was identified as the Pole whose 'minced . . . palpitating limbs' were given as 'food for the pigs'.[36] There were many other tales of this sort.[37] The Polish experience in 1830 and 1831 even contributed a popular verb to working-class political jargon: to Polandise. It was used most frequently in connection with Ireland, a nation dubbed 'the Poland of the West'. A verse from Ernest Jones' *Labourer* illustrates how the parallel was drawn:

> Why weeps your sorrowing sister Ireland
> Still bleeding unredressed,
> 'Neath *Russell*, England's Nicholas
> The Poland of the West?[38]

Romantic gore and newly discovered class consciousness, loudly exchanged, fuelled the fraternisation of Poles and Chartists in the early forties. Poles were ubiquitous in London working-class activities, hailed by press and platform. They provided a grand source of entertainment and a broadening interest, but more important, the commemoration of their struggles gave reasons for Chartists and other exiles, particularly the Germans, to draw closer together. The Poles of the Great Emigration acted as a magnificent catalyst for Chartist internationalism, particularly in the creation of its most important manifestation, the Fraternal Democrats.

II THE GERMAN EXILES

While it goes too far to say that the Fraternal Democrats were an Anglo-German Bund,[39] it cannot be denied that German exiles and their friends were the most well known and important foreigners to the Chartist members of the Fraternal Democrats. They were even more influential than the Poles, whose role was often merely to provide the *cause célèbre* to bring Chartists and Germans together. At meetings and demonstrations held in behalf of the Polish cause, Chartists often spent their time exchanging ideas and sentiments with German rather than Polish exiles. Moreover, there were no Poles as prominent in the Fraternal Democrats as Karl Schapper was. Louis Oborski, secretary of the Polish section of the Fraternal Democrats, certainly was not. The most important visiting Continental theorist, from the Chartists' point of view, was a German, Wilhelm Weitling. From the point of view of posterity, the most important Continental theorists to visit the Fraternal Democrats were also German—Marx and Engels. These people, Marx, Engels, Schapper and Schapper's associates, including Joseph Moll and Heinrich Bauer, made the deepest impression upon British Fraternal Democrats, an impression different in nature and style from that of the Poles. Besides, Polish socialists were in Portsmouth; the German socialist society was in London.

Who led whom is, of course, a moot point. Some Germans, then and thereafter, complained of British workers' theoretical immaturity; others stressed how Germans learned from advanced class relationships and struggles in England.[40] The homeland of the German workers was experiencing the initial stages of industrialism; before 1848 almost all of Germany's productive workers were still artisans, and many of them continued to be, like so much of their homeland, charmingly medieval.[41]

Most of the German workers known to Harney and Jones were true exiles, that is, they had been expelled from elsewhere. Others were in the metropolis for part of their traditional journeyman's *Wanderjahre*.[42] They tended to excel in certain trades, including furniture making and tailoring.[43] Their politics tended to be *Handwerkerkommunismus*—literally, hand worker's communism—the subject of much criticism from Marx and Engels.[44]

The three most important German exiles in London, Karl Schapper, Heinrich Bauer, and Joseph Moll, came to London in 1839 after participating in an unsuccessful uprising in France.[45] Before that date, Paris had been the centre for German communists, but since many of them had been implicated or killed in the 1839 rising, the centre shifted to London for a time. They arrived in the English metropolis well-seasoned in the techniques of Parisian conspiracy from secret organisations dedicated to revolution. There was little of this for them to learn in London, for British radicals and continental revolutionaries were far apart in method. The former relied upon openness, public meetings, free speech, mass demonstrations, addresses, and petitions. Their ultimate hopes were placed upon an enlightened public opinion. By contrast, Europeans depended upon secret, mystical organisations and the promise of successful violence. British leaders tended to be good men on the platform, or good journalists—hearty, outspoken types, whose most common fault was egotism. Many European leaders were, in sharp contrast, disciplined, ascetic, and, in numerous instances, fanatically devoted to their cause. While Chartism certainly suffered from unsteady leadership, muddled programmes, and verbosity, Chartists were spared from experiencing the paranoid atmosphere of continental secret societies. Chartism's goals were inscribed on banners that rippled at public meetings.[46]

Whether or not continental societies were linked and involved in a European-wide conspiracy is a matter for historical debate and speculation. As it might be expected, sources are difficult to interpret and reliable sources are few.[47] While the objective existence of an international conspiracy is in question, its subjective existence is not, for it was real in the minds of police agents, churchmen and statesmen, including Metternich. It was also real in the faith of conspirators cut off from reality by the veils of mysticism and secrecy. At any rate, the *Société des Saisons* existed both objectively and subjectively, and the Germans had been able to model their *Bund der Gerechten*, or League of the Just, upon it. Undoubtedly some of the League's features came from the *Burschenschaften* and German journeymen's secret societies modelled on French *compagnonnages*.[48] It seems that the British environment did not immediately bring an end to the League's melodramas, for the Germans kept passwords, mystic signs, and secret names for each member. They also retained the organisation's elaborate hierarchy with its odd names.[49]

Even though they kept these trappings temporarily, the League's members readily took to the political opportunities London offered—public meetings and free association. Actually, their organisation was protean, for in some countries they had formed singing or gymnastic societies as a cover for the League of the Just. In London it was unnecessary to sing or tumble in order to deal with politics, and a German Worker's Educational Society was brought into being in 1840.[50] It was known to Chartists by that name or as the 'German Democratic Society'. Schapper, Bauer and Moll were its principal founders, and, for a time, Ernest Jones and Julian Harney were among the several non-Germans who held membership.[51] Inside the covering group the League of the Just existed as a secret, small group, perpetuating the old ritualistic mysteries[52] and in contact with Wilhelm Weitling in Switzerland and the revived Parisian section.[53] The outer group had attractive functions for German workers in London in the forties: one night each week was given over to choral singing, one night to political discussion, and other evenings featured lectures of one kind or another. Members could use a library that had several hundred volumes, a grand piano, maps, and even some medical instruments. Moreover, the Society paid sick benefits, and sold tobacco, food, and drink co-operatively.[54] Its meeting place, the rooms at the rear of the White Hart Tavern, Drury Lane, are worth describing, because they were the same rooms used by the Fraternal Democrats. The main room, according to the *Northern Star's* description, was 'large and spendid', decorated with 'graceful scrolls, figures, and flowers, associated with medallion portraits of Shakespeare, Schiller, Mozart, and Albert [*sic*] Dürer'. In the centre of the wall above the chairman's seat was 'an extensive view of Hampstead Heath. . .'. On one side was a statue of liberty and on the other a statue of justice. Maps decorated other wall surfaces, and, upon occasion, 'wreaths and festoons of laurel and other evergreens' were interwoven. The rooms were particularly cheerful at Christmastime, when a swarm of children descended upon the scene.[55]

In 1847 this apparently harmless German Workers' Educational

Society ceased to house the League of the Just because it was transformed into the Communist League, or *Kommunistenbund*. What is more, the League was the original audience for the Communist Manifesto. For these reasons, much has been written about these German conspirators, for, according to several Marxist historians, they becamse the first true disciples in 1847. Unfortunately, much that has been printed about the Communist League is questionable history, suffering from distortions traceable not only to the emotional commitments of some writers or to the conscious or unconscious constraints of dogma, but also to the paucity of evidence. Nicolaevsky found materials 'meagre in quantity, . . . extremely inadequate as to quality' when he wrote an article entitled 'Toward a History of the Communist League, 1847–1852', and declared that 'the main body of materials . . . has been lost'.[56] Perhaps the best source is still Engels' own account. He claimed that some of the London leaders of the League of the Just had come to see the inadequacy of both French equalitarian communism and Weitling's Christian communism at the time they began to realise the correctness of Marxist 'scientific' communism. Previous to 1847, Marx and Engels had pressed their theoretical outlook upon the London artisans 'by word of mouth, by letters and through newspapers'.[57] The upshot was that Joseph Moll travelled from London to Brussels in 1847 in order to invite them to join the League of the Just and help transform it. Moll also offered Marx and Engels an opportunity to present a manifesto of their principles to German workers at a specially assembled gathering in London. When they complied, the world gained the Communist Manifesto and the League of the Just became the Communist League, shorn of most of its colourful trappings—a small loss in exchange for everlasting fame.[58]

No other organisation of exiles was as close to the Fraternal Democrats as these Germans. There were lower-class Italians in London, many of whom were, as one Chartist reported, either organ grinders, vendors of terracotta statues or shoplifters.[59] Several Mazzinian organisations existed to help the poorer sons of Italy in London, but Mazzini was not as close to the Fraternal Democrats as he was to their Chartist enemies.[60]

A rather obscure French socialist society, *La Société Democratique Française*, existed in London in the forties, but its members in general were not workers. Their interests were almost entirely absorbed in French politics, but nevertheless some of their meetings were thrown open to Chartists and exiles. Reports appeared from time to time in the *Northern Star* in very abbreviated form. In 1847 they joined the Germans' organisation.[61] Many members had already left for France by then, drawn back by a proclamation of amnesty. One historian has remarked that those remaining were 'without much weight',[62] a description which certainly fits the two Frenchmen from its ranks who became 'regulars' in the Fraternal Democrats: Dr Camille Berrier-Fontaine and Jean Michelot.[63] Like the Pole most prominent in the Fraternal Democrats, Oborski, their contributions to meetings were less than profound and rarely reported at any length.

Working-class radicals from other lands—Russia, Scandinavia, the Low Countries, and Turkey—exercised no special influence on the Fraternal Democrats and did not have organisations of their own. Instead, they tended to join the German Workers' Educational Society.

III   A TRIUMVIRATE OF LEADERS AND THEIR NEWSPAPER

London's left-wing exiles, particularly the Germans and the Poles, made the Fraternal Democrats possible, but that organisation's inspiration, tone, set of attitudes, and driving force can be traced to a triumvirate of leaders and their extensive use of the *Northern Star*, the most popular of all the Chartist newspapers. One leader was a German artisan; one was a working-class Englishman and one was a middle-class Englishman of a decidedly proletarian point of view. These three, Karl Schapper, G. J. Harney, and Ernest Jones respectively, made most of the speeches at Fraternal Democrats' meetings, introduced most of the resolutions, prepared the addresses, and, in general, kept the organisation together.

Karl Schapper was a poor vicar's son who had been to the University of Giessen to study forestry. His students' *Burschenschaft* decisively influenced him, and when it joined in an unsuccessful attempt to overthrow the Frankfurt Diet in 1832, Schapper was forced into exile. In 1834 he showed up with Mazzini's forces in Savoy where he became one of the Germans who helped found Young Europe in Switzerland later that year. When Swiss police chased him out on account of his political activities, Schapper moved to Paris, where he became oriented more and more towards utopian communism and Babouvism and away from the national-democratic teachings of Mazzini. Gaol and expulsion from France followed his participation in an unsuccessful Blanquist rising in 1839. He arrived in London in 1840 and remained until the revolutions of 1848 drew him to the continent again.[64]

By the time he became a Fraternal Democrat he was highly class conscious, as these remarks from a speech of 1845 indicate:

One thing the people might be sure of, they would never get their rights either by relying on the middle class, or merely talking about liberty. (Cheers.) The middle classes had always used the people as instruments, and then flung them away. The middle classes had always deceived and persecuted the working classes. (Hear, Hear.) The people must have recourse to force. . . . Let the working men trust nobody but themselves. . . .[65]

He was a decided internationalist. In one speech he declared his wish that 'the age may speedily arrive when there will be for all men but one country—the earth; but one family—mankind. . .'. He had a high regard for international gatherings because 'we shall learn to know each other, and by regarding each other as brethren . . . establish the rights of men in all nations'.[66] Like most continental leftists, Schapper was far from pacifism. In 1848, stimulated by the first news of fresh revolutions, he thundered:

He [Schapper] repudiated the cant of peace! He was for liberty first, and then peace. . . . There must be a Holy War for the destruction of tyrants, and then when they are swept from the earth, then—peace; but, until then—war![67]

Schapper made a strong impression on Engels when they first met in 1843. Engels later described him as a vigorous, energetic, resolute, outgoing man, but with a 'somewhat obtuse' mind that tended to become extraordinarily stubborn.[68] As one modern Soviet historian has put it, rather tactfully, 'Schapper's way to scientific communism was long and difficult. It was the way of a man who acquired theoretical concepts laboriously. . . .'[69] Anyway, Schapper was actually the first proletarian revolutionist Engels knew. Despite his university sabre scar, there was no doubt about Schapper's credentials. He was a huge, muscular worker who had laboured as a brewer's apprentice in Switzerland and as a compositor in Paris and London. His closest associates in the British metropolis were also proletarian revolutionists. Heinrich Bauer was a Franconian shoemaker and Joseph Moll was a watch-maker from Cologne.[70]

The key member of the triumvirate was G. J. Harney, a proletarian from the time of his birth in east London.[71] Bad health prevented a career as a seaman, but not before he visited Lisbon and Brazil as a teenager. He became shopboy to Henry Hetherington, under whom he enjoyed an excellent apprenticeship in radical politics and journalism, coming under the influence of Bronterre

O'Brien. Harney emerged as a leader in the East London Democratic Association, or, as it was later known, the London Democratic Association. This group of Chartists comprised militants who came to link their political fortunes with Feargus O'Connor and were considered as rabble by the artisans of the LWMA. Harney wanted this organisation to play the role of the Jacobin Club at the Chartist Convention of 1839. G. D. H. Cole referred the early Harney as Chartism's *'enfant terrible*—a young enthusiast, addicted to flaunting the red cap of liberty at public meetings . . . a revolutionary by sentiment as well as conviction'.[72] Harney's strength was in his prolific and forceful writing—he could fill whole sections of the *Northern Star* each week with rather lively material whose thinness and dogmatic assertiveness were partly overcome by style. Gammage who did not like him, reports that he was a poor speaker.[73] Harney, a short man, inclined to be overdressed, spoke very frequently, often at great length, and usually with heavy reliance upon strong, emotional phrases and gestures. Estimates of him by Chartists or modern historians vary considerably. Harney's own estimate of his abilities, written in a letter to Engels at the height of the Chartist's career, was decidedly modest.[74]

Ernest Jones was a gentleman, what the Fraternal Democrats called 'working class by adoption'.[75] He wrote poems, now-forgotten novels, supported himself as a barrister, belonged to the Church of England, and led a fairly comfortable life until he made sacrifices for the Chartist cause. Before 1848, Jones was second to Harney in Chartist internationalism; after that date, he was probably first. Jones was admirably well suited to carry on this activity, for it was said that he was eloquent in German and French.[76] He had been raised in Germany, where his father had been stationed as a British cavalry officer. Moreover, Jones continued to maintain a lively interest in European history throughout his life. He was usually at hand to speak at the international meetings of Harney and his friends, or to sit as chairman at functions held jointly by Chartists and exiles. An able speaker and writer, his contributions appeared regularly in the *Northern Star*. There is no indication that he did not mix well with proletarians.[77] G. D. H. Cole found him 'sincere, honest, singleminded and proud', the force which kept Chartism alive for ten years after 1848.[78]

While Harney liked to deal with the problems of class consciousness, Jones' speciality was the problem of nationality. He regarded several states in Europe as artificial creations that had been determined haphazardly by the clashing ambitions of dynasts over the previous centuries. He found so-called 'racial groups'—Scandinavians, Teutons, Slavs, Italians, Franks, and Celts—to be genuine communities. He wanted Europe reconstructed with 'normal' boundaries, so that true 'racial' nations could be formed, or, as he put it, somewhat grotesquely, 'kingdoms' had to be replaced with 'kindoms'. Beyond that was the realisation that all men were related, so nationality was 'one great lever' or one major step towards the time when all men would be brothers.[79] Similar views were, of course, quite common in his century.

Just as the Fraternal Democrats depended upon the energies of Jones, Harney and Schapper, this triumvirate of leaders all relied upon the *Northern Star* for publicity, to the extent that the history of the organisation is inseparable from this newspaper. For most Chartists and all historians, the Fraternal Democrats live through its pages. Harney, the sub-editor from 1843, on, opened the columns of this most remarkable Chartist newspaper to carry tens of thousands of words about the organisation, primarily in the form of full-length accounts of meetings, which included most of the speeches, all of the resolutions, declarations and addresses. Of course, Harney's editorial pen was busy everywhere in these accounts. It was not until 1844, just after the newspaper had moved from Leeds to London, that the *Northern Star* announced its commitment to foreign affairs. Before that date, such concerns had not been any more important in the *Star* than in any other Chartist newspaper. As Harney apologised, 'regard was almost exclusively had to British exertions, and little pains . . . [were] . . . taken to make the English democrat aware of the part that was being played by his brethren on the different stages of the political world'. But now,

. . . the *Northern Star* has endeavoured to let the English working man commune with the 'struggling' portion of his 'order' in all parts of the world; . . . recording their successes to exhilarate the toiling, to animate the apathetic, and to confirm the wavering; and setting forth their defeats as beacons to warn where to pause and where to avoid. . . . We know that the *Star* finds its way into almost all civilised states; . . . and we also know that it is . . . making the different sections of the grand army acquainted with their respective operations and tactics, and enabling all to value the importance of the conflict . . . as one of universal moment.[80]

Even though circulation dropped to less than a sixth of what it had been during the newspaper's best year after this commitment was made,[81] the *Northern Star* remained the closest thing to a national newspaper the Chartists had, for their other journalistic ventures were short-lived and seemed unable to retain popularity.[82] Harney described its role in 1847 with typical immodesty:

We have been the first to denounce oppression . . . and to vindicate the oppressed, no matter what their country or religion. . . . The hypocritical villainies of the 'Fagin' of France, the atrocities of the assassin Metternich, and the rascalities of Palmerston, have alike been exposed by us to the scorn and indignation of mankind. Happily we have not laboured in vain. In France, Germany, in Switzerland and the United States, the *Northern Star* is known and respected, as the organ of British democracy, the advocate of universal liberty and the defender of the rights of all men, without regard to colour, clime or creed.[83]

The *Star's* popularity had been built up by featuring harangues by Feargus, the usual police reports, and reports of scattered meetings and obscure speeches by obscure Chartists.[84] Critics found it a terrible example of yellow journalism, filled with exaggerations, distortions and attempts to exploit the emotions of readers rather than develop their intellects. R. G. Gammage, the chronicler of Chartism, regretted how the *Northern Star* excited the vanity of ordinary speakers by describing their orations as 'eloquent, argumentative' and had them 'dressed up' as if they were 'parliamentary harangues fashioned to the columns of the daily press'. In this manner, 'men of very mediocre abilities appeared to people at a distance to be oracles of political wisdom'.[85] A damaging criticism appeared in an anonymous letter in O'Brien's *National Reformer*.[86] The writer attended a meeting in Glasgow which consisted of what he called lifeless, dull speeches given before almost empty benches. The *Star's* report of the meeting, he pointed out, was delivered with the usual clichés of that newspaper—the speeches were 'brilliant'; they were received with 'thunderous applause'; and the house was 'crowded to suffocation'. Any regular, critical reader of the *Northern Star* knows the point of the letter writer's complaint.

Such criticisms must be taken very seriously since the *Northern Star* is virtually the only major source of information about the Fraternal Democrats. If they held a meeting it almost invariably was reported as being 'crowded to excess' with a 'wildly enthusiastic' audience. Beyond this, it is obvious that the speeches of Harney's friends, or persons with his point of view, received the most space in the *Star's* columns. Other speakers might be reduced to a one-sentence summary or omitted altogether. The effect of this was that the speeches reported in the *Northern Star* from meetings of the

Fraternal Democrats echoed each other. Moreover, reports rarely displayed controversy or debate. Whenever a dissenting voice was raised, a rare and striking phenomenon in the newspaper's reports anyway, the dissenter was swamped by the arguments of Harney and his friends.[87] According to the *Northern Star*, addresses and resolutions were nearly always passed unanimously. All of this gives the Fraternal Democrats a monolithic nature. This only major primary source for the Fraternal Democrats must be handled with care, something which has not always been done by historians who have taken them at face value as they advertised themselves in these pages.

IV THE FRATERNAL DEMOCRATS: ORIGIN, ORGANISATION AND OUTLOOK

The ingredients for a brief history of the Fraternal Democrats have been considered—exiles, particularly the German democrats and left-wing Poles from the Great Emigration; the leaders, Jones, Harney and Schapper; and the organ of the group, the *Northern Star*. All were mixed together in the London environment, an environment that encouraged foreigners and Englishmen to mingle openly and freely if they desired. Many did, sharing banquets and agendas of public meetings, often celebrating or commemorating one or another popular event. In this atmosphere of almost recreational politics, amidst toasts, speeches, conversations and songs, the Fraternal Democrats came into existence.

Curiously, the birth of the organisation was unheralded, even by the *Northern Star*. In fact, no news about the Fraternal Democrats appeared in that newspaper until the group had been in existence for six months.[88] This fact begs for an explanation, considering how Harney was never a man to hide from the light of publicity. A. R. Schoyen, Harney's biographer, has offered the explanation that the Fraternal Democrats feared the jealousy of the Chartist executive, which might come to consider them a new, rival centre of working-class leadership. Schoyen added that foreigners might have been apprehensive as well, fearing that the British government might refuse them further asylum on account of such political activities.[89] Since Schoyen wrote, fresh evidence has come to light with the publication of the Harney papers. A letter from Harney to Engels in March, 1846, confirms his argument. Harney described how the Fraternal Democrats were 'progressing' and declared: 'After a deal of trouble and discouragement I think I shall succeed in this. We were for some time regarded with much prejudice and jealousy by the Chartists, but this is wearing away.' Harney explained that the members of the Chartist executive came to the Fraternal Democrats in fear that they 'would take the popular leadership out of their hands. . . . We said, "You lead, we will follow." Our policy is not to push ourselves, but our principles, and compel others to adopt them.' In this spirit, the Fraternal Democrats and the Chartist executive formed a joint committee to get up a public meeting to celebrate the Cracow uprising.[90] There is further evidence to support Schoyen's explanation. An 'Address to the Democrats of All Nations from the Fraternal Democrats' in 1846, declared:

Once for all we explicitly state, that we repudiate all ideas of forming any 'party'. . . . We desire not to rival, but to aid all men who are honestly combined to work on the emancipation of the people.[91]

In January 1848, Karl Schapper raised the question at one of their meetings 'whether it was in the province' of the Fraternal Democrats to 'address the working men of Britain upon questions of Chartism'. He said 'he feared that the society's motives might be misconstrued . . . people might think that the Fraternal Democrats wished to usurp the functions of the Chartist executive'.[92] He was answered by Philip McGrath, a member of both the Fraternal Democrats and the Executive, who 'begged to assure his friend Schapper that there could be no rivalry between the Fraternal Democrats and the Chartist Executive'.[93]

Although the founding of the Fraternal Democrats was not announced, the celebration at which the organisation emerged was well publicised. It was a public supper held at the City Chartist Hall on September 22, 1845, on the anniversary of the establishment of the first French Republic of 1792. The importance of this particular meeting should not be overestimated in regard to the feelings of internationalism and workers' solidarity, as if they generated then and there, at that confrontation of Chartists, foreign workers and their exiled friends. Actually, the principles of the Fraternal Democrats had been anticipated by many articles and editorials in the *Northern Star*.[94] In addition, Chartists and foreigners had fraternised several times previously, on a scale similar to that of September 22, 1845. For instance, when Wilhelm Weitling came to England in 1844, there was a welcoming meeting at which Owenites, radicals, Chartists, German communists and other foreigners came together.[95] Even more important was a meeting held at the Crown and Anchor

Tavern in July 1844, to celebrate the anniversary of the storming of the Bastille. The *Star*'s reporter observed:

So many working men . . . [of various countries] . . . thus united, as it were in one family meeting, and in whom amity and cordiality were displayed no less in words than in looks, tones, and gestures, formed a truly delightful and exhilarating spectacle.[96]

Then again, two months later, a meeting of 500 people convened at Highbury Barn Tavern to 'witness the fraternisation of nations'.[97] Therefore the meeting which launched the Fraternal Democrats was but one out of many.

Ironically, Thomas Cooper took the chair at the founding meeting. He was destined to become the foremost Chartist enemy of the organisation. Harney was one of the principal speakers, and his remarks consisted largely of a Babouvist reinterpretation of the French revolution. Along the way he did express these internationalist sentiments:

We loathe and scorn those barbarous clap-traps 'natural enemies' and 'national glory'. (Loud cheers.) We denounce all wars, except those into which nations may be forced against domestic oppressors or hostile invaders. (Applause.) More than that, we repudiate the word 'foreigner'—it shall not exist in our Democratic vocabulary. (Great cheering.)[98]

The meeting was actually covered more extensively in Friedrich Engels' *Rheinische Jahrbücher* than in the *Northern Star*. Engels was quite enthusiastic about what he saw there, and felt pleased that workers were progressing rapidly towards international fraternisation.[99] Even so, there was nothing really extraordinary in the speeches—nothing that had not been said before. Weitling was his usual dull self, reading, in wretched English, a speech about utopian communism. Actually, the speeches at the previous year's anniversary meeting had much more to say about internationalism. At any rate, at the next anniversary celebration, September 22, 1846, this announcement was made: 'The present festival announces the termination of the first year's existence of the Fraternal Democrats!'[100]

It might be better to say that the Fraternal Democrats 'emerged' than that they were 'founded' in September 1845, because the society undoubtedly grew out of many social gatherings. The organisation was probably the product of many long conversations, dinners, long speeches, songs, toasts, and, one suspects, much beery, back-slapping camaraderie. There is nothing at all to suggest that the Fraternal Democrats were in any way mysterious, revolutionary, or even clandestine after 1846.

The strongest evidence indicating that the Fraternal Democrats were primarily social and open is that the organisation was initially formless. It had no council, no committee, no officers, no rules, no regulations, and no fixed membership. Anyone could attend.[101] As with so many other organisations, the Fraternal Democrats tightened up somewhat with time. In March 1846, names of members were enrolled 'for the purpose of maintaining the character of the assembly and preventing the intrusion of improper persons'. In addition, new candidates for membership had to be recommended by two members and sanctioned by a majority vote in favour of their admittance. Still, any member could invite a 'friend' to take part in the proceedings. At the same time, six secretaries were appointed 'for the purpose of authenticating all documents issued to the public'. A British, German, French, 'Slavonic', Scandinavian, and Swiss secretary were elected, providing a structure that has been noted by some historians as a model for the International. Other officers were declared unnecessary because the Fraternal Democrats were not 'a society or a party, but merely an assemblage of men belonging to different countries', gathered together for 'the purpose of mutual information'.[102] In 1847, weekly contributions of a halfpenny were introduced and then discontinued in favour of an annual one shilling fee payable upon receipt of membership cards. Some members, including Karl Schapper, argued for a contribution of sixpence. If some members were in financial difficulty they could pay for their cards by instalments at the rate of one penny weekly. By December, 1847, the Fraternal Democrats had a set of rules that included these provisions: 'Democrats of all nations, wherever residing, may become members. . .'. Those who proposed prospective members were held responsible for 'the democratic principles and moral character' of their nominees. Meetings were to be held on the first Monday of each month, and the 'invited friends' were to be introduced to the group. Incidentally, the names of the 'friends' had to be known to the chairman prior to the meeting—an interesting provision—but any member of the National Charter Association or of the German, French, or Polish democratic societies was automatically a 'friend' and could enter freely. The order of business was in the standard parliamentary form. Financial statements were to be submitted triennially and an annual balance sheet was planned. In order to handle the financial matters and

F

reports, a committee of the general secretaries plus one additional member from each country was created.[103] This was as far as the Fraternal Democrats were ever institutionalised, and even by 1848, when the group flew apart, it was still rather open.

The official reasons given for the founding of the organisation were basically concerned with improving communications among peoples. They were presented in an 'Address of the Fraternal Democrats to the Democrats of All Nations', September 1846:

> In all countries the friends of progress are mainly dependent for their knowledge of passing events upon the public journals, the great majority of which represent the interests of usurping governments and privileged classes. . . . From this cause the democrats of different countries have been comparatively ignorant of each other's progress, and from ignorance or misconception have often acted sectionally, or even in opposition to each other. . . . Impressed with these ideas, and seeing that in this great metropolis was gathered men from all parts of the earth, . . . the founders of this society saw in . . . friendly union . . . the practicality of establishing a nucleus of thought and combination of mind which would impart to all associated more accurate and enlightened views of the state of the masses in all countries, and the course of action most advisable to elevate them above the bondage and misery to which class domination has everywhere consigned them.[104]

The old faith of rational democracy, the faith of Richard Carlile, rings in such statements. In effect, the repetitious message, subject of scores of fraternal speeches, was that men must overcome difficulties in communication and spread knowledge in order to attain the good. The burden assumed by the Fraternal Democrats was the task of enlightenment. To carry out this mission they issued dozens of addresses and declarations that burst into print in the *Northern Star* and in several foreign newspapers—the French *Débat Social* and *Réforme* and the *Deutsche Brüsseler Zeitung*. These pronouncements were also regularly submitted for insertion in several London newspapers, but they were almost invariably turned down.[105] When they attempted to raise money, as in 1847, it was not to help some planned European insurrection, but to pay for missionaries who were to tour the countryside preaching universal brotherhood.[106] Even without missionaries, the Fraternal Democrats gained members and affiliates from over twenty towns in Britain,[107] partly through open advertisements for them.[108] In London, active membership went up in 1847 and 1848, but no figures were ever published. Harney, Jones, their Chartist friends, some of the Germans of the League of the Just, and a number of ubiquitous

Poles, plus a scattering of individuals of various nationalities provided a hard core of members.[109] All told, the Fraternal Democrats were an educational and propagandistic body rather than a band of conspirators aimed at European-wide revolution. Except for a degree of *Gemütlichkeit*, they were in essence quite English.

Some picturesque details probably helped to make the society attractive to London workers. Their motto, 'All Men Are Brethren' —the same motto of the Polish and German democratic societies— was printed in twelve languages on their membership cards.[110] Their Drury Lane meeting place was decorated with the German, Polish, French, and Hungarian flags. There was also a painted, gas-illuminated, full-length transparency of a 'female figure' representing liberty and equality. She trampled on the 'hydra of corruption', and held a red cap aloft. Behind her the rising sun of liberty banished the darkness of war and tyranny. All of this was surrounded by a golden wreath of oak leaves and acorns, complete with a ribbon bearing the society's motto in a dozen languages.[111]

Thanks to the *Northern Star*, most of the speeches, toasts, resolutions, and declarations given life beneath that figure have not been consigned to oblivion. They have survived, edited, but still at great length. They were so repetitious that it can almost be said that they adhered to a liturgy of a simple internationalism. This is the case for all of the six major public declarations that the Fraternal Democrats drew up and published before the revolutions of 1848.[112] Perhaps the best way to present the content, or essence of the content, of this profusion of propaganda is to reproduce a statement of principles prepared by the Fraternal Democrats in December 1847.[113] Much can be read into these principles, and some of them can be traced back to Robbespierre, Babeuf, the French utopian socialists—via O'Brien, perhaps—and something can be seen of the influence of Marx and Engels as well:

We renounce . . . all political hereditary inequalities and distinctions of 'caste'; consequently, we regard kings, aristocrats, and classes monopolising political privileges in virtue of their possession of property, as usurpers and violators of the principle of human brotherhood. Governments elected by, and responsible to, the entire people is our political creed.

We declare that the earth with all its natural productions is the common property of all; we therefore denounce all infractions of this evidently just and natural law as robbery and usurpation. We declare the present state of society, which permits idlers and schemers to monopolise the fruits of the earth and the productions of industry and compels the working classes to labour for inadequate rewards and even condemns them to social slavery, destitution and degradation, is essentially unjust. That labour and rewards should be equal is our social creed.

We condemn the 'national' hatreds which have hitherto divided mankind, as both foolish and wicked; foolish, because no one can decide for himself the country he will be born in, and wicked, as proved by the feuds and bloody wars which have desolated the earth, in consequence of these national vanities. Convinced, too, that national prejudices have been, in all ages, taken advantage of by people's oppressors, to set them tearing the throats of each other, when they should have been working together for their common good, this society repudiates the term 'Foreigner', no matter by or to whom applied. Our moral creed is to receive our fellow men, without regard to 'country', as members of one family, the human race; and citizens of one commonwealth—the world.

V   THE FRATERNAL DEMOCRATS AND THE CRACOW UPRISING

At private and public meetings and in the editorial columns of the *Northern Star* the Fraternal Democrats expressed their concern with a variety of issues in a variety of foreign countries. The affairs of France, Switzerland, North America, Spain, Portugal, Greece, the Near East, Italy, Germany, and even an uprising in the Caucasus mountains received their rather profuse verbal attention.[114] Despite such a diversity of interests, an overwhelming majority of the meetings and speeches were given over to a single topic—Polish affairs. Simultaneously with the emergence of the Fraternal Democrats there occurred a fresh and highly exciting uprising in Poland, and so the organisational and propagandistic efforts of the Fraternal Democrats reached their height in a great outburst of perfervid Polonophilism.

In February 1846, Polish revolutionaries gained a brief success in the Free State of Cracow and neighbouring Austrian Galicia. For a few weeks a radical, democratic 'Provisional Government', headed by John Tyssowski, gained control and issued a famous document, the Cracow Manifesto. What made this insurrection different from that of 1830, and so attractive to the British working class, was the revolutionaries' emphasis on social democracy. According to their celebrated Cracow Manifesto, the peasants of the new Poland were to be free owners of the land they cultivated. Although the leaders were mostly of noble birth, their democratic leanings endeared them to the Polish Democratic Society in England. Nevertheless, a feature complicating the 1846 insurrection was Austrian encouragement and bribery of Polish peasants for a gruesome slaughter of the rebellious Polish gentry in what has been called 'the greatest peasant jacquerie' since the days of the French revolution of 1789.[115]

When news of the uprising arrived in England it did not kindle an intense enthusiasm for the Polish cause among any segment of English society except the working class. No one in Parliament expressed sympathetic feelings towards the Provisional Government, while *The Times* implied on several occasions that the principles of communism had been at work in the city.[116] Even some of the Poles in exile did not hail the event; Czartoryski Poles disavowed the 'wild theories of government' in the Cracow Manifesto.[117] The effect of the situation was that the response to the Cracow insurrection served to underline class-conscious groupings that had developed since the Poles of the Great Emigration had come to Britain. The Fraternal Democrats' celebration therefore marks at once one of the most class-conscious manifestations of their activities.

Chartist internationalists and their friends among the exiles of various nations went into action immediately after they heard that a 'democratic' Polish rebellion had begun. They were ecstatic. Their first impulse was to call mass meetings and raise money. The Fraternal Democrats were able to get two members of the Chartist executive and several South London Chartists to appear in order to work out plans for mass demonstrations. As a result, they elected an international committee to arrange events, produced an address to the people of Great Britain on the insurrection, and sent a formal request to the National Charter Association for another address. It appeared shortly thereafter, and plans went ahead for a series of demonstrations in London of a 'thoroughly democratic character'. Meanwhile, the *Northern Star* collected the money that had been raised for the brave Poles of Cracow.[118]

The first great public meetings took place late in March 1846, one at the Crown and Anchor Tavern and the other simultaneously at the Chartist Hall, Blackfriars Road.[119] Philip McGrath, a workman and a member of the Chartist Executive, took the chair at the crowded Crown and Anchor. Polite apologies were received from a number of prominent radicals who had been invited, including Duncombe, Bowring, Hume, and Mazzini. Two dozen other 'public characters' similarly invited, did not bother to reply—a point not missed by the chairman. He inferred that this demonstrated that the democratic Poles' only true support came from British workers. Several resolutions were passed at this meeting and a petition was drawn up, signed, and sent to the Queen.[120]

One of the results of the Crown and Anchor meeting was the birth of a new working-class international organisation, the Democratic

Committee for Poland's Regeneration. Under its authority, more meetings, resolutions and addresses were produced. It was new, but its active members were the same people who carried on in the Fraternal Democrats, namely Harney, Jones, Schapper, Oborski, and Clark. Moreover, the Democratic Committee for Poland's Regeneration met in the same place in which the Fraternal Democrats customarily gathered, the German Hall in Drury Lane. After the excitement over the Cracow uprising subsided, the Democratic Committee had joint meetings with the Fraternal Democrats. All of this justifies the judgement of Harney's biographer, which is that the new group was, in effect, a subcommittee of the Fraternal Democrats.[121]

Fund-raising was a problem. Early in April an article in the *Northern Star* called upon members and supporters not to be discouraged on account of the unemployment that made the raising of large subscriptions impossible just then. The Committee could at least watch every act of the oppressors, and not let any 'act of cruelty' go unnoticed through alerting public opinion. The article mentioned the desire to send a statement of the current wrongs committed against Poland to every Member of Parliament, but regretted that funds for paper and postage were hard to acquire.[122]

The rules of the committee were uncomplicated: meetings were to take place every month; reports were to be published in the 'democratic journals'; a quarterly report on 'the progress and prospects of Poland's Regeneration' was to be given, along with a report on the finances of the organisation. Whenever necessary, it was to call special meetings—otherwise public meetings would be arranged to commemorate events in recent Polish history. The means that the Committee for Poland's Regeneration sought to employ were entirely propagandistic. They sought, first and foremost, to create 'an enlightened public opinion' about Poland, and, to bring this about, they wanted to circulate reports, addresses, and tracts. Petitions to the legislature were also to be prepared. Besides this, they intended to give 'pecuniary assistance' to 'patriotic' Polish exiles. There was one vague clause, which stated that the Polish cause was to be aided by 'every practicable means'. Outside of this probably innocuous clause, there was nothing in their statement of purpose that could possibly be construed as un-English.[123]

Shortly after they were formed they passed a rule to allow honorary members from all over Britain to join and assist in publishing the Committee's documents and, of course, help raise funds.[124]

Ernest Jones became the permanent chairman at that time, and Feargus O'Connor accepted the post of treasurer, a remarkable appointment, since it was the closest relationship that the great Chartist leader ever had with Chartist internationalism.[125]

All told, the activities of the Democratic Committee for Poland's Regeneration in conjunction with the Fraternal Democrats produced a torrent of spoken and written words. A petition to Queen Victoria was included in this output, a document which called for the use of British force to help restore Poland and derided the policy of non-intervention:

> ... for some years past, the British government has affected to act upon what is called 'the principles of non-intervention . . .', a principle your petitioners repudiate, because they hold that the intervention of the strong to save the weak from oppression is a duty as much binding upon nations as upon individuals.[126]

A significant portion of all that was said and written about the Cracow insurrection by these internationalists concerned that remarkable document, the Cracow Manifesto. The most appealing part was this:

> Let us conquer a state of society, in which every man shall enjoy his share of the fruits of the earth according to his merits [earnings] and his capacity, in which no exclusive privilege of any kind whatever will be allowed to remain . . . in which . . . every man disabled by nature in the use of his bodily or mental functions will find without humiliation, the unfailing assistance of the whole social state. . . .[127]

Subsequently it became a commonplace for some Polish exiles and their British working-class cohorts to pledge their devotion to the principles of the Cracow Manifesto, as a democratic test. Harney spoke of it in what can be called proto-Marxist terms:

> We applaud the Cracow Manifesto because it prepares the way for the destruction of class usurpation . . . the social and political elevation of the people must now be the grand object of revolutionary struggles. . . .[128]

> [It] . . . recognised the social as well as the political rights of man and held forth to the multitude the assurances of a real reward for the sacrifices they are called upon to make for their country's regeneration.

The thorniest issue for the Fraternal Democrats was the Galician massacres, because the respectable press trumpeted about the slaughter of democratic Polish insurgents by the masses they were trying to liberate. Chartists like Harney and some of the democratic Poles simply could not accept this fact—it went directly against principles that they held sacred. The Galician massacres were therefore explained away. Sometimes the killers were made out to be Austrian soldiers disguised as peasants. At other times they were declared to be serfs from Austrian crown lands who had been Austrian soldiers.[129] Harney's explanation was that the atrocities had been committed by 'felons taken out of the gaols, whose leader, the notorious Szela, had been a house-burner, a child-violator, and a murderer'. The assassins were Polish, he admitted, but 'wretches whom oppression had brutalised—a class existing in all countries', who murdered 'for a certain quantity of brandy and a stipulated price for each head'. Surely, he insisted, these were not the kinds of men who were like ordinary Polish peasants.[130] Unlike his English cohorts, Karl Schapper did not try to explain away the manner in which Polish peasants turned upon the revolutionaries of 1846. He called this turn of events the 'bad harvest' of the 'bad seed sown in 1830'.[131] Even so, some of the democratic Poles who could not accept this view pleaded that the Galician massacre was a fabrication manufactured by the Czartoryskites.[132] Furthermore the *Northern Star* accused German papers, apparently the source of information for the respectable press in England, of lying.

A less difficult issue remains: if the Polish cause was a national cause, how could the Fraternal Democrats become so enthusiastic if their basic commitment was not to nationalism but to internationalism? Fraternal Democrats generally followed Marx in regarding nationalism as an intermediate stage in development. According to this view, national liberation provided a necessary stage in some countries, including Poland and Italy. As Harney put it, national feelings were 'indispensable to rekindle life in those countries'. Upon occasion, nationalism had 'saved mankind from universal and irredeemable slavery'. For more advanced countries, these national feelings need not be 'rekindled' or even kept alive, because in such places they were atavistic. People living in France or England should look towards the higher destiny of internationalism instead. Needed in a given area or not, nationalism was secondary to the fundamental problem that existed throughout the world, which was, according to Harney, the problem of 'enslaved and plundered labour'.[133]

VI MARX AND ENGELS AND THE FRATERNAL DEMOCRATS

While celebration of this new Polish uprising was the most important activity for the Fraternal Democrats themselves, it did not become the major source of notoriety and significance for the society in the eyes of historians. Connections with Marx and Engels claim this distinction. Many writers have been interested in the Fraternal Democrats simply because Marx and Engels were for a time associated with some of the leaders of the organisation. As might be expected, the keenest Marxists among them have exaggerated the importance of the German theoreticians to the organisation.[134] While the assiduous attentions of Marx and Engels to the intellectual development of Harney and Jones and other members cannot be denied, it is safe to say that they provided but two more voices in a chorus of democratic republicanism. Sometimes they blended into the other voices and sometimes they were drowned out by them.

Actually, Marx and Engels began to work with some Chartists who became Fraternal Democrats before that organisation existed. In fact, Engels' friendship with Harney began in 1843, which means that this relationship predates even Engels' collaboration with Marx by some months. Engels came to England for the first time in 1842, ostensibly to complete his commercial training for a position in a European cotton mill partly owned by his father. He was already in reaction against bourgeois society, and his interests in the condition of the British working class had made him quite familiar with the *Northern Star* and the ideas of its editor. So, when in Leeds in 1843, Engels appeared in the *Northern Star* office to meet Harney. A friendship was soon cemented.[135] When Engels brought Marx to England in 1845, in order that he might observe industrial conditions at first hand and learn more about the teachings of English economists, Harney was introduced to him. The next time Harney met Marx was in 1847, when the German was back in England attempting to organise the Communist League, and, at the same time, trying to work the Fraternal Democrats into a planned federation of communist societies.

Marx and Engels were ambivalent about Harney, the Fraternal Democrats, and the Chartists in general. While they regarded England's new industrial proletariat as the most advanced working class in Europe, they were upset at what they called the 'unrevolutionary' and 'specifically British nature' of the movement.[136] The Fraternal Democrats, whom they regarded as the most advanced members of the most developed proletariat, stressed too much brotherhood and too little class war to suit the German theoreticians.[137] Even so, Marx and Engels were ever ready to praise the *Northern Star*, the Fraternal Democrats, and Harney himself in public. It was in the privacy of their correspondence that the theoreticians were acidly critical.[138] An example of their praise was carried in the *Star* in July 1846:

We hesitate not a moment in declaring that the *Star* is the only English newspaper . . . which knows the real state of parties in England; which is really and essentially democratic; which is free from national and religious prejudice; which sympathises with the democrats and working men . . . all over the world . . . and . . . is the only English paper really worth reading for the continental democrats. We hereby declare that we shall do everything in our power to extend the circulation of the *Northern Star* on the Contenent, and to have extracts from it translated in as many continental papers as possible.[139]

In 1847 Marx was engaged in a tri-lingual correspondence with socialist leaders throughout Europe, including August Blanqui and Karl Schapper, seeking the acceptance of his doctrines and trying to purge what he called the sentimentalities of artisan communism. As he explained to Proudhon in 1846, he wished to:

. . . put the German socialists in contact with the French and English socialists. . . . In this way it will be possible to air differences of opinion. An exchange of ideas will ensue and impartial criticism secured. It is a step which the social movement should take . . . to free itself of its national limitations.[140]

Marx worked on both steps from Brussels, as the representative and vice-president of the *Association Démocratique*, a society 'having for its purpose the union and brotherhood of all people . . . without distinction as to country or profession'. It was, like the Fraternal Democrats, primarily an educative, propagandistic body. It sent out addresses, manifestos and petitions. Membership tended to be drawn much more from middle-class intellectuals than that of the Fraternal Democrats. Part of its rules called for affiliation with other societies in Belgium and abroad, and to an extent they were successful, although some Belgian democrats raised xenophobic criticisms.[141]

Perhaps the most important meeting ever held by the Fraternal Democrats took place on November 29, 1847, in the familiar rooms of the German Workers' Educational Society. It certainly has not been ignored by historians, although they must all rely upon the *Northern Star*'s extensive account of the meeting.[142] At the same time that Dr 'Charles' Marx was being welcomed by the Fraternal Democrats, Dr Karl Marx's plans were being anxiously awaited by the members of the League of the Just. Of the two appointments that Marx had in London, the meeting with the Fraternal Democrats, which gained far more publicity at the time, came to nothing, and the meeting with the League of the Just, unrecorded then, has become famous. Marx's plans to affiliate the *Association Démocratique* and the Fraternal Democrats went up in smoke, along with the Fraternal Democrats as an organisation, in 1848. The Communist Manifesto lives on.

Once again it was the Polish cause that served as the *raison* to bring democrats of various nationalities together. The November 29 meeting of the Fraternal Democrats was held in conjunction with the Democratic Committee for Poland's Regeneration to celebrate the anniversary of the Polish uprising of 1830 and a considerable portion of the speeches had nothing at all to do with Marx and his proposals for affiliation with the *Association Démocratique*. Many of the speeches were the familiar ones about the Polish cause. It was Karl Schapper who drew attention to Marx:

He [Schapper] had some glorious news for them. A Democratic Society that was a Society of Fraternal Democrats had been established in Brussels, and that society had sent a deputy, the learned Dr Marx, to represent them at this meeting. (Great applause.)

He then read Marx's credentials, which gave him 'full power' on behalf of the committee to establish 'relations of correspondence and sympathy'.

Schapper went on to speak about the Poles and the Cracow Manifesto, and after another speaker, an English Chartist whose topic was how the world would be better when the Charter was law, Marx came forward and delivered a speech in German, of which the edited, poorly translated version that appeared sandwiched between other speeches in the small print of the *Northern Star* a few days later has been in part quoted or at least cited time and time again by all sorts of writers. Here is that version in its entirety:

He had been sent by the democrats of Brussels to speak in their name to the Democrats of London, and through them to cause to be holden a congress of nations—a congress of working men, to establish liberty all over the world. (Loud cheers.)

The middle classes, the Free Traders, had held a congress, but their fraternity was a one-sided one, and the moment they found that such congresses were likely to benefit the working men, that moment their fraternity would cease, and their congresses be dissolved. (Hear, Hear.)

The Democrats of Belgium felt that the Chartists of England were the real democrats, and that the moment they carried the six points of that Charter, the road to liberty would be opened to the whole world. Effect this grand object, then, you working men of England, and you will be hailed as the saviours of the whole human race. (Tremendous cheering.)

Harney then rose to move this resolution:

> That this meeting rejoices to learn of the establishment of a Society of
> Fraternal Democrats in Brussels, and responding to the alliance offered by
> that society, receives its delegate, Dr Marx, with every feeling of fraternal
> regard; and their meeting hails with exultation the proposition to hold a
> Democratic Congress of all nations, pledging itself to send delegates to that
> congress whenever summoned by the Fraternal Democratic Societies of
> London and Brussels.

After a rambling speech by Charles Keen, Engels rose and delivered
an oration which was, from the account of it in the *Northern Star*,
primarily on Poland. It did, however, conclude on this note:

> He [Engels] had resided for some time in England, and was proud to boast
> himself a Chartist 'name and all'. (Great cheering.) Who were now the
> chief oppressors? Not the aristocracy, but the wealth takers and scrapers,
> the middle class. (Loud cheers.) Hence, it was the duty of the working
> classes of all nations to unite and establish freedom for all. (Rapturous
> applause.)

Engels was followed by 'Citizen' Tedesco from the *Association
Démocratique* who had accompanied Marx and Engels to London. He
noted that 'the men of Belgium looked on the English democrats as
a leading party, and trusted they would obtain the great measure,
the People's Charter'. Then, after a few more speeches primarily on
the Polish cause, the most important meeting held by the Fraternal
Democrats came to an end with the singing of the 'Marseillaise' by
Joseph Moll.

The Harney papers have revealed that the foremost Chartist
internationalist worked in close collaboration with Marx and
Engels to affiliate the Fraternal Democrats with the *Association
Démocratique* and also reorganise the League of the Just. While
Marx and Engels were preparing these arrangements, Harney was
busy quelling rumours among the German workers in London that
some 'literary characters' had established a society excluding working men. Harney himself was concerned lest his collaboration with
Marx and Engels be against 'popular interests'. In no way did he
want to 'appear as a conspirator' behind the backs of 'the long
trusted, incorruptible . . . martyr men of the German movement'.[143]

Harney prompted the Fraternal Democrats to produce an
official reply to the proposal of affiliation with the *Association
Démocratique*. It appeared shortly after the famous meeting of

November 29, and the most significant sections from this lengthy document were these:

Your delegate, our esteemed friend and brother, Dr Marx, will inform you of the enthusiasm which hailed his appearance, and the reading of your address. . . . We accept your proffered alliance with feelings of unspeakable pleasure. . . . The conspiracy of kings should be met by the counter-combination of the peoples.

Whenever the Democratic Congress may assemble, you may rely upon the English Democracy being represented thereat. It must be the work of your society in connection with ours to assemble the representatives of our brethren throughout Europe.

Your delegate, Dr Marx, will inform you of the arrangements we have entered into with him to render effective the union of the two associations.

The oppressed people of the several European countries may propose to themselves various modes of accomplishing their emancipation; they may differ as to the peculiar forms of the free political systems they seek to establish, and they may not agree on the social reforms necessary to render liberty a reality; on these points, unity of sentiment and action may be neither possible nor necessary. . . . These two principles—*Popular Sovereignty* and *Universal Fraternity*—may bind the veritable Reformers of all countries in one invincible phalanx. . . . We are aware that it is the *veritable* people, the proletarians, the men whose sweat and blood are poured out daily under the slavery imposed upon them by the present system of society . . . [to whom] . . . we must look for the establishment of universal brotherhood.

It is the interest of the landlords and the moneylords to keep the nations divided; but it is the interest of the Proletarians, everywhere oppressed by the same kind of taskmasters, and defrauded of the fruits of their industry by the same description of plunderers, it is their interest to unite.

From the loom, the anvil, and the plough, from the hut, the garret, and the cellar, will come forth, are even now coming forth, the apostles of fraternity, and the destined saviours of humanity.

Hurrah for Democracy! Hurrah for the Fraternity of nations.[144]

One week later, it was announced in the *Northern Star* that the Fraternal Democrats had unanimously passed these resolutions:

That the holding of a Democratic Congress of all nations is desirable.

That the Democratic Association of Brussels be requested to convene, in conjunction with this society; the said congress to be holden in Brussels on the 25th of September next—the anniversary of the Belgian Revolution.

That the Brussels society be requested to prepare the programme of business, for the consideration of the said Congress; other recognised bodies of Democrats to have the power to offer propositions in addition to those contained in the programme.

That it be suggested to the first Congress that the second Congress (in 1849) be summoned to meet in London.[145]

News of fresh revolutions in 1848 disrupted all of these plans permanently, as democratic exiles in London rushed away to their respective homelands in order to participate in dramatic events. Many more important hopes, plans and dreams than those of the Fraternal Democrats were lost forever in 1848.

VII Feargus O'Connor's role

Marx, Engels, Harney, Schapper, and Jones all had to work around a famous and important personage whose displeasure could have ruined their manifestations of fraternal internationalism. That person was the Lion of the North, the great and controversial demagogue, Feargus O'Connor, the most important leader during the lifespan of the Fraternal Democrats. What he thought about Europe, its people and its recent history and how he responded to Chartist internationalism are important primarily because Feargus succeeded magnificently as a demagogue. Some recent efforts have been made to rehabilitate O'Connor's reputation, partly, it may be supposed, because historians regard renovation and demolition as standard operations in their profession, and because the earliest sources, particularly Lovett and Gammage, condemned him so soundly and were followed in this by standard academic historians.[146] In short, he had many enemies among the Chartist craftsmen of the shops and the latter-day Whiggish craftsmen of Academe. Either as a speaker or as a columnist, O'Connor was, by modern standards or by the utterly serious middle-class standards of his day, crude, bombastic, illogical, shallow, and vacillating. He loved blarney and the applause it brought. He made wild predictions and uttered countless inane and declamatory phrases. Yet there was much more to his leadership than these very things which made him despicable to the LWMA. He was a superb entertainer on the platform—commanding, fluent, and witty. He could communicate his unbounded belief in himself, in his listeners, and in their mutual cause. He had amazing rapport. His charisma thrilled multitudes. To his many enemies, it was simply demagogery, but to the starving weavers and overworked 'hands' he was the incarnation of hope. More than that, his dramatic rapport enabled him to develop forms of political organisation among poorly educated workers who had only recently been introduced to politics. Feargus O'Connor was the opiate but also the organiser of the Chartist masses.[147]

At this point a possibly apocryphal scene must be described: one day in October 1845 in a northern Italian village, a travelling English gentleman peered out of the window of his coach as it approached a group of players bowling in the dusty street. As the coach passed them, one of the players bent over the pins suddenly stood straight. At that, the Englishman riding by fell back in his seat wide-eyed and exclaimed: 'Feargus O'Connor, by God!'[148]

So it possibly was. Feargus was on his version of a Grand Tour in 1845, which included visits to Italy, Belgium, Prussia, several other German states, France, and Switzerland. Historians have noticed this visit only in passing, despite the fact that Feargus dispatched a remarkable series of letters from abroad, letters that appeared prominently in his popular Chartist newspaper.[149] By itself an account of the trip would be something of a vignette, seemingly of no particular importance, even if vaguely interesting. None the less, it has significance. Why did O'Connor go to the continent? Did he wish to bring Chartists and continental agitators into a closer alliance? Did he wish to imbibe the revolutionary thoughts of the radical continental theoreticians, such as Weitling, Blanc, Marx, and Engels? Definitely not. He went to study land utilisation because he was a monomaniac at that time over his 'Land Plan', a scheme to settle British workers on small farms. The irony of this is that in the very year the Fraternal Democrats were founded, the foremost Chartist leader was abroad seeking ways to restore the old world of hearty, well-fed, manly, independent yeomen, rather than seeking ways to help usher in the new world of class-conscious proletarian internationalists.

Mark Hovell's *History of the Chartist Movement* contains the blithe declaration that Feargus O'Connor 'simply did not go to Belgium to study its agriculture . . .' because he 'had treaty' with a 'band of German democratic communists' including Marx and Engels.[150] This body was supposed to have welcomed him with a 'congratulatory address'. Hovell's source is the *Northern Star* of July 25, 1847. There is no *Northern Star* bearing that date, but there was an issue of July 25, 1846, which did contain an address signed by the 'German Democratic Communits of Brussels', and among them were Marx and Engels. It dealt with one of O'Connor's Nottingham speeches, lauded the *Northern Star*, and remarked upon O'Connor's feud with Thomas Cooper. It said nothing about the Chartist chieftan's visit to Europe, and for a good reason—the trip had been the previous year. Perhaps Mark Hovell would have corrected this slip had he lived through the First World War and finished his book himself. Unfortunately, several historians have picked up this item and compounded his error.

The net effect of O'Connor's European travels was to strengthen his enthusiasm for the Land Plan, which was designed to create small holdings from estates purchased with lottery funds.[151] At the end of his journey he concluded, 'I have seen as much as required to convince me of the correctness of my views on the all important subject of *The Land*.'[152] To prove his point, O'Connor told of the 'thriving, happy' people he had observed living in many places on the continent where the land was cultivated mainly by small farmers. O'Connor wished that his friends among the overworked, overcrowded British working class could see the 'straight, majestic-looking peasants' in Belgium and elsewhere.[153] His basic conclusion on this issue was that European land was bad compared to English land, but European peasants were healthy and happy because small-scale ownership and cultivation were widespread. If continental styles of cultivation could be practised on the richer soils of England by workers on small holdings, untold prosperity was bound to accrue to them.[154] Moreover, abundance would come from the 'superior strength of Englishmen over any people that I have ever seen, except the Irish'.[155]

Beyond strengthening his confidence in the Land Plan, O'Connor's journey deepened his reactionary attitudes toward the new industrial economy of Britain. He compared what he had seen in some places in England—'barren valleys, barren hills, barren slopes, all made barren in consequence of their proximity to the quicker money-maker—the tall chimney'—with what he observed in Europe. There he had seen 'the result of man's labour, when unchecked by mechanical power. . .'.[156] However, while in Ghent, he noticed with alarm that 'the devil chimneys are beginning to spread . . .' and hoped that 'capitalists will never be able to entice the virtuous peasantry from their peaceful homes'.[157]

Despite his overwhelming preoccupation with agrarian matters, Feargus's prolix style led him to make several political observations while on the continent. They reveal him to be something of a British nationalist, convinced that special benefits were conferred by English laws and institutions. He had been in a republic—Switzerland—and his freedom to talk politics had been curtailed in several cantons, or so he claimed.[158] Near an old Roman arena outside Milan, Feargus remarked to a friendly native that the structure would make a fine place for a public meeting. The Italian told him that troops would arrive to disperse such a meeting immediately upon its convocation. Incidents of this sort convinced him that 'even . . . in the midst of the most degrading slavery, we possess advantages which no other people in Europe do possess—the advantages of meeting and saying what we like. . . . In no other country do people meet. They are governed wholly and entirely by the press of the factions, and by military despotism.'[159]

Sharp xenophobic feelings accompanied this patriotism from time to time. One editorial of 1847, written by O'Connor bore the following heading, underlined and in bold type: CHARTISTS MUST ADMIT OF NO FOREIGN QUESTION OR QUARRELS OR DISPUTES, BEING MIXED UP WITH YOUR CAUSE. . . . HAVE NOTHING WHATEVER TO DO WITH ANY FOREIGN MOVEMENT. He added, 'Let Englishmen and Irishmen and Scotchmen work together for England, Ireland and Scotland—let Frenchmen work for France, Russians for Russia, and Prussians for Prussia. I WILL WORK ONLY FOR HOME SWEET HOME.'[160]

In a way, O'Connor's reaction to foreigners was reminiscent of William Cobbett. Both men peppered their speeches and writings with anti-semitic and anti-foreign remarks. Both were eager to proclaim the blessings of being English. O'Connor's editorial of July 1847 contained these typical remarks:

I contend, without fear of contradiction, that the English people are better prepared for liberty than any people, not only in Europe but in the world, and I say, with vanity, that I have brought them to that state. The French are not prepared for liberty, and for this single reason—because the people have not had the privilege of meeting and discussing their grievances. . . .[161]

He did not hestitate to express similar sentiments at internationalist gatherings:

Foreigners, for the most part, contend for a Republic, while we contend for our Charter, which is an improved principle of Republicanism. (Loud cheers.) . . . England was setting an example to the world. . . .[162]

O'Connor's patriotic convictions and his obsession with the Land Plan seem to have been strengthened by his trip to Europe. Therefore Feargus and the Fraternal Democrats were proclaiming separate paths to the millenium from 1845 to 1848, which seems odd, considering that Harney and the other English leaders were his lieutenants, and that his own newspaper gave them such immense publicity. He did, of course, show up at most of the important international public meetings, often to sit in a place of honour. On some of these occasions he delivered ambivalent or mildly enthusiastic speeches. On one occasion he publicly debated with members of the Fraternal Democrats: At the first anniversary banquet, in 1846, he took issue with Karl Schapper, who had declared that democrats of all nations should struggle first for freedom from middle-class oppressors. Feargus retorted that 'political liberty must be the precursor of social equality and religious freedom'.[163]

Such debate was rather exceptional. In general, Feargus peacefully coexisted with Chartist internationalism and kept his remarks guarded and ambiguous when associating with them. For example, at one public meeting in London he congratulated the organisers on the presence of many foreigners and said:

... No matter where a man's country, what his creed, or what his colour, provided he was a friend to democracy, he hailed him and called him brother. (Loud cheers.) While these were his sentiments, he begged to be distinctly understood upon the question of fraternisation which had been so frequently enforced by previous speakers. While he had studiously avoided what was considered to be the fraternisation of the people of all nations, he had as studiously endeavoured to insure freedom for all countries. (Cheers.)[164]

He was more positive as a principal speaker at a gala banquet of the Fraternal Democrats:

I have never sought to limit the struggle for liberty to country, creed or colour: for I have invariably declared that I cared not where the country, what the colour, or which the creed, of the patriot was—that if he loved liberty and struggled for it, I would call him brother and take him by the hand. (Loud cheers.)[165]

This was as far as O'Connor ever went in hailing the cause of proletarian internationalism. He was glad to cheer on patriots everywhere, but he was interested primarily in the fight at home and thought that everyone else should be similarly engaged, wherever their homes might be. Yet he did render a great service to Chartist internationalism by leaving Harney alone so that his editor could cram the *Northern Star* with views of and news about the Fraternal Democrats. When Engels badgered Harney with complaints about his leader, the Chartist internationalist wrote back asking the German not to be 'too hard' with O'Connor because 'he never interferes with what I write in the paper nor does he know what I write until he sees the paper.'[166] This arrangement was important. Much of the existence of the Fraternal Democrats would have been lost to history otherwise.

VIII   THE FRATERNAL DEMOCRATS' RIVALS

The Fraternal Democrats did not have a monopoly on Chartist internationalism because two other organisations existed embodying fraternal union between Chartists and exiles from 1844 to 1848, the Democratic Friends of All Nations and its successor, the People's International League. In these societies William Lovett and Thomas Cooper emerged in leading roles matching those of Harney and Jones in the Fraternal Democrats and, in place of Marx and Engels, the competitors had Giuseppe Mazzini.

An important consideration is that Lovett and his friends, including James Watson, John Cleave, W. J. Linton, Henry Hetherington, and, after his dramatic struggle with Feargus O'Connor, Thomas Cooper, did not participate in the Fraternal Democrats or the Democratic Committee for Poland's Regeneration. They called separate meetings to celebrate notable events in European history, and attempted to form their own kind of organisations to carry on international fraternisation. While Jones and Harney did not attend or in general give much publicity to these meetings of Lovett's friends, or vice-versa, many European exiles attended both sets. It is difficult to say whether London workmen would drift into both kinds of international meetings, or whether they, like the London leaders, practised discrimination. Probably most were oriented towards only one variety of Chartist internationalism, for the split in London between O'Connorites and anti-O'Connorites carried over into many working-class activities. At any rate, British workers interested in fraternisation with European exiles actually had a choice of meetings and celebrations, institutions and leaders, and, to an extent, programmes. The significance of this is that London Chartist internationalism of the forties actually had two faces, just as Chartism, throughout England, had many faces.

The LWMA counterpart predated the Fraternal Democrats but it did not last as long. William Lovett and his friends helped to found the Democratic Friends of All Nations in 1844, in conjunction with German, Polish, French, and Italian exiles. Early in 1845, the organisation stated its principles in an 'Address to the Friends of Humanity and Justice among all Nations', a document written largely by Lovett and printed by John Cleave and sold by Henry Hetherington and James Watson. Among the officers who signed the address were two foreigners who would become 'regulars' at the Fraternal Democrats—Louis Oborski and 'Charles' Schapper.[167]

On the whole, the document was a vague, general statement that contrasts sharply with the militant proletarian declarations about the international class struggle for which the Fraternal Democrats have been so often noted and quoted by historians. Like many other documents that emanated from LWMA leaders, it sought to avoid frightening away any radical middle-class support or membership. In this respect, the Democratic Friends of All Nations served as another attempt to bring about Chartist and middle-class co-operation. In specific provisions, they called for free trade and peace. It was strong in its condemnation of Eastern European serfdom and American slavery. In accordance with Lovett's well-known views, it called for education rather than revolution. While the Fraternal Democrats had singled out the 'profitocracy' as one of the chief causes of human misery, this declaration of the Democratic Friends pointed to general human 'selfishness, force and fraud'. Moreover, the 'deep rooted evils of society' were not attributed to a maldistribution of property—a common claim of the Fraternal Democrats—but to 'exclusive political power, class legislation, defective knowledge, corrupt rulers, bad laws, unjust privileges, and monopolies of various kinds'. While the Fraternal Democrats called upon workers or proletarians 'in spirit', the Democratic Friends of All Nations appealed to 'men and women of all nations'. Perhaps the only part of the address that sounded anything like the Fraternal Democrats' declaration of principles was in the opening lines, which read: 'All men being "brethren" should surely seek to promote each others' happiness, whatever may be their individual country, creed or colour.'

One clause involving the exercise of moral force instead of physical force became a topic of serious contention within the organisation and helped to bring on Lovett's withdrawal and the rapid demise of the group:

Not that we would invite you to outbreaks of violence, for we have faith in the mental and moral combinations of men being able to achieve victories for humanity beyond the force of armies to accomplish. What is wanting are men armed in all the moral daring of a just cause, and resolved at all risks to pursue and achieve their righteous object.

Such a statement might offend some sabre-rattling Chartists in 1844—but it surely offended Frenchmen, Poles, Italians, and Germans whose chief preoccupation in exile was fomenting or dreaming about violent revolutions in their respective homelands.[168]

When the Democratic Friends of All Nations quietly died shortly thereafter, many of its dissidents joined the Fraternal Democrats while other members went into a new organisation involving Lovett, the People's International League. Both of these organisations kept Lovett and his friends in contact with that outstanding intellectual leader of Italian liberalism and nationalism, Guiseppe Mazzini. Lovett and Hetherington had endeared themselves to Mazzini through their role in an incident known to history as the 'Mazzini Letters Scandal'. England's Home Secretary, Sir James Graham, had ordered the opening of Mazzini's letters, and as an end result of this—or so Mazzini claimed—a number of Italian patriots died at the hands of the Austrians. To detect tampering, Lovett and Hetherington sent a decoy letter to Mazzini, containing tiny pieces of material folded in a particular way. Mazzini opened this in the presence of witnesses, and claimed proof of interference in his mail. Meanwhile Duncombe exposed the matter in the House of Commons and brought about some criticism of the Home Secretary and a general public outcry.[169] The scandal was vigorously decried by the *Northern Star*, which claimed that the aristocrats of England did not really care for England's honour or Italy's liberty and that only the working class sincerely took the cause of Italian freedom to heart.[170]

By a lucky accident Lovett's ill-fated coffee shop venture was situated nearly opposite Mazzini's free and struggling elementary school for impoverished Italian boys, and so the Chartist leader knew Mazzini from the thirties onward.[171] Mazzini also worked up a journal, the *Apostolato Populare*, for a group of poor Italian workmen in London, who, it is claimed, comprised the first workingmen's organisation of that nationality. They met once each week at the home of W. J. Linton, the famous Chartist wood engraver. These ventures were but a few products of the whirlwind of organisational and journalistic activity carried on by this eminent Italian nationalist while in London. One of the organisations that he fostered was the People's International League—which was apparently not one of his more important concerns.[172]

The Cracow uprising, so significant for the Fraternal Democrats, also played an important part for the League, because the organisation sprang from a public meeting of April 28, 1846, dedicated to protesting the destruction of the Polish free state. The radical M.P., Dr Bowring, was in the chair, and the following resolution was settled upon:

That an Association be now formed, to be called the 'People's International League', the objects of which shall be as follows:—'To enlighten the British Public as to the Political Condition and Relations of Foreign Countries. To disseminate the Principles of National Freedom and Progress. To embody and manifest an efficient Public Opinion in favour of the right of every

People to Self-government and the maintenance of their own Nationality. To promote a good understanding between the Peoples of all Countries,'

The executive council of the League was all-British and reveals the kinds of members it drew: three were members of the LWMA; five were young lawyers in sympathy with the Chartist movement; two, Duncombe and Bowring, were M.P.s, and three others, Stansfield, P. A. Taylor, Jr., and the Unitarian orator, W. J. Fox, would become Members of Parliament in the future. Perhaps the most prominent Chartist council member, besides Lovett, was Thomas Cooper, fresh from gaol.[173]

The League regarded British xenophobia as its special target, as this portion from an address of its council indicates:

The insularity of England among the family of European nations is more than that of mere geographical position. Self-contained and self-contented, her people, as a people, seldom extend an enlightened regard or warm sympathy beyond the narrow sphere of cares and interests involved in the progressive development of the internal powers and resources of their own country . . . foreign relations . . . [are] . . . regarded as the exclusive and peculiar province of statesmen and diplomatists. . . .

The British working class was especially singled out for having 'absolutely no symptom of public opinion' on foreign affairs, which meant that they applied no check to important decisions made capriciously by government ministers. To counter apathy and ignorance, the League proposed to 'place England in a position of knowledge and matured opinion' on such subjects. Englishmen should know how 'the progressive destinies of Europe are being worked out, so that whenever European affairs call for interference they may be in no doubt as to the course' to be followed. The Mazzinian influence on the council was indeed strong: 'The question now at issue throughout Europe, at the bottom of all European movements, is the question of nationality—of national rights and duties.' The Congress of Vienna was singled out as a root cause of European difficulties.[174]

With such aims in view, just what did the League accomplish? Fortunately, a report of all the organisation's activities since its founding was published late in 1847, just before the revolutions of 1848 permanently disrupted the group.[175] Like the Fraternal Democrats and the Democratic Friends of All Nations, the League specialised in education and propaganda. Its original address was forwarded to each member of both Houses of Parliament, every British newspaper, many foreign newspapers, many public institutions and to thousands of individuals, British and foreign. Eventually it was translated into French, Spanish, German, Italian, and Polish. Another publication, a pamphlet on the *Sonderbund* crisis in Switzerland, was similarly distributed, with copies also going to every member of the Swiss Diet. It evoked sympathetic public demonstrations in four Swiss cities and brought resolutions of support from several Swiss associations. Councillors of the League wrote to numerous contacts abroad in order to gain correct information. A total of seventeen free public lectures were delivered and among the lecturers were two Chartists, W. J. Linton and Thomas Cooper. Membership went up to four hundred and included Charles Dickens.[176]

The organisation had to endure sharp attacks from left and right. *The Times* as well as the Fraternal Democrats was bitterly hostile. The League was described in *The Times* as a 'mean and pitiful imitation' of the 'great original', the Anti-Corn Law League. Readers were assured that 'no society that was ever formed combines more of impudence and impotence. . .'. It endeavoured 'to graft on every foreign tree some of the slips and cuttings which are lopped off and discarded as wild excrescences from the exuberant growth of politics in England'. Their nostrums were part of 'the refuse of exaggerated Radicalism', a 'poisonous trash' and 'blundering bombast' which might do less harm when diffused 'over the whole universe'. *The Times* took particular relish in ridiculing the base of the League's operations, a floor rented at 85 Hatton Garden, which was the same address as Linton's wood engraving shop, and close to Mazzini's school. *The Times* declared that it was preposterous to have 'a branch of the foreign office' there, to seek solutions to diplomatic questions 'by ringing the first, second, or top bell, as the case may be, and enquiring for the People's International League, or any of its executives who may happen to be found on the premises'. Might 85 Hatton Garden 'become a grand political mart, from which constitutions will be supplied wholesale, retail and for exportation?' How could they express 'a desire that every people should maintain its own nationality' while attempting to bring 'the public opinion of one country to bear on the condition of another . . .?' They were out 'to thrust changes upon foreign nations', whether they were 'disposed to adopt innovations or not', which was 'forcing freedom down everybody's throat, as a medicine is administered to children. . .'. Such foolishness grew out of the nature of the membership in the League. It consisted of some Chartists—*The Times* mentioned Henry Vincent and James Watson

in particular—and other 'great unknowns and little-knowns. . .'.
Was it not 'a little ridiculous' of such 'a parcel of people' to 'dictate
to the inhabitants of other nations on the subject of their own
government' when they 'have evinced an utter incapacity for dealing with the politics of their own country . . .?' There was only one
object of the League that evoked some sympathy from *The Times*:
emigration for those who could not find 'profitable investment of
their facilities'. *The Times* hoped that the Council would 'be among
the earliest who . . . will "leave their country for their country's
good", and their own also'.[177]

On the other hand, the Fraternal Democrats were displeased by
what they called the League's "namby-pamby liberalism', and they
were incensed that the League had held up English middle-class
freedoms as examples to European nations. These very freedoms,
Harney insisted, were the cause of distress in England.[178] Harney
called League members 'humbugs' and, early in 1846, ridiculed
their plans for a 'genteel' Polonophilistic meeting. Undoubtedly
his friends heckled and harassed the League from time to time in a
manner reminiscent of the treatment meted out to the Anti-Corn
Law League.[179] One incident is recorded of a workman protesting
against the insertion of the word *free* as an adjective to describe
Britain in a resolution proposed at a League meeting. It was
struck out.[180] Finally, at a festival of the Fraternal Democrats,
Ernest Jones warned Chartists to stay away from the distracting
'People's International League Hole'.[181]

Part of the reason for this enmity was the attraction of the
People's International League for so-called 'moral force' Chartists.
Such Chartists often had grave reservations about each new European revolution, although they were likely to favour the aims of the
side in rebellion. The People's International League helped them
out of this dilemma by allowing them to declare that violence was
the only means that Poles, or Italians, or Greeks had to free themselves. British workers, on the other hand, had recourse to better
means to achieve their ends, namely public meetings, petitions,
elections, etc., and they should use them instead of violence. A
moral force Chartist put it succinctly when he said: 'If I were in
Poland, where liberty of speech is denied, the first weapon I could
grasp I would seize upon to annihilate every monster that blackened
the soil of my country.'[182] Certainly Mazzini was skilful in advocat-
ing revolution on the Continent without offending either moral
force Chartists or middle-class followers. The publications of the

League, which were never far removed from Mazzini's draft, spoke of Europe as a 'sleeping volcano' and identified 'the will of the people' with the 'will of God'. Yet Englishmen were urged only to 'welcome' and 'hail' nationalistic outbreaks, on the assumption that both the oppressors and oppressed on the continent were going to use force anyway, and England had the responsibility of tilting the scales of combat by throwing 'the weight of peaceful, but firm and generous assertion of the principles of Eternal Truth and Justice' into the scales.

There is no thought in this of any armed intervention in the affairs of Europe, no thought of England embroiling herself. Let her only speak out firmly and decidedly: her voice will be listened to. . . . Her present apathy encourages aggression, and so does more than aught else to make the sword the sole arbiter of right. It is emphatically for Peace that the League is founded.[183]

Even such care in exposition did not keep Mazzini from being attacked, but the shafts were apt to come only from respectable sources.[184] Even though Harney had no use for the People's International League, he did not attack Mazzini. In fact, the Italian leader was usually invited to important meetings of the Democratic Committee for Poland's Regeneration, and his articles had been gladly welcomed in the *Northern Star*.[185] Even so, Mazzini did not have much to do with Harney, the Fraternal Democrats or the Democratic Committee for Poland's Regeneration.

Mazzini's contacts were with another set of Chartists, and among them Thomas Cooper stands forth not only as a rival to O'Connor as a leader, but also as a rival to Harney as a Chartist internationalist. Thomas Cooper was one of the more colourful Chartists, a classic nineteenth-century autodidact and something of a working-class Renaissance man. He worked as a cobbler, schoolteacher, preacher, journalist, lecturer, author, and along the way he found time to start musical, Shakespearian, and political societies. He began as a Primitive Methodist and became a secularist and vehement O'Connorite. A stay in gaol brought him to moral force positions and, after several years, he was reconverted from secularism to Bible Christianity. When his long life ended he was remembered as a popular preacher and very minor man of letters.[186] His Chartist career was but an episode in this long, busy life, and centred on Leicester, where chronically depressed framework knitters lived. He broke vehemently with Feargus O'Connor in 1846, and while his denunciation of Feargus had nothing to do with

Chartist internationalism at first,[187] his attack on O'Connor also became an attack on the Fraternal Democrats and the Democratic Committee for Poland's Regeneration. This drew fire from Feargus himself, some of the foreigners prominent in these organisations and their Chartist contingents.[188] Engels wrote from Brussels, calling Cooper a 'disguised bourgeois' who was busy striving to insinuate himself with the middle classes while he propounded 'such base and infamous old women's doctrines as that of non-resistance'.[189]

Cooper's concern with Europe and European exiles was pronounced both before and after this break. He knew several foreign languages, many exiles, and became chairman at several international gatherings and a noted lecturer on certain foreign topics.[190] He played an important part in the Democratic Friends of all Nations and the People's International League, where Mazzini undoubtedly influenced him strongly. At a public meeting held in November 1845, he had this to say concerning the necessity of rousing British interest in Italy's freedom:

The time for burying selfish thoughts, for annihilating selfish associations, for forgetting the bad and depraving maxims that we 'take care of number one' and that 'charity begins at home', for devoting all our energies to self-sacrifice and unceasing struggle for the good of *all*, was now at hand— nay, he would dare to say it was come. (Enthusiastic cheering.)[191]

His lecture on the Swiss question contained these sentiments:

Are not all men our brethren? Do we not grow ashamed of the old 'national antipathies', so diligently taught and prompted in our forefathers by their rulers? . . . The true cosmopolitan spriit—a nobler spirit than even the patriotic—is, I trust, deepening its influence in the hearts and minds of my countrymen.[192]

Cooper's internationalism did not include enthusiasm for the Cracow uprising. In fact, he strenuously opposed working-class celebrations over the event. Cooper denied that the Poles were fighting to recover freedom—he insisted that they never had it:

That there either is now, or has been lately, a truly patriotic struggle, I have yet to learn. I read of peasants slaughtering their countrymen and expecting a reward from the Austrians for it—but it seems to me strange patriotism.

He also had little use for the Cracow Manifesto:

A 'Manifesto' promulgating Communist doctrines is also related to have been issued at Cracow by a small number of men, no doubt desirous of establishing those doctrines, and connected, it is quite evident, with the Poles, Germans, French, etc., professing the same doctrines in Paris and

London; but the inhabitants of Poland seem so very far from heartily espousing their views. . . . The means . . . the insurgents had at their disposal were manifestly so disproportioned to their enterprise, that I wondered to find even advocates for physical force crying up to the rash undertaking so loudly.[193]

Furthermore, Cooper raised the same argument against working-class enthusiasm for the Cracow uprising that had been used against Urquhart's Foreign Policy Movement earlier by O'Connor and others. He though it was foolish for Chartists to allow the Polish cause to divert them away from efforts to place 'members of their own class in Parliament'. Energies should not be spent on 'any new wild-fire scheme that happens to be got up'. Therefore he urged Chartists to stay away from public demonstrations over the Cracow insurrection:

I malign no man's motives for attending. . . . I can only claim the liberty . . . to say that I think Chartism was in no wise benefited but injured, by them.

Harney's reply to this attack was rather weak. He derided Cooper's 'surface view of the Polish question'—a description that might have better fitted his own outlook—and accused Cooper of xenophobia:

I can only understand this as an exhibition of that 'Old English' selfishness which has created so much hatred against England on the Continent. Because an Englishman is born on this side of a ditch and a Pole on the other, therefore the former is not to assist the latter! 'Ourselves, and the devil take the rest' appears to be Mr Cooper's idea of Chartism. I must say such "Chartism" has not my sympathy.[194]

These exchanges represent but one aspect of one faction fight in a movement that saw many episodes of such strife. Yet from the standpoint of Chartist internationalism, Cooper's attack, combined with the organisational work of Lovett, Hetherington, Watson, and their friends clearly indicate that the Fraternal Democrats did not have a monopoly on this aspect of Chartist activity. If heightened class consciousness produced the Fraternal Democrats and their collaboration with Marx and Engels, it also produced another variety of Chartist internationalism, a kind that kept the door open to other classes, and called for the growth of an enlightened British public opinion above all else, a public opinion not drawn exclusively from working-class ranks.

IX THE FRATERNAL DEMOCRATS IN PERSPECTIVE:
SOME CONCLUSIONS

George Julian Harney first saw the news of the French revolution of 1848 on a placard at Charing Cross. He recalled that he 'ran like a lunatic' to Karl Schapper's and pulled his bell 'like a bedlamite'.[195] Later, news of Louis Philippe's abdication reached the Fraternal Democrats while they were in session. An eye-witness recalled that the effect was 'electrical' as:

Frenchmen, Germans, Poles, Magyars, sprang to their feet, embraced, shouted, and gesticulated in the wildest enthusiasm. Snatches of oratory were delivered in excited tones, and flags were caught from the walls, to be waved exultingly, amidst cries of 'Hoch! Eljen! Vive la République!' Then the doors were opened, and the whole assemblage descended to the street, and, with linked arms and colours flying, marched to the meeting-place of the Westminster Chartists, in Dean Street, Soho. There another enthusiastic fraternisation took place, and great was the clinking of glasses that night in and around Soho and Leicester Square.[196]

As the revolutions spread, continental Fraternal Democrats rushed off to participate in their respective homelands while British members were swept into a hectic and ill-fated revival of the Chartist movement. All hoped to realise the dreams of the organisation in that year, but at its end those visions were shattered all over Europe. The end of Europe's springtime also saw the end of the Fraternal Democrats as an international organisation. While there was a society by that name in existence under Harney's leadership after 1848, it was composed entirely of Englishmen out of fear of deportation facing foreigners under a new Alien Act.[197]

Almost three and one half years separate the founding of the Fraternal Democrats from their disruption by revolutions in 1848. During that time, a number of persons and groups made the organisation what it was—Harney, Jones, Schapper, Marx, Engels, O'Connor, the Polish democrats, and the German communists. A study of each as they related to the organisation as well as a consideration of rival internationalists has placed the Fraternal Democrats in some perspective and moved away from the manner in which they advertised themselves and the way historians have absorbed these advertisements. One additional consideration of importance has only been touched upon so far—the London environment.

It seems that London was the only place in the British Isles where foreigners were regularly incorporated into Chartist organisations, as well as the only city where concern for foreign affairs was institutionalised by working-class leaders. Chartists in the provinces might pay their shilling and become affiliated members of the Fraternal Democrats and thereby find their names in the *Northern*

Star, or they might get up local public meetings for the brave Poles
upon occasion, but that was as far as Chartist internationalism went
outside of London, except for the Urquhart stir of the late thirties
and early forties and the general tumult of celebrations in 1848.
London was not a Paris, not a heart and centre of radical democracy. As Gammage put it, 'the rest of France' would move at the
bidding of Paris, but London had to be 'impelled by some external
power'.[198] How could workers be inflamed in dingy, largely empty
halls in the way that they were out on the moors, roaring through
great torchlit meetings?[199] The Fraternal Democrats never held
meetings in torchlight! Chartist London was very different from
the rest of Chartist England—it was at once a vast and internally
divided environment. It was in contrast to the kinds of Chartism
that appeared from time to time in some places in the north and
midlands, Chartism that was monolithic, coherent and vigorous.
There are good reasons for this contrast. First of all, London was so
large that it really consisted of several towns in which radical agitations usually remained uncoordinated and local. Secondly, despite
the existence of some heavy industry, many workers toiled at a
great number of small trades in varied, stratified occupations. Many
were quite well off; many more were on the fringes of existence. In
the midlands and the north, much less heterogeneous conditions prevailed, because workers were often grouped around a few staple
industries, which meant that a bad local situation or grievance
would probably affect a high percentage of the workers. This is what
gave Chartism the terrible force it was able to display there from
time to time, which worked itself out in creating the highest social
tension and the most violence. Lancashire hands out of bread were
far more awesome as a revolutionary force than skilled London
artisans steeped in Thomas Paine, Babeuf, or whatever they
picked up from continental revolutionaries in exile. While London's
leading Chartists busied themselves in committees, northern
Chartists manufactured pikes and drilled at night. At worst,
London's leaders appeared to northern Chartists as corrupt atheists
or inept talkers, ineffective revolutionists in spirit only or moral
force 'old women'. Surely Harney, Jones, and their favourite
Chartist organisation shared in some of this disapprobation from the
provinces.[200]

If London's Chartism did not display the coherence, stamina and
unity that the Chartist movement occasionally possessed in the
north, it did offer other advantages. In large cities groups can more

readily be found to accept and appreciate new, varied, or novel ideas. Internationalist groups such as the Fraternal Democrats could easily get established in London. The important thing to keep in mind about this, however, is that a group such as the Fraternal Democrats could flourish in London, propagate their new ideas and yet be cut off from most of the workers in England, and, for that matter, they could very well have existed cut off from the vast majority of workers in the metropolis.[201]

This consideration of the nature of the London environment serves to reduce the significance of the Fraternal Democrats substantially. Several other factors share this reductive facility, and foremost among them is chronology. The activities of the Fraternal Democrats and their competitors fell into a period when Chartism's most important years were over. Despite the Chartist surge and flurries of 1848, the movement had been in decline and decay throughout Britain when the Chartist internationalists came forward with their organisations and pledges of universal proletarian brotherhood.[202]

The decline of the Chartist movement was matched by a decline in the circulation of the *Northern Star*, and many who purchased copies in the years of the Fraternal Democrats were primarily concerned with news of the Land Plan.[203] In the very years that proletarian internationalism was being expounded, thousands of workers shared Feargus O'Connor's obsession and put their hopes, interest, and shillings into the Land Plan's great lotteries. That the greatest Chartist leader could be so close to the Fraternal Democrats and yet so tepid about their causes gives a reason to suspect that the general rank and file up and down the land were as little concerned with their internationalism.

O'Connor's lieutenants at this time joined the Fraternal Democrats and supported the organisation from their positions on the Chartist executive. But they—McGrath, Clarke, Doyle and Wheeler —were an Irish Mafia, daring and eloquent, but newcomers to the movement in London and with little real following in the metropolis.[204]

The Fraternal Democrats did not need O'Connor's political connections to build up membership. The nineteenth century was a century for joiners, which multiplied all sorts of political and social organisations. There were some new groups for singers, temperance advocates, and tumblers as well as internationalists. Perhaps this phenomenon was, as some historians have argued, a result of the search for new definitions of position in life in an era where so many old, stratified, traditional bonds were breaking.

Those who joined Chartist internationalism found that this phase of the movement shared many characteristics of the whole movement: Chartist internationalism was divided into groups that would and groups that would not co-operate with middle-class radicals; it was educative; it was factious; it relied upon free speech, public meetings, petitions, demonstrations, addresses, and a free press. But while Chartist internationalism shared these characteristics of the whole movement, Chartism in general did not share their peculiar characteristic of internationalism. To put it quite simply, internationalism was not common to Chartism, and no number of quotations from G. J. Harney or from the addresses of the Fraternal Democrats can ever make it so. The impassive Chartist background generally has the effect of shrinking the efforts and achievements of Harney and his friends to much smaller proportions than those by which they chose to regard themselves. To substantiate this contention, it is worth noting that only the *Northern Star* and Ernest Jones' *Labourer* had a deep commitment to internationalism among Chartist newspapers, and even the *Star* itself was uncommitted until 1844.[205] The same can be said about Chartist leaders. The speeches, editorials, and letters of most of them show that Europe was generally ignored. Northern leaders, Joseph Rayner Stephens and Richard Oastler in particular, ignored European affairs almost entirely. Moreover, a key test of internationalism is whether working-class leaders were willing to draw analogies between British and European situations when they faced important problems and crises. Outside of the members of the Fraternal Democrats and the People's International League, they were not.

Another indication of the limited nature of Chartist internationalism may be weakness of its opposite, overt xenophobia in the movement. What there was of it was directed at named foreigners from the upper classes. Chance remarks in Chartist speeches and editorials indicate a common conviction that it was better to be English than to be foreign, but besides this, foreign workers, either in their homelands or resident in England, were generally not the subjects of xenophobic attacks. In the case of foreign workers in London this was probably due to the fact that they were not present in great enough numbers to have their status change from that of interesting novelty to economic threat. Workers overseas were regarded as fellow-sufferers, not responsible for the competition of cheap foreign goods, or they might be considered impersonally in economic calculations. Certainly some latent but passive xenophobia must have been below the surface. Otherwise, the Fraternal Democrats, Democratic Friends of All Nations, Democratic Committee for Poland's Regeneration, and People's International League would not all have sounded so much as if they were preaching new learning when they called upon workers to overcome national prejudices and ancient hostilities.

Finally, how could working-class internationalism be important if the People's International League could complain of '*absolutely* no symptom of public opinion' from the working class on foreign affairs and if Thomas Cooper could declare that the common attitude was 'grumbling contempt of other nations or indifference to the questions that agitate them?'[206]

All of these points serve to minimise the importance of Chartist internationalism and its foremost devotees, the Fraternal Democrats. Even so, they surely must derive considerable significance just from their collaboration with Marx and Engels—the point implied, mentioned, and stressed by many writers. The Fraternal Democrats, in this view, were the Chartists most informed by these great men, and therefore the most advanced segment of the whole Chartist movement. They were the bright, foamy crest, the forerunners of a wave of proletarian internationalism that was swelling in their direction. Even this aspect of Chartist internationalism is subject to considerable shrinkage when viewed in perspective. A key question is: how Marxist or proto-Marxist were they? Historians who have celebrated their 'advanced' position have carefully selected suitably 'advanced' portions of their addresses and speeches, usually the parts most vigorously class-conscious. The following excerpt have been quoted time and again by historians of the left:

The 'Proletarians of France' received an address which included these highly class-conscious expressions just before the revolution of 1848:

The Democratic movement in this country is emphatically a proletarian movement. The result will be a social reformation which will render political equality no longer an illusion. This movement, therefore, menaces all classes of the enemies of Labour. The privileged orders, consequently, are alarmed. Their alarm is increased by the extraordinary attitude of late assumed by the working millions of this country towards the nations of the continent. Isolated from their continental brethren, the working classes of Great Britain have, until within a few years past, been indifferent or hostile to other nations. But now, from the Seine to the Danube, from the Tagus to the Tiber, every movement for veritable liberty calls forth the good wishes of this people. . . . In all countries, the working men are subjected to political proscription and social suffering; their enemies are the same, and their interests are identical. Let, then, the Proletarians of all lands forget and mutually forgive the wicked and bloody feuds of the past, and work together for that happy future which shall witness their deliverance. . . .[207]

In the same month, just before news of the new revolutions in France arrived, George Julian Harney declared at a public meeting:

Now that the claws of kings are clipped, and aristocrats have had their teeth drawn, the people find in the bourgeoisie their most deadly enemy; an enemy which by turn uses fraud and force to delude and crush the proletarians. . . . The rule of the bourgeoisie is doomed; . . . their kingdom will be given to the proletarians.[208]

Harney had renounced all prospects of an alliance with the middle-class reformers just before, at a soirée:

Unite with the middle class? Unite rather with wolves, bloodhounds and tigers, honest monsters compared with that class whose conspiracies created the reign of terror and ruined the French Republic . . . whose treason to the people of this country is the cause of all the evils and miseries suffered at this moment by the working class.[209]

At another occasion, he stressed how workers' distress was international:

In each country the tyranny of the few and the slavery of the many are variously developed, but the principle in all is the same. . . . In all countries the men who grow wheat live on potatoes. The men who rear cattle do not taste flesh food. The men who cultivate the vine have only the dregs of its noble juice. The men who make clothing are in rags. The men who build the houses live in hovels. The men who create every necessity, comfort and luxury are steeped in misery.[210]

These were certainly militant proto-Marxist statements, at the very least, but what about the rest of the vast flood of internationalist propaganda pouring into the *Northern Star*? The quotations just cited were but a tiny fraction of the Fraternal Democrats' output, which, upon examination, turns out to be largely old-fashioned, consisting of democratic rhetoric couched in vague romantic effusions. The clichés of the Enlightenment and the French revolution are liberally sprinkled throughout. A sterling example is the song, 'All Men Are Brethren', written by Harney himself for the organisation:

> Hail to the flag of Fraternity flying,
> 'Nail'd to the mast' our bright banner waves,

> Kingly and Lordly brigands defying
> Breaking our fetters we scorn to be slaves.
>
> By the scourge of oppressors long we've been driven,
> Long have we bent 'neath the yoke and the chain;
> Our labour, our blood, our lives have been given
> To pamper the tyrants who scoff at our pain.
> The earth they have plunder'd
> Mankind they have sunder'd
> Nation 'gainst nation excited to war.
> But no more disunited,
> Our wrongs shall be righted,
> 'All men are Brethren! hip! hip! Hurrah!'
>
> Tremble, ye purple-clad, princely oppressors,
> Woe to ye, haughty and gold-grasping lords
> Curs'd be your false-hearted priestly abettors—
> More fatal their frauds than your blood-reeking swords.
> Like the cataract dashing,
> The avalanche crashing,
> The on-rushing millions shall scatter you far.
> Like the hurricane roaring,
> Their voices are soaring:
> 'All Men are Brethren! hip! hip! Hurrah!'[211]

Consider, too, this anniversary toast of the Fraternal Democrats, which was proposed in 1847:

May the society of the Fraternal Democrats, founded to propagate the principles of the French Republic, progress triumphantly, and advance in this and every other land the principles of Equality, Liberty, and Fraternity.[212]

In his private correspondence with Engels, Harney remained very independent intellectually, and expressed such views as regret at the calm disposition of the English people and his firm belief that 'a revolution in this country would be a vain and foolish project'.[213] When Engels effusively flattered him, Harney responded by claiming a more modest role, and in so doing claimed a more modest significance for the Fraternal Democrats themselves:

To myself my proper position appears clear; I am a 'pioneer', the teacher of 'strange doctrines', the proclaimer of principles which startle the many, and are but timidly acknowledged even by the few; and the office of the pioneer is surely useful, and as surely not inglorious.[214]

Was Harney really much of a pioneer? Radicals and liberals were also working in areas of interest to the Fraternal Democrats, which were, essentially, concern for refugees, vehement disapproval of foreign despotisms and their deeds and pacifism when 'unjust threatened. In taking up such causes, the Fraternal Democrat adding their voices to those of Lovett, O'Brien, Richard Cobden, and many others.

In a way it is really beside the point to demonstrate that the Fraternal Democrats were not Marxists or proto-Marxists to any marked degree, because Marxism itself was only being developed when the organisation flourished. Surely Marx and Engels learned much more from the Chartists than any group of Chartists learned from them, because the movement comprised the first independent working-class drive for democracy that they had the opportunity to observe.[215] Indeed, Chartist internationalism of the early forties was a young man's activity. Harney and Jones were 31 and 29 respectively at the outbreak of the revolutions of 1848. Marx would turn 30 in the year of revolutions, and Engels would turn 28. Schapper was the eldest of the leaders, but he was only 35.[216]

So the Fraternal Democrats dealt with Marx when he, too, was something of a proto-Marxist, and at a time when a teeming mass of ideas were being produced by a great number of theoreticians. The Fraternal Democrats only wanted to add Marx and Engels to the interesting people they knew, and include them in their busy round of speeches, addresses, songs, and drink. Their activities were harmless social politics and certainly not the stuff out of which revolutions were made.

Surely one particular contribution of the young Marx and the young Engels to the Fraternal Democrats which has been frequently cited by numerous writers was a heightened sense of class consciousness. Yet how much more class conscious and 'proletarian' were Harney's addresses of 1846 to 1848 than those of the LWMA before 1840?[217]

It must be concluded that the Fraternal Democrats do lose much of their self-advertised significance when they are viewed in perspective. Instead of being the bright, bubbly crest of a wave of internationalism, they resemble a foaming eddy in a movement that was a diverse, eclectic, irregular, restless hodgepodge. Nevertheless, the Fraternal Democrats were a small part of something greater and truly significant. Chartism, for all its shortcomings and failures, was educational for British workers. An educational process succeeds by degrees, and its accomplishments are hard to measure. Like Chartism in general, the Fraternal Democrats were educational and, in the same manner, successful to an unknown degree.

X AN EPILOGUE: TIVERTON

An almost forgotten episode in 1847 was in many ways more indicative of future working-class involvement with European affairs than the celebrated activities of the Fraternal Democrats. Before the century was over, male British workers could vote and, in the next century, the Labour party produced its own Foreign Secretaries. Historians have found their harbingers in the commemorative dinners, mass demonstrations of support for one or another European cause, the new vocabulary of international class consciousness, and the guiding vision of continental theoreticians. Yet it was not in the smoke filled taverns and halls of London where the Chartists and exiles hailed each other but in the Devon town of Tiverton, quiet then and quiet now, that an event took place which can be seen as a true harbinger of the more significant future development.[218]

A Chartist butcher named William Rowcliffe, a man with a local reputation for baiting Lord Palmerston on the hustings, was responsible for inviting George Julian Harney down to Tiverton to contest an election in Palmerston's own constituency.[219] Under the restrictive franchise of the day, Chartists who stood for seats had little hope of winning at the polls, but they stood a chance of winning the traditional show of hands preceding the poll and gaining a psychological boost thereby. What is more, they had the opportunity to address a wider audience, one that might include lords, squires, manufacturers, businessmen and farmers—persons who would ordinarily shun mass meetings and tavern gatherings given over to agitation for the Six Points.[220]

In many ways Palmerston and Harney were unfairly matched: Harney was only thirty; Palmerston sixty-three, with forty years of experience in Parliament behind him, a man noted for his formidable wit, repartee, and sarcasm. Harney's experience in public speaking had been gained primarily from appearances before enthusiastic throngs of workers who were willing to overlook his shortcomings on the platform. In bearing the two men were markedly dissimilar: Palmerston was at ease, urbane, and nonchalant, dressed in a bright blue coat and white trousers. Harney approached the contest in utter seriousness, formal in manner and sober in garb. Actually, neither man conformed to the upper-middle-class norms of respectability that were becoming increasingly important in Victoria's England. Harney was a democrat and a radical; Palmerston was an old Regency buck, rational, cynical, and jaunty—in contrast to so many sober, pious, and deeply serious Victorians who typified their age. Palmerston's popularity was in large measure due to his appeals to the deep tribal instincts of nationalism. He had a feeling and flair for cultivating and manipulating popular opinion, for he knew how to get his dispatches and pronouncements into middle-class homes via the newspapers. When dealing with the public, the old Regency buck was actually a man of the next century. Not even his opponent at Tiverton in 1847 could escape his magic entirely.

Their contest was noticed to the extent that several London reporters were sent to cover it, since they heard that the young Chartist intended to launch a general attack on Palmerston's foreign policy.[221] Harney arrived several days before the nomination and warmed his supporters with nightly speeches delivered from the window of a friend's house. Perhaps Palmerston, lodged close by, heard them. Anyway, when the day of open nominations arrived a crowd estimated at three thousand gathered before the hustings.[222] After a brass band had paraded past the parish church, Lord Palmerston made his appearance and the nominations began. A change in procedure then occurred: since Palmerston was a sitting member he should have spoken first. Because he had heard of Harney's planned attack on his foreign policy, Palmerston wanted his speech to serve as a reply.[223] A hubub ensued, for some of Harney's friends urged him not to forego his right of speaking last, but Harney, declaring that he 'wanted only fair play', agreed to speak first.[224]

Thereupon commenced the speeches which took up most of the seven hours of the whole proceedings. Coverage varied, with the respectable press conceding several columns to Palmerston and a paragraph or two to Harney, a process reversed in the *Northern Star*. The *Star* added its own flourishes, such as informing its readers in an aside that certain words of Harney 'and the manner of the speaker, who, looking directly at Lord Palmerston, seemed to hurl his accusations at the "noble Lord" ', produced an extraordinary sensation in the crowd. 'The Whigs were silenced and Palmerston bit his lip and turned whiter even than usual.'[225] Palmerston's witty, sarcastic style needed no such editorial assistance, either in the respectable press or in the pamphlet form in which his speech was circulated.[226] Taken together, the clashing speeches present the Chartist and Whig positions on the great questions of foreign policy. Harney accused the Whigs of professing to be the peace party, while bearing a record stained with a number of aggressive, expensive 'little' wars. Harney put the blame for the Opium War squarely on British merchants and free traders, whose 'insolence at last roused the Chinese to acts of retaliation' which were taken as a 'pretext' for a 'murderous onslaught. . .'. Therefore the British 'played the part of pirates and cut-throats to make the Chinese swallow poison'. The campaigns in Afghanistan were similarly nefarious. In the attempt to establish a ruler there who would collaborate, British blood had been needlessly shed, and the Afghans were subjected to 'numerous insults and cruel outrages', including those perpetrated on Afghan women. As Harney put it, 'it is a well ascertained fact that no man's wife or daughter was safe from the intrigues or violence of men calling themselves British officers'. There was no use in justifying British aggression on the grounds of affording greater safety to the Indian Empire. British workers had no stake in it, and besides, if the campaign were waged to create a barrier against Russian designs it failed miserably because Afghans, hitherto indifferent, were now ready to become Russian allies.

Harney did not hesitate to plunge into the complex Near Eastern Question. In his view, war in Syria had been undertaken to preserve the Turkish Sultan from Mehemet Ali. Harney professed that he had 'no great veneration' for the Egyptian rebel, but—a curious argument for a Chartist—'there was at least order in that country (Syria) under his rule, and persons and property were safe'. The Sultan's restoration, accomplished with Palmerston's aid, led to 'anarchy and misery' and 'horrible excesses'. Palmerston might declare that the deposition of Mehemet Ali was done to 'preserve the integrity of the Turkish Empire', but it was this rebel who was 'the only man capable of rallying the Mohammedan race against the Russians'. At that point Harney felt it necessary to declare that he did not accept Urquhart's well known accusation that Lord Palmerston was a Russian agent: 'For myself, I never believed anything of the sort. . . . I never believed Lord Palmerston to be any worse than the rest of his order.'

No speech of Harney's in 1847 could really be complete without a lament for the lost Free State of Cracow. Harney accused Palmerston of proclaiming 'cringing rubbish' in the place of a vigorous protest and sending 'waste paper' to the courts of the three eastern despots. As a result, the despots could 'grin contemptuous defiance' at 'this might of England, sovereign of the ocean, conqueror of

Napoleon . . . Oh! Shame! Shame!' What would he have done facing such a situation? A war for Cracow would be insufficient, but a war for all Poland was necessary. But 'the time is not yet. (cheers.)' He would have withdrawn ambassadors from Berlin, Vienna and St Petersburg and proclaimed: 'We will have no part with crowned faith-breakers and royal perjurers.' Once the alliance of England with despotic governments was broken he would 'seek to establish an alliance with the peoples of the world. (renewed cheering.)' No longer would the 'British lion play jackal' to the despots, as in the case of the sacrifice of Italian patriots to the Austrians in the scandalous case of the Mazzini letters.

Palmerston's response consisted of a broad, detailed defence of his foreign policy, a speech answering Harney point for point and aimed at showing how he fostered liberal constitutionalism and free trade throughout the world. As it might be expected, his defence was laced with patriotic braggadocio, pointed wit, and sarcastic barbs. Harney's accusation that his foreign policy aimed at the establishment of tyranny and despotism was dismissed in this fashion:

There is really something amusing in the novelty; for, after I have been accused all over Europe of being the great instigator of revolution—(laughter.)—the friend and champion of all popular insurrections, the enemy of all constituted authorities—after I have been charged with disturbing the peace of Europe by giving encouragement to every revolutionary and anarchical style of men—(renewed laughter.)—it is somewhat amusing to hear charges the very reverse made against me by my present opponent.[227]

Palmerston went on defending his policies, country by country, but seemed less at ease in treating non-European areas. He described British aid to Turkey as 'merely giving a few thousand muskets' to the Turks and landing 'a few hundred marines' to aid them, with the exhortation: 'Go it boys!—If you want to get rid of Mehemet Ali, here we are to back you; if you intend to act, now's your time—(a laugh.)' Campaigns in Afghanistan were defended on the grounds of protecting India, and Harney's remarks about the conduct of British troops there drew scornful remarks from the foreign secretary:

Mr Harney has, as I think with somewhat bad taste, launched into most wounding, and, as I sincerely believe, unfounded charges, against the officers of the British army. I believe he is totally in error in supposing that there is any foundation for such charges. British officers are men of honour; they behave gallantly in the field and honourably in quarters. . . .

Palmerston's explanation of the Opium War was dashing: the Chinese had 'protective and prohibitory' regulations to prevent 'the

importation of' an article that the people wanted. In such circumstances 'men will be found to risk a great deal to bring it in. . . '.
Then, suddenly, the authorities turned on the 'men who had been
their partners in this smuggling trade' and locked them up. That
was how thirty or forty British merchants came to be locked up
under the threat of starvation. Faced with this, Britain could stand
for 'no nonsense. (Laughter.) . . . We said "This won't do! this is no
go, gentlemen of China." (a laugh.)'

His rejoinder on the Cracow uprising came towards the end of his
remarks. He handled Harney's criticism of the mildness of the
British protest by declaring: 'I think that in the case of nations . . .
as well as of individuals, there is no dignity or wisdom in threatening
to do what you are not prepared, and may not be able, to accomplish'. The events surrounding the extinction of Cracow may have
been deplorable, but it was 'childish' to talk of going to war with
three great powers to re-establish the Republic of Cracow.

The foreign secretary concluded with a flourish:

My constituents here, and the country generally, will judge whether my
conduct has been right or wrong; and, strong in my own conscious rectitude,
and . . . firmly convinced that in the humble share which I have had in the
administration of the foreign affairs of this country, I have contributed to
the spread of constitutional liberty among foreign nations, and that there
are many millions of mankind who are now happier, better, and more
prosperous and contented in consequence of [it] . . . —I fearlessly commit
my cause to my old friends at Tiverton and abide without apprehension or
uneasiness the result of a poll, if a poll should be demanded by my opponent.

Harney made no such demand, but Palmerston did, once a show
of hands indicated, amidst a 'tumult of cheering', that Harney had
won. The poll took place the next day, but Harney refused to stand
for it, despite Palmerston's taunt to 'try his strength and test his
principles' by the contest. Harney simply declared that he had won
the election and left the scene.[228]

It had been a remarkable contest. The courtesies extended on
both sides were notable, considering the sharp blows struck by each
man.[229] Such graces might be expected of Palmerston's style, but
the way Harney accommodated himself to the process is reminiscent
of the stiff politness of some of the earliest working-class Members of
Parliament of the late nineteenth century. He even asked Palmerston
to 'give his compliments to Lord Morpeth' because Harney remembered Morpeth's kindnesses during a previous election contest in
Yorkshire. Palmerston answered by whisking his hat from his head

and bowing. The crowd roared.[230] In old age Harney had glowing praise for Palmerston's fairness and courtesy that day at Tiverton, and even noted that the mayor 'presided with perfect impartiality'. In Harney's recollection, the crowd was courteous as well, 'with but few exceptions' from amongst Palmerston's supporters. When Harney's followers in the crowd threatened disturbance, and interrupted Palmerston with shouts and cries, the foreign secretary 'folded his arms and smilingly enjoyed the fun'.[231]

Perhaps there is something poignant about Harney's statement that 'some day I may be in his Lordship's place' as foreign secretary of Great Britain. If the *Star* may be believed, the declaration produced 'sneering and laughter from Palmerston and great cheering from the people'.[232] When it was his turn, Palmerston replied:

But with all respect for him, and with the utmost desire to act with the most perfect courtesy towards him, I am not prepared at present either to give up to him my pretensions here or to put him into the Foreign Office—(laughter.) The day may come, indeed, as he has said, when he may be the director of the foreign policy of this country; and one thing I will promise him, that when that day comes I will not misrepresent his policy as, I think, he has misrepresented mine—(laughter, cries of 'Bravo' and some interruption.)[233]

They never saw each other again, but in the mellowness of old age the opponents recalled their contest with fondness. Harney wrote in 1894 that it was 'one remembered incident of my Chartist career which I can look back on with unalloyed satisfaction'. He admitted then that his speech 'was not all words of wisdom', but declared that most of his views on foreign topics remained similar.[234] After Palmerston's death Harney was told about an incident that had occurred in the House of Commons during the time that the Chartist leader was in America. Radical visitors were in the lobbies, soliciting subscriptions for sick and indigent radicals from Liberal members. As Palmerston approached:

Said one of the party—'Here comes Pam, let us try him'. The idea was pooh-pooh'd; but it was carried out by the suggester. Lord Palmerston . . . responded with his usual kindly liberality. . . . He had faced towards the chamber of the Commons, when suddenly turning back, he enquired, 'Can you tell me what has become of an old Chartist acquaintance of mine, Mr George Julian Harney?' . . . An older man of the group said he believed Julian Harney was in America. Lord Palmerston rejoined, 'Well, I wish him good fortune; he gave me a dressing down at Tiverton some years ago and I have not heard of him since; but I hope he is doing well.'[235]

Harney wrote his reminiscences long after the violent fires of youth had been banked, long after he had ceased to aspire to the role of

Marat in an English revolution. His zeal and the zeal of countless British workers had cooled in the prosperous, triumphant years of Victorian capitalism, a time which saw the broadening of the political base and a time when nationalism filled much of the place that the youthful Harney had decreed for working-class internationalism. Perhaps these remarks from Harney's pen in 1894 may serve to indicate the victory of nationalism and imperialism, as well as the victory of Lord Palmerston himself:

One word more. Could Lord Palmerston have been living now, and still member for Tiverton, I have no doubt of his attitude in relation to the Home Rule question. At an election, had he been opposed by a Gladstonian, and had I appeared at Tiverton, it would not have been as another opponent, but as a supporter of his candidature, proud . . . to stand on the same Imperial platform to combat for the integrity of the United Kingdom and the maintenance of the British Empire against all enemies—whether foreign foes or domestic traitors.[236]

Notes to Chapter 4

1 *Northern Star*, June 8, 1839, p. 3.

2 Excellent accounts of aspects of the history of Polish exiles in Britain are in articles by Peter Brock: 'Polish democrats and English radicals, 1832–1862: a chapter in the history of Anglo-Polish relations', *Journal of Modern History*, vol. 25, no. 2 (June 1953), pp. 139–56; 'The Polish revolutionary commune in London', *Slavonic and East European Review*, vol. xxxv, no. 84 (December 1956), pp. 116–28; 'The birth of Polish socialism', *Journal of Central European Affairs*, vol. xiii, no. 3 (October 1953), pp. 213–31; 'Joseph Cowen and the Polish Exiles', *Slavonic and East European Review*, vol. xxxii, no. 78 (December 1953), pp. 52–69; 'Polish socialists in early Victorian England: three documents', *The Polish Review*, vol. vi, no. 1–2 (1961), pp. 33–52. Other sources are Günther Weber, *Die polnische Emigration im neunzehnten Jahrhundert* (Essen, 1937); John Howes Gleason, *The Genesis of Russophobia in Great Britain* (Cambridge, Mass., 1950); Robert F. Leslie, *Polish Politics and the Revolution of November, 1830* (London, 1956); Henry Weisser, 'Polonophilism and the British working class, 1830–1845', *The Polish Review*, vol. xii, no. 2 (Spring 1967), pp. 78–96; 'The British working class and the Cracow uprising of 1846', *The Polish Review*, vol. xiii, no. 1 (Winter 1968), pp. 3–19. The exact number of exiles is uncertain. It probably never exceeded 10,000 and was probably somewhat less. Paris had many more of them than London.

3 See the biography by Marian Kukiel, *Czartoryski and European Unity, 1770–1861* (Princeton, 1955). There are scattered references to him and his followers in Weber, *op. cit.* and Leslie, *op. cit.*, p. 270.

4 From 1834 to 1838 this group disposed of funds set aside by the government for relieving indigent Polish émigrés, and could, if it wished, remove some Poles from the list of beneficiaries. See Brock, 'Polish democrats and English radicals', p. 141.

5 Leslie, *Polish Politics and the Revolution of November, 1830*, p. 269.

6 Brock, 'Polish democrats and English radicals', pp. 140–7; A. Müller-Lehning, *The International Association, 1855–1859*, p. 9; Julius West, *A History of the Chartist Movement*, p. 229; There is a simplified chart of the differences between the two wings in Weber, *Die polnische Emigration im neunzehnten Jahrhundert*, p. 71.

7 Leslie, *Polish Politics and the Revolution of November, 1830*, pp. 270–9, describes four groups of Polish exiles in Paris at the time.

8 It was Harney's boast in later life that 'since he was seventeen years of age he

had enjoyed the confidence of the Polish exiles'. See the *Northern Star*, December 26, 1846; Brock, 'Joseph Cowen and the Polish exiles', p. 57; Schoyen, *The Chartist Challenge*, pp. 51, 135. Many Polish left-wingers were in *Młoda Polska*, or 'Young Poland', and tended to associate with British middle-class radicals and moral force Chartists rather than with the Chartist left. In addition there were two groups of socialist exiles; one composed of gentry, was on the Isle of Jersey and the other, one hundred and forty rank and file, settled in barracks at Portsmouth. The Portsmouth group formed an organisation of considerable importance in Polish history, *Lud Polski*, or 'The Polish People'. Brock, 'The birth of Polish socialism', p. 217.

9 One Russian exile described him as 'a figurehead . . . not very bright. . .'. Brock, 'The Polish revolutionary commune in London', p. 123. Regardless of some rumours which stated that he fell while fighting in 1848, Oborski lived to a ripe old age.

10 An uninspiring example of an Oborski speech is in the *Northern Star* of February 21, 1846, p. 6.

11 Harney was in Sheffield at this time and probably inspired the document. It appeared in the *Northern Star*, December 13, 1841, p. 7.

12 See Peter Brock, 'Polish Democrats and English Radicals', pp. 139–56.

13 *London Mercury*, December 4, 1836, p. 91.

14 The Polish Democratic Manifesto appeared in the *London Mercury*, April 6, 1837, and the East London Democratic Association response in the issue of June 4, 1837.

15 *Northern Star*, December 13, 1841, p. 7. *Lud Polski's* rejection of the Literary Association is in the *Chartist Circular*, pp. 73–80, 171, 194.

16 *Northern Star*, December 30, 1843. Also December 13, 1845, p. 7; December 4, 1847, p. 1; February 26, 1848, p. 3.

17 *Northern Star*, December 13, 1845, p. 7; Philip McGrath's remarks in the *Northern Star* of March 28, 1846, p. 1; Ernest Jones' remarks in the issue of May 16, 1846, p. 8. See also April 4, 1846, p. 4.

18 See the address of the 'Polish Exiles United Under the National Banner' in the *Northern Star* of March 28, 1846, p. 4.

19 For a Chartist response, see *Northern Star*, December 13, 1846, p. 7. The espousal of an exclusive Anglo-Polish working-class consciousness went too far for some Chartists and radicals. *The Reasoner*, Holyoake's publication, of June 10, 1846, p. 18, expressed impatience with exclusive, dogmatic class consciousness.

20 *Northern Star*, December 5, 1846, p. 18.

21 *Northern Star*, May 23, 1846, p. 8.

22 The meeting was held in the National Hall on May 20, 1846, and reported in the *Northern Star* of May 23, 1846, p. 8.

23 *Northern Star*, March 21, 1846. Quoted in Rothstein, *From Chartism to Labourism*, p. 136; Brock, 'Polish Democrats and English Radicals', p. 150.

24 *Northern Star*, February 27, 1847, p. 7.

25 *Northern Star*, November 15, 1845, p. 7. Lelewel's remarks are in the issue of December 4, 1847, p. 1; an address of *Lud Polski* in *Northern Star*, December 13, 1846, p. 7; also the issues of May 23, 1846, p. 8.

26 *Northern Star*, December 13, 1845, p. 7; see also the address of the Democrats of Sheffield, *Northern Star*, December 13, 1841, p. 7. Poland was usually regarded as a frontier of civilisation (*Northern Star*, December 30, 1843, p. 4).

27 *Northern Star*, October 16, 1847, p. 1.

28 See Schapper's remarks in the *Northern Star*, March 28, 1846, p. 1, an article on the subject in the same issue, and another article in the *Northern Star* of December 30, 1843, p. 4.

29 *Northern Star*, November 20, 1841. Another old idea expressed in the forties was that the English people themselves would be the ones who would save or restore Poland, but they had to achieve their political rights in England first. See the *Operative*, November 11, 1838, p. 21; *Northern Star*, June 15, 1844, p. 6; December 13, 1841, p. 7.

30 G. S. R. Kitson-Clark, 'The romantic element, 1830–1850', in J. H. Plumb ed., *Studies in Social History: A Tribute to G. M. Trevelyan* (London, 1957).

31 *Northern Star*, December 13, 1841, p. 7.

32 *Northern Star*, June 15, 1844, p. 6.

33 *Northern Star*, November 29, 1845, p. 7. *The Times* had criticised such incidents as 'overcharged'.

34 *Northern Star*, February 28, 1848, p. 3.

35 *Northern Star*, February 14, 1843.

36 *Northern Star*, August 28, 1847, p. 4.

37 For other noteworthy examples, see the *Northern Star*, March 21, 1846, p. 8; the *Destructive and Poor Man's Conservative*, November 30, 1833.

38 It was probably written by Jones. See also, the *Northern Star*, December 4, 1847, p. 5, where Irishmen were depicted as 'people who have suffered all and perhaps more than all suffered by the Poles. . .'. Irishmen and Poles were similar in that each had 'the most infernal means' tried upon them to 'force them to abjure their religion, language, laws, and customs . . .'.

39 Werner Brettschneider, *Entwicklung and Bedeutung des deutschen Frühsozialismus in London* (Königsberg, 1936), comes closest to making this claim, p. 40.

40 Hermann Schlütter, *Die Chartisten-Bewegung*, stressed the uniqueness of English class consciousness (p. 217). Rothstein saw the Germans leading British workers towards a higher understanding of their situation. 'Weitling and Schapper', he wrote in *From Chartism to Labourism*, p. 28, 'were never tired of bringing home to their English brothers that the proletariat of the world is one and has only one enemy, the international bourgeoisie. . . .' Brettschneider, *Entwicklung und Bedeutung des deutschen Frühsozialismus in London*, p. 42, makes the point that German handworkers in London led Chartism towards internationalism, overcoming 'narrow, insular views'. On the other hand, Herwig Förder, *Marx und Engels am Vorabend der Revolution* (Berlin, 1960), p. 128, claims that English workers, because of their advanced class relationships, made German workers in London think beyond their handworkers' communism to more modern class consciousness. From such statements and from the nature of the situation it can be readily concluded that each group learned much from the other.

41 To be sure, big industry had made its appearance along the Rhine, in Saxony and Silesia, and handloom weavers had burst into rebellion in a few places. There was even a riot against labour-saving machinery in Aachen. See Theodore S. Hammerow, *Restoration, Revolution, Reaction: Economics and Politics in Germany, 1815–1871* (Princeton, 1958); Carl Wittke, *The Utopian Communist: A Biography of Wilhelm Weitling* (Baton Rouge, 1950); P. H. Noyes, *Organization and Revolution: Working Class Associations in the German Revolutions of 1848–1849* (Princeton, 1966), pp. 15–54. Noyes observed (pp. 9, 20) that 'by the time of the 1848 uprisings . . . only the beginnings' of industry were present. The working class 'was made up largely of guild artisans who sought to carry out old skilled trades in the face of increasing threats from domestic and foreign factories'.

42 Literally, 'wandering years'. J. Watson, *Young Germany: An Account of German Communism and a Report of the Proceedings at a Banquet Given by the English Socialists to Commemorate Wilhelm Weitling's Arrival in England* (London, 1844) (title abbreviated!).

43 Tailors were like British shoemakers in their undeniable penchant for radical politics and many of them had some direction given to their *Wanderjahre* by the actions of unfriendly governments.

44 Marx and Engels felt that this was a narrow-minded, anti-intellectual and unsuitable outlook for a world where an industrial proletariat was becoming increasingly common. See Gustav Mayer, *Friedrich Engels: A Biography* (London, 1956), p. 165; Franz Mehring, *Karl Marx—The Story of His Life* (New York, 1935), pp. 161–73; Engels, *Germany: Revolution and Counter-Revolution*, p. 125; E. Kandel and S. Lewiowa, 'Marx und Engels als Erzieher der ersten proletarischen Revolutionäre', in E. P. Kandel, ed., *Marx und Engels und die ersten proletarischen Revolutionäre* (Berlin, 1965), pp. 10–11.

45 Engels, *Germany: Revolution and Counter-Revolution*, p. 120; Wittke, *The Utopian Communist*, p. 29; Müller-Lehning, *The International Association*, p. 10; H. Forder, *Marx und Engels am Vorabend der Revolution*, p. 128.

46 Continental leaders often created disciples during incarceration, which frequently gave mystical bonds to conspiratorial organisations. It was not uncommon for continental leaders to be unknown to the rank and file, for security, and ideological goals were sometimes known only to the highest-ranking members.

See Elizabeth L. Eisenstein, *The First Professiona Revolutionist: Filippo Michelie Buonarroti, A Biographical Essay* (Cambridge, Mass., 1959). Eric Hobsbawm makes the point that as Continental societies became increasingly proletarian ritual sharply declined. He uses the changes that came over the German workers in London in the forties as one of his examples in *Primitive Rebels: Studies in Archaic Forms of Social Movement in the 19th and 20th Centuries* (Manchester and New York, 1959; latest ed. 1971), pp. 167–74.

47 Eisenstein, *The First Professional Revolutionist*, bibliographical notes.

48 Wittke, *The Utopian Communist*, p. 20; Müller-Lehning, *The International Association*, pp. 10–11; Engels, *Germany: Revolution and Counter-Revolution*, pp. 119–22. Engels claimed that the German organisation was really a branch of the French secret society for some time. For a contemporary source, scarcely trustworthy, see Thomas Frost, *The Secret Societies of the European Revolution, 1776–1876*, 2 vols. (London, 1876).

49 The hierarchy had the names, from highest echelon down, of burning point, order, provincial camp, bivouac and tent. Wittke, *The Utopian Communist*, mentions that such terms are less awkward in German (p. 26).

50 To German exiles and historians it was or is variously known as the *Londoner Arbeiterbildungsverein, Londoner Bildungsverein, Deutsche Bildungsverein für Arbeiter, Bildungs Gesellschaft für Arbeiter* and *Deutsche Bildungs-Gesellschaft für Arbeiter*.

51 John Saville, ed., *Ernest Jones: Chartist* (London, 1952), p. 84; H. Förder, *Marx und Engels am Vorabend der Revolution*, p. 128; Engels, *Germany: Revolution and Counter-Revolution*, p. 124. At first membership was scanty, but during the life-span of the Fraternal Democrats it was probably around 700. The organisation actually continued in existence until 1917.

52 Fehling, *Karl Schapper und die Anfänge der Arbeiterbewegung bis zur Revolution von 1848* (Rostock, 1922), p. 6.

53 *Ibid.*

54 Wittke, *The Utopian Communist*, p. 101.

55 The first part of the description is in the *Northern Star*, February 13, 1847, p. 6, and the very last in the issue of January 1, 1848, p. 3. Also Saville, *Ernest Jones, Chartist*, p. 88.

56 B. Nicolaevsky, 'Toward a history of the Communist League, 1847–1852', *International Review of Social History*, 1 (1956), pp. 235–7. Numerous entries in the bibliography are sources studied for this topic, but Nicolaevsky's premiss about the paucity of documentary material is confirmed by them.

57 Engels, *Germany: Revolution and Counter-Revolution*, pp. 128–9. Noyes, *Organization and Revolution*, p. 41, discounts the influence of Marx on them.

58 Engels, *Germany: Revolution and Counter-Revolution*, pp. 128–30; Mayer, *Friedrich Engels*, p. 4; Müller-Lehning, *The International Association*, pp. 10–11; Fehling, *Karl Schapper*, p. 90; Förder, *Marx und Engels am Vorabend der Revolution*, p. 128.

59 W. J. Linton, *European Republicans, Recollections of Mazzini and His Friends* (London, 1892), p. 55.

60 Mazzini's relations with the Chartists are taken up in a subsequent section of this chapter.

61 Max Nettlau, 'Marxanalekten: II. Zu Marx' und Engel's Aufenthalt in London, Ende 1847', in Carl Grünberg, ed., *Archiv für die Geschichte des Socialismus und Arbeiterbewegung*, vol. 8 (Leipzig, 1919 and 1921), p. 392; A. Lehning, 'Discussions à Londres sur le Communisme Icarien', *Bulletin of the International Institute for Social History* (1952), p. 94.

62 Fehling, *Karl Schapper und die Anfänge der Arbeiterbewegung bis zur Revolution von 1848*, p. 56.

63 For these Frenchmen see the brief sketches in Jean Maitron, ed., *Dictionnarie biographique du mouvement ouvrier francais, première partie, 1789–1864*. Berrier-Fontaine is described in vol. 1 (Paris, 1964), p. 204, and Michelot in vol. III (Paris, 1966), p. 95.

64 One dissertation on Schapper is August Fehling, *Karl Schapper und die Anfänge der Arbeiterbewegung bis zur Revolution von 1848, ein Beitrag zur Geschichte des Handwerkerkommunismus* (Rostock, 1922), which has been criticised in a recent Soviet article, S. Lewiowa, 'Karl Schapper', in E. Kandel, ed., *Marx und Engels und die*

ersten proletarischen Revolutionäre (Berlin, 1965), pp. 76–119. Criticisms of Fehling's account are in the end notes on p. 503.

65 *Northern Star*, November 15, 1845, p. 7.

66 *Northern Star*, February 14, 1846.

67 *Northern Star*, February 26, 1848, p. 3.

68 Engels, *Germany: Revolution and Counter-Revolution*, p. 120. For another description of him, see the *Northern Star*, October 3, 1846, p. 6.

69 S. Lewiowa, 'Karl Schapper', *loc. cit.*, p. 93.

70 For a biographical article on Moll, see N. Beloussowa, 'Joseph Moll', in E. Kandel, ed., *Marx und Engels und die ersten proletarischen Revolutionäre*, pp. 42–75.

71 There is a fine full length biography of Harney, A. R. Schoyen, *The Chartist Challenge: A Portrait of George Julian Harney* (London, Melbourne, and Toronto, 1958). Cole has a portrait of him in *Chartist Portraits*, pp. 268–99. Both sources have been criticised by W. Kunina, 'George Julian Harney', in E. Kandel, ed., *Marx und Engels und die ersten proletarische Revolutionäre*, pp. 421–55. In a note on p. 546 the Soviet historian complains that Cole treated him like a 'white raven'. Schoyen is accused of not placing his relations with Marx and Engels in the proper light because of anti-communist bias. A useful collection of primary material has recently been published: Frank Gees Black and Renee Métivier Black, eds., *The Harney Papers* (Assen, 1969). It includes a letter stating that he joined the German Democratic Society in 1846 (Harney to Engels, March 30, 1846, item 247, p. 242).

72 Cole, *Chartist Portraits*, p. 268. For Harney's use of French revolutionary symbolism, see Schoyen, *The Chartist Challenge*, pp. 14, 38, 44, 48, 50, 53, 62, 65, 82. Like most Chartists, he was inconsistent in holding his position towards the use of force, and tended to moderate with age and hardship.

73 R. G. Gammage, *The History of the Chartist Movement*, p. 37.

74 Engels had flattered him by calling him 'international . . . revolutionary . . . energetical . . . proletarian . . . more of a Frenchman than an Englishman . . . atheistical, Republican and Communist. . .'. Engels wanted him to assume a greater role of Chartist leadership. Harney confided to Engels that he did not have the physical or oratorical prerequisites for leadership. Nor did he have 'great animal courage, contempt of pain and death' and knowledge of military affairs. He concluded that he was 'but one of the humble workers in the great movement of progress'. Black and Black, *The Harney Papers* Harney to Engels March 30, 1846, item 247, pp. 241–2. Other estimates are in Lovett, *Life and Struggles* (1920 ed.), p. 125; Thomas Frost, *Forty Years' Recollections* (London, 1880), p. 103. Many provincial Chartists saw him as a 'professional' Chartist, regularly paid by O'Connor for his efforts, and, as one derisively remarked, Harney had 'never known what real work was' (Richard Otley, a Sheffield Chartist, quoted in John Salt, *Chartism in South Yorkshire* (Sheffield, 1967), p. 22). Rumours circulated and persisted that Harney had been hired as a police spy, even while he was hounded and prosecuted by the authorities.

75 *Northern Star*, March 7, 1846, p. 6. There is a good biographical sketch of him in the long introduction to John Saville, ed., *Ernest Jones: Chartist: Selections from the Writings and Speeches of Ernest Jones with Introduction and Notes* (London, 1952). Cole has a chapter on him in *Chartist Portraits* and there is a recent Soviet historian's essay on him: W. Galkin. 'Ernest Jones' in E. Kandel, ed., *Marx und Engels und die ersten proletarischen Revolutionäre*. The Jones papers at Columbia University definitely indicate an atmosphere of gentility in the Jones household. It is unfortunate that Ernest Jones' Diary, in manuscript at the Manchester Central Reference Library, is so taciturn. Only brief and matter-of-fact references are given for his activities as a member of the Fraternal Democrats and other organisations involving foreigners. The diary covers the years 1839 to 1847.

76 George Howell, 'Diary and Newspaper Clippings about Ernest Jones, Chartist, Poet and Orator', *Columbia University Microfilms*. Jones noted in his *Diary* that on November 17, 1846, and January 12, 1847, he 'lectured to the German Democrats in German'. One German exile's appreciation of him is recorded in Friedrich Lessner, 'Vor 1848 und nachher. Errinerungen eines alten Kommunisten', *Deutsche Worte*, *Monatshefte*, XVIII, 1898, p. 110.

77 An introduction to his poems in the *Northern Star* of July 4, 1846, p. 3, noted: 'We must have high hopes for the future when such men as Ernest Jones cast their

lot with the people.' Gammage conceded his favourable impression on Chartists but explained: 'An aristocrat is always most acceptable to the working class, even by democrats, and the young sprig of aristocracy, promoted, as O'Connor would have said, to the ranks of the democracy, was received with enthusiasm'. Gammage complimented his oratorical powers and ability to flatter, but expressed mistrust as well (*History of the Chartist Movement*, 1969 ed.), p. 282. A laudatory evaluation is in G. J. Holyoake, *Sixty Years of an Agitator's Life* (London, 1892), pp. 248–54.

78 Cole, *Chartist Portraits*, p. 300; also, P. W. Slosson, *The Decline of the Chartist Movement*, p. 200.

79 *The Labourer*, vol. II, pp. 212–15.

80 *Northern Star*, May 4, 1844, p. 4. The new location of the *Star's* offices in Great Windmill Street was indeed propitious for such a commitment because the German Workers' Educational Society was quite close.

81 During the most exciting months of 1839, circulation was over 50,000 per week, which slid to 30,000 by the end of that year and down to 6,000 by 1846, based upon stamp returns: Donald Read and Eric Glasgow, *Feargus O'Connor, Irishman and Chartist* (London, 1961), pp. 59–62. See also Schoyen, *The Chartist Challenge*, pp. 124–7; Eric Glasgow, 'The establishment of the *Northern Star* newspaper', *History*, XXXIX (February and June 1954), pp. 54–67. Since it was very common for groups of readers to share a single copy, greater significance must be given to these figures. In its best months of all, the *Star* could rival *The Times* in circulation.

82 There were actually fewer popular radical newspapers during the Chartist period than in the early thirties. The *Northern Star*, stamped, and priced at $4\frac{1}{2}d$, was unique in paying its way for a considerable time. D. J. Rowe, 'The London Working Men's Association and the People's Charter', *Past and Present*, 36 (April 1967), p. 77.

83 *Northern Star*, November 13, 1847, p. 3.

84 To quote one hostile contemporary: 'It was almost the only paper that the Chartists read, and it had in consequence a very extended circulation.' O'Connor's editorial letters were 'generally . . . full of claptrap. . . . But the turgid claptrap took. The people of that period seemed to relish denunciation, and O'Connor gave them plenty of it' (W. E. Adams, *Memoirs of A Social Atom*, p. 204).

85 R. G. Gammage, *The History of the Chartist Movement* (1969 ed.), p. 17.

86 *The National Reformer and Manx Weekly Review of Home and Foreign Affairs*, January 16, 1847, p. 47. O'Brien and O'Connor were feuding at this time.

87 A good example is found in a controversy with Thomas Cooper. To Cooper's single letter in the *Star*, Harney replied with several editorials and reproduced the speeches of the leading members of the Fraternal Democrats condemning Cooper. *Northern Star*, April 25, 1846, p. 7. For the only example of a controversy at a meeting of the Fraternal Democrats, see the *Northern Star* of July 27, 1846, p. 5. The controversy with Cooper is presented in full later in this chapter.

88 They first indicated their existence by publishing an address to the working classes of Great Britain and the United States over the Oregon controversy, which appeared in the *Northern Star* of March 7, 1846, p. 6. According to an article of September 26, 1846, p. 1, the organisation celebrated its first anniversary in September 1846.

89 A. R. Schoyen, *The Chartist Challenge*, pp. 137–8.

90 Black and Black, *The Harney Papers*, Harney to Engels, March 30, 1846, item 247, p. 244.

91 *Northern Star*, September 26, 1846, p. 1.

92 *Northern Star*, January 8, 1848, p. 1.

93 McGrath maintained that addresses of the society on the subject were 'of the utmost importance' and very welcome. Even so, the public airing of this question indicates that suspicions about the Fraternal Democrats were held by some O'Connorite Chartists. At other times the internationalists had more or less to pledge allegiance to the Charter: *Northern Star*, March 7, 1846, p. 6; March 21, 1846, p. 1; November 20, 1847, p. 5; Charles Keen's speech, *Northern Star*, December 4, 1847, p. 1; Harney's speech, *Northern Star*, August 14, 1847, p. 7. Also, Rothstein, *From Chartism to Labourism*, p. 132.

94 The old idea of a holy alliance of the people was broadcast in an editorial of September 9, 1843, p. 4; an article of May 4, 1844, entitled the 'Movement'

stressed the need of that newspaper to take a greater interest in foreign affairs, because the struggle of the 'millions' was world wide. Engels joined the list of *Northern Star* correspondents in 1844. There was also an article, 'The Fraternity of Nations', June 22, 1844.

95 See Watson, *Young Germany . . . A Memoir of Wilhelm Weitling . . .*; Müller-Lehning, *The International Association*, p. 11; Wittke, *The Utopian Communist*; Emil Kaler, 'Wilhelm Weitling, seine Agitation und Lehre', *Sozialdemokratische Bibliothek*, XI (Zürich, 1887), pp. 72–3. It is generally conceded that Weitling's reputation was much greater than that of Marx at this time. Although he was in England for over a year and a half, he spent most of his time smoking and drinking with his fellow-Germans and supporting himself as a tailor and dressmaker. He lectured now and then and attended meetings of the League of the Just, but his favourite topics often were mechanical inventions and plans for a new world language. He seems to have had little to do with London Chartism.

96 *Northern Star*, July 27, 1844, p. 6. The French democrats had the meeting and funds were collected at it for Spanish refugees. There were other such occasions before September 22, 1845, including a meeting to celebrate the anniversary of the Democratic Association. See the *Northern Star* of August 16, 1845, p. 8.

97 A full report is in the *Northern Star* of September 28, 1844, p. 1 It too celebrated the founding of the first French Republic on September 22, 1792.

98 *Northern Star*, September 27, 1845, p. 5.

99 *Rheinische Jahrbücher zur gesellschaftlichen Reform*, vol. II, 1846, pp. 1–19.

100 *Northern Star*, September 26, 1846.

101 The publication of rules in the March 21, 1846 issue of the *Northern Star* shows that until that date the society existed without any.

102 *Northern Star*, March 21, 1846, p. 1. Also, March 7, 1846, p. 6.

103 *Northern Star*, December 18, 1847, p. 4.

104 *Northern Star*, September 26, 1846.

105 Harney announced in July 1846 that *The Times, Morning Chronicle, Morning Advertiser, Daily News, Sun, Standard, Globe* and *Douglas Jerrold's Weekly Newspaper* had rejected a recent declaration of the Fraternal Democrats (*Northern Star*, July 25, 1846, p. 8). In December the *Morning Advertiser* and the *Sun* published the Fraternal Democrats' 'Address to the Democrats of Europe' (*Northern Star*, December 26, 1846, p. 5). Harney complained to Marx and Engels on July 20, 1846, that 'no paper will print anything they give birth to except the *Northern Star*' (Black and Black, *The Harney Papers*, p. 246).

106 The results were disappointing. Some Chartists groups responded by pleading their financial difficulties. For example, the Chartist Council of Preston regretted inability to comply, but noted that 'no one possessing the heart of an Englishman' could do otherwise than 'feel he is performing a noble duty' in contributing to the missionaries' fund, 'but such is the misery that surrounds the working classes in this district that no other subject is at present thought of' (*Northern Star*, July 17, 1847, p. 3).

107 Schoyen, *The Chartist Challenge*, p. 140. Lists of members with addresses appeared in the *Star* from time to time. Both large and small communities were represented. See the *Northern Star* of July 24, 1847, p. 7, for an example. The *Star* of July 25, 1846 contained a proposal of the Fraternal Democrats that 'Democrats . . . not residing in London might become members after two nominate them and a majority of those present at the nominating meeting approve of them'.

108 Short advertisements, complete with little pointing fingers, were inserted in the *Northern Star* from time to time, reading something like this: 'Persons in England, or elsewhere, wishing to become members of the above society, are requested to forward their names, etc., to G. Julian Harney, *Northern Star* office. . . .'

109 Oborski regularly signed for the Poles; a Scandinavian, Peter Holm, for his region; J. Schabelitz usually signed for Switzerland; J. A. Michelot signed for the French democrats.

110 It appeared in English, French, and German on the top; Dutch, Danish, and Swedish on the left; Italian, Spanish, and Romanian on the right; Russian, Polish, and Hungarian at the bottom. Thomas Frost wondered whether they had members enough to correspond with the languages on their cards (Thomas Frost, *Forty Years' Recollections*, p. 125).

111 *Northern Star*, February 13, 1847, p. 4.
112 'Address to the Working Class of Great Britain and the United States', *Northern Star*, March 7, 1846, p. 6; 'Address to the Democrats of All Nations', September 26, 1846, p. 1; 'Address to the Democrats of Europe', October 2, 1847, p. 1; 'Address to the National Diet of Switzerland', December 18, 1847, p. 5; 'Address to the Democrats of Great Britain', January 8, 1848, p. 1; 'Address to the Proletarians of France', February 5, 1848, p. 1.
113 *Northern Star*, December 18, 1847, p. 4. Much of the same was declared in their 'Address to the Democrats of All Nations', September 26, 1846, p. 1.
114 For major expressions of concern over French affairs, see the *Northern Star* of July 18, 1846, p. 8, an editorial against Louis Philippe, September 11, 1847, p. 4; a portion of an address, October 2, 1847, p. 1; a speech by Harney, October 30, 1847; p. 1, also July 25, 1846, p. 8; September 26, 1846, p. 1; December 26, 1846, p. 5; for Switzerland, see the address to Switzerland, December 18, 1847, p. 5, and October 2, 1847, p. 1; North America, March 7, 1846, p. 6, July 11, 1846, p. 7; Spain, an editorial of August 21, 1847, p. 7; Portugal, July 10, 1847, p. 7, August 7, 1847, p. 5, August 21, 1847, p. 7; Greece, October 2, 1847, p. 1; the Near East, July 11, 1846, p. 7; Italy, an extensive speech by Ernest Jones, September 25, 1847, p. 8; October 16, 1847, p. 1, and October 2, 1847, p. 1; Germany (Prussia), October 2, 1847, p. 1; the Caucasus, October 2, 1847, p. 1.
115 For aspects of the Cracow uprising, see *The Cambridge History of Poland, 1697–1935*, vol. II (Cambridge, 1951), pp. 342–4, 352–64; Robert A. Kann, *The Multinational Empire: Nationalism and National Reform in the Habsburg Monarchy, 1848–1918*, vol. I (New York, 1950). For the career of John Tyssowski, see M. Neomisia Rutowska, 'John Tyssowski', *Bulletin of the Polish Institute of Arts and Sciences in America*, vol. II, no. 4 (July 1944), pp. 1128–42. For this subject in general, see Henry Weisser, 'The British working class and the Cracow uprising of 1846', *The Polish Review*, vol. XIII, no. 1 (Winter 1968), pp. 3–19. The Cracow Manifesto is presented in this as an appendix, and the document is the version printed in the *Northern Star* of February 26, 1848, p. 3. The suppression of the regime was another example of how the unstable Austrian Empire used class against class to hold itself together. After heavy fighting, the 425 square miles of the Free State of Cracow were annexed to Austrian Galicia.
116 *The Times*, March 12 and 13, 1846. Also debates in the House of Lords, Hansard, *Parliamentary Debates*, third series, vol. 85, pp. 574–7; vol. 87, pp. 1361–78; vol. 88, pp. 602–21; House of Commons, vol. 85, pp. 958–9; vol. 88, pp. 816–38. Even radicals, such as Joseph Hume, had little enthusiasm for the revolutionary regime itself.
117 Peter Brock, 'Polish Democrats and English Radicals, 1832–1862', p. 149.
118 The German Workers' Educational Society met and raised £4 10s 6d for the insurgents. The Fraternal Democrats, meeting shortly thereafter, were only able to muster £2 2s 3d (*Northern Star*, March 21, 1846, p. 1). Schapper made the point in the *Star* of March 28, 1846, p. 1, that this represented a considerable sum in light of the prevalent unemployment. The address of the National Charter Association is in the *Star* of March 21, 1846, p. 8.
119 The Crown and Anchor meeting was reported in the *Northern Star* of March 28, 1846, p. 1; the Chartist Hall meeting, April 4, 1846, p. 1.
120 It is reproduced in full in the *Northern Star* of March 28, 1846, p. 1.
121 Schoyen, *The Chartist Challenge*, p. 138.
122 *Northern Star*, April 4, 1846, p. 4. Eventually they attempted to send copies to members of the Chartist Convention instead, according to the issue of September 12, 1846.
123 *Northern Star*, June 6, 1846, p. 1. There is no evidence that the committee did anything other than busy itself with propaganda. It published a pamphlet entitled 'Poland and the Seizure of Cracow' which strongly criticised Lord Palmerston. For other meetings, see the *Star* of December 12, 1846, p. 2 and August 15, 1846, p. 7. For other emphasis of the committee on the importance of public opinion, *Northern Star*, March 21, 1846, p. 8; May 16, 1846, p. 5.
124 *Northern Star*, July 16, 1846, p. 8.
125 Schoyen, *The Chartist Challenge*, p. 140, noted that 'however tenuously, O'Connor had associated himself with the aims of the Fraternal Democrats'.

126 *Northern Star*, March 28, 1846, p. 1. One meeting of the Democratic Committee for Poland's Regeneration passed a resolution to this effect and sent a copy of it to Lord Palmerston (*Northern Star*, December 6, 1847, p. 7).

127 *Northern Star*, February 26, 1848, p. 3.

128 *Ibid*. Earlier Harney had been less precise. See his remarks in the issue of March 28, 1846, p. 1; December 4, 1847, p. 1. For another note on the Cracow Manifesto, see Henry Weisser, 'New light upon the Cracow Manifesto', *The Polish Review*, vol. XVI, no. 2 (Spring 1971), pp. 103–4.

129 *Northern Star*, May 23, 1846, p. 8.

130 *Northern Star*, August 28, 1847, p. 4.

131 *Northern Star*, December 4, 1847, p. 1.

132 *The Reasoner*, February 22, 1848, pp. 202–4.

133 For Harney's remarks on nationalism, see the *Northern Star*, February 14, 1846, and Dona Torr, ed., *History in the Making*, vol. I, pp. 246–7. For an analysis, see Rothstein, *From Chartism to Labourism*, p. 134.

134 The claim of E. A. Stepanowa, *Friedrich Engels, sein Leben und Werk* (Berlin, 1958), p. 56, is that Marx and Engels helped to found the Fraternal Democrats! In recent years other Soviet historians have taken pains to show how Marx and Engels as active leaders of the working classes before 1848, busily engaged in struggling against utopian communism, handworkers' communism, and other 'unscientific' variants. A most explicit statement is E. Kandel and S. Lewiowa, 'Marx und Engels als Erzieher der ersten proletarischen Revolutionäre' in *Marx und Engels und die ersten proletarischen Revolutionäre*. Another study in the same work, W. Kunina, 'George Julian Harney', goes to great lengths to show how Marx and Engels worked with 'advanced' Chartists to improve their theoretical views. So did Reg Groves in 'The class leadership of Chartism', *Labour Monthly*, XI (April 1929), pp. 243–4.

135 Schoyen, *The Chartist Challenge*, p. 130, notes that Engels found Harney's doctrinal beliefs vague enough to be acceptable. Harney was favourably impressed with Engels. According to Cole, *Chartist Portraits*, p. 61, Harney found Engels 'laughter-loving . . . a joy inspirer . . .' who spoke remarkably good English.

136 Engels, *Germany: Revolution and Counter-Revolution*, p. 124. Engels complained earlier of theoretical immaturity in *The Condition of the Working Class in England*, reprinted in *Karl Marx and Frederick Engels on Britain*, 2nd ed. (Moscow, 1962), p. 274. Also, Morton H. Cowden, 'Early Marxist views on British labour, 1837–1917', *The Western Political Quarterly*, XVI (1963), pp. 34–52.

137 Cole, *Chartist Portraits*, p. 285. Engels informed Marx in October, 1846 that he had sent a 'mild attack' to Harney on the subject of the peacefulness of the Fraternal Democrats and urged the Chartists to keep up a brisk correspondence with Marx. Karl Marx and Friedrich Engels, *Selected Correspondence* (London, 1941), p. 38.

138 There are numerous scattered references to Harney, Jones, and, to a lesser extent, O'Brien and O'Connor in A. Bebel und Ed. Bernstein, eds., *Das Briefwechsel zwischen Friedrich Engels und Karl Marx, 1844 bis 1883* (Stuttgart, 1913), especially vol. I. See Engels to Marx, September 28, 1847, p. 65, November 15, 1847, p. 82 for remarks about the Fraternal Democrats. Engels boasted about the Fraternal Democrats in his article, 'The Chartist Movement', which appeared, among other places, in the French newspaper, *La Réforme* (November 22, 1847). He wrote that 'this fraternal society . . . [of] . . . the most distinguished democrats . . . had openly come out against any act of oppression. . .'. *Karl Marx and Frederick Engels on Britain*, p. 343. Harney was 'Citizen hip-hip-hurrah' in their private correspondence.

139 *Northern Star*, July 18, 1846, p. 8.

140 Karl Marx and Friedrich Engels, *Selected Correspondence*, pp. 32–3.

141 The *Association Démocratique* was founded in November, 1847. Brussels, like London, had a multi-national population and served as a refuge for exiles. Jacob Katz and several radical lawyers and publicists were members. See Louis Bertrand, *Histoire de la démocratie et du socialisme en Belgique depuis 1830*, vol. I (Brussels and Paris, 1906); Walter Haenisch, 'Karl Marx and the Democratic Association of 1847', *Science and Society, a Marxian Quarterly*, vol. II, no. 1 (Winter 1937). Haenisch noted (p. 90) that a Belgian leader decried the foreigners who wanted to give them

'lessons'. Marx replied in the *Deutsche Brüsseler Zeitung*, December 19, 1847, that the group 'had no other purpose than to exchange ideas and agree on the principles which would bring about unity and fraternity among peoples'. It was the 'duty' of foreigners 'to state their opinions frankly'; and it was absurd to call them 'instructors' everytime they fulfilled their duty to the society.

142 *Northern Star*, December 4, 1847, p. 1. Literally dozens of sources mention or describe or cite this account. See Appendix for works dealing with working-class internationalism. Material for these pages is drawn directly from the *Star* rather than from any secondary sources. Prior to this meeting, Marx had become somewhat familiar with Chartist internationalists. The *Northern Star* of October 16, 1847, p. 1, carried a speech he had hoped to deliver to an international free trade congress. Although he was prevented from doing so, a Belgian, George Weerth, claimed that British workers were not truly represented there, an opinion which gained favourable notice from some groups of British workers. For this, see the *Northern Star* of October 9, 16, and 30, 1847.

143 Black and Black, *The Harney Papers*, Harney to Engels, March 30, 1846, item 247, pp. 242-3. Also Harney to Marx, December, 1847, item 246, p. 247; Harney to Engels and Marx, July 20, 1846, item 248, p. 245.

144 *Northern Star*, December 11, 1847.

145 Harney, Schapper, Oborski, Jones, and Keen were appointed as a deputation to lay the proposition for a Democratic Congress before the Chartist executive and the Metropolitan Chartist Delegate Committee. Another deputation was appointed to present the subject to the German society, according to the *Northern Star* of December 18, 1847, p. 4. The issue of January 1, 1848, p. 4, announced that the Metropolitan Delegate Council had agreed 'unanimously and enthusiastically'.

146 See R. G. Gammage, *History of the Chartist Movement* (1965 ed.), pp. 13-14, 246-53, 261-9; William Lovett, *Life and Struggles of William Lovett, passim*; Thomas Cooper, *The Life of Thomas Cooper, Written by Himself*, pp. 179-80, 271-3, 277; Mark Hovell, *The Chartist Movement*, pp. 92-8; Cole, *Chartist Portraits*, pp. 300-36. Some contemporaries were appreciative, as, for example, W. E. Adams, in *Memoirs of a Social Atom*, p. 157, who declared: 'Hundreds of thousands of working men were almost as devoted to him as the better spirits of Italy at a later date were devoted to Joseph Mazzini. When he addressed in the rich brogue of his native country the "blistered hands and unshorn chins of the working classes" he appeared to touch a chord which vibrated from one end of the kingdom to the other.'

147 Some attempt at rehabilitation may be found in Donald Read and Eric Glasgow, *Feargus O'Connor, Irishman and Chartist* (London, 1961), p. 30 especially. John Saville's introduction to Gammage, *History of the Chartist Movement*, p. 62, expressed the opinion that Feargus was responsible 'above all others' for the 'wide diffusion' of a 'consciousness of a collective political spirit' among ordinary people. See also sympathetic remarks by Asa Briggs, 'Chartism reconsidered', in M. Roberts, ed., *Historical Studies, Papers Read Before the Third Conference of Irish Historians* (London, 1959), p. 47; A. L. Morton, 'The rediscovery of Chartism', *Marxism Today* (March 1960), p. 85.

148 *Northern Star*, October 11, 1845, p. 1. O'Connor related the story, so it may very well be an example of his often genial 'blarney'.

149 His first letter from the continent appeared in the *Northern Star* of September 20, 1845, and they ceased by early November.

150 Hovell, *The Chartist Movement*, pp. 285-6.

151 A recent study of the Land Plan is Alice Mary Hadfield, *The Chartist Land Company* (Newton Abbot, 1970); also Joy MacAskill, 'The Chartist land plan', in Asa Briggs, ed., *Chartist Studies*, pp. 304-41; W. H. G. Armytage, 'The Chartist land colonies, 1846-8', *Agricultural History*, XXXII (1958), pp. 87-96; Donald Read and Eric Glasgow, *Feargus O'Connor, Irishman and Chartist* (London, 1961), pp. 109-116; John Saville, 'The Chartist land plan', *Society for the Study of Labour History Bulletin*, 3 (Autumn 1961), pp. 10-12.

152 *Northern Star*, October 11, 1845, p. 1.

153 *Northern Star*, September 27, 1845, p. 1.

154 *Northern Star*, October 11, 1845, p. 1; November 8, 1845, p. 1; September 27, 1845, p. 1. For greater detail, see Henry Weisser, 'The role of Feargus O'Connor in

Chartist internationalism, 1845–8', *The Rocky Mountain Social Science Journal* VI (April 1969), pp. 82–90.

155 *Northern Star*, October 4, 1845, p. 1.

156 *Northern Star*, October 11, 1845, p. 1.

157 *Northern Star*, September 27, 1845, p. 1.

158 *Ibid.*

159 *Northern Star*, June 6, 1846, p. 5.

160 *Northern Star*, July 24, 1847, p. 1. Like other Chartists who were not internationalists, he made incidental references to Europe from time to time. His maiden speech as a Member of Parliament mentioned the example of Poland, in comparison with Ireland. See Hansard, *Parliamentary Debates*, third series, 15 (1833), p. 453, quoted in Read and Glasgow, *Feargus O'Connor, Irishman and Chartist*, p. 30. Feargus had a family connection with Europe in that his uncle, Arthur O'Connor, served Napoleon as a general and married the daughter of the philosopher Condorcet, and eventually settled on an estate in France. Treason was charged against him because he had discussed the invasion of Ireland with a French general in 1796.

161 *Northern Star*, July 17, 1847, p. 1.

162 *Northern Star*, November 15, 1845, p. 1.

163 *Northern Star*, September 26, 1846, p. 1. He also took issue with Harney, who had joined Schapper in designating the middle class as man's greatest enemy. Feargus replied, rather vaguely, 'I think man's greatest enemy is disunion. . . .'

164 *Northern Star*, November 15, 1845, p. 1. He had been more emphatic and less ambiguous in an editorial of 1844: 'I have always most doggedly and scrupulously refused to form any alliance with any section of foreigners for political purposes, while I have diligently pointed out the master grievance of every nation, allowing each to apply its own national mind for the attainment of the great corrective— *Self Government*' (*Northern Star*, August 17, 1844, p. 1).

165 *Northern Star*, September 26, 1846, p. 1.

166 Black and Black, *The Harney Papers*, Harney to Engels, March 30, 1846, item 247, p. 241. Harney wanted Engels to be more cautious in transmitting such letters to him so that he could be kept out of a 'very awkward' position with O'Connor. Marx and Engels responded to O'Connor in different ways in public and in private. They openly flattered him, as in the congratulatory address appearing in the *Northern Star* of July 18, 1846, p. 8. In their correspondence they showed exasperation over such things as the Land Plan. In planning the Democratic Congress, Engels wanted to get it out of London, to keep Feargus from directing it towards his 'nonsense'. *Karl Marx and Friedrich Engels Werke*, vol. 27, Engels to Marx, Paris 14/15 November, 1847, p. 102.

167 The document is in pamphlet form in the British Museum under 'London, Miscellaneous Organisations'. A small portion is reproduced in Lovett, *Life and Struggles*, pp. 256–7 (1967 ed.).

168 *Ibid.* Lovett recalled that these views were so unpopular that he had to withdraw from the organisation.

169 According to W. J. Linton, *Threescore and Ten Years, 1820 to 1890, Recollections* (New York, 1894), pp. 50–3, there was considerable public indignation. Letters were posted 'not to be Grahamed' on the outside. Henry Vincent typified Chartist indignation when he declared: 'We have heard that slaves, on touching English soil, become as free as the nobles of the land; and why, then, should the correspondence of Europeans, presumed to be born free, be outraged for the wishes of any tyrant . . .' (William Dorling, *Henry Vincent: A Biographical Sketch*, London, 1879, p. 50). Also, Lovett, *Life and Struggles* (1967 ed.), pp. 247–8; An explanation of this case, and the phenomenon in general, is in F. C. Mather, *Public Order in the Age of the Chartists* (Manchester, 1959), p. 224.

170 *Northern Star*, November 29, 1845, p. 1; also August 16, 1845, p. 8; September 6, 1845, p. 7.

171 Lovett, *Life and Struggles*, p. 72. Mazzini came to what he called 'a sunless and musicless land' in 1837, aged 31, miserably poor and lonely. After a time in debt and despair, he gained a circle of friends and started to work with poor Italians in the metropolis. His free elementary school, opened in 1841, became a meeting place for various foreign exiles, including Poles, and their English friends.

172 For Mazzini's activities in London in these years see M. C. Wicks, *The Italian Exiles in London, 1816–48* (Manchester, 1937), especially pp. 186–95; E. E. Y. Hales, *Mazzini and the Secret Societies: the Making of a Myth* (New York. n.d.); Bolton King, *The Life of Mazzini* (London and Toronto, 1902). There are two studies in Italian of this period in his life: Emilia Morelli, *Mazzini in Inghilterra* (Florence, 1938) and *L'Inghilterra di Mazzini* (Rome, 1965). Mazzini's autobiographical materials and letters in English do not mention the People's International League, a point also made by Emilia Morelli on p. 94 of the latter works.

173 'Report of a Public Meeting . . . To Explain the Principles and Objects of the Peoples' International League', Pamphlet in the Cowen Collection, Newcastle-upon-Tyne City Libraries, item A13.

174 'Address of the Council of the Peoples' International League' (London, 1847), Cowen Collection, item A 8. It also appeared in *The Reasoner*, May 1846, no. 52, and, in part, in William Shirrefs' *The People's Press and Monthly Historical Newspaper*, vol. 1, 1847, pp. 210–12. Other addresses and papers of the League are in the Cowen Collection, including item A 10, 'The Swiss Question: A Brief Statement of Facts' (London, 1847); A13, 'Report of a Public Meeting Held at the Crown and Anchor Tavern . . . November 15, 1847. . .'. Item A9 is a circular letter from W. J. Linton to accompany a tract. It cited the glaring ignorance of the British public and blamed it on 'the loose and garbled accounts of the Press'. Without the influence of an informed public opinion, British foreign policy was 'the creature of irresponsible diplomacy', which was 'out of harmony' with the British 'popular sympathies'.

175 The account is contained in a 'Report of a Public Meeting Held at the Crown and Anchor Tavern . . . November 15, 1847 . . .' (Cowen Collection, item A13), p. 4.

176 Morelli, *L'Inghilterra de Mazzini*, p. 95. The Crown and Anchor meeting was supposed to have had 1,500 persons attending. See also Linton, *Memories*, p. 100; *European Republicans, Recollections of Mazzini and His Friends*, p. 62.

177 *The Times*, June 7, 1847, p. 4. Mazzini's reaction to the attack was composed. He wrote: 'I think it is a good thing that *The Times* gave a detailed attack against a society that hasn't yet had great publicity, for it is clear that they feel the importance of it.' Still, he was worried about the effect it might have had on some of the councillors, according to Morelli, *L'Inghilterra di Mazzini*, p. 94. On November 16, 1847, p. 6, *The Times* reported the Crown and Anchor meeting in a matter-of-fact manner, without editorial comment.

178 Schoyen, *The Chartist Challenge*, p. 153.

179 Black and Black, *The Harney Papers*, Harney to Engels, March 30, 1846, item 247, pp. 244–5. Harney declared that 'we stepped in and settled their hash for them. It is not likely that they will hold a meeting at all.'

180 'Report of a Public Meeting Held at the Crown and Anchor Tavern . . . November 15, 1847 . . .' (Cowen Collection, item A13), p. 13. The protest was featured in the *Northern Star's* brief report of the meeting, November 20, 1847, p. 2.

181 *Northern Star*, September 25, 1847, p. 8.

182 *Northern Star*, March 28, 1846, p. 1. Bronterre O'Brien's views were not far from this position. He urged public meetings to raise funds for the purchase of gunpowder to be sent to Poles fighting around Cracow. He explained his position in the *National Reformer and Manx Weekly Review of Home and Foreign Affairs*, March 13, 1847, p. 8, by putting words in the mouth of the Irishman Pat, who said, 'Moral force is all very well, but has it less effect if you have a smart shillelagh at the back of it?'. This 'shillelagh, or something like it', was what 'the friends of Poland require'.

183 Address of the Council of the People's International League (Cowen Collection, item A8), pp. 10–11, 14. An explanation of the League's position also appeared in *The People's Press*, August 2, 1847, p. 212, for 'the satisfaction of the scrupulous'.

184 See the defence of Mazzini in 'Report of a Public Meeting . . . at the Crown and Anchor . . . of the People's International League' (Cowen Collection, item A13), pp. 12–13.

185 Mazzini's long essay, 'Italy, Austria and the Pope', was published in serial form in the *Northern Star*, beginning with the issue of September 6, 1845.

186 Perhaps the best account of Cooper's life is G. D. H. Cole, *Chartist Portraits*, pp. 187–217. R. J. Conklin, *Thomas Cooper the Chartist* (Manila, 1935), is more concerned with literature than history. Then there is Cooper's autobiography, *The Life of Thomas Cooper* (London, 1875).

187 Cole, *Chartist Portraits*, p. 211, indicates that it was mainly Cooper's distrust of the land scheme and O'Connor himself that led to the break.

188 For the censuring of Thomas Cooper, see the *Northern Star*, June 27, 1846, p. 5. Cooper apparently had some strength in the Fraternal Democrats, because an attempt was made to stay the censure until more information about the dispute between Cooper and O'Connor could be gathered. Those who made this motion, Joseph Dunn and D. Ross, were not heard of in accounts of the Fraternal Democrats henceforth.

189 The censure was included in an address from the *Association Démocratique*. Apparently Marx and Engels had taken an active role against Cooper. In a letter from Harney to Engels, March 30, 1846, the Chartist leader complained that Engels omitted to include 'some resolutions' he thought proper to pass against Cooper. Black and Black, *The Harney Papers*, item 247, p. 243. See also the remarks of the editors on p. 246, note 2.

190 According to *The Life of Thomas Cooper Written by Himself*, pp. 105–6, he knew Latin, French, Italian, and some German. He studied at a Mechanics' Institute with an Italian who had been a veteran of Carbonari conspiracies. He even had an argument with William Wordsworth in 1846 over the merits of Louis Philippe (pp. 293–4). It seems that Cooper's interest in foreign affairs was not constant throughout his Chartist career. His *Midland Counties Illuminator*, for instance, an earlier journalistic venture, carried almost nothing about Europe.

191 *Northern Star*, November 15, 1845, p. 7.

192 *The Reasoner*, vol. III, 1847, p. 574. The lecture was delivered at the National Hall, October 3, 1847.

193 *Northern Star*, April 25, 1846, p. 7.

194 *Ibid*. Actually, Cooper's 'moral force' objections to Cracow celebrations was well answered by Holyoake's *Reasoner*, June 10, 1846: 'He who is an advocate of moral force should attend a Polish meeting, if not to applaud the Poles for their resistance, to execrate the Russians for their oppressions. . . . Surely Mr Cooper execrates the aggressor. . . . The men of peace ought to crowd a Polish meeting . . . to protest against violence upon the part of the oppressor, since they condemn it on the part of the oppressed.'

195 Black and Black, *The Harney Papers*, Harney to Engels, February 23, 1894, item 369, p. 355. In the same letter he mused over how he had then believed in 'what, alas! to my bitter sorrow, I cannot believe now—. . . the sovereign people'.

196 Thomas Frost, *Forty Years' Recollections, Literary and Political* (London, 1880), pp. 128–9.

197 F. C. Mather, *Public Order in the Age of the Chartists* (Manchester, 1959), p. 33, contends that the act was aimed at the threat of an Irish rebellion. Rothstein, *From Chartism to Labourism*, pp. 143–4 attributed the ruination of the Fraternal Democrats to the Home Secretary's powers of deportation under the new act. Harney, writing in the *Democratic Review of British and Foreign Politics, History and Literature*, November 1849, p. 201, observed that 'on the Government proposing the alien bill of 1848, the society was called together, dissolved, and reconstituted solely of natives of the British Isles, in order to release the continental members from their obligations to, and connection with, the association'. See the *Northern Star* of April 22, 1848, p. 5; May 6, 1848, and May 27, 1848, p. 6. The Alien Bill is in *A Collection of Public General Statutes* 11 Vict., c. 20, pp. 205–8. The Lord Lieutenant or the Secretary of State could deport aliens without trial and such aliens could be arrested and gaoled without bail pending deportation. Aliens resident for over three years and diplomatic households were excluded from these provisions.

198 Gammage, *The History of the Chartist Movement*, pp. 46–7. Recent studies point to the diversity and divisions of working-class politics in the metropolis from 1830 to 1848, politics that featured bitter rivalries, the incessant formation of factions and the unending clashes of these groupings. These studies are D. J. Rowe, 'The failure of London Chartism', *Historical Journal*, XI, 3 (1968), pp. 472–87; 'Chartism and the Spitalfields silk-weavers', *Economic History Review*, second

series, xx, 3 (December 1967), pp. 482–93. Rowe explains in both articles why there was a lack of a powerful London Chartist organisation, stressing hugeness and diversity. See also Iorwerth Prothero, 'Chartism in London', *Past and Present*, 44 (August 1969), pp. 76–105, which claims that the two traditions of London Chartism, one major group following Lovett and another following Harney, have been exaggerated. London Chartism featured many more groups, and it was carried over into the forties with much local vigour. Lesser known leaders actually counted for more than the celebrated ones.

199 Rowe, 'Chartism and the Spitalfields silk-weavers', p. 492.

200 Robert Lowery, from the North, called London 'a sink of corruption—the wealth of the aristocracy was spent there' and since artisans 'lived by their extravagance', how could they be as 'virtuous' as workmen in provincial towns? See Brian Harrison and Patricia Hollis, 'Chartism, liberalism and the Life of Robert Lowery', *English Historical Review*, vol. 82, 1967, p. 512. Of course, the contrast is overdrawn for emphasis. Militancy, complete with arms preparation, was sporadic but very desperate in London in 1848.

201 See below, p. 166. Iorwerth Prothero, 'Chartism in London', p. 80, makes the point 'that even if most of the prominent Chartist leaders, including four of the five members of the Chartist executive belonged to the Fraternal Democrats, 'this does not mean they dominated London Chartism . . . the main stream in the 1840s consisted of localities of the National Charter Association'.

202 While decline seems certain, Chartists themselves and historians have disputed the degree of decline from 1845 to the end of 1847. Harney, late in his long life, wrote an article for F. J. Snell's *Palmerston's Borough* entitled 'Who were the Chartists?'. In it he declared that 'in spite of manifold errors, and the repressive effects of political persecution, Chartism was still a power in the land when writs were issued for the General Election in 1847' (p. 83). Another Chartist, B. Wilson of Salterhebble, concurred, in *The Struggles of an Old Chartist: What He Knows and the Part He Has Taken in Various Movements* (Halifax, 1887), p. 10. Thomas Frost, another contemporary, disagreed and said the movement 'languished, and its continued existence was scarcely known, except to readers of the *Northern Star*'. (*History of the Chartist Movement*, chapter VIII, *Bradford Observer Budget*, Newspaper Clippings, n.d.)

203 Other schemes also absorbed the interest of the *Star*'s readers in these years, including the Anti-Enclosure Association, the Irish Democratic Association and the Anti-Gold Law League.

204 Rachel O'Higgins, 'The Irish influence in the Chartist Movement', *Past and Present*, 20, November 1961, p. 90.

205 The rest of the Chartist periodicals generally took up only a small percentage of their space with European matters, in a manner similar to that of the ultra-radical publications of the twenties. There might be a column of news items taken from other newspapers, an occasional editorial, a pacifistic tirade now and then, or a long, confused letter from a group of irate Poles condemning another group of Poles.

206 *The Reasoner*, vol. III, 1847, p. 573, from a lecture of Cooper's that was delivered on October 3, 1847.

207 *Northern Star*, February 5, 1848, p. 8.

208 *Northern Star*, February 26, 1848, p. 3.

209 *Northern Star*, February 5, 1848, p. 1.

210 Rothstein, *From Chartism to Labourism*, p. 135, quoted from the *Northern Star* of February 14, 1846. For the treatment of the Fraternal Democrats at the hands of numerous Marxist historians, see Appendix.

211 *Northern Star*, September 19, 1846, p. 3. Harney intended it to be sung to the air of 'Roderigh Vich, Alpine Dhu', the Boat Song in Scott's 'Lady of the Lake'.'

212 *Northern Star*, September 25, 1847, p. 8.

213 Black and Black, *The Harney Papers*, Harney to Engels, March 30, 1846, item 247, p. 240. Marxist theory acknowledges that mass class consciousness is only likely to develop when the overthrow of capitalism has become immediately feasible, but mass action has to crystallise around a revolutionary group which acts upon the fringe until proper conditions develop. The argument which can be made about the Fraternal Democrats is that they were not revolutionary, even if they were on the fringe.

214 *Ibid.*, pp. 241–2.

215 Some lament that Marx was born too late to supply theory for the mass stages of Chartism, and that he discovered 'scientific' principles only when the tide had reached its ebb. See Salme A. Dutt, *When England Arose: The Centenary of the People's Charter*, Key Books, no. 6 (London, 1939), p. 59; Neil Stewart, *The Fight for the Charter* (London, n.d.), p. 209; A. L. Morton, 'The interpretation of Chartism', *Marxism Today*, June 1961, p. 183.

216 By 1848 O'Brien, Cooper, and Lovett were in their forties; Hetherington was 56; Wooler was 62; and both Richard Carlile and William Cobbett were dead.

217 Compare the addresses of the LWMA in the previous chapter with the addresses of the Fraternal Democrats in this chapter. Iorwerth Prothero, 'Chartism in London', p. 95, notes that Lovett's pronouncements to overseas workmen were equally proletarian.

218 It should be pointed out that both A. R. Schoyen and Julius West mentioned this incident in their books. Incidentally, the author visited Tiverton recently to examine the site of this event.

219 F. J. Snell, *Palmerston's Borough: A Budget of Electioneering Anecdotes, Jokes, Squibbs and Speeches* (London and Tiverton, 1894), pp. 78–9.

220 Only one Chartist candidate, Feargus O'Connor, was actually returned, but Nottingham's new member in 1847 had displayed pretensions at gentility and claimed descent from Irish kings.

221 Schoyen, *The Chartist Challenge*, p. 150; Snell, *Palmerston's Borough*, p. 98.

222 Snell, *Palmerston's Borough*, p. 79. He quotes 'a witness not identified with the Chartist cause' who also declared that the crowd was two-thirds in favour of Harney. Harney invited Palmerston to a meeting with young Chartists but he declined it (Black and Black, *The Harney Papers*, Lord Palmerston to G. Julian Harney, Tiverton, July 31, 1847, item 83, p. 65).

223 Snell, *Palmerston's Borough*, p. 79.

224 *Ibid.*, p. 85 (Harney's memoir); Gammage, *History of the Chartist Movement*, p. 284.

225 *Northern Star*, August 7, 1847, p. 1. References to Harney's speech below are drawn from this source.

226 'Speech of Lord Viscount Palmerston, Secretary of State for Foreign Affairs, to the Electors of Tiverton, 31 July, 1847', 2nd edition (London, 1847).

227 'Speech of Lord Viscount Palmerston . . . to the Electors of Tiverton. . . .' The following quotations are drawn from pages 23 to 38. Taken together, less than half of the foreign secretary's oration was given over to a defence of his foreign policy. He spent time on other topics and made numerous digressions, even including comments on the dispute over the statue of Wellington in Hyde Park.

228 Snell, *Palmerston's Borough*, p. 80.

229 At one point, Palmerston accused Harney of 'conduct unworthy of a fellow countryman', and ignorance, explaining that Harney had appeared 'to have got by rote a certain number of empty declamatory phrases . . . a jargon and jingle of words . . . which have no reference to facts, which have no bearing upon anything that has happened. . .'.

230 Snell, *Palmerston's Borough*, p. 86.

231 *Ibid.*, pp. 80 and 87.

232 *Northern Star* August 7, 1847.

233 'Speech of Lord Viscount Palmerston . . . to the Electors of Tiverton. . .', p. 22.

234 Snell, *Palmerston's Borough*, p. 87.

235 *Ibid.*, p. 88. Quoted from Harney's memoir. The story is also in W. E. Adams, *Memoirs of a Social Atom*, pp. 222–3. Palmerston also helped Feargus O'Connor's indigent sister, according to George Jacob Holyoake, *Sixty Years of an Agitator's Life*, p. 80.

236 Snell, *Palmerston's Borough*, p. 88.

Appendix
The historiography of Chartist internationalism

Chartist internationalism has been celebrated by a number of historians, especially those of a Marxist orientation, but usually not as a separate subject.[1] It has appeared as a rather peripheral topic in the histories of the labour movement, Chartism, communism, or internationalism, or as background material for some biographers. In most cases the Fraternal Democrats and their Chartist leaders, George Julian Harney and Ernest Jones, have been singled out as the 'most advanced' representatives of the working-class movement, mileposts along the progressive way from the French revolutionary internationalism of Robbespierre[2] to the proletarian internationalism of socialist societies today. Since this notoriety exists, it is worthwhile to examine the Marxist positions on internationalism and specific applications of it to the Fraternal Democrats.

Marxism has placed stress on working-class internationalism from the beginning. The *Communist Manifesto* proclaimed it as an important feature that distinguishes communists from all other working-class parties.[3] Older, bourgeois internationalism broke down as nationalistic, competitive, property-oriented states emerged. By contrast, working-class internationalism was truly pacifistic, because workers had no private property and interests to divide them from the working people of other countries. Since workers had a common enemy, capital, their exploitation would serve to unite them internationally, as well as with the 'colonial slaves' and the peasant masses of lands exploited by overseas interests. Opposition and exploitation were not the only causes of working-class internationalism: knowledge of Marxism determines it; the more it permeates the working-class movement in any country, the more ties those workers will have with working people of other countries.[4] In all of these developments there is a progressive, cumulative nature. The working class itself was formed at a time when a world economy and new, swift worldwide relations came into being. Its internationalism, at first instinctive, became conscious, manifesting itself increasingly in support for workers striking in another country, in international resistance to political repression and in support for struggles of national liberation. As class-conscious awareness and Marxist 'scientific' teaching spread, internationalism grew from the handful of working-class internationalists in the early Communist League to the present day system of socialist states commanding a third of the world's allegiance.

Such is the Marxist position. Perhaps the most quoted specific applications of this position to Chartism have come from Theodore or Fiodor Rothstein, whose *From Chartism to Labourism*, as well as the similar 'Aus der Vorgeschichte der Internationale', has been quarried regularly.[5] A central argument of his was that the truly vital elements of Chartism were internationalist because the class struggle had already developed, and working-class internationalism had to exist as a natural part of the class struggle.[6] According to Rothstein, the Fraternal Democrats 'carried on . . . a vigorous agitation for the ideas of international proletarian solidarity and international mass action for freedom both in England and abroad'.[7] Harney and Jones were 'revolutionary internationalists in the modern sense of the term'[8] and the views of such leaders were 'entirely free from bourgeois ideology' on the subjects of nationalism and internationalism:

They emphasised that nationalism is necessary only for the more active prosecution of the proletarian class struggle, and that internationalism is the corollary of the identity of the proletarian cause in all countries.[9]

G. M. Stekloff quoted Rothstein's material extensively for his *History of the First International*, and added some points of his own. He declared: 'The beginnings of internationalist sentiment and the awareness of the international solidarity of the workers developed in Britain, simultaneously with the development of class consciousness in general. . .'. Chartism was permeated with 'democratic' internationalism that was not proletarian and suffered from hindrance by insularity. Then, through the 'chaos of vague revolutionism' and 'bourgeois-democratic' internationalism of the exiles in London, 'a purely proletarian trend' began to emerge. It evolved further in the Fraternal Democrats, to the extent that:

The leaders of the Fraternal Democrats were free from bourgeois ideology. They taught that nationality was necessary for the more effective guidance of the class war, but that internationalism would result from the triumph of the proletarian movement in all lands. Furthermore, they proclaimed the international solidarity of the workers as an essential preliminary to the victory of the proletariat over the bourgeoisie.[10]

Many explicit pronouncements about Chartist internationalism were made by Salme A. Dutt in the *Labour Monthly* on the eve of the second world war.[11] He found the creation of the Fraternal Democrats 'the greatest historical achievement of Chartism in the fight of the working class for internationalism and for world peace',[12] and observed:

The internationalism of the working class grew and took its shape with the development of class consciousness, with the understanding of the common interest and common task of the workers of the whole world. . . . Already in the eighteen-thirties the British working-class movement began to express this advance towards proletarian internationalism, though a deeper understanding was first reached towards the end of the Chartist movement. . . . A closer contact with the revolutionary refugees strengthened the understanding, especially among the London Chartists, of proletarian internationalism which reached its concrete expression in the formation in 1845 of the first international organisation, 'The Society of Fraternal Democrats'.[13]

In one of the earliest histories of Chartism, written in German, Hermann Schlütter declared that 'it was the influence of the Fraternal Democrats and influence that the communists in their ranks obtained over the Chartists which was the cause of a sudden shift that took place in the Chartist movement. The change made communist doctrines as well as a clear comprehension of historical development come forth in the movement.'[14] In his view, 'the English workers had advocated peace since class had formed and class consciousness developed' because 'a feeling of international solidarity was aroused'.[15]

These themes, with some variations, have been presented by numerous other writers. A Marxist study course booklet of 1932 assured readers that the Chartists 'laid the ideological and organisational foundation stone of international solidarity', and that Jones and Harney represented 'the transition stage from Chartism to scientific socialism'.[16] Reg Groves, an inter-war historian of the movement, concurred, as did A. L. Morton and George Tate in several publications, and Neil Stewart, author of *The Fight for the Charter* and R. Palme Dutt, not to be confused with Salme A. Dutt.[17] Perhaps the latest word of this nature is found in Collins and Abramsky, *Karl Marx and the British Labour Movement*:

. . . at least for the first two years of its existence, the society's [the Fraternal Democrats] importance in giving organised expression to the idea of proletarian internationalism can hardly be exaggerated. To Harney and the Fraternal Democrats must go much of the credit for the fact that in the

1850s and 1860s the British workers were more responsive to international issues than at any time before or much of the time since.[18]

Post-war Soviet historians have been more modest than earlier Marxist writers or Marxist writers in Britain in making claims for the importance of Chartist internationalism. They lay stress on the immaturity of the phenomenon, and declare that the Fraternal Democrats were without a 'very clear programme' and were 'still far' from true proletarian internationalism even if they were taking steps in that direction. The importance of Marx and Engels acting upon 'the best representatives' of the movement is, of course, given great weight.[19]

Marxist historians have not gone unanswered. Less committed historians have questioned the importance and significance of the Fraternal Democrats and the extent to which they led or influenced the Chartist movement in general. G. D. H. Cole thought that Chartism was far behind the Fraternal Democrats in internationalism. He insisted that Chartism arose out of purely British conditions and was 'for the most part led by men who had but a dim awareness of any affinity among the workers on the Continent. . . '.

The masses who shouted and marched against the hated Bastilles and the hated power-factories felt but dimly Harney's enthusiasm for continental revolutions; and even slogans of world-wide workers' solidarity meant little to them. They threw up leaders made in their own image, and concerned more with the immediate local struggle than with either theories or world-wide appeals. . . . The main body of Chartists in the industrial areas were too much engaged with their own sufferings and oppressions to spare more than a cheer for continental victories—or, more often, for the victims of continental tyranny who were able to find asylum in Great Britain. . . . Harney's perpetual . . . desire to regard British working-class action as merely part of a world-wide proletarian uprising were apt to seem unrealistic, and to make little appeal outside a narrow circle of convinced revolutionaries.[20]

Preston William Slosson, author of a monograph on the later stages of Chartism that appeared during the first world war, offered this opinion:

The evidences of Chartist interest in the democratic movements in continental Europe and America are numerous and striking; indeed, if the Chartist periodicals may be supposed to have had any influence on their readers, Chartism must have done more than any other factor to form the opinions of radical working men upon the questions of foreign policy.

But the degree of attention which the Chartists bestowed upon events in other countries was not constant, being very much greater after the revolutionary year of 1848 than it had ever been before. . . .

In the years when the Chartist movement in England seemed nearest success and when the revolutionary movements in other European countries seemed far from being equally strong, the majority of the Chartists confined their attention to the domestic situation. But even in those days not a few of the party leaders followed with the greatest sympathy the progress of democracy abroad.[21]

Asa Briggs has taken note of an 'unmistakable shift in emphasis' in the last years of the movement which led some Chartists, 'notably Jones and Harney', to search for 'social democracy' by looking abroad and expressing 'international commitment and action'. In so doing, these Chartists were led to 'propound a foreign policy of their own. . .'. Nevertheless, Briggs declared that the 'changing outlook of the Chartist leaders' was 'not necessarily shared . . . by the old Chartist rank and file'.[22] Similarly balanced was the recent assessment of Iorwerth Prothero: 'The Fraternal Democrats were undoubtedly important, though much of the significance given them has been retrospective, because of the adherence of certain communists like Schapper and Moll, and their contacts with Marx and Engels'[23].

Several other writers have discounted the claims of the Fraternal Democrats in their estimations of the role of the organisation: John Price, author of a history of the international labour movement for the Royal Institute of International Affairs, called them a 'small association' of 'local and transitory' importance.[24] Another historian who discounted their significance was Arthur Müller-Lehning, whose monograph focused on the International Association of 1855 to 1859, another forerunner of the International. He viewed the Fraternal Democrats as one of several 'manifestations of international solidarity', a vehicle for 'propaganda for universal alliance'. He regarded his own subject instead of the Fraternal Democrats as 'the first international organisation of a proletarian and socialist character'.[25]

While there might be disagreement over just how significant the Fraternal Democrats were, historians of various persuasions concede that they were some sort of forerunner or harbinger of the First International, or, at the very minimum estimate, a signpost in that direction. Julius Braunthal, an Austrian social democrat and author of a multi-volume *History of the International*, stressed this aspect of the organisation:

In its organisational structure the Society of Fraternal Democrats was a complete prototype of the later, historic International. . . . It was a genuine workers' international, which upheld the ideal of international solidarity. . . . Rightly, Theodor Rothstein ends his account of the society's history with the remark that, but for the frustration which stemmed from the triumph of reaction in 1848, the Society of the Fraternal Democrats would have developed into the First International.[26]

These, then, have been the judgements of historians and other writers. Some have been incidental, some hasty, some cautious, and many assessments stand in contradiction. It is hoped that this study has helped to bring about some clarifications.

Notes to Appendix

1 There have been only two articles devoted specifically to this subject: Salme A. Dutt, 'Chartism and the fight for peace', *Labour Monthly*, vol. xxi (June 1939), pp. 367–74 and Henry Weisser, 'Chartist internationalism, 1845–8', *The Historical Journal*, xiv, no. 1 (1971), pp. 49–66.

2 Robespierre's proposed amendment to the Declaration of the Rights of Man included these provisions: '34. The men of all countries are brothers, and the different peoples must help one another, according to their power, as citizens of the same State. 35. Whoever oppresses a single nation declares himself the enemy of all. 36. Whoever makes war on a people in order to check the progress of liberty and annihilate the rights of man must be prosecuted by all, not as ordinary enemies, but as rebels, brigands and assassins. 37. Kings, aristocrats, tyrants, whoever they be, are slaves rebelling against the sovereign of the earth, which is the human race, and against the legislator of the universe, which is nature.' Quoted from George Rudé, ed., *Great Lives Observed: Robespierre* (Englewood Cliffs, 1967), p. 57.

3 It stated: 'The Communists are distinguished from other working-class parties by this only: 1. In the national struggles of the proletarians of the different countries, they point out and bring to the fore the common interests of the entire proletariat, independent of all nationality. 2. In the various stages of development through which the struggle of the working class against the bourgeoisie has to pass, they always and everywhere represent the interests of the movement as a whole.' Quoted from *The Communist Manifesto* as published in Arthur P. Mendel, ed., *Essential Works of Marxism* (New York, London, and Toronto, 1965), p. 25.

4 According to *Fundamentals of Marxism-Leninism Manual* (2nd revised ed., Moscow, 1963), 'whoever has mastered Marxist doctrine is bound to be an internationalist, to strive consciously for the unity and co-operation of the working people of all nations'. Proletarian internationalism is defined as 'the scientifically-confirmed ideology of the community of interests of the working classes of all countries and nations; . . . a definite *form taken by the relations* between the national detachments of the working class' (pp. 305–6).

5 Fiodor Rothstein, *From Chartism to Labourism: Historical Sketches of the English Working Class Movement* (London, 1929); 'Aus der Vorgeschichte der Internationale', *Ergänzungshefte zur neuen Zeit*, Nr. 17 (October 1913). Rothstein, born in Russia, lived in England from 1891 to 1920. He later was a bureaucrat and minister of the Soviet Union.

6 'It was precisely in England that the proletariat became keenly aware not only of solidarity with foreign workers but of the indispensability of this solidarity in the struggle with bourgeois society.' 'Aus der Vorgeschichte der Internationale', p. 2.

7 Rothstein, *From Chartism to Labourism*, p. 133.

8 *Ibid.*, p. 139.

9 *Ibid.*, p. 136.

10 G. M. Stekloff, *History of the First International* (New York, 1928), pp. 14–23. (The lengthy quotation is from p. 23.)

11 Salme A. Dutt, 'Chartism and the fight for peace', pp. 367–74.

12 *Ibid.*, p. 373.

13 *Ibid.*, pp. 368 and 369. On p. 370 he remarks that 'the best exponents of pro-letarian internationalism during the Chartist struggles were Harney and Jones. Their expressions of internationalism are already free from bourgeois ideology and are very close to modern proletarian internationalism. . . .'

14 Hermann Schlütter, *Die Chartisten-Bewegung: ein Beitrag zur sozialpolitischen Geschichte Englands* (New York, 1916), p. 186. On p. 212 he explained: 'Naturally, it came to be seen and realised that the interests of the working class of one country, and, beyond that, the interests of the workers of all nations were the same. This realisation soon made itself generally recognised.'

15 *Ibid.*, p. 215.

16 'The English industrial revolution and Chartism', *Marxist Study Courses*, course two, 'Working class history', Lesson two (London, 1932), pp. 46 and 47.

17 Reg Groves, *But We Shall Rise Again: A Narrative History of Chartism* (London, 1939), pp. 161 and 164 in particular; William Z. Foster, *History of the Three Inter-nationals: The World Socialist and Communist Movements from 1848 to the Present* (New York, 1968), p. 45. A. L. Morton and George Tate, *The British Labour Movement A History* (London, 1956), p. 45, wrote that the Chartists had 'recognised the identity of the popular cause in all lands, and a whole series of organisations had existed to promote . . . international solidarity', something which had 'a powerful and long standing . . . tradition' in Britain. Also A. L. Morton, 'The interpretation of Chartism', *Marxism Today* (June 1961), p. 181; 'The rediscovery of Chartism', *Marxism Today* (March 1960), pp. 83–7; Neil Stewart, *The Fight for the Charter* (London, n.d.), p. 52; R. Palme Dutt, *The Internationale* (London, 1967), p. 32.

18 C. Abramsky and H. Collins, *Karl Marx and the British Labour Movement* (London, 1965), p. 9.

19 See Yuri V. Kovalev, 'Chartist literature', *Communist Party of Great Britain, Historians' Group*, Pamphlet no. 17 (Spring 1960); Kira Tatarinova, 'Soviet historians on Chartism', *Society for the Study of Labour History Bulletin*, 5 (Autumn 1962), pp. 27 and 29; W. Kunina, 'George Julian Harney', in E. Kandel, ed., *Marx und Engels und die ersten proletarischen Revolutionäre* (Berlin, 1965), pp. 422 and 429.

20 G. D. H. Cole, *Chartist Portraits* (London, 1941), pp. 269–70. Cole was much less ambiguous when he wrote on this subject for his *History of Socialist Thought*: 'Through these contacts [with foreign exiles and Marx] the Jones–Harney wing of the movement developed a strongly internationalist attitude—which indeed had been present in Harney's thought from the beginning. The Chartist left . . . came to consider itself much more as the British wing of an international revolutionary movement and to take much more notice of continental Socialist and Communist ideas' (vol. 1, *The Forerunners, 1789–1850* (New York, 1965), pp. 150–1).

21 Preston William Slossen, *The Decline of the Chartist Movement* (New York, 1916), p. 200.

22 Asa Briggs, 'National bearings', in Asa Briggs, ed., *Chartist Studies* (London, 1959), p. 290.

23 Iorwerth Prothero, 'Chartism in London', *Past and Present*, 44 (August 1969), p. 80.

24 John Price, *The International Labour Movement* (Oxford, 1945), p. 7.

25 Arthur Müller-Lehning, *The International Association, 1855–1859: A Contri-bution to the Preliminary History of the First International* (Leiden, 1938), pp. 1 and 41.

26 Julius Braunthal, *History of the International*, vol. 1, 1864–1914 (New York, 1967), pp. 67–8 and 73. Collins and Abramsky found the Fraternal Democrats 'the first serious attempt to found a Labour International' which, despite 'limited scope . . . paved the way' for the International Working Men's Association (*Karl Marx and the British Labour Movement*, p. 3). Similarly, John Saville has written of this 'vigorous tradition' of internationalism as a 'basic belief' carried over into subse-quent decades: John Saville, introduction to R. G. Gammage, *History of the Chartist Movement* (New York, 1967 ed., p. 44).

Bibliography

COLLECTIONS AND PAPERS

The Cowen Collection, Newcastle-upon-Tyne Central Reference Library.
The Ernest Jones Papers, *Seligman Collection*, Columbia University.
Ernest Jones, *Diary, 1839–47*, Manchester Central Reference Library.
Ernest Jones, *Scrapbook of Newspaper Cuttings, etc., on Ernest Jones*. Manchester Central Reference Library.
The Hovell Collection, University of Manchester Library.
The Place Collection, British Museum, Add. MSS., various between 27,819 and 36,626; *the Place Collection of Newspaper Cuttings*, sets 9, 39, 55, 66.

PAMPHLETS

Address from the National Association for Promoting the Improvement of the People to the Working Classes of the United Kingdom on the Subject of the Militia. London: John Cleave, 1846.
All Men Are Brethren. An Address to the Friends of Humanity and Justice Among All Nations by the Democratic Friends of All Nations. London: J. Cleave, 1845.
Anon., *Ernest Jones. Who is He? What Has He Done?* Manchester: A. Heywood, 1868.
Anon., *The Life and Death of Ernest Jones, the Chartist Reformer: a Memoir*. Manchester: John Heywood, 1869.
Anon., *The Real Chartist. Patriotically Addressed to the Consideration of All Republicans, Chartists, Reformers, Radicals, Whigs, Tories and Conservatives, by a Working Man*. London: 1848.
Anon., *What the Chartists Are Like. A Letter to English Workingmen by a Fellow Labourer*. London: 1848.
Anon., *The Life of John Frost, Esq.*, 7th ed., with additions. London: Thomas White, John Cleave, 1840.
Cannon, John, *The Chartists in Bristol*. Bristol: Bristol Branch of the Historical Association, Local History Pamphlets, no. 2, 1964.
Carlile, Richard, *The Character of a Soldier:* by Philanthropos, 2nd ed. London: 1822.
Davies, David P., *A Short Sketch of the Life and Labours of Ernest Jones, Chartist, Barrister and Poet, to which is added several of his Poems*. Liverpool: The Journal of Commerce Printing Works, 1897.
Frost, John, *History of the Chartist Movement*. Manchester Central Library: Newspaper Cuttings Chiefly Relating to Chartism and Local History of Hypperholme.
Lovett, William, and Collins, John, *Chartism: a New Organization of the People Embracing a Plan for the Education and Improvement of the People, Politically and Socially*. London: J. Watson, 1840.

Mazzini, Joseph, *Italy, Austria and the Pope, a Letter to Sir James Graham, Bart.* London: 1845.

Paine, Thomas. *Address to the Republic of France, September 25, 1792.* London: W. Holland, 1792.

Palmerston, Lord Viscount, *Speech of Lord Viscount Palmerston, Secretary of State for Foreign Affairs, To the Electors of Tiverton on the 31st July, 1847,* 2nd ed. London: Smith, Elder & Co., 1847.

People's International League, *Address of the Council of the People's International League.* London: Palmer and Clayton, 1847.

People's International League, *Italy, Switzerland and Austria.* Dundee: M'Cosh, Park and Dewars, 1847.

People's International League, *Report of a Public Meeting Held at the Crown and Anchor Tavern, Strand, on Monday, November 15, 1847, 'To Explain the Principles and Objects of the People's International League'.* London: People's International League, 1847.

Salt, John, *Chartism in South Yorkshire.* Pamphlet 1, Local History Series, Sheffield: University of Sheffield Institute of Education, 1967.

Watson, J., *The Life and Character of Henry Hetherington.* London: J. Watson, 1849.

Watson, J., *Young Germany: an Account of the Rise, Progress and Present Position of German Communism, with a Memoir of Wilhelm Weitling, its Founder—and a Report of the Proceedings at the Banquet Given by the English Socialists in the John Street Institution, London, September 22, 1844, to Commemorate his Escape from the Persecution of the Prussian Government and Arrival in England.* London: 1844.

BRITISH WORKING-CLASS NEWSPAPERS

(Editors and years consulted given in parenthesis)

The Black Dwarf (T. J. Wooler, 1817–24).

The British Statesman (O'Brien, 1842–3).

The Briton (1819).

Bronterre's National Reformer in Government, Law, Property, Religion and Morals (O'Brien, 1837).

Carpenter's Political Letters (Wm. Carpenter, 1830–1).

The Cap of Liberty (1819–20).

The Charter (1839–40).

The Chartist Circular (Glasgow, 1839–42).

Cleave's Weekly Police Gazette (John Cleave, 1835).

Co-Operative Magazine (1827–8).

The Cosmopolite (1832).

The Crisis (Owenite, 1832–4).

The Democratic Review of British and Foreign Politics, History and Literature (G. J. Harney, 1849–50).

The Destructive and Poor Man's Conservative (Hetherington, 1833).

The English Chartist Circular and Temperance Record for England and Wales (1839).

The Gauntlet—A Sound Republican Weekly Newspaper (Carlile, 1833–4).

The Gorgon (John Wade, 1818–19).

The Herald of the Rights of Industry (Manchester, 1832).
Hetherington's Twopenny Dispatch and People's Police Register (1836).
The Isis (Carlile, 1832).
The Labourer: a Monthly Magazine of Politics, Literature, Poetry, etc. (Jones and O'Connor, 1847–8).
The Labourer's Friend and Handicraft Chronicle (1821).
The London Democrat (Harney, 1839).
The London Dispatch (Hetherington, 1836–8).
The London Mercury (John Bell, 1836–7).
The London Working Man's Association Gazette (1839).
McDouall's Chartist and Republican Journal (Heywood, Hetherington, Hobson, 1841).
Midland Counties Illuminator (Thomas Cooper, 1841).
The Medusa or Penny Politician (1819).
The Movement (G. J. Holyoake, 1843–5).
The National (W. J. Linton, 1839).
The National Association Gazette (Hetherington, 1842).
The National Instructor (1850).
The National Reformer and Manx Weekly Review of Home and Foreign Affairs (O'Brien, 1846–7).
The Northern Liberator (Newcastle upon Tyne, 1837–8).
The Northern Star (Harney and O'Connor, 1837–52).
Notes to the People (Ernest Jones, 1851–2).
The Operative (O'Brien, 1838–9).
Pamphlets for the People (J. A. Roebuck, 1835).
Penny Papers for the People (Hetherington, 1830–1).
The People's Conservative and Trades' Union Gazette (Hetherington, 1833–4).
People's Press and Monthly Historical Newspaper (Shirrefs, 1847–8).
The Pioneer (Owenite, 1833–4).
Political Letters and Pamphlets (William Carpenter, 1830–3).
The Political Register (William Cobbett, 1802–35).
The Politician (Henry Gibb, 1841).
The Poor Man's Advocate (Manchester, 1832).
The Poor Man's Guardian (Hetherington, 1831–8).
The Prompter (Richard Carlile, 1830–1).
The Radical (1831).
The Reasoner (Holyoake, 1846–8).
The Red Republican (Harney, 1850).
Reid's Glasgow Magazine (1834).
The Republican (Carlile, 1819–25).
The Republican or Voice of the People (Hetherington, 1831).
Sherwin's Political Register (1817–18).
The Southern Star (O'Brien, 1840).
The Spirit of the Age (1848–9).
The Ten Hours' Advocate and Journal of Literature and Art (Manchester, Doherty, 1831–4).
The White Hat (1819).
The Working Man's Friend and Political Magazine (James Watson, 1832–3).

OTHER NEWSPAPERS CONSULTED

L'Atelier, Organ Special des Ouvriers.
Daily News.
Le Débat Social, Organe de la Démocratié.
Demokratisches Taschenbuch für das Deutsche Volk.
Deutsche Brüsseler Zeitung.
Deutsche Londoner Zeitung.
The Examiner.
The Globe.
The Leeds Mercury.
The Manchester Guardian.
The Morning Chronicle.
Neue Rheinische Zeitung, Organ der Demokratie.
The Spectator.
The Times.

ARTICLES

Armytage, W. H. G., 'The Chartist land colonies, 1846–8', *Agricultural History*, vol. XXXII, no. 2 (April 1958), pp. 87–96.

Aveling, Edward, 'George Julian Harney: a straggler of 1848', *The Social Democrat, A Monthly Socialist Review* (January 1847), pp. 2–8.

Beloussowa, N., 'Joseph Moll', in E. P. Kandel, ed., *Marx und Engels und die ersten proletarischen Revolutionäre* (Berlin: Dietz Verlag, 1965), pp. 42–74.

Briggs, Asa, 'Chartism reconsidered', in M. Roberts, ed., *Historical Studies, Papers Read Before the Third Conference of Irish Historians* (London: Conference of Irish Historians, 1959), pp. 42–59.

— 'The language of class in early nineteenth century England', in Asa Briggs and John Saville, eds., *Essays in Labour History*, London: Macmillan, 1960.

— 'The local background of Chartism', in Asa Briggs, ed., *Chartist Studies* (London, New York and Toronto: Macmillan and St Martin's Press, 1967 ed.), pp. 1–28.

— 'Middle class consciousness in English politics, 1780–1846', *Past and Present*, 9 (April 1956), pp. 65–74.

Brock, Peter, 'The birth of Polish socialism', *Central European Affairs*, vol. XIII, 1953, pp. 213–31.

— 'Joseph Cowen and the Polish exiles', *The Slavonic and East European Review*, vol. XXXII, no. 78 (December 1953), pp. 53–69.

— 'Polish democrats and English radicals, 1832–62: a chapter in the history of Anglo–Polish relations', *Journal of Modern History*, vol. XXV (1953), pp. 139–56.

— 'The Polish revolutionary commune in London', *Slavonic and East European Review*, vol. XXXV, no. 84 (December 1956), pp. 116–28.

— 'Polish socialists in early Victorian England: three documents', *The Polish Review*, vol. VI, no. 1–2 (1961), pp. 33–52.

Cadogan, Peter, 'Harney and Engels', *International Review of Social History*, vol. 10, no. 1 (1965), pp. 66–104.

Cowden, Morton H., 'Early Marxist Views on British Labor, 1837–1917', *The Western Political Quarterly*, xvi (1963), pp. 34–52.

Currie, R. and Hartwell, R. M. 'The making of the English working class?', *Economic History Review*, vol. 18, no. 3 (December 1965), pp. 633–43.

Drahn, Ernst, 'Zur Vorgeschichte des kommunistischen Manifests und der Arbeiterinternationale', *Die Neue Zeit*, vol. 37 (1919), pp. 131–8.

Dutt, Salme A., 'Chartism and the fight for peace', *Labour Monthly*, vol. 21 (June 1939), pp. 367–74.

Engels, Friedrich, 'The Chartist movement', *La Réforme*, November 22, 1847.

— 'Das Fest der Nationen in London', *Rheinische Jahrbücher zur gesellschaftlichen Reform*, vol. II, 1846, pp. 1–19.

Galkin, W., 'Ernest Jones', in E. P. Kandel, ed., *Marx und Engels und die ersten proletarischen Revolutionäre* (Berlin: Dietz Verlag, 1965), pp. 456–96.

Gash, Norman, 'The July revolution in England', Richard Pares and A. J. P. Taylor, eds., *Essays Presented to Sir Lewis Namier* (London: Macmillan, 1956).

Glasgow, Eric H., 'The establishment of the Northern Star Newspaper', *History*, vol. 39 (February and June 1954), pp. 55–67.

Groves, Reg, 'Chartism and the present day: the illusion of reformism', *Labour Monthly*, vol. 11 (January 1929), pp. 47–56.

— 'The class leadership of Chartism', *Labour Monthly*, vol. 11 (April, 1929), pp. 240–4.

Grünberg, Carl, 'Bruno Hildebrand über den kommunistischen Arbeiterbildungsverein in London', in Carl Grünberg, ed., *Archiv für die Geschichte des Sozialismus und der Arbeiterbewegung*, vol. 11 (Leipzig, 1919–21), pp. 445–59.

— ed., 'Die Londoner Kommunistische Zeitschrift und andere Urkunden aus dem Jahren 1847/1848', *Hauptwerke des Sozialismus und der Sozialpolitik*, Neue Folge, Heft 5 (Leipzig: C. L. Hirschfeld, 1921).

Haenisch, Walter, 'Karl Marx and the Democratic Association of 1847', *Science and Society, A Marxian Quarterley*, vol. II, no. 1, Winter 1937, pp. 83–102.

Harley, J. H., 'David Urquhart', *Contemporary Review*, vol. 118 (September 1920), pp. 400–4.

Harrison, Brian and Hollis, Patricia, 'Chartism, liberalism and the life of Robert Lowery', *English Historical Review*, vol. 82 (July 1967), pp. 503–35.

Hill, Christopher, 'The Norman yoke', in John Saville, ed., *Democracy and the Labour Movement, Essays in Honor of Dona Torr* (London: Lawrence and Wishart, 1954).

Hobsbawm, E. J., 'The labour aristocracy in nineteenth century Britain', in *Labouring Men: Studies in the History of Labour*, 3rd ed. (London: Weidenfeld and Nicolson, 1968), pp. 272–315.

— 'Methodism and the threat of revolution in Britain', in *Labouring Men: Studies in the History of Labour*, 3rd ed. (London: Weidenfeld and Nicolson, 1968), pp. 23–33.

Howell, George, 'Ernest Jones, the Chartist, poet, orator, patriot and politician', *The Delaware Reporter* (February 29, 1899).

Kandel, E. P., 'Eine schlechte Verteidigung einer schlechten Sache', *Beiträge zur Geschichte der deutschen Arbeiterbewegung*, Heft 2 (1963), pp. 290–303.

— and Lewiowa, S., 'Marx und Engels als Erzieher der ersten proletarischen Revolutionäre', in E. P. Kandel, ed., *Marx und Engels und die ersten proletarischen Revolutionäre* (Berlin: Dietz Verlag, 1965), pp. 5–40.

Kellett, E. E., 'The press', in G. M. Young, ed., *Early Victorian England*, London: Oxford University Press, 1934.

Kitson-Clark, G., 'Hunger and politics in 1842', *Journal of Modern History*, vol. 25 (December 1953), pp. 355–74.

Kovalev, Yuri V., 'Chartist literature', *Our History, Communist Party of Great Britain, Historians' Group*, pamphlet 17 (Spring 1960).

Krzyzanowski, Ludwik, 'Joseph Conrad's Prince Roman: fact and fiction', in Ludwik Krzyzanowski, ed., *Joseph Conrad: Centennial Essays* (New York: Polish Institute of Arts and Sciences in America, 1960), pp. 27–69.

Kunina, W., 'George Julian Harney', in E. P. Kandel, ed., *Marx und Engels und die ersten proletarischen Revolutionäre* (Berlin: Dietz Verlag, 1965), pp. 421–55.

Lehning, A., 'Discussions à Londres sur le communisme Icarien', *Bulletin of the International Institute for Social History*, 1952, pp. 87–109.

Lessner, Friedrich., 'Vor 1848 und nachher, Erinnerungen eines alten Kommunisten', *Deutsche Worte, Monatschefte*, xviii (1898), pp. 97–112.

Lewiowa, S., 'Karl Schapper', in E. P. Kandel, ed., *Marx und Engels und die ersten proletarischen Revolutionäre* (Berlin: Dietz Verlag, 1965), pp. 76–119.

MacDonald, H. Malcolm, 'Marx, Engels and the Polish national movement', *Journal of Modern History*, vol. xiii, no. 3 (September 1941), pp. 321–7.

Maehl, William H., Jr., 'Augustus Hardin Beaumont: Anglo-American radical, 1798–1838', *International Review of Social History*, vol. xiv, part 2 (1969), pp. 237–50.

— 'Chartist disturbances in north-eastern England', *International Review of Social History* (1963), pp. 389–414

Mahon, John, 'Marx, Engels and the London workers', *Marxism Today* (September 1964), pp. 266–74.

Mehring, Franz, 'Der Bund der Kommunisten', *Die Neue Zeit*, vol. 29, part 2 (April 1911), pp. 65–71.

Morris, Max, 'Chartism and the British working class movement', *Science and Society*, vol. 12, no. 4 (Autumn 1948), pp. 400–17.

Morton, A. L., 'The interpretation of Chartism', *Marxism Today* (June 1961), pp. 177–83.

— 'The rediscovery of Chartism', *Marxism Today* (March 1960), pp. 83–7.

Na'aman, Shlomo, 'Zur Geschichte des Bundes der Kommunisten in der zweiten Phase seines Bestehens', *Sonderdruck aus dem Archiv für Sozialgeschichte*, vol. 5 (1965). Hanover: Verlag für Literatur und Zeitgeschehen.

Neale, R. S., 'Class and class consciousness in early nineteenth century England: three classes or five?', *Victorian Studies*, vol. xii, no. 1 (September 1968), pp. 4–32.

Nettlau, Max, 'Londoner deutsche kommunistische Diskussionen, 1845', in Carl Grünberg, ed., *Archiv für die Geschichte des Socialismus und der Arbeiterbewegung*, vol. 10 (Leipzig, 1919–21), pp. 362–91.

Nettlau, Max, 'Marxanalekten: II. Zu Marx' und Engel's Aufenthalt in London, Ende 1847', in Carl Grünberg, ed., *Archiv für die Geschichte des Socialismus und der Arbeiterbewegung*, vol. 8 (Leipzig, 1919–21), pp. 392–401.

Nicolaevsky, B., 'Toward a history of "The Communist League" 1847–52', *International Review of Social History*, vol. 1 (1956), pp. 234–52.

O'Higgins, Rachel, 'The Irish influence in the Chartist movement', *Past and Present*, 20 (November 1961), pp. 83–96.

Plummer, Alfred, 'The place of Bronterre O'Brien in the working class movement', *Economic History Review*, vol. II, no. 1 (January 1929), pp. 61–80.

Prothero, Iorwerth, 'Chartism in London', *Past and Present*, 44 (August 1969), pp. 76–101.

Prothero, Iorwerth, and Rowe, D. J., 'Debates: the London Working Men's Association and the People's Charter', *Past and Present*, 38 (December 1967), pp. 169–76.

Rjasanoff, N., 'Karl Marx und Friedrich Engels über die Polenfrage', in Carl Grünberg, ed., *Archiv für die Geschichte des Socialismus und der Arbeiterbewegung*, vol. 6 (Leipzig, 1919–21), pp. 175–81.

Rose, J. H., 'The Unstamped Press, 1815–36', *English Historical Review*, vol. 12 (1897), pp. 711–26.

Rothstein, Th., 'Aus der Vorgeschichte der Internationale', *Ergänzungshefte zur Neuen Zeit*, 17 (October 31, 1913).

Rowe, D. J., 'Chartism and the Spitalfields silk weavers', *Economic History Review*, vol. XX, second series, no. 3 (December 1967), pp. 482–93.

— 'The Chartist convention and the regions', *Economic History Review*, vol. XXII, second series, no. 1 (April 1969), pp. 58–74.

— 'The failure of London Chartism', *The Historical Journal*, vol. XI, no. 3 (1968), pp. 472–87.

— 'The London Working Men's Association and the "People's Charter" ', *Past and Present*, 36 (April 1967), pp. 73–85.

Rutkowska, Sister M. Neomisia, 'John Tyssowski', *Bulletin of the Polish Institute of Arts and Sciences in America*, vol. II, no. 4 (July 1944), pp. 1128–42.

Salt, John, 'Local manifestations of the Urquhartite movement', *International Review of Social History*, vol. XIII, part 3 (1968), pp. 350–65.

Saville, John, 'Chartism in the year of revolution, 1848', *Modern Quarterly*, vol. 8, no. 1 (Winter 1952–3), pp. 23–33.

— 'The Chartist land plan', *Society for the Study of Labour History Bulletin*, 3 (Autumn 1961), p. 4.

Soffer, R. N., 'Attitudes and allegiances in the unskilled north, 1830–50', *International Review of Social History*, vol. 10, no. 3 (1965), pp. 429–54.

Tatarinova, Kira, 'Soviet historians on Chartism', *Society for the Study of Labour History Bulletin*, no. 5 (Autumn 1962) pp. 27–32.

Tholfsen, Trygve R., 'The Chartist crisis in Birmingham', *International Review of Social History*, vol. 3, part 2 (1958), pp. 461–81.

Thompson, Dorothy, 'Notes on aspects of Chartist leadership', *Society for the Study of Labour History Bulletin*, no. 15 (Autumn 1969), pp. 28–33.

Webb, R. K., 'The Victorian reading public', *Pelican Guide to English Literature*, ed. Boris Ford, vol. 6, *From Dickens to Hardy*. Harmondsworth and Baltimore: Penguin Books, 1963, pp. 205–27.

— 'Working class readers in Victorian England', *English Historical Review*, vol. 65 (1950), pp. 333–51.

Weisser, Henry, 'The British working class and the Cracow uprising of 1846', *The Polish Review*, vol. XIII, no. 1 (Winter 1968), pp. 3–19.

— 'Chartist Internationalism, 1845–8', *The Historical Journal*, vol. XIV, no. 1 (1971), pp. 49–66.

— 'Polonophilism and the British working class, 1830–45', *The Polish Review*, vol. XII, no. 2 (Spring 1967), pp. 78–96.

— 'The role of Feargus O'Connor in Chartist Internationalism', *The Rocky Mountain Social Science Journal*, vol. 6, no. 1 (April 1969), pp. 82–90.

— 'New light on the Cracow manifesto: a note', *The Polish Review*, vol. XVI, no. 2 (Spring 1971), pp. 103–4.

BOOKS

Abramsky, C. and Collins, H., *Karl Marx and the British Labour Movement*. London: Macmillan, 1965.

Adams, W. E. *Memoirs of a Social Atom*. New York: A. M. Kelley, 1968 ed.

Altick, R. D., *The English Common Reader: a Social History of the Mass Reading Public, 1800–1900*. Chicago: University of Chicago Press, 1959.

Armytage, W. H. G., *The Liberal Background to the Labour Movement*. London: Ernest Bann, 1951.

Artz, Frederick B., *Reaction and Revolution, 1814–32*. New York and London: Harper, 1934.

Aspinall, A., *Politics and the Press, 1780–1850*. London: Hone and Van Thal, 1949.

Barker, Ambrose G., *Henry Hetherington, Pioneer in the Freethought and Working Class Struggles of a Hundred Years Ago for the Freedom of the Press*. London: Pioneer Press, n.d.

Bebel, A. and Brenstein, E. eds., *Der Briefwechsel zwischen Friedrich Engels und Karl Marx, 1844 bis 1883*. 4 vols., Stuttgart, 1913.

Beer, M., *A History of British Socialism*, vol. II. London: George Allen and Unwin, 1953.

Berlin, Isiah., *Karl Marx: his Life and Environment*. London: Oxford University Press, 1948.

Bernstein, Eduard, ed., *Documente des Socialismus, Hefte für Geschichte, Urkunden, und Bibliographie des Socialismus*. Berlin: Verlag der Socialistischen Monatshefte, 1902.

Bertrand, Louis, *Histoire de la Démocratie et du Socialisme en Belgique depuis 1830*, vol. I. Brussels and Paris: Dechenne, 1906.

Black, Frank Gees and Black, Renee Métivier, eds., *The Harney Papers*. Assen: Van Gorcum, 1969.

Braunthal, Julius., *Geschichte der Internationale*, vol. I. Hanover: Dietz, 1962; *History of the International*, vol. I. New York and Washington: Frederick Praeger, 1967.

Brettschneider, Werner., *Entwicklung und Bedeutung des deutschen Frühsozialismus in London*. University of Königsberg Ph.D. Dissertation: Wilhlem Postberg, Bottrop, 1936.

Briggs, Asa, ed., *Chartist Studies*. London: Macmillan, 1959, 1967.
— *History of Birmingham*. London: Oxford University Press, 1952.
Brown, Philip Anthony, *The French Revolution in English History*. London: Crosley Lockwood and Son, 1918.
Cobbett, William, *Eleven Lectures on the French and Belgian Revolutions and English Boroughmongering, Delivered in the Theatre of the Rotunda, Blackfriars Bridge*. London: W. Strange, 1830.
Cole, G. D. H., *Attempts at General Union: a Study in British Trade Union History, 1818–34*. London: Macmillan, 1953.
— *British Working Class Politics, 1832–1914*. London: George Routledge and Sons, 1941.
— *Chartist Portraits*. London: Macmillan, 1941, 1965.
— *The Life of William Cobbett*. London: Hone and Van Thal, 1947.
— *Richard Carlile*. London: Fabian Society Biographical Series, no. 13, 1943.
— *A History of Socialist Thought*, vol. I, *The Forerunners, 1789–1850*. London: Macmillan, 1959.
— and Cole, Margaret, eds., *The Opinions of William Cobbett*. London: The Cobbett Publishing Co., 1941.
— and Filson, A. W., *British Working Class Movements, Select Documents, 1789–1875*. London: Macmillan, 1959; New York: St Martins Press, 1965.
Collett, C. D., *A History of the Taxes on Knowledge*. London: T. Fisher Unwin, 1899.
Cone, Carl B., *The English Jacobins: Reformers in the Late 18th Century England*. New York: Scribner, 1968.
Conklin, Robert J., *Thomas Cooper the Chartist, 1805–1892*. Manila: University of the Philippines Press, 1935.
Cooper, Thomas, *The Life of Thomas Cooper*. London: Hodder and Stoughton, 1875.
— *Thoughts at Fourscore, and Earlier, a Medley*. London: Hodder and Stoughton, 1855.
Cukierman, Liza, *Die polenfreundliche Bewegung in Frankreich im Jahre 1830–1831*. Warsaw: 1926.
Darvall, Frank Ongley, *Popular Disturbances and Public Order in Regency England*. London: Oxford University Press, 1934.
Deane, Phyllis, *The First Industrial Revolution*. London: Cambridge University Press, 1967.
De La Hodde, Lucien, *History of Secret Societies and the Republican Party of France from 1830 to 1848*. Philadelphia: J. B. Lippencott and Co., 1886.
Dolléans, Edouard, *Le Chartisme, 1830–48*. Paris: H. Floury, 1913.
— *Histoire de la Démocratie et du Socialisme*. Paris: 1936.
Dorling, William, *Henry Vincent, a Biographical Sketch*. London: James Clarke, 1879.
Duncombe, Thomas H., ed., *The Life and Correspondence of Thomas Slingsby Duncombe*. London: Hurst and Blackett, 1868.
Dutt, R. Palme, *The Internationale*. London: Lawrence and Wishart, 1964.
Dutt, Salme A., *When England Arose: the Centenary of the People's Charter*, Key Books, no 6. London: Fore Publications, 1939.

Eisenstein, Elizabeth L., *The First Professional Revolutionist: Filippo Michelle Buonarroti, a Bibliographical Essay*. Cambridge, Mass.: Harvard University Press, 1959.

Fehling, August Wm., 'Karl Schapper und die Anfänge der Arbeiterbewegung bis zur Revolution von 1848, von der Burschenschaft zu Kommunismus'. Rostock: Ph.D. dissertation, 1922.

Fejtö, Francois, ed., *The Opening of an Era, 1848—an Historical Symposium*. London: Alan Wingate, 1948.

Förder, Herwig, *Marx und Engels am Vorabend der Revolution*. Berlin: Akademie Verlag, 1960.

Foster, William L., *History of the Three Internationals: the World Socialist and Communist Movements from 1848 to the Present*. New York: Greenwood Press, 1968.

Frost, Thomas, *Forty Years' Recollections, Literary and Political*. London: Sampson, Low, Searle, and Rivington, 1880.

— *The Secret Societies of the European Revolution, 1776–1876*. London: Tinsley Brothers, 1876.

Fundamentals of Marxism Leninism Manual, 2nd revised ed. Moscow: Foreign Languages Publishing House, 1963.

Gammage, R. G., *The History of the Chartist Movement from its Commencement to the Present Time*. Newcastle upon Tyne: Browne and Browne, 1894; New York: Augustus M. Kelley, 1969.

Glasgow, Eric, and Read, Donald, *Feargus O'Connor, Irishman and Chartist*. London: Edward Arnold Publishers, 1961.

Gleason, John Howes, *The Genesis of Russophobia in Great Britain*. Cambridge, Mass.: Harvard University Press, 1950.

Groves, Reg, *But We Shall Rise Again: a Narrative History of Chartism*. London: Secker and Warburg, 1939.

Hadfield, Alice Mary, *The Chartist Land Company*. Newton Abbot: David and Charles, 1970.

Halecki, O., *A History of Poland*. New York: Roy Publishers, 1943.

Hales, E. E. Y., *Mazzini and the Secret Societies: the Making of a Myth*. New York: P. J. Kennedy and Sons, n.d.

Halèvy, Elie, *A History of the English People*, vols. I, II and III. London: 1941–7; New York: Peter Smith, 1950.

Hall, Charles, *The Effects of Civilization on the People in European States*. London: 1813.

Hamburger, Joseph, *James Mill and the Art of Revolution*. New Haven and London: Yale University Press, 1963.

Hamerow, Theodore, *Restoration, Revolution, Reaction: Economics and Politics in Germany 1815–71*. Princeton: Princeton University Press, 1958.

Hammond, J. B. and Hammond, Barbara, *The Age of the Chartists, 1832–54: a Study in Discontent*. Hamden, Conn.: Anchor Books, 1962.

Harvey, Rowland Hill, *Robert Owen, Social Idealist*. University of California Press, 1958.

Hobsbawm, E. J., *The Age of Revolution, 1789–1848*. London: Weidenfeld & Nicolson; Cleveland and New York: The World Publishing Co., 1962.

— *Labouring Men: Studies in the History of Labour*. London: Weidenfeld & Nicolson, 1964.

Hobsbawm, E. J., *Primitive Rebels: Studies in Archaic Forms of Social Movement in the 19th and 20th Centuries.* Manchester: Manchester University Press, 1959; New York: The Norton Library, 1965 ed.

Hollis, Patricia, *The Pauper Press: a Study in Working-Class Radicalism of the 1830s.* London: Oxford University Press, 1970.

Holyoake, G. J., *Bygones Worth Remembering.* London: T. Fisher Unwin, 1905.

— *Life and Character of Henry Hetherington.* London: Reasoner Office, 1849.

— *Life and Labours of Ernest Jones, Esq., Poet, Politician and Patriot.* London: F. Farrah, 1869.

— *Sixty Years of an Agitator's Life.* London: T. Fisher Unwin, 1892.

Hovell, Mark, *The Chartist Movement.* Manchester University Press, 1950 ed.

Hutchison, Keith, *Labour in Politics.* Edinburgh: The Riverside Press, 1925.

Institut für Marxismus–Leninismus beim Zentralkomitee der Sozialistischen Einheitspartei Deutschlands, *Geschichte der deutschen Arbeiterbewegung.* Vol. 1, *Von den Anfängen der deutschen Arbeiterbewegung bis zum Ausgang des 19. Jahrhunderts.* Berlin: Dietz Verlag, 1966.

Jackson, Thomas Alfred, *Trials of British Freedom.* London: Lawrence and Wishart, 1945.

Jephson, Henry, *The Platform, its Rise and Progress.* London: Macmillan, 1892.

Kaler, Emil, *Wilhelm Weitling, seine Agitation und Lehre in geschichtlichen Zusammenhange dargestellt,* Sozialdemokratische Bibliothek, xi. Hottingen–Zurich: Volksbuchhandlung, 1887.

Kandel, E., *Marx und Engels und die ersten proletarischen Revolutionäre.* Berlin: Dietz Verlag, 1965.

Kann, Robet A., *The Multi-National Empire: Nationalism and National Reform in the Habsburg Monarchy, 1848–1918,* vol. 1. New York: Columbia University Press, 1950.

King, Bolton, *The Life of Mazzini.* Everyman's Edition, London and Toronto: J. M. Dent; New York: Dutton, 1902.

Kissinger, Henry A., *A World Restored: Metternich, Castlereagh and the Problems of the Peace, 1812–22.* Boston: Houghton, Mifflin Co., 1957.

Kukiel, Marian, *Czartoryski and European Unity, 1770–1861.* Princeton: Princeton University Press, 1955.

Leary, Frederick, *The Life of Ernest Jones.* London: Democrat Publishing Office, 1887.

Leslie, Robert F., *Polish Politics and the Revolution of November, 1830.* London: The Althone Press, 1956.

Linton, W. J., *European Republicans: Recollections of Mazzini and his Friends.* London: Lawrence and Bullon, 1892.

— *Memories.* London: Lawrence and Bullon, 1895; published in New York as *Threescore and Ten Years, 1820–90, Recollections.* Scribners, 1894.

Lorwin, Lewis L., *The International Labor Movement.* New York: Harper and Brothers, 1953.

— *Labor and Internationalism.* New York: The Macmillan Co., 1929.

Lovett, William, *Life and Struggles of William Lovett in His Pursuit of Bread, Knowledge and Freedom.* London: G. Bell and Sons, 1920; Macgibbon & Kee, 1967.

Maccoby S., *English Radicalism*, vol. I, *1786–1832*, vol. II, *1832–52*. London: George Allen and Unwin, 1955 and 1935.

McCord, Norman, *The Anti-Corn Law League*. London: Allen and Unwin, 1958.

Maenchen-Helfen, Otto and Nicolaievsky, Boris, *Karl Marx, Man and Fighter*. New York: J. P. Lippincott, 1936.

Maitron, Jean, ed., *Dictionnaire Biographique du Mouvement Ouvrier Français. Premiere Partie, 1789–1864*, vols. 1 and 3. Paris: Éditions Ouvrières, 1964–6.

Marshall, Dorothy, *English People in the Eighteenth Century*. London, New York and Toronto: Longmans, Green & Co., 1956.

Martin, Kingsley. *The Triumph of Lord Palmerston: a Study of Public Opinion in England Before the Crimean War*. London: George Allen and Unwin, 1924.

Marx, Karl, *Enthüllungen über den Kommunisten-Prozess zu Köln*. Hottingen–Zürich: Volksbuchhandlung, 1885.

Karl Marx and Friedrich Engels on Britain. Moscow: Foreign Languages Publishing House, 1954, 1962.

Marxist Study Courses, course two, *Working Class History*, lesson two, 'The English industrial revolution and Chartism'. London: Martin Lawrence, 1932.

Mather, F. C., *Public Order in the Age of the Chartists*. Manchester: Manchester University Press, 1959; New York: A. M. Kelley, 1967 ed.

Mayer, Gustav, *Friedrich Engels—a Biography*. London: Chapman and Hall, 1936.

Mehring, Franz, *Karl Marx—The Story of His Life*. New York: Covici Friede, 1935.

Mendel, Arthur P., *The Essential Works of Marxism*. London, New York and Toronto: Bantam Books, 1965.

Mitchell, Charles, *The Newspaper Press Directory*. London: Charles Mitchell, 1846.

Morelli, Emilia, *Mazzini in Inghilterra*. Studi e documenti di storia risorgimento, XVI. Florence: Felice Le Monnier, 1938.

— *L'Inghilterra di Mazzini*. Italiano Biblioeteca Scientifica, Serie II, *Memorie*, vol. XVI. Rome: Instituto per la storia del risorgimento, italiano, 1965.

Morton, A. L. and Tate, George, *The British Labour Movement, a History*. London: Lawrence and Wishart, 1956.

Müller-Lehning, A., *The International Association, 1855–9: a contribution to the Preliminary History of the First International*. Leiden: E. J. Brill, 1938.

Neiman, Fraser, 'W. J. Linton, 1812–97', unpublished Harvard Ph.D. thesis, 1938.

Noyes, P. H., *Organization and Revolution: Working-Class Associations in the German Revolutions of 1848–9*. Princeton: Princeton University Press, 1966.

Osborne, John W., *William Cobbett: his Thought and his Times*. New Brunswick, New Jersey: Rutgers University Press, 1966.

Paine, Thomas, *The Rights of Man*. London and New York: J. M. Dent and Sons, 1963 ed.

Pankhurst, R., *The Saint Simonians: Mill and Carlyle*. London: Sidgwick and Jackson, 1957.

Pares, Richard, and Taylor, A. J. P., eds., *Essays Presented to Sir Lewis Namier*. London: Macmillan, 1956.

Patterson, A. Temple, *Radical Leicester: a History of Leicester, 1780–1850*. Leicester: Leicester University College, 1954.

Perkins, Harold, *The Origins of Modern English Society, 1780–1880*. London and Toronto: Routledge & Kegan Paul and the University of Toronto Press, 1969.

Plumb, J. H., ed., *Studies in Social History: a Tribute to G. M. Trevelyan*. New York: Longmans, Green, 1955.

Plummer, Alfred, *Bronterre: a Political Biography of Bronterre O'Brien, 1804–64*. London: George Allen and Unwin, 1971.

Postgate, R., *The Worker's International*. London: Harcourt, Brace and Howe, 1920.

Postgate, Raymond and Vallance, Aylmer, *Those Foreigners: the English People's Opinion on Foreign Affairs as Reflected in their Newspapers since Waterloo*. London: George C. Harrop and Co., 1937.

Price, John, *The International Labour Movement*. Oxford: Royal Institute of International Affairs, Oxford University Press, 1945.

Read, Donald, *The English Provinces, 1760–1960: a Study in Influence*. London and New York: Edward Arnold and St Martin's Press, 1964.

— *Press and People, 1790–1850—Opinion in Three English Cities*. London and New York: Edward Arnold and St Martin's Press, 1961.

— and Glasgow, Eric. *Feargus O'Connor, Irishman and Chartist*. London: Edward Arnold, 1961.

Reddaway, W. F., Renson, J. H., Halecki, R. and Dyboski, R., eds., *The Cambridge Modern History of Poland, 1697–1935*. London: Cambridge University Press.

Reybaud, M. Louis, *Études sur les reformateurs ou socialistes modernes*, 2nd ed., vol. II. Paris: Guillaumin et Cie, 1848.

Rheinische Jahrbücher zur Gesellschaftlichen Reform, vol. II, Bellevue bei Constanz, 1846.

Robinson, Gertrude, *David Urquhart: Some Chapters in the Life of a Victorian Knight Errant of Justice and Liberty*. Oxford: Basil Blackwell, 1920.

Rosenblatt, Katherine Golding, *The Chartist Movement in its Social and Economic Aspects*. New York: Columbia University Press, 1916.

Rothstein, Fiodor, *From Chartism to Labourism, Historical Sketches of the English Working Class Movement*. London: M. Lawrence, Ltd., 1929.

Rudé, George. *The Crowd in History, 1730–1848: a Study in Popular Disturbances in France and England*. New York: John Wiley and Sons, 1964.

— *Great Lives Observed: Robespierre*. Englewood Cliffs, N.J.: Prentice Hall, 1967.

Saville, John, ed., *Democracy and the Labour Movement; Essays in Honor of Dona Torr*. London: Lawrence and Wishart, 1954.

— *Ernest Jones: Chartist. Selections from the Writings and Speeches of Ernest Jones with Introduction and Notes*. London: Lawrence and Wishart, 1952.

Schenk, H. G., *The Aftermath of the Napoleonic Wars, the Concert of Europe—an Experiment*. London: Oxford University Press, 1947.

Schlütter, Hermann, *Die Chartistenbewegung, ein Beitrag zur social-politischen Geschichte Englands*. New York: Socialist Literature Company, 1916.

Schoyen, A. R., *The Chartist Challenge: a Portrait of George Julian Harney*. London: Heinemann, 1958.

Searby, Peter, *Coventry Politics in the Age of the Chartists, 1836–48*. Coventry: Allesley Press, 1964.

Sencier, Georges, *Babouvisme après Babeuf, sociétés secrètes et conspirations communistes, 1830–48*. Paris: Marcel Rivière, 1912.

Seton-Watson, Hugh, *Britain in Europe, 1789–1914: a Survey of Foreign Policy*. London: Cambridge University Press, 1937.

Slosson, Preston William, *The Decline of the Chartist Movement*. New York: Columbia University Press, 1916.

Smelser, N. J., *Social Change in the Industrial Revolution*. Chicago: University of Chicago Press, 1959.

Snell, F. J., *Palmerston's Borough: a Budget of Electioneering Anecdotes, Jokes, Squibs and Speeches*. London: Horace Marshall and Son, 1894.

Spitzer, Alan, *The Revolutionary Theories of Louis Auguste Blanqui*. New York: Columbia University Press, 1957.

Stekloff, G. M., *History of the First International*. London: Lawrence Martin, 1928.

Stepanowa, E. A., *Friedrich Engels, sein Leben und Werk*. Berlin: Dietz Verlag, 1958.

Stern, Alfred, *Geschichte Europas seit den Verträgen von 1815 bis zum Frankfurter Frieden von 1871*. Stuttgart and Berlin: Cotta, 1913–28.

Tawney, R. H., *The British Labour Movement*. New Haven: Yale University Press, 1925.

Temperley, Harold, *The Foreign Policy of Canning, 1822–7*. London: G. Bell & Sons, 1925.

Thompson, E. P., *The Making of the English Working Class*. London: Victor Gollancz, 1963; New York: Vantage Books, 1966.

— *The Struggle for a Free Press*. London: A People's Press Publication, 1952.

Torr, Dona, ed., *History in the Making*, vol. I, *From Cobbett to the Chartists, 1815–48*. London: Lawrence and Wishart, 1956.

Von Sala, Moriz Freiherrn, *Geschichte des polnischen Aufstandes vom Jahre 1846*. Wien: Carl Gerold's Sohn, 1867.

Wakefield, A. B., *Ernest Jones, the People's Friend*. Halifax: Womersley Exchange Printing Works, 1891.

Wallas, Graham, *The Life of Francis Place*. New York: Alfred A. Knopf, 1919.

Wearmouth, Robert F., *Some Working-Class Movements of the Nineteenth Century*. London: Epworth Press, 1948.

Webb, R. K., *The British Working Class Reader, 1790–1848: Literacy and Social Tension*. London: George Allen and Unwin, 1955.

Weber, Günter, *Die polnische Emigration in neunzehnten Jahrhundert*. Essen: Essener Verlanganstalt, 1937.

Webster, Sir Charles, *The Foreign Policy of Castlereagh, 1815–22*, 2nd ed. London: 1947.

— *Britain, the Liberal Movement and the Eastern Question*. London: G. Bell & Sons, 1951.

Wermuth, D. Jur. and Stieber, Dr. Jur., *Die communisten Verschwörungen des neunzehnten Jahrhunderts*. Berlin: 1853.

West, Julius, *A History of the Chartist Movement*. London: Constable, 1920.

White, R. J., *Waterloo to Peterloo*. New York: The Macmillan Co., 1957.

Wicks, Margaret C. W., *The Italian Exiles in London, 1816–48*. Manchester. Manchester University Press, 1937.

Wickwar, William H., *The Struggle for the Freedom of the Press, 1819–32*. London: George Allen and Unwin, 1928.

Wiener, Joel H., *The War of the Unstamped: the Movement to Repeal the British Newspaper Tax, 1830–6*. Ithaca and London: Cornell University Press, 1969.

Williams, David, *John Frost, a Study in Chartism*. Cardiff: University of Wales Press, 1939.

Wilson, Alexander, *The Chartist Movement in Scotland*. Manchester: Manchester University Press, 1970.

— *Scottish Chartist Portraits*. Wakefield: Micro-Methods, Inc., 1965.

Winkler, Gerhard, ed., *Dokumente zur Geschichte des Bundes der Kommunisten, Beiträge zur Geschichte und Theorie der Arbeiterbewegung*, Heft 15. Berlin: Dietz Verlag, 1957.

Wittke, Carl, *The Utopian Communist: a Biography of Wilhelm Weitling, Nineteenth Century Reformer*. Baton Rouge: Louisiana State University Press, 1950.

Wright, Leslie C., *Scottish Chartism*. Edinburgh and London: Oliver and Boyd, 1953.

Wyncoll, Peter, *Nottingham Chartism; Nottingham Workers in Revolt During the Nineteenth Century*. Nottingham: Nottingham Trades Council. 1966.

Index

Abramski, C., 195
addresses, to and from Europe and Europeans
  Chartist, 5, 32, 67–78, 86, 88, 92, 108 (n. 11, n. 15), 121, 123, 129, 132, 135, 138, 149, 155–6, 167–8, 183 (n. 88), 185 (n. 112), 192 (n. 217)
  working-class, pre-Chartist, 5, 7, 32, 35–7, 50, 53–7, 60 (n. 14), 64 (n. 96), 88–9
Afghanistan, 76, 174, 175
Albert, Prince Consort, 89, 90
Alexander I, Tsar of Russia, 14
Algeria, 76, 83
Alien Bill, Alien Act, 26, 164, 190 (n. 197)
Althrop, Viscount (Spencer, John Charles), 38
America, United States of, 11, 39, 73–4, 76, 83, 86, 93, 133, 140, 156, 177
Anti-Corn Law League, 97, 99, 114 (n. 144), 159, 160 (see also Corn Laws; free trade)
anti-Semitism, see Jews
Apostolato Populare, 157
armies
  criticisms of, 25, 41, 75–6, 83, 153
  in revolutions, 17, 18, 29 (n. 61), 48, 100–1, 174
artisan communism, 126, 146, 180 (n. 40)
Aspinall, Arthur, 21
assassination, 41, 80, 106, 117 (n. 213)
Association Démocratique (of Brussels), 146–8, 151, 186–7 (n. 141), 190 (n. 189)
Attwood, Charles, 105, 117 (n. 201)
Attwood, Thomas, 105, 117 (n. 201)
Austria and Austrians, 10, 13, 15, 19, 20, 24, 30 (n. 71, n. 78), 82, 94–5, 113 (n. 123), 124, 140, 144, 157, 162, 175, 185 (n. 115)
  intervention in Italy, 19, 20, 24, 30 (n. 71, n. 78)

Babouvism, 78, 136, 139, 165, 181 (n. 46)

Ballot, 44, 46, 93
Bauer, Heinrich, 125–7, 130
Beaumont, Arthur James, 87, 89
Beaumont, Augustus Hardin, 72, 87–9, 108 (n. 17)
Belgium, 47–8, 57, 69–71, 73, 85, 112 (n. 98), 146, 151–2, 186 (n. 141)
  revolution of 1830, 34, 43, 47–8, 62 (n. 66), 69, 87, 149
  workers in Belgium, 48, 67–9, 70–2, 108 (n. 15), 114 (n. 148), 147–8 (see also Katz, Jacob)
Bell, John, 88
Beniowski, Major Bartolomiej, 99, 101–2, 115 (n. 178, n. 179), 116 (n. 180, n. 183), 118
Bernard, James, 88, 89, 111 (n. 84)
Berrier-Fontaine, Camille, 111 (n. 72), 129
Birmingham Political Union, 93
Black Dwarf, 9, 11, 13–14, 18–19, 24–5, 28 (n. 20)
Blanc, Louis, 151
Blanqui, August 129, 146
Bonaparte, Joseph, 21–2
Bonaparte, Napoleon, 12–15, 22, 28 (n. 29, n. 33, n. 35), 95, 174–5, 188 (n. 160)
Boroughmongers, 10, 14, 17, 19, 20–3, 26, 28 (n. 11), 33, 42–7, 65 (n. 111)
Bourbons, in general, 10, 12–13, 22, 26, 29 (n. 46), 42, 44–5, 62 (n. 48)
  Bourbon police, 40, 85, 91, 112 (n. 104) (see also police)
  Bourbon 'system', 26 (see also centralisation)
Bowring, Sir John, 111 (n. 71), 141, 157, 158
Braunthal, Julius, 60 (n. 14), 197–8
Brazil, 130
Briggs, Asa, 197
Britain, in general, 4, 8, 9, 11, 22, 26–7, 33, 34, 65 (n. 111), 70, 74, 75, 82, 84–5, 98, 144, 152–3, 160
  Constitution, 9, 27, 82, 152
  foreign policy, 1, 4, 11, 14–15, 20, 23,

Britain, foreign policy (*cont.*)
27, 28–9 (n. 37), 30 (n. 78), 52,
57–9, 63 (n. 83), 58–9, 75–6, 81,
94–7, 104, 158–60, 173–8, 189
(n. 174), 196
republicanism, 101, 153
revolution in, 16, 34, 39, 53, 63 (n.
81), 99–103, 170
British Museum, 74
British Statesman, 83
British working class, *see* working class;
Chartism
Brougham, Henry, first Baron
Brougham and Vaux, 38
Bund der Gerechten, 126–8, 138, 146–8,
181 (n. 48, n. 49), 184 (n. 95)
Buonarotti, Filippo Michelle, 78, 181
(n. 46)
Burschenschaften, 127, 129

Cap of Liberty, 11
Canning, George, 15
Carbonari, 16, 119, 190 (n. 190)
Carlile, Richard, 3, 11, 13–15, 17–19,
23–6, 27 (n. 3), 28 (n. 20, n. 27),
30 (n. 71), 32, 42, 138, 192 (n. 216)
Caroline, Queen of England, 8
Carpenter, William, 33–5
Cartwright, Major John, 7, 66
Castlereagh, Viscount (Stewart,
Robert), 14–15, 26, 28 (n. 33), 62
(n. 65), 95–6
Caucasus and Caucasians, 140
Central National Association, 88, 89
centralisation, workers' fears of, 74, 85,
89, 92, 110–11 (n. 67)
Charles X, King of France, 38, 44–6, 93
Charlotte, Princess, 90
Charter, The, 89, 92–3
Chartism, in general, 66, 84, 110 (n.
63), 145, 147, 165–6, 171–2, 191
(n. 202), 194, 197
Chartist movement
addresses, to and from Europe, 5, 32,
67–78, 86, 88, 92, 108 (n. 11, n.
15), 121, 123, 129, 132, 135, 138,
149, 155–6, 167–8, 183 (n. 88), 185
(n. 112), 192 (n. 217)
belligerency, 81, 130, 143, 189 (n.
182) (*see also* Chartist movement
and interventionism; Chartist
movement and war, 'just')
class consciousness, 1, 68–72, 77–8,
80–2, 120–3, 125, 130–1, 144, 149,

155–6, 163, 168–9, 171–2, 179
(n. 19), 180 (n. 40), 194–5
Conventions, 79, 84–7, 110 (n. 64),
131, 185 (n. 122)
and education, 68–70, 73–5, 77, 156,
158, 167, 171
and emigration, 83, 160
Executive of, 134–5, 141, 166, 183
(n. 93)
exiles and, *see* exiles; *names of individual exiles; the names of exiles'
organisations*
and foreign policy, 58–9, 75–6, 81,
84–7, 104, 158–60, 173–8, 189
(n. 174), 196
French Chartists, 93
fund-raising for European affairs, 72,
108–9 (n. 19), 138, 141–2, 184 (n.
106), 185 (n. 118), 189 (n. 182)
and internationalism, 25, 32, 48, 68–
73, 76–9, 81, 84, 92–3, 101, 107,
109 (n. 30), 112 (n. 109), 120–1,
125, 130–2, 135–7, 139, 143–4,
148–9, 154–5, 162–3, 165–8, 171,
175, 179
and interventionism, calls for, 89,
143, 161 (*see also* Chartist movement, belligerency; Chartist movement and war, 'just')
and the Land Plan, 49, 151–3, 166,
188 (n. 166)
and London, 4, 11, 66, 107 (n. 1),
108 (n. 5), 120, 126, 134, 138, 155,
164–6, 190–1 (n. 198), 191 (n. 200,
n. 201)
and Marx, 144–50, 186 (n. 137, n.
138) (*see also* Marx, Karl; Marxism, or scientific communism;
Marxist comments and views of
Chartists (including proto-Marxism))
meetings on foreign affairs, 32, 72,
106–7, 118–19, 125, 131–2, 134–6,
141, 146–8, 153, 155, 157
and middle-classes: co-operation
with, 95, 156, 167; resentment of,
80–2, 94–5, 97, 104, 130, 147–8,
156, 162, 169, 188 (n. 163)
and moral force, physical force
issues, 79–80, 110 (n. 63), 156,
160, 163, 165, 190 (n. 194)
and nationalism: British, 70, 74–5,
82, 85, 96–7, 144, 152–3, 167, 178;
foreign, 131–2, 140, 157–61, 194

organisations of, for internationalism, *see* Fraternal Democrats; Democratic Friends of All Nations; Democratic Committee for Poland's Regeneration; People's International League; *for other organisations in the movement, see* London Working Men's Association; National Association; National Charter Association; East London Democratic Association
and pacifism, 68, 70, 73–7, 81–3, 95–6, 109 (n. 27), 112 (n. 109), 113 (n. 131), 136, 140, 156, 188 (n. 168), 191 (n. 205)
and polonophilism, 73, 77, 106–7, 119–25, 140–4, 147, 160, 165, 180 (n. 38), 190 (n. 194)
press of, 25, 75, 78–9, 84, 87–9, 93, 118, 138, 183 (n. 82), 191 (n. 205) (*see also individual publications, including Northern Star; Labourer; London Democrat; London Dispatch; Midland Counties Illuminator*)
and resentment of foreigners, *see* xenophobia
and revolution, 69, 99, 100–3 (*see also* revolution)
Sturgite conference, 95
and war, 'just', 25, 51, 63 (n. 88), 76, 81, 130, 143, 175, 179 (n. 29), 189 (n. 182)
xenophobia in, 85, 89–91, 97–8, 106, 153, 158, 162–3, 167–8
Chateaubriand, François René, Viscount de, 21
China, 76, 96, 97, 174, 175, 176
Church of England, 131
Clark, James, 142, 166
class consciousness
Chartist, 1, 68–72, 77–8, 80–2, 120–3, 125, 130–1, 144, 149, 155–6, 163, 168–9, 171–2, 179 (n. 19) 180 (n. 40), 194–5
resentment of middle classes, 36, 38–41, 52, 58, 61 (n. 29, n. 33), 64 (n. 107), 80–2, 94–5, 97, 104, 130, 147–8, 156, 162, 169, 188 (n. 163)
rhetoric of, 1, 24, 32, 33, 139
working-class, pre-Chartist, 1–4, 6 (n. 1), 24, 27, 27 (n. 5), 32–3, 35–43, 50–3, 57, 62 (n. 48)
Cleave, John, 36, 52, 61 (n. 41), 72, 155
Cobbett, William, 7–15, 17, 19, 21–4,

26, 27 (n. 9, n. 10), 28 (n. 11), 28–9 (n. 37), 29 (n. 58), 30 (n. 73, n. 78, n. 86), 30–1 (n. 88), 31 (n. 90), 32–4, 40, 62 (n. 65, n. 66), 66, 153, 192 (n. 216)
and the July revolution, 42–7, 62 (n. 43, n. 48, n. 49, n. 51, n. 56)
Cobden, Richard, 113, 171
Cole, G. D. H., 43, 131, 196, 199 (n. 20)
Collins, H., 195
communism
artisan, 126, 146, 180 (n. 40)
egalitarian, 128, 186 (n. 134)
scientific and Marxist, 128, 130, 186 (n. 134) 191 (n. 213), 192 (n. 215), 193–5, 198 (n. 3, n. 4)
utopian, 128, 135–6, 139, 162–3, 186 (n. 134)
Communist League (*Kommunistenbund*), 128, 145, 181 (n. 56), 194
Communist Manifesto, 128, 147, 193, 198 (n. 3)
Congress of Vienna, 10, 28 (n. 14), 28–9 (n. 37), 47, 62 (n. 65), 158
Constitution, of Britain, 9, 27, 82, 152, Cooper, Thomas, 78, 104, 136, 151 155, 158–9, 161–2, 168, 183 (n. 87), 190 (n. 186, n. 187, n. 188, n. 189, n. 190, n. 194)
Copenhagen Tea Gardens, 35, 36
Corn Laws, 46, 97–9, 114 (n. 144, n. 148, n. 149, n. 156)
Cracow, Free State of, *see* Cracow Uprising
Cracow Manifesto, 140–1, 143, 147, 162, 186 (n. 128)
Cracow Uprising, 135, 140–4, 157, 162–3, 174, 176, 185 (n. 115, n. 116, n. 118, n. 123), 189 (n. 182)
criminal libel, law of, *see* libel laws
Crisis, The, 53–4
Crown and Anchor tavern, 7, 135–6, 141
czars, *see* tsars
Czartoryski, Prince Adam 119, 141, 144, 178 (n. 3)

Davison, Thomas, 11, 26
Debat Social, 138
Deism, 4, 9, 14, 28 (n. 20)
Democratic Association of Brussels (*Association Démocratique*), 146–8, 151, 186–7 (n. 141), 190 (n. 189)

Democratic Committee for Poland's Regeneration, 141–3, 147, 155, 161–2, 168, 185 (n. 123), 186 (n. 126)

Democratic Friends of All Nations, 155, 158, 162, 168

Destructive and Poor Man's Conservative, The, 106

Deutsche Brüsseler Zeitung, 138

Dey of Algiers, 26

Dickens, Charles, 159

Doherty, John, 34, 51

Doyle, Christopher, 166

drink and drinking, 36, 84

Duncombe, Thomas Slingsby, 141, 157–8

Dutt, R. Palme, 195

Dutt, Salme A., 195

East London Democratic Association, 121, 130

eastern Europe, in general, 49, 106, 156 (*see also* individual countries)

Eastern Question, 58, 65 (n. 113), 140, 174

education, working class and, 3, 68–70, 73–5, 77, 156, 158, 167, 171

Egypt, 95–6, 174 (*see also* Ibrahim Pasha)

emigration of British workers, 26, 83, 160

Engels, Friedrich, 32, 79, 125–6, 128, 130–1, 134, 136, 139, 145–51, 154–5, 162–4, 168, 170–1, 180 (n. 44), 182 (n. 71, n. 74), 184 (n. 85, n. 94), 186 (n. 134–8), 188 (n. 166), 190 (n. 185, n. 189), 196–7

England, *see* Britain

exaltados, 17

exiles, in general, including foreigners who may not be exiles technically, 4, 35, 48, 78, 84, 86, 129, 134–5, 137, 156, 162, 164, 167, 172, 194–5, 199 (n. 20)

French, 86, 90–1, 111 (n. 72), 128–9, 155–6, 162–3, 184 (n. 96)

German, 125–9, 134, 138, 155–6, 162–4, 180 (n. 40), 182 (n. 76)

Italian, 90–1, 128, 155–6, 188 (n. 171)

Polish, 48–9, 53, 100, 102, 104, 107, 115 (n. 172), 118–25, 134, 138, 141, 155–6, 162–4, 178 (n. 2, n. 7), 178–9 (n. 8), 188 (n. 171), 191 (n. 205)

Swiss, 91

see also French Democratic Society; German Workers' Educational Society; Polish Democratic Society; Fraternal Democrats. *For foreign workers in foreign countries, see* workers

Ferdinand VII, King of Spain, 13, 17, 20

Fieschi, Guiseppe, 80

foreign policy

Chartism and, 58–9, 75–6, 81, 94–7, 104, 158–60, 173–8, 189 (n. 174), 196

liberal views, 22, 32, 45, 49, 52–3, 63–4 (n. 92), 81–3, 90, 93, 113, 150, 160–1, 170–1, 175 (*see also* middle class; foreign affairs)

working-class criticisms of, pre-Chartist, 1, 4, 11, 14–15, 20, 23, 27, 28–9 (n. 37), 30 (n. 78), 52, 57–9, 63 (n. 83)

foreigners, *see* exiles; xenophobia; workers

Fox, William J., 158

France, in general, 5, 8–14, 17, 22, 24–5, 28 (n. 11, n. 27), 36, 40, 42, 45, 47, 54, 72–3, 75–8, 80, 83, 85–8. 93, 95–6, 108 (n. 13), 112–13 (n, 118), 113 (n. 126), 126, 129–30, 133, 140, 144, 151, 153, 165

and the July revolution, 20, 23, 32–47, 49, 51, 53, 54, 59 (n. 2), 61 (n. 33, n. 35), 62 (n. 49, n. 51, n. 56), 64 (n. 108), 67, 80, 85, 87 (n. 30), 68, 72, 93–4, 117 (n. 213), 133, 164, 190 (n. 190) (*see also* French)

and Louis Philippe, 38, 40, 41, 61 (n. 30), 68, 72, 93–4, 117 (n. 213), 133, 164, 190 (n. 190) (*see also* French)

Fraternal Democrats

and the Cracow Uprising, 140–4, 185 (n. 118)

and Feargus O'Connor, 150–4

general comments, 5, 6, 8, 111 (n. 72), 127–30, 132–4, 182 (n. 75), 183 (n. 87)

and the historians, 193–8, 199 (n. 26)

and Marx and Engels, 144–50, 186 (n. 137, n. 138)

origin, organisation and outlook, 134–40, 183 (n. 93), 184 (n. 101, n. 107, n. 108, n. 109, n. 110), 185 (n. 112)

in perspective, 163–72, 191 (n. 213), 192 (n. 217)
rivals of, 154–63, 190 (n. 188)
Freemasons, 119
free trade and protection, 81, 97–9, 114 (n. 144, n. 156, n. 161), 147, 156, 175, 187 (n. 142)
French
'Chartists', 93
Democratic Society (La Société Démocratique Française), 111 (n. 72), 128–9,
exiles, 86, 90–1, 111 (n. 72), 128–9, 137, 155–6, 162–3, 184 (n. 96)
first revolution, 1789 up to Napoleon, 4–6, 10–13, 16, 19, 58, 66, 78–80, 106, 135–6, 140, 169–70, 184 (n. 97), 193; Jacobinism, 5, 12, 31 (n. 92), 131; symbols and trappings from, 36–7, 46, 84, 110 (n. 64), 131, 139, 148
intervention in Spain in 1823, 7, 17, 20–3, 25, 30 (n. 80)
July revolution, 20, 23, 32–47, 49, 51, 53–4, 59 (n. 2), 61 (n. 33, n. 35), 62 (n. 49, n. 51, n. 56), 64 (n. 108), 67, 80, 85, 87
juste milieu, 38, 94, 113 (n. 126)
revolutionary wars, 10, 11, 19–23, 28 (n. 20), 44–5, 83, 120
Whigs, 38, 40, 42, 61 (n. 30), 93
workers, in France, 36–43, 54–5, 60 (n. 20), 61 (n. 33), 62 (n. 48), 73, 75, 77–8, 80, 99–100, 114 (n. 148), 168
Frost, John, 100–1
Frost, Thomas, 184 (n. 110)
fund-raising, working-class, for European affairs, 1, 5, 7, 22–3, 43, 50, 57–8, 62 (n. 49), 63 (n. 85), 72, 108–9 (n. 19), 138, 141–2, 184 (n. 106), 185 (n. 118), 189 (n. 182)

Galicia and Galician massacres, 140, 143–4, 162
Gammage, R. G., 131, 133, 165, 183 (n. 77)
Gash, Norman, 33, 43, 45, 59 (n. 2)
German
Democratic Society of London, see German Workers' Educational Society
exiles, 125–9, 134, 138, 155–6, 162–4, 180 (n. 40), 182 (n. 76)

hall, Drury Lane, 127, 142
workers, in Germany, 69, 71, 148, 180 (n. 40)
Workers' Educational Society, 111 (n. 72), 127–9, 137, 139, 181 (n. 50, n. 51), 183 (n. 80), 185 (n. 118)
Germany, in general, 25, 39, 48, 73, 90–2, 105, 125, 129, 131, 133, 140, 180 (n. 41)
Prussia, see Prussia
Gleason, John Howes, 52, 103
Gorgon, The, 8, 11, 16, 26
Graham, Sir James, 157
Grand National Consolidated Trade Union, 53
great emigration of Poles, see Polish exiles
great unstamped press, see unstamped press
Greece, in general, 73, 112 (n. 98), 140, 160
revolution in, 15, 17, 20–1, 87, 96
Groves, Reg, 100, 195

Halèvy, Elie, 33, 45, 59 (n. 2)
Hamburger, Joseph, 33
Handwerkerkommunismus, 126, 146, 180 (n. 40)
Hardy, Thomas, 5, 66
Harney, George Julian, 5, 32, 78, 92, 101, 104, 110 (n. 64), 114 (n. 144), 120–4, 127, 129–36, 138, 142–5, 148, 150, 153–6, 161, 163–5, 167, 169, 171–8, 178 (n. 8), 182 (n. 71, n. 74), 186 (n. 135), 187 (n. 145), 188 (n. 163, n. 166), 190 (n. 195), 191 (n. 198), 192 (n. 222, n. 229), 193–7, 199 (n. 13, n. 20)
Hetherington, Henry, 3, 31 (n. 90), 32, 34–5, 37–8, 40–1, 47–8, 51–2, 56–7, 61–2 (n. 41), 72, 79, 106, 130, 155, 157, 163, 192 (n. 216)
Hibbert, Julian, 35–6, 38, 60 (n. 18)
Hobsbawm, Eric J., 16
Holy Alliance, 14–15, 19–20, 26, 28–9 (n. 37), 58, 70, 92, 95, 112 (n. 115)
Holyoake, George Jacob, 103, 179 (n. 19)
Home Rule, 178
Hovell, Mark, 85, 151
Hume, Joseph, 38, 141, 185 (n. 116)
Hunt, Henry, 8, 33, 38, 61 (n. 41), 66

Ibrahim Pasha, 58

industrialisation, in general, 2, 4, 6, 9, 98, 114 (n. 148), 125, 152, 180 (n. 41)

International, First, 197, 199 (n. 26)

International Association, 197

internationalism
Chartist, 25, 32, 48, 68–73, 76–9, 81, 84, 92–3, 101, 107, 109 (n. 30), 112 (n. 109), 120–1, 125, 130–2, 135–7, 139, 143–4, 148–9, 154–5, 162–3, 165–8, 171, 175, 179; historiography of, 193–9
rhetoric of, 1, 4–5, 24, 138, 140, 169, 170
working-class, pre-Chartist, 1, 4–5, 24–7, 31 (n. 92), 38–9, 48, 53–7, 60 (n. 14), 64 (n. 96, n. 104); see also working class addresses, to and from Europe; Chartist addresses, to and from Europe; Fraternal Democrats; meetings, working-class, on foreign affairs

intervention
Austrian, in Naples, 19–20, 24, 30 (n. 71, n. 78)
British, called for, or opposition to, 20, 24, 27 (n. 4), 51–2, 57–8, 89, 143, 161
French, in Spain, 7, 17, 20–3, 25, 30 (n. 80)

Ireland and the Irish, 23, 39, 47, 83, 85, 112 (n. 98), 124, 152, 166, 180 (n. 38), 188 (n. 160), 190 (n. 197)

Italian
exiles, 90–1, 128, 155–6, 188 (n. 171)
workers, in Italy, 157

Italy, in general, 24, 48, 54, 73, 129, 132, 140, 144, 150–2, 157, 160, 175
revolutions in 1820, 7, 8, 15, 17, 19, 20, 24, 30 (n. 71, n. 78)

Jacobinism, 5, 12, 31 (n. 92), 131

Jews, in general, 49, 51, 102, 105, 116 (n. 181), 123
anti-Semitism, 22, 30–1 (n. 88), 31 (n. 103), 40, 42, 153

Jones, Ernest, 32, 78, 104, 122–3, 127, 129, 131–2, 134, 138, 142–3, 145, 150, 155, 160, 164–5, 167, 171, 182 (n. 75, n. 76), 182–3 (n. 77), 187 (n. 145), 193–5, 197, 199 (n. 13, n. 20)

Journal du Peuple, 72

July revolution, 1830, 20, 23, 32–47, 49,

51, 53–4, 59 (n. 2), 61 (n. 33, n. 35), 62 (n. 49, n. 51, n. 56), 64 (n. 108)

juste milieu, 38, 94, 113 (n. 126)

Katz, Jacob (*sometimes spelt Kats*), 67–8, 72, 108 (n. 9), 108–9 (n. 19), 186 (n. 141)

Keen, Charles, 148

Kommunistenbund (Communist League), 128, 145, 181 (n. 56), 194

Labour Party, 172

Labourer, 124, 167

Lafayette, Marquis de, 35–7, 61 ⟨n. 39⟩, 102

Land Plan, 49, 151–3, 166, 188 (n. 166)

Law of Criminal Libel, *see* libel laws

law reform, 71, 156

League of the Just, 126–8, 138, 146–8, 181 (n. 48, n. 49), 184 (n. 95)

Leicester, 161

Lelewel, J., 122

Levant, 83

libel laws, 3, 26, 32

liberal opinions on foreign affairs, 22, 32, 45, 49, 52–3, 63–4 (n. 92) 81–3, 90, 93, 113, 150, 160–1, 170–1, 175

Linton, William James, 108 (n. 6), 155, 157, 159

Literary Association of the Friends of Poland, 115–16 (n. 179), 116 (n. 180), 119, 121, 178 (n. 4)

London, in general, 4, 11, 66, 107 (n. 1), 108 (n. 5), 120, 126, 134, 138, 155, 164–6, 190–1 (n. 198), 191 (n. 200, n. 201)

London Conference of 1830, 47–8

London Corresponding Society, 5, 66–7

London Democrat, 101

London Democratic Association (East London Democratic Association), 121, 130

London Dispatch, 68, 72, 87–8, 90

London Working Men's Association, 66–79, 87, 92, 107–8 (n. 5), 109 (n. 35), 131, 150, 155–6, 158, 192 (n. 217)

Louis Philippe, King of France, 38, 40–1, 61 (n. 30), 68, 72, 93–4, 117 (n. 133), 164, 190 (n. 190)

Louis XVIII, King of France, 13

Lovett, William, 32–3, 60 (n. 13), 61 (n. 41), 66–7, 72–4, 77–8, 92, 104,

106, 108 (n. 6), 109 (n. 7), 155–8, 163–4, 177, 188 (n. 168), 191 (n. 198)

Lowery, Robert, 103, 115 (n. 179), 117 (n. 201), 191 (n. 200)

Lud Polski, 123, 179 (n. 8)

McDouall, Peter Murray, 91
Maceroni, Francis, 100
McGrath, Philip, 135, 141, 166, 183 (n. 93)
Marx, Karl, 32, 79, 81, 102, 125–6, 128, 139, 145–50, 155, 163–4, 168, 171, 180 (n. 44), 181 (n. 57), 182 (n. 91), 184 (n. 105), 186 (n. 134, n. 137, n. 138), 186–7 (n. 141, n. 142), 188 (n. 166), 190 (n. 189), 192 (n. 215), 196–7, 199 (n. 20)
Marxism, or scientific communism, 128, 130, 186 (n. 134), 191 (n. 213), 192 (n. 215), 193–5, 198 (n. 3, n. 4)
Marxist comments and views of Chartists (including proto-Marxism), 81, 122, 142, 146–9, 168, 171
Marxist historians, 128, 191 (n. 213), 192 (n. 215), 194–6
Masons, 16
Mazzini, Guiseppe, 79, 119, 128–9, 141, 155–8, 160–2, 187 (n. 146), 188–9 (n. 171), 189 (n. 172, n. 177, n. 185)
Mazzini letters scandal, 157, 175, 188 (n. 169)
Medusa, The, 11, 14, 25
meetings, working class, on foreign affairs, 7–8, 22–3, 32–9, 43, 50, 57, 60 (n. 14, n. 21), 72, 106–7, 118–219, 125, 131–2, 134–6, 141, 146–8, 153, 155, 157–8, 172, 190 (n. 194)
Mehemet Ali, 174–5
Metropolitan Political Union, 67
Metternich, Prince Clements von, 14, 20, 126, 133
Mexico, 83
Michelot, Jean, 111 (n. 72), 129, 184 (n. 109)
middle class(es)
and foreign affairs, 17, 19, 160–1 (*see also* liberal opinions on foreign affairs)
press, 3, 17–19, 29 (n. 40), 30 (n. 80), 45, 52–3, 60–1 (n. 27), 63–4 (n. 92) 76, 81, 90, 93, 102, 113 (n. 120), 144, 161, 173, 184 (n. 105)

working-class co-operation with, 23, 95, 156, 167
working-class resentment of, 36, 38–9, 40–1, 52, 58, 61 (n. 29, n. 33), 64 (n. 107), 80–2, 94–5, 97, 104, 130, 147–8, 156, 162, 169, 188 (n. 163)
Midland Counties Illuminator, 95
military
criticisms of, 25, 41, 75–6, 83, 153 (*see also* pacifism)
in revolutions, 17–18, 29 (n. 61), 48, 100–1, 174
Mill, James, 33
missionaries
Chartist, 109 (n. 34), 138, 184 (n. 106)
St Simonian, 56–7, 64 (n. 99, n. 100, n. 103)
Urquhartite, 103, 105
Młoda Polska, 179 (n. 8)
moderados, 17, 81
Moll, Joseph, 125–8, 130, 148
Monmouthshire, *see* Newport Rising
moral force Chartism, 79–80, 110 (n. 63), 156, 160, 163, 165, 190 (n. 194)
Morning Chronicle, 93
Morton, A. L., 195
Müller-Lehning, Arthur, 197

Napier, Charles, 100
Naples, *see* Neapolitan revolution of 1820
Napoleon, *see* Bonaparte, Napoleon
Napoleon, Joseph, 21–2
National Association, 73, 78, 109 (n. 30)
National Association Gazette, 89, 99, 112 (n. 109)
National Charter Association, 73, 137, 141
national guard, 25, 40–2, 60 (n. 20), 61 (n. 34), 87, 93
National Reformer, 80, 133
National Union of the Working Classes, 37, 50, 58, 61 (n. 41)
nationalism
foreign, 131–2, 140, 157–61, 194
working-class, 26–7, 33, 39, 47, 70, 74–5, 82, 85, 96–7, 144, 152–3, 167, 173, 178
Neapolitan revolution of 1820, 7–8, 15, 17, 19–20, 30 (n. 71, n. 73, n. 78)
Nelson, Horatio, 90

Netherlands, 47–8, 57, 85
   Belgian revolution against the, 34,
   43, 47–8, 62 (n. 66), 69, 87, 149
New Poor Law, 83, 85, 89, 91, 100
Newport Rising, 88, 99–101, 115 (n.
   171, n. 172, n. 176), 115–16
   (n. 179)
newspapers, *see* press
Nicholas I, Tsar of Russia, 54, 90,
   106–7, 124
Nicolaevsky, Boris, 128
Northern Liberator, 87, 103, 113 (n. 120)
Northern Star, 2, 25, 79, 90, 92, 96, 98,
   104–6, 118, 121, 129, 131–6,
   138–42, 144–8, 151, 154, 157, 161,
   164, 166–7, 169, 173, 177, 183 (n.
   80, n. 82, n. 84, n. 87), 183–
   184 (n. 94), 184 (n. 105), 189
   (n. 185)
Norway, 73–4, 86, 94, 113 (n. 122)

Oastler, Richard, 91, 167
Oborski, Louis, 116 (n. 183), 120, 122,
   125, 129, 142, 155, 178 (n. 9), 184
   (n. 109), 187 (n. 145)
O'Brien, James Bronterre, 31 (n. 90),
   32–3, 40, 42, 44, 61 (n. 28, n. 29),
   78–84, 88, 99, 109–10 (n. 41), 114
   (n. 160, n. 161), 130–1, 133, 139,
   171, 189 (n. 182), 192 (n. 216)
O'Connell, Daniel, 79, 118
O'Connor, Feargus, 2, 49, 73, 79, 84,
   88, 91–3, 98, 99, 104–5, 107 (n. 1),
   112 (n. 98, n. 116), 114 (n. 156),
   131, 133, 143, 150–4, 161–4, 166,
   183 (n. 77, n. 84), 185 (n. 125),
   187 (n. 146, n. 148), 188 (n. 160,
   n. 163, n. 164), 188 (n. 166), 190
   (n. 187, n. 188), 192 (n. 220)
Opium wars, 174–6
Oregon Boundary dispute, 76
organisations, *see specific organisations,*
   for internationalism: Fraternal
   Democrats; Democratic Friends of
   All Nations; Democratic Committee for Poland's Regeneration;
   People's International League;
   for Chartism: London Working
   Men's Association; National Association; National Charter Association; East London Democratic Association; *pre-Chartist:*
   National Union of the Working
   Classes

Ottoman Empire, *see* Turkey
Owenism, 53–7, 67, 78, 135

pacifism
   Chartist, 68, 70, 73–7, 81–3, 95–6,
      109 (n. 27), 112 (n. 109), 113 (n.
      131), 136, 140, 156, 188 (n. 168),
      191 (n. 205)
   working-class (non-Chartist), 25–6,
      57–8, 193
Paine, Thomas, 4–5, 6 (n. 4), 9, 11–12,
   24, 32, 57, 66–7, 86, 165
Palestine, 102
Palmerston, third Viscount Palmerston
   (Temple, Henry John), 96–7, 102–
   105, 116 (n. 188), 117 (n. 197),
   133, 172–8, 185 (n. 123), 192
   (n. 222, n. 227, n. 229, n. 235)
Pankhurst, R., 56
patriotism, working-class, *see nationalism*
Peel, Sir Robert, 98
Penny Paper for the People, 33, 35, 40, 42,
   47, 51–2, 57
*People's Conservative and Trades Union
   Gazette*, 58–9
People's International League, 155–7,
   162, 167–8, 189 (n. 174, n. 177,
   n. 179)
Peterloo massacre, 8
physical force Chartism, and moral
   force Chartism, 79–80, 110 (n. 63),
   156, 160, 163, 165, 190 (n. 194)
Pioneer, the, 54–5
Place, Francis, 33, 72, 79
platform, the, 4, 8, 125–6, 150, 172
Plummer, Alfred, 79
Poland, 48, 50, 52, 54, 73, 92, 96, 99–
   100, 113 (n. 124), 119–20, 123–4,
   140, 142, 144, 148, 160, 162–3,
   175, 179 (n. 29), 186 (n. 160), 189
   (n. 189), 190 (n. 194)
police, 40, 85, 89, 91, 107, 110–11
   (n. 67), 112 (n. 104)
Polignac, Prince Jules de, 38, 44–6, 62
   (n. 59)
Polish
   Democratic Society, 120–2, 137,
      139–40
   exiles, 48–9, 53, 100, 102, 104, 107,
      115 (n. 172), 118–25, 134, 138,
      141, 155–6, 162–4, 178 (n. 2, n. 7),
      178–9 (n. 8), 188 (n. 171), 191
      (n. 205)
   revolution of 1830, 32, 34, 48–53, 63

(n. 83), 63–4 (n. 92), 102, 121–4, 140, 144, 147
workers, in Poland, 49
Political Register, 2, 10, 13, 21, 28 (n. 20), 42, 44
polonophilism, 39, 48–9, 52–3, 63 (n. 79), 73, 77, 106–7, 119–25, 140–4, 147, 160, 165, 180 (n. 38), 190 (n. 194)
Poor Laws, 83, 85, 89, 91, 100
Poor Man's Guardian, 2, 3, 35, 37, 40–1, 56
Pope and the Papacy, 10, 13, 94
Portugal, 24, 29 (n. 58), 54, 57, 73, 130, 140
 revolution of 1820, 7, 8, 15, 17
press
 Chartist, 25, 75, 78–9, 84, 87–9, 93, 118, 138, 183 (n. 82), 191 (n. 205)
 (*see also Northern Star; Labourer; London Democrat; London Dispatch; Midland Counties Illuminator and other individual newspapers*)
 middle-class, 3, 17–19, 29 (n. 40), 30 (n. 80), 45, 52–3, 60–1 (n. 27), 63–4 (n. 92), 76, 81, 90, 93, 102, 113 (n. 120), 144, 161, 173, 184 (n. 105) (*see also Morning Chronicle; Times*)
 ultra-radical, 7–31, 76, 83, 191 (n. 205)
 unstamped, 3, 32, 40–1, 50, 52, 57
 working-class, in general, 1–4, 7–31, 33, 35, 41, 55–8
Price, John, 197
protection and free trade, 81, 97–9, 114 (n. 144, n. 156, n. 161), 147, 156, 175, 187 (n. 142)
Prothero, Iorwerth, 197
proto-Marxism, Chartist, 81, 122, 143, 146–9, 168, 171
Prussia, 13, 15, 74, 91, 94, 95, 105, 151, 153, 175

reform of the House of Commons, 5, 10–12, 16–17, 27, 30 (n. 78), 32–35, 38, 42–3, 46, 50, 52, 59 (n. 2), 93
Réforme, 138
Republican, 11, 16, 18
Republican, or Voice of the People, 35
republicanism
 British, 101, 153
 continental, 14, 17, 25, 35–6, 38,

47–8, 51, 57, 61 (n. 39), 63 (n. 70), 94, 111 (n. 72), 153
revolution, in general, 4, 5, 15–18, 25, 29 (n. 46), 33–4, 41–2, 51, 57, 60 (n. 13), 69, 87, 115 (n. 164), 139, 145, 156, 160, 171, 175, 197
 Belgian, of 1830, 34, 43, 47–8, 62 (n. 66), 69, 87, 149
 British, 16, 33–4, 39, 53, 63 (n. 81), 99–103, 170
 Chartism and, 69, 99, 100–3
 French, first, 1789 up to Napoleon, 4–6, 10–13, 16, 19, 58, 66, 78–80, 106, 135–6, 140, 169–70, 184 (n. 97), 193
 Greek, 15, 17, 20–1, 87, 96
 July of 1830, 20, 23, 32–47, 49, 51, 53–4, 59 (n. 2), 61 (n. 33, n. 35), 62 (n. 49, n. 51, n. 56), 64 (n. 108)
 military as a revolutionary force, 17–19, 21 (n. 61), 48, 100–1, 174
 Neapolitan, of 1820, 7, 8, 15, 17, 19, 20, 30 (n. 71, n. 73, n. 78)
 of 1848, continental, 129, 149–50, 158, 163–5, 190 (n. 195), 191 (n. 200), 196
 Polish, of 1830, 32, 34, 48–53, 63 (n. 83), 63–4 (n. 92), 102, 121–4, 140, 144, 147
 Portuguese, of 1820, 7, 8, 15, 17
 rhetoric of, 5, 16–18, 33–4, 51, 115 (n. 164)
 Spanish, of 1820, 7–9, 12, 15–23, 25, 27 (n. 3), 29 (n. 61), 30–1 (n. 88)
rhetoric, working-class
 on class, 1, 24, 32–3, 139
 on internationalism, 1, 4–5, 24, 138, 140, 169–70
 on Poland, 49–52, 118, 123–4
 on revolution, 5, 16–18, 33–4, 51, 115 (n. 164)
Rights of Man, 6 (n. 4), 12
Robespierre, Maxmilien, 12, 61 (n. 33), 78–9, 109–10 (n. 41), 139, 194
Roebuck, John Arthur, 72, 198 (n. 1)
Romanticism, 123–4
Rothschild family, 50
Rothstein, Fiodor or Theodore, 64 (n. 108), 194, 198, 198 (n. 5)
Rotunda, 33, 43, 45–7, 50, 52, 60–1 (n. 41)
Rowcliffe, William, 172
Rural Police Bill, *see* police
Russell, Lord John, first Earl Russell, 38, 110–11 (n. 67), 124

Russia, 13, 15, 42, 49–50, 83, 91–2, 94, 95–6, 101, 103, 105–6, 119, 123–4, 153, 174–5 (*see also* tsars, of Russia)
Russophobia, 20, 26, 38, 42, 50, 59, 84, 95, 100–7, 113 (n. 135), 118, 123–4, 190 (n. 194)

Saint-Simonians, 56–7, 64 (n. 99, n. 100, n. 103)
Schapper, Karl, 32, 79, 125–7, 129–30, 132, 134–5, 137, 142, 144, 146–8, 153–5, 164, 171, 180 (n. 40), 181–2 (n. 64), 185 (n. 118), 187 (n. 145), 188 (n. 163), 197
Schlütter, Hermann, 109 (n. 35), 195
Schoyen, A. R., 134–5, 142
secret societies, in general, 16, 126–7 180–1 (n. 46)
    Carbonari, 16, 119, 119 (n. 190)
    Communist League, 128, 145, 181 (n. 56), 194
    League of the Just, 126–8, 138, 146–8, 181 (n. 48, n. 49), 184 (n. 95)
    Société des droits de l'Homme, 87
    Société des Saisons, 126, 181 (n. 48)
Sherwin's Political Register, 11, 14, 24, 26
slavery, 156
Slosson, Preston William, 196
Société Democratique Française (French Democratic Society), 111 (n. 72), 128–9, 137
Société des droits de l'Homme, 87
Société des Saisons, 126, 181 (n. 48)
Somerville, Alexander, 100
Spain, 17–18, 24, 29 (n. 58), 54, 57, 64 (n. 107), 81, 113 (n. 126), 140
    revolution of 1820, 7–9, 12, 15–23, 25, 27 (n. 3), 29 (n. 61), 30–1 (n. 88); French intervention in, 7, 17, 20–3, 25, 30 (n. 80)
Spectator, The, 102
stamp duty, 3
Stekloff, G. M., 194
Stephens, Joseph Rayner, 91, 112 (n. 100), 167
Stewart, Neil, 195
Stuart, Lord Dudley, 115–16 (n. 179), 119
Sturgite Conference, 95
Sweden, 74, 112 (n. 100)
Switzerland, 73–4, 86, 111 (n. 71), 129–30, 133, 140, 151–2, 159, 162
Syria, 97, 174

szlachta, 49–50, 63 (n. 76), 140

Tate, George, 195
Tawney, R. H., 78
Taylor, Dr John, 85–7, 89, 111 (n. 73, n. 78)
Temperley, Harold W. V., 21
Thompson, Dorothy, 81
Thompson, Edward P., 12–13, 31 (n. 92), 40, 53, 60 (n. 18), 61 (n. 28), 78, 80
Times, The, 141, 159–60, 183 (n. 81), 189 (n. 179)
Tiverton (election of 1847), 172–8, 192 (n. 218)
Tories, 3, 39, 45, 58–9, 95, 97, 104
Tory radicalism 9, 28 (n. 20), 102
Trevelyan, George Macaulay, 42
tsars of Russia *see* Alexander I, Nicholas I
    in general, 10, 26, 38, 50, 52, 58, 95, 105–6, 113 (n. 135), 117 (n. 213), 120, 124
Turkey and Turks, 26, 58, 82, 91, 95, 103, 105, 116 (n. 193), 174–5
Twopenny Dispatch and People's Police Register, 40–1
Twopenny Trash, 34, 42, 44, 46
Tyssowski, John, 140

ultra-radical press, 7–31, 76, 83, 191 (n. 205)
United States, *see* America, United States of
unstamped press, 3, 32, 40–1, 50, 52, 57
Urquhart, David, 84, 99, 100, 102–7, 116 (n. 185, n. 186, n. 187, n. 188, n. 192, n. 193, n. 194), 117 (n. 196, n. 197, n. 198, n. 200, n. 201, n. 202, n. 209, n. 211), 165, 174
Urquhartite organisations, 103–6, 163, 165
utopian communism, 128, 135–6, 139, 162–3, 186 (n. 134)

Victoria, Queen of England, 89–90, 107, 141, 143
Vincent, Henry, 72, 115–16 (n. 179), 120, 159, 188 (n. 169)
Voice of the People, 34, 51, 63 (n. 82), 65 (n. 111)

Wade, John, 8, 11, 26
Wales, *see* Newport rising

Wanderjahre, 126, 180 (n. 42, n. 43)

wars, just, 25, 51, 63 (n. 88), 76, 81, 130, 143, 175, 179 (n. 29), 189 (n. 182) (*see also* working-class belligerency)

Watson, James, 35, 39, 52, 61 (n. 41), 72, 155, 159, 163

Webster, Sir Charles Kingsley, 102

Weitling, Wilhelm, 79, 125, 127–8, 136, 151, 180 (n. 41), 184 (n. 95)

Wellington, Duke of (Wellesley, Arthur), 33, 45, 90

Wheeler, Thomas, 166

Whigs
British, 3, 39, 40, 52, 58–9, 78, 80, 82–3, 93–5, 97, 104, 113 (n. 126), 119, 173
'French', 38, 40 .42, 61 (n. 30), 93
'Spanish', 64 (n. 107)

White Hat, 11, 26

Wilkes, John, 66

Wooler, Thomas, 9, 11, 14, 18–20, 23–4, 30 (n. 71), 31 (n. 90), 32, 40, 192 (n. 216)

Worcell, Stanislaus, 79

workers (excluding exiles and workers abroad from their native countries)
American, 73, 76
Belgian, 48, 67–9, 70–2, 108 (n. 15), 114 (n. 148), 147–8
Dutch, 69, 71
European, in general, 97–9, 114 (n. 148, n. 153)
French, 36–43, 54–5, 60 (n. 20), 61 (n. 33), 62 (n. 48), 73, 75, 77–8, 80, 99, 100, 114 (n. 148), 168
German, 69, 71, 148, 180 (n. 40)
Polish, 49
Prussian, 99
Swiss, 99, 111 (n. 71)

working class, British
addresses, to and from Europe: Chartist, 5, 32, 67–78, 86, 88, 92, 108 (n. 11, n. 15), 121, 123, 129, 132, 135, 138, 149, 155–6, 167–8, 183 (n. 88), 185 (n. 112); pre-Chartist, 5, 7, 32, 35–7, 50, 53–7, 60 (n. 14), 64 (n. 96), 88–9
belligerency, 20, 24–5, 27 (n. 3), 51–2, 63 (n. 88), 81, 130, 143, 189 (n. 182) (*see also* Chartist movement and; interventionism, Chartist movement and; wars ''ust')

and Chartist internationalism, 25, 32, 48, 68–73, 76–9, 81, 84, 92–3, 101, 107, 109 (n. 30), 112 (n. 109), 120–1, 125, 130–2, 135–7, 139, 143–4, 148–9, 154–5, 162–3, 165–8, 171, 175, 179; historiography of, 193–9

class consciousness: Chartist, 1, 68–72, 77–8, 80–2, 120–3, 125, 130–1, 144, 149, 155–6, 163, 168–9, 171–2, 179 (n. 19), 180 (n. 40), 194–5; pre-Chartist, 1–4, 6 (n. 1), 24, 27, 27 (n. 5), 32–3, 35–43, 50–3, 57, 62 (n. 48); rhetoric of, 1, 24, 32, 33, 139

and education, 3, 68–70, 73–5, 77, 156, 158, 167, 171

and emigration, 26, 83, 160

and exiles, *see* exiles; *names of individual exiles; names of exiles' organisations*

and foreign policy: Chartism and, 58–9, 75–6, 81, 94–7, 104, 158–60, 173–8, 189 (n. 174); pre-Chartist, 1, 4, 11, 14–15, 20, 23, 27, 28–9 (n. 37), 30 (n. 78), 52, 57–9, 63 (n. 83)

and fund-raising for European affairs, 1, 5, 7, 22–3, 43, 50, 57–8, 62 (n. 49), 63 (n. 85), 72, 108–9 (n. 19), 138, 141–2, 184 (n. 106), 185 (n. 118), 189 (n. 182)

and intervention, calls for, opposition to, 20, 24, 27 (n. 4), 51–2, 57–8, 89, 143, 161

meetings on foreign affairs, 7–8, 22–3, 32–9, 43, 50, 57, 60 (n. 14, n. 21), 72, 106–7, 118–19, 125, 131–2, 134–6, 141, 146–8, 153, 155, 157–8, 172, 190 (n. 194)

and middle classes: co-operation with, 23, 95, 156, 167; resentment of, 36, 38–9, 40–1, 52, 58, 61 (n. 29, n. 33), 64 (n. 107), 80–2, 94–5, 97, 104, 130, 147–8, 156, 162, 169, 188 (n. 163)

and nationalism, 26–7, 33, 39, 47, 70, 74–5, 82, 85, 96–7, 144, 152–3, 167, 173, 178

and nationalism, foreign, 131–2, 140, 157–61, 194

organisations, *see specific organisations; for internationalism:* Fraternal Democrats: Democratic Friends of All Nations; Democratic Committee

Working class, Brit. organisations (*cont.*)
for *internationalism* (*cont.*)
for Poland's Regeneration;
People's International League;
for Chartism: London Working
Men's Association; National Association; National Charter Association; East London Democratic Association; *pre-Chartist:*
National Union of the Working
Classes
pacifism: Chartist, 68, 70, 73–7, 81–3,
95–6, 109 (n. 27), 112 (n. 109), 113
(n. 131), 136, 140, 156, 188 (n.
168), 191 (n. 205); pre-Chartist,
25–6, 57–8, 193
patriotism, *see* nationalism
polonophilism, 39, 48–9, 52–3, 63
(n. 79), 73, 77, 106–7, 119–25,
140–4, 147, 160, 165, 180 (n. 38),
190 (n. 194)
and pre-Chartist internationalism,
1, 4–5, 24–7, 31 (n. 92), 38–9, 48,
53–7, 60 (n. 14), 64 (n. 96, n. 104)

press, 1–4, 7–31, 33, 35, 41, 55–8;
Chartist, 25, 75, 78–9, 84, 87–9, 93,
118, 138, 183 (n. 82), 191 (n. 205)
(*see also Northern Star; Labourer; London Democrat; London Dispatch; Midland Counties Illuminator and other
individual newspapers*); ultra-radical,
7–31, 76, 83, 191 (n. 205); unstamped, 3, 32, 40–1, 50, 52, 57
rhetoric of internationalism of, 1,
4–5, 24–7, 31 (n. 92), 38–9, 48,
53–7, 60 (n. 14), 64 (n. 96, n. 104)
Russophobia, 20, 26, 38, 42, 50, 59,
84, 95, 100–7, 113 (n. 135), 118,
123–4, 190 (n. 194)
and war, 'just', 25, 51, 63 (n. 88), 76,
81, 130, 143, 175, 179 (n. 29),
189 (n. 182)
xenophobia, *see* xenophobia

xenophobia, working-class, 7, 22, 23,
25–6, 54, 85, 89–91, 97–8, 106,
146, 153, 158, 162–3, 167–8

Young Europe, 129